Owen H. King
8/79

Modern Accounting Principles and Practices: A Professional Handbook

Modern Accounting Principles and Practices: A Professional Handbook

Thomas D. Wood, Ph.D., CPA
Franklyn H. Sweet, Ph.D., CPA

Prentice-Hall, Inc.
Englewood Cliffs, New Jersey

Prentice-Hall International, Inc., *London*
Prentice-Hall of Australia, Pty. Ltd., *Sydney*
Prentice-Hall of Canada, Ltd., *Toronto*
Prentice-Hall of India Private Ltd., *New Delhi*
Prentice-Hall of Japan, Inc., *Tokyo*
Prentice-Hall of Southeast Asia Pte. Ltd., *Singapore*
Whitehall Books, Ltd., *Wellington, New Zealand*

"This publication is designed to provide accurate and authoritative information in regard to the subject matter covered. It is sold with the understanding that the publisher is not engaged in rendering legal, accounting or other professional service. If legal advice or other expert assistance is required, the services of a competent professional person should be sought.

. . . From the Declaration of Principles jointly adopted by a Committee of the American Bar Association and a Committee of Publishers and Associations."

Library of Congress Cataloging in Publication Data

Wood, Thomas D
Modern accounting principles and practices.

Bibliography: p.
Includes index.
1. Accounting. I. Sweet, Franklyn Haley, joint author. II. Title.
HF5635.W873 657'.02'02 77-28600
ISBN 0-13-586214-0

Printed in the United States of America

To Dora Nelle
and
Melba

ABOUT THE AUTHORS

Thomas D. Wood is Professor and Chairman of the Accounting Department of the University of South Alabama. He has a B. S. C. in Accounting from Spring Hill College (Mobile, Alabama), and an M.A. and Ph.D., from the University of Florida. He has written several articles in Accounting Journals. He is a CPA and consulting partner in the firm of Wallace and Wood. He is co-author of *A Profile of Alabama CPA Firms* and has made a number of speeches at professional society meetings.

Franklyn H. Sweet is a professor of accounting at the University of South Alabama with B.S. and M.S. degrees from the University of Alabama and a Ph.D. from the University of Texas (Austin). He is a CPA in the State of Alabama. He has had professional experience with a well-known mail order chain and years of experience in the public accounting field. During his many years in academe, he has served as an accounting department chairman at two universities and a college and as a vice-president for finance and administration for several years at the University of South Alabama.

A WORD FROM THE AUTHORS

Everyone with accounting and financial responsibilities is faced with the staggering task of keeping up with current developments, new reporting rules and increasing requirements imposed by regulatory agencies. This means continuing education is essential to the professional. Continuing education includes attendance at seminars, workshops and conferences, as well as self-study courses and regular reading of professional journals. Alloting time to "keeping up," coupled with a normal workload, introduces the risk that certain essential procedures, techniques, or principles will be forgotten and lost, overlooked or sidestepped as indecipherable in the available time. Herein lies the purpose of this book.

Purpose of this Book

This is an advanced practice book for public, corporate and industrial accountants. It is a highly practical use-oriented resource, not a handbook in the traditional sense. It has been carefully constructed on the foundation of "narrative, example and explanation."

The very latest concepts and practices concerning carefully selected topics are presented in the format previously indicated. The topics were selected using three criteria:

The first criterion was that of concern for the needs of the widest variety of practitioners in the public, industrial and institutional sectors.

The second criterion was that of identifying topics involving fairly complex procedures that do not come up often enough to require the accountant to be thoroughly familiar with them on a day-to-day basis.

The third criterion was that of selecting topics wherein the theory and practice were narrowly enough defined so that one or two concise examples can offer practical "how-to-do-it" illustrations that would represent the majority of the technical situations encountered.

Approach Used

While it is necessary to include some discussion of concepts and principles in each case, these are limited to exactly what the accountant needs to know in the particular situation and serve merely as a refresher. Background information in depth and extended theoretical discussion are scrupulously avoided. The reader is referred to the bibliography for references to more extended treatment of the respective topics.

Auditing Problems

The section on auditing deals with three topics rather difficult to handle in a routine fashion. Some of the questions about these topics for which answers have been provided are:

1. How to provide for practical separation of asset custody and record-keeping.
2. How to flow chart the proposed system for study and review.
3. How to provide for internal check on transactions from employee to employee.
4. Evaluating information gained from the flow charts.
5. How to review and evaluate the firm's organization.
6. How to relate weaknesses in internal control to audit procedures.
7. A simplified approach to estimation sampling for variables.
8. Using attribute sampling.

This section also contains complete examples of worksheets necessary for documentation of sampling results.

Budgets—Forecasting—Control

The second section deals with financial forecasting, planning and control techniques. Solutions to a variety of practical problems regularly confronting accountants are presented along with illustrations of how to do it. The user will find such information as:

1. Laying the groundwork for developing a good budget.
2. Using methods and information sources for preparing sound forecasts.
3. A flow chart for the budget preparation program.
4. A complete set of worksheets, with explanations, for actual preparation of the budget is illustrated.
5. The three most modern and commonly used approaches to the evaluation of alternative capital additions plans.
6. How to set up for effective cash planning.
7. Illustrations of the basic cash budget.
8. An illustration of working papers for day-to-day cash control.
9. Working papers for development of long-range cash projections.
10. A practical approach to computing the E.O.Q. and E.O.P.
11. A summary of the most useful inventory control techniques currently in use.

Developing Financial Statements and Reports

The third section covers special topics requiring the recasting of financial statements, including:

1. Full discussion of current financial statement treatment of revaluations.
2. A comprehensive illustration of a firm's accounting through the entire bankruptcy procedure.
3. A complete description of the accountant's role at each step of bankruptcy.

4. A complete illustration of the most up-to-date technique for conversion of conventional statements to remove the effect of price-level changes.
5. The use of a set of standardized and streamlined worksheets to aid in the conversion process.
6. A complete illustration of a worksheet technique for preparation of the statement of changes in financial position on both the working capital basis and the cash basis.

Cost Accounting

The fourth section treats cost accounting for the small manufacturing plant. Job order costs, process costs and standard costs are presented in a simplified form without sacrificing necessary accuracy and reliability in the development of cost information.

In this section will be found:

1. Easy methods of accounting by jobs for material and labor.
2. An illustration of the development of a flexible overhead budget.
3. A complete illustration of job order cost accounting for a small manufacturing firm.
4. Flow charts of various types of process cost flows.
5. The calculation of equivalent units.
6. A detailed analysis of the composition of the cost of production report.
7. A complete illustration of process cost accounting in a five-department chemical plant with illustrated cost of production reports covering a variety of realistic situations, such as:
   a. Units added, increasing volume.
   b. Change in units of measure.
   c. Units lost in process.
   d. Units held in department.
   e. Inventory in process.
8. A flow chart depicting the flow of costs in a standard cost system.
9. Modern methods of accounting for material and labor variances.
10. Overhead variance analysis simplified.
11. Three methods of analyzing variances.

Summary

Following the examples and explanations will provide real savings in both research and work time, while at the same time providing techniques, methods, and ideas which are essential to a competent professional. Finally, the user will find much use is made of short-cut approaches without sacrificing sound, well-grounded accounting principles; in fact, principles are made operational for the accountant who does not have enough time in his day.

Thomas D. Wood
Franklyn H. Sweet

ACKNOWLEDGEMENTS

The authors gratefully acknowledge the assistance of a number of individuals who contributed their talents to this book. Those who merit special mention are: Dr. Carl C. Moore, Dr. Fred A. Petro, Mr. Michael J. Salmon, Ms. Vivian J. Blackwell and Mr. James Franz, all of whom critiqued particular chapters; Ms. Margaret Piercy, who proofed much of the original manuscript and re-instructed the authors in the use of the English language; Ms. Debbie Feeney, who set up and typed most of the charts as well as part of the manuscript; and Ms. Mary Gordon Smith Fonde, Ms. Joan Haig, and Mr. Joseph E. Lawrence, Jr., CPA, who contributed proofing, typing, or original ideas.

TABLE OF CONTENTS

A Word from the Authors 9

1. HOW TO DESIGN AND INSTALL INTERNAL CONTROL SYSTEMS 17

Some principles of system design (17) • Three "links" in the accounting control system (18) • Constructing an organization chart (19) • A description of duties and responsibilities (19) • The importance of the organization chart (22) • Identifying the originators of information (23) • The flow chart (24) • An example of flow charting (24) • The purchasing function (25) • Processing of vendor invoices and freight bills (28) • The disbursements function (30) • Payment of freight bills, travel and truck maintenance (30) • Petty cash (30) • Charge sales (34) • Cash receipts (39) • Cash sales (39) • Collections on account (39) • Other cash receipts and reporting (42) • The charge of accounts (42) • How to help management overcome staff resistance to ICS installation (42) • After the system is installed (44)

2. EVALUATING AN INTERNAL CONTROL SYSTEM 47

Why evaluating an internal control system is difficult (47) • A standard for measuring internal control systems (48) • The first step in the evaluation of an internal control system (49) • Understanding the organization plan (49) • A worksheet example of describing duties and responsibilities (50) • Understanding the information flow (50) • Understanding the chart of accounts (52) • Step two—the evaluation process (52) • Recognizing weakness in the organization plan (53) • Evaluating the information flow (55) • Detecting weaknesses in the information flow (55) • An example of evaluating a flow chart (57) • Evaluating the chart of accounts (59) • What to do about evaluating people (60) • Evaluating skills (60) • Evaluating will and intent (61) • Documenting the evaluation (62) • Internal control questionnaires (64) • Evaluating computerized systems (64) • Techniques for testing control of input data (64) • Testing control over output data (65) • Testing control over processing (65) • Testing for control over the program and the computer (66) • Steps in evaluating a computer-based accounting system (66) • Some internal control problems of very small firms (67) • A check list of internal control techniques for very small businesses (68) • How much "system" does a small firm need? (68)

3. MODERN STATISTICAL SAMPLING APPLICATIONS 99

Using sampling techniques in practice (99) • The purpose of statistical sampling (99) • Sampling theory simplified (100) • Steps in determining sample size (100) • An example of determining sample size (102) • Using random number tables (103) • How to apply systematic sampling in an audit (103) • Sampling items that have been grouped (105) • The versatility of stratified random sampling (105) • Evaluating the sample result (105) • The usefulness of discovery sampling (107) • A simplified method of estimating totals (108) • Documenting statistical sampling through working papers (111) • Some particular applications of sampling techniques (111) • Applying sampling techniques to the cash audit (111) • Testing cash disbursements (112) • An example of using discovery sampling in the audit of cash receipts (113) • Applying sampling techniques to the audit of accounts receivable (114) • An example of selecting a confirmation sample (114) • Applying statistical sampling to auditing inventory (119) • Other applications of statistical sampling techniques (119)

4. THE FINANCIAL BUDGET—A PRACTICAL APPROACH 129

Preliminary ground—the first phase (129) • Basic planning information—the second phase (130) • Forecasting the environment (131) • The economic forecast (131) • The sociological forecast (132) • The technological forecast (133) • The controller's/public accountant's role (134) • The budgeting program—the third phase (135) • The sales budget (137) • The production budget (137) • The administrative expense budget (138) • The distribution expense budget (139) • Other income and expense items (139) • The cash budget (139) • The master budget (140) • Illustrative and budget working papers (140) • Sales budget forms (141) • Production budget forms (142) • Distribution and administrative expense budget forms (148) • Cash budget forms (148) • Budget assembly forms (152)

5. PLANNING AND CONTROLLING CAPITAL ADDITIONS 155

Planning relationships (155) • Planning for facilities (155) • The capital expenditure management process (156) • Controlling capital additions (156) • The post-completion audit (157) • Financing capital additions (158) • Evaluating investment alternatives (159) • Basic evaluation approaches (159) • Pay-back approach (159) • Return on investment (arithmetic basis) approach (161) • Return on investment (discounted basis) approach (161) • Equipment alternatives—an illustration (163) • Equipment alternatives—a second illustration (166) • Illustration—determining the lowest cost method of financing (168) • Illustration—keep or replace equipment (173)

6. CASH PLANNING AND CONTROL 179

Selling cash management to managers (179) • Preparation for cash management (180) • Where to start (180) • Analyzing collections of receivables (180) • Other receipts and disbursements (183) • Cash management illustrated (184) • Basic cash budget (184) • Using the cash control schedule (186) • The usefulness of long-range projections (191) • Long-range projections—an illustration (191) • The importance of good bank relations (192) • Summary (194)

7. EFFECTIVE INVENTORY CONTROL 195

How can inventory control save money? (195) • Inventory control systems—perpetual inventories (197) • Using the control (198) • The ABC method

(198) • Some other tools for controlling inventory effectively (199) • What record-keeping is required? (201) • Some special problems of controlling manufacturing inventories and what to do about them (202) • EOQ—a simplified model for controlling the number of inventory orders (202) • Four methods of determining when to order inventory (208) • The visual inspection method (208) • Reserve stock system (208) • Minimum—maximum system (208) • The economic order point method (209) • Determining lead time (210) • Determining average usage and safety stock (210) • EOQ and EOP—a comprehensive example (211) • Some techniques for evaluating the firm's inventory control system (213) • What inventory control measures should the accountant recommend? (213)

8. PREPARATION OF BANKRUPTCY AND RECEIVERSHIP STATEMENTS 215

When the business runs into financial difficulty (215) • Remedies for the insolvent short of bankruptcy (215) • The protection of bankruptcy (216) • Involuntary bankruptcies and acts of bankruptcy (216) • Steps taken to obtain relief under Chapter XI (217) • The role of the accountant (218) • Preparing the statement of affairs (219) • Understanding the statement of affairs (221) • The purpose of the deficiency statement (221) • Accounting for the trustee (223) • Entries at the beginning of the trustee's term (224) • Recording transactions of the trustee (225) • Using a worksheet (229) • Preparing financial statements from the worksheet (229) • Interpreting the trustee's income statement (231) • Liquidating the firm—the statement of realization and liquidation (232) • Working with the statement of realization and liquidation (233) • Translating transactions into statement language (236) • Preparing interim statements during liquidation (244)

9. A STREAMLINED APPROACH TO PRICE-LEVEL CONVERSION TECHNIQUES 245

The problem of inflation accounting (245) • Background in brief (245) • What is the price-level problem? (245) • Some approaches to solving the problem (246) • Current replacement value approach (246) • Replacement cost information requirements (247) • Some additional information (248) • Current fair-value approach (248) • Historical development of price-level adjusted statements (249) • The price index as a benchmark (250) • Monetary and nonmonetary classification of assets and liabilities (251) • An illustration of purchasing power loss (252) • How to handle the foreign currency problem (254) • Income tax restatement (254) • Restatement of investments and bonds (254) • Estimated liabilities (254) • Inventories (255) • A complete illustration of price-level conversion (255) • Summary (258)

10. A SIMPLIFIED METHOD FOR THE PREPARATION OF THE STATEMENT OF CHANGES IN FINANCIAL POSITION 289

Purpose (289) • Two versions of the statement (290) • A comprehensive illustration (290) • Arrangement of the worksheet (291) • Transferring information from worksheet to changes statement (292) • Requirements of APB no. 19 (292)

TABLE OF CONTENTS

11. USING JOB ORDER COST IN A SMALL MANUFACTURING PLANT 299

Job order vs. process cost system (299) • What a job order cost system can do for a small manufacturer (300) • The manufacturing cost accumulation cycle (300) • Minimum reporting requirements according to GAAP and for the IRS (301) • Cost accounting terminology (301) • How much record-keeping in a job order cost system? (303) • Materials requisition (303) • Time ticket (303) • Job cost sheet (305) • Finished goods perpetual record card (305) • Accounting for materials and labor cost (305) • Labor cost record-keeping and idle time (307) • Accounting for manufacturing overhead (308) • How to select the basis for applying overhead (308) • Choosing the level of activity to be used (309) • Steps in estimating normal capacity (310) • Cost behavior—fixed and variable costs (311) • Why does each firm's cost need analysis? (311) • The high-low method of segregating fixed and variable elements of semi-variable costs (312) • When to use a flexible budget (315) • Developing a flexible budget (315) • The mechanics of applying overhead—an example (316) • Overhead variance—differences between actual and predetermined overhead (316) • Understanding overhead variances (317) • What do the variances mean? (318) • How to account for variances (318) • An example of allocating variances (319) • A comprehensive example of job order cost accounting (320) • A description of the illustrative firm and its operation (321) • The accounting process (321) • A note to practitioners (327)

12. A QUICK REVIEW OF PROCESS COST ANALYSIS 329

Characteristics of process costing (329) • Process cost plans—general (330) • Calculation of equivalent units (333) • Procedures for accumulating costs (333) • The cost of production report (334) • Illustrative case—description (337) • Grinding department (338) • Mixing department (340) • Cooking department (344) • Refining department (347) • Packaging department (350) • Costing of inventories (353) • A final word (354)

13. A PRACTICAL APPROACH TO STANDARD COSTING 355

What are the advantages of using standard costing? (355) • The two elements composing standard costs (356) • Who sets the standards? (356) • The philosophy of standards—how high? (356) • Use of standard cost card (356) • Standard costs and financial accounting (358) • A simplified illustration of standard cost flows (358) • Standard costs in the accounts—the "partial" plan (360) • The "dual" plan (361) • Accounting for standard costs of materials (361) • Computing and recording price and quantity variances (361) • Accounting for standard costs of direct labor (363) • Computing and recording rate and efficiency variances (363) • Some causes of labor variances and how to identify them (364) • Accounting for standard costs and factory overhead (365) • Three methods of analyzing and recording overhead variances (365) • The two-variance overhead analysis (366) • The three-variance overhead analysis (368) • The four-variance overhead analysis (369) • Completing the standard cost accounting process (371) • Some reporting considerations (373) • Summary (374)

Bibliography **375**
Index **377**

CHAPTER 1

HOW TO DESIGN AND INSTALL INTERNAL CONTROL SYSTEMS

This chapter provides a general framework to guide accountants in the design and installation of internal control systems. It is necessarily "general" because every system must be constructed to fit the peculiarities of the individual firm. However, this framework may be applied to practically all firms. It stresses the best of current practice in ICS design.

SOME PRINCIPLES OF SYSTEM DESIGN

The functions of designing and installing internal control systems are inseparable. This is true because almost any system the accountant conceives must be superimposed on a firm that has procedures, organization and paper flow already in operation and, often, solidly imbedded in the "modus operandi" of the individuals who make up that firm. It is a common characteristic of many people that they take on a proprietary attitude about their work, however mundane. In fact, it is often true that the more routine a function, the more proprietary the attitude of the individual who performs that function. The point is that a first principle of internal control system design and installation is: *the accountant must consider the individuals as well as the firm.*

Another principle of system design is: *the internal control system should not be more complex than is necessary to accomplish the stated objectives.* There is a trade-off here between the cost of operating the sytem and the benefits it provides. Too much system is as cumbersome as it is expensive, and can produce nearly as many inefficiencies and opportunities for error as too little system. A corollary to this is that paper flow should be designed on a need-to-know basis.

That is, whenever a form or document is to be introduced into the system it should be done only after asking: who needs to see this document and why?

A third principle of system design is, obviously, that *it must accomplish its objectives.* They are:

1. To protect the resources of the firm against unauthorized or improper use, and
2. To provide reliable accounting data for informed decisions. To this end, SAS No. 1 concludes that accounting control is designed to provide reasonable assurance that:
   (a) Transactions are executed in accordance with management's general or specific authorization.
   (b) Transactions are recorded as necessary
      (1) to permit preparation of financial statements in conformity with generally accepted accounting principles or any other criteria applicable to such statements and
      (2) to maintain accountability for assets.
   (c) Access to assets is permitted only in accordance with management's authorization.
   (d) The recorded accountability for assets is compared with the existing assets at reasonable intervals and appropriate action is taken with respect to any differences.[1]

The system should provide for the separation of duties of personnel so that no complete transaction is handled by one individual; nor should an individual who handles cash have access to accounting records. Of course, in very small firms, this is next to impossible. (The necessity for this provision is obvious and will not be discussed further.)

Two points raised by SAS No. 1 need emphasis. First, an accounting control system provides *reasonable assurance* of the above, not certainty. This means that no system can totally eliminate errors or the potential for misappropriations. The system should give a high degree of comfort in that such possibilities are minimized, and if errors or misappropriations should occur, they will come to light in the course of the operation of the system. Second, the influence of management on accounting controls is as important as it is inescapable. No system is better than the people who make it work, especially those in the firm who have the ultimate authority and responsibility. Thus, an accounting internal control system is *management's* system—not the accountant's. Once installed, *management* and the firm's employees make it operational.

THREE "LINKS" IN THE ACCOUNTING CONTROL SYSTEM

There are three links to an accounting control system: an organization chart, a flow chart, and a chart of accounts. An organization chart is a picture of the lines of authority

[1]*Statement on Auditing Standards,* Number 1 (American Institute of Certified Public Accountants, 666 Fifth Avenue, New York, N.Y.) copyright 1973, p. 20.

within the firm and a description of the responsibilities of each level of the firm's hierarchy. This latter function of an organization chart is sometimes referred to as a job description, but this is a narrower view than intended here as will be seen later in this chapter. A flow chart is a picture, usually in symbols, of the movement of accounting information through the firm's hierarchical structure. The information is in the form of or is supported by documents or paperwork. A chart of accounts is, of course, a listing of all the accounts in the firm's general ledger. Ultimately, the accounting information generated rests here, and the accounts form the basis for financial reports. While all of this is merely a repetition of what every accountant already knows, it is important to set the stage for an understanding of the interdependence of these three elements as overlays superimposed on one another, each adding to the completed picture.

1. Constructing an Organization Chart

The first building block, and at the "bottom" of the overlays, is an organization chart. To illustrate the construction of an organization chart, and indeed an entire accounting control system, assume a firm of nine members, one of whom is the president-general manager (and, perhaps, sole shareholder). In this firm, ultimate authority and responsibility rest with him. He employs a bookkeeper, a secretary, a stockclerk (or warehouseman), an assistant manager who also makes floor sales, two inside salesmen, an outside salesman, and a delivery truck operator. The firm sells automotive parts in both the retail and wholesale markets. Most of the sales volume is over-the-counter to small auto repair shops on account, although some sales are made for cash. The firm's outside salesman services several retail parts stores in smaller towns nearby. All sales to these stores are made on account. The parts are sent by motor freight from the firm's warehouse. The outside salesman furnishes his own transportation for which he is reimbursed periodically. The deliveryman makes regular "runs" to larger retail shops and one local parts store supplied by the firm.

The firm's annual volume approximates $2 million, with inventory of about $250,000. Receivables average $235,000, and payables $100,000. Cash discounts are not allowed to customers, but are ordinarily taken when offered by suppliers. The firm rents its premises on a long-term lease and has an investment of about $50,000 in fixtures, equipment, automotive equipment and leasehold improvements. The firm has a cash register on which all sales made for cash are "rung-up."

Of course, the techniques described below are standard or what "ought to be." Whatever system is already in operation is not considered here. The practicing accountant, however, cannot ignore the existing system; rather he must work through or around it. Therefore, the accountant should view what follows as "optimum" and make the necessary adjustments to fit the individual situation.

A Description of Duties and Responsibilities

The illustrative firm's organization chart and description of duties and responsibilities may take the form shown in Figure 1-1:

Figure 1-1 **Organization Chart**

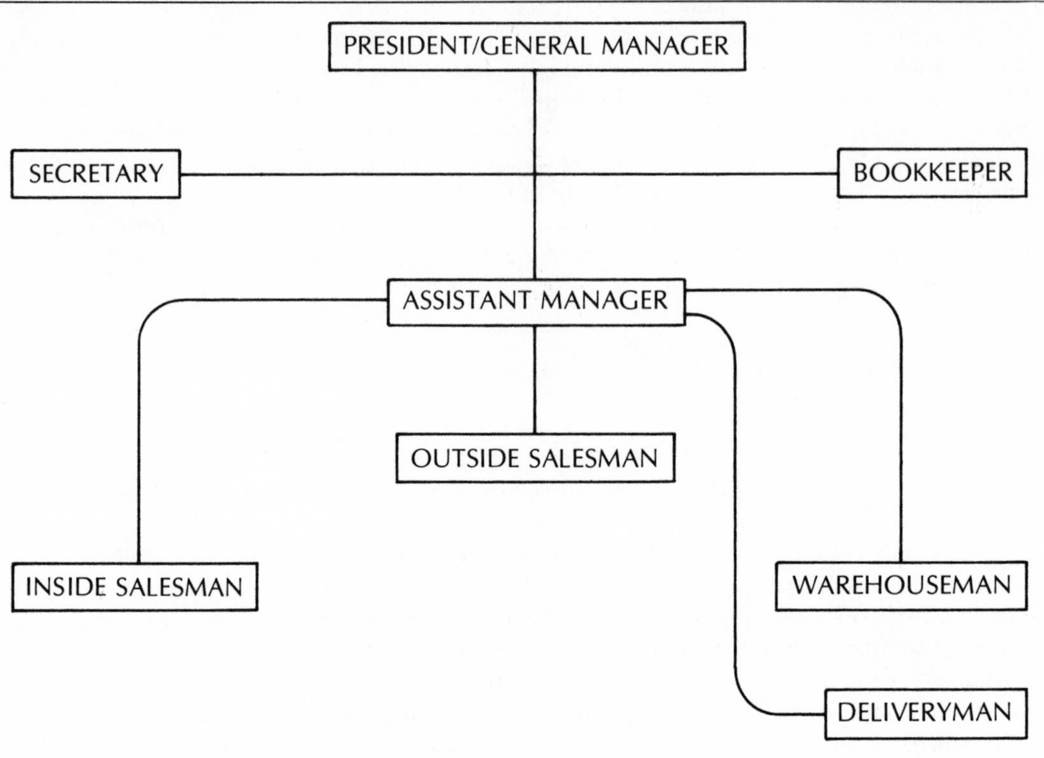

Position	Description of Duties and Responsibilities
President/ General Manager	1. Delegates authority as necessary. 2. Responsible for overall operation of the firm. Primary responsibilities include: a. Handling public relations and firm advertising. b. Managing cash and budgeting. c. Reporting to governmental agencies and other third parties (e.g. banks). d. Handling credit and collections. e. Maintaining physical facilities. f. Establishing personnel policy. g. Marketing the firm's products. h. Supervising bookkeeping function. 3. Specific duties are: a. Signing all checks. b. Establishing pay rates. c. Supervising bookkeeper and secretary.
Assistant Manager	1. Primary responsibilities include: a. Training personnel under his supervision.

Position	Description of Duties and Responsibilities
	b. Enforcing policy with respect to personnel under his supervision. c. Making recommendations for hiring, raises and terminations. d. Authorizing overtime. e. Balancing cash register daily and preparing daily deposit. f. Making sales during peak periods. g. Substituting for absent inside salesmen. h. Originating requests for display merchandise from warehouse. i. Approving merchandise for return from customers. j. Approving merchandise for return to supplier. k. Initiating purchase orders. l. Approving petty cash disbursements. m. Approving travel reimbursement and routine delivery expenses.
Bookkeeper	1. Primary responsibilities include: a. Preparing financial reports for president/ general manager. b. Paying bills on time. 2. Duties include: a. Maintaining books of original entry (cash receipts, cash disbursements, sales, purchases and general journals). b. Posting subsidiary accounts receivable and payable ledgers. c. Making payroll. d. Preparing and mailing customers' statements. e. Comparing invoices with receiving report and preparing invoices for payment.
Secretary	1. Primary responsibilities include: a. Documenting filing system. b. Disbursing petty cash. c. Reception. 2. Duties include: a. Filing, typing, answering telephone. b. Preparing bank reconciliation. c. Opening mail. d. Preparing listing of monies received by mail.
Warehouseman	1. Primary responsibility includes: receiving, storing and shipping inventory. 2. Duties include: a. Tracing incoming shipment items to purchase orders.

Position	Description of Duties and Responsibilities
	b. Arranging inventory items in storage areas. c. Filling customer orders according to sales invoice and filling requests for display merchandise. d. Originating delivery ticket per sales invoice. e. Maintaining inventory records and submitting requests for stock replenishment.
Deliveryman	1. Primary responsibility: delivering merchandise to customer. 2. Duties include: a. Having regular, routine maintenance of delivery equipment taken care of. b. Comparing delivery ticket with merchandise and obtaining customer's signature on delivery ticket. c. Making daily bank deposit.
Inside Salesmen	1. Primary responsibility includes: serving customers who come into the store or who telephone. 2. Duties include: a. Ringing accurately on the cash register each cash sale made. b. Originating sales invoices for charge sales.
Outside Salesman	1. Primary responsibilities include: a. Serving existing customers on established routes. b. Generating new customers through solicitation. 2. Duties include: a. Making regular periodic visits to customers' locations. b. Planning and making scheduled calls on potential customers. c. Accurately preparing customer orders and orginating sales invoices in accordance with the orders. d. Submitting regular reports of calls and orders taken.

The Importance of the Organization Chart

Preparing an organization chart and description of duties and responsibilities similar to the one shown has important advantages to the accountant designing an internal control system. By understanding the lines of authority and areas of responsibility, he can:

1. Identify the originators of documents supporting the firm's financial transactions.
2. Determine what the information needs are and to whom the data should be directed.

3. Design a paper flow to accomplish the foregoing, and
4. Develop a chart of accounts in which to summarize the transactions generated.

IDENTIFYING THE ORIGINATORS OF INFORMATION

Identifying the individuals who originate information in the form of documents is essential to sketching the flow of the data. Not only does this procedure indicate the source, but it also establishes responsibility for accuracy and timeliness. In the illustrative firm, information origination is as follows:

Personnel	Accounting Information Originated	Supporting Document
Outside Salesman	Customer orders	Sales invoices
	Firm travel expense	Travel reimbursement voucher
	Returned goods	Credit memoranda
Inside Salesmen	Customer orders	Sales invoices and/or cash register tapes
	Returned goods	Credit memoranda
Deliveryman	Firm delivery expense	Invoices from suppliers
Warehouseman[2]	Filled customer orders for delivery.	Delivery tickets
	Goods received from suppliers and returned goods from customers	Receiving report
Secretary	Disbursements of petty cash	Petty cash voucher
	Cash receipts	Listing of cash received by name of payer
Bookkeeper	Payroll sheet	Time clock cards
	Check disbursements	Suppliers' invoices, payroll sheet, petty cash vouchers, travel expense vouchers, customer credit memoranda
Assistant Manager	Terminations and additions/ overtime	Memoranda
	Goods returned to supplier, ordering goods.	Debit memoranda, purchase order
	Transferring goods to display area.	Memoranda

[2]A perpetual inventory system is not assumed in this example. If it were, the warehouseman would originate inventory movement information.

	Sales and cash received over-the-counter. Checks received in mail.	Daily sales and cash receipts report, cash register tape, deposit slip
President/General Manager	Discretionary expenditures. Loans & other non-operating cash in-flows. Rates of Pay	Suppliers' invoices, etc. signed notes, deposit slip Memoranda

It is important to note that only three of the firm's personnel have authority to commit the firm's resources to outsiders—the president/general manager, the assistant manager, and the deliveryman. The latter's authority is restricted to routine operation of the delivery truck. Ultimately, of course, because he must sign all checks, the president/general manager approves all disbursements of cash. Another aspect of the plan of organization is the separation of responsibilities and the requirement of approval by the upper echelon of management.

Each individual obtains whatever information is necessary to discharge his or her responsibilities, and this information is well-established by the organization plan. The number of copies of forms or documents can also be easily determined. Generally, the information can flow from the originator-to user-to rest, with no one individual burdened with extraneous data.

2. The Flow Chart

The second building block in designing an accounting control system is to prepare an information system flow chart. This follows easily from the preceding step. Information flow is essentially a flow of paper work in the form of memoranda, invoices, purchase orders, receipts and so forth, and involves not only the *kind* of paper work and its origin, but also its *direction.* Moreover, while it cannot be shown as an integral part of the flow chart itself, *timeliness* is also an obvious requirement for smooth information flow.

An Example of Flow Charting

A comprehensive illustration of flow charting for the firm described earlier in this chapter follows. The objective will be to build a complete accounting information flow chart by analyzing each of four functions of the company: purchasing; disbursing cash; sales; and receiving cash. The sub-function payroll is described and flow charted in Chapter 2. Not every operation involving accounting information flow is included. For example, the operation of transferring inventory from warehouse to showroom and those of transferring returned sales and returned purchases are omitted to keep this section within manageable proportions. Symbols in flow charting to indicate the operation and documents have been fairly well formalized by others, and those traditional symbols will be used here. Standard symbols and their meanings as used in this illustrative case are shown in Figure 1A-1 in the appendix, page 45*.

---

*Note: Where figure references contain the designation "A" as in Figure 1A-1, refer to the appendix of each chapter to locate that figure.

THE PURCHASING FUNCTION. (FIGURES 1-2 AND 1-3)

The simplest approach to flow chart construction is to begin with the originator of the accounting information. From the preceding description of duties and responsibilities it is seen that the assistant manager originates purchase orders; consequently the purchasing function begins with him. The warehouseman has been delegated the authority to request inventory replenishment. The assistant manager may check inventory bins himself or have the warehouseman perform this duty periodically. Purchase orders emanate from this activity.

The initial purchasing decision is whether the inventory should be ordered or not. This is the responsibility of the assistant manager. If the order is to be placed, he has a purchase order prepared in triplicate. Two copies are sent to the vendor and the third is kept in a temporary file by the warehouseman. A request for inventory replenishment may either be approved or denied for several reasons. If denied (the item is to be discontinued), the request is returned to the warehouseman and discarded. The reason for denying the request is probably noted thereon for the information of the warehouseman.

The operation just described may be flow charted as in Figure 1-2.

From a systems point of view, the initial steps of the purchasing system for this company provide several advantages: (1) the assistant manager who is responsible for the inventory, also has the authority to approve or disapprove the purchase of inventory; (2) the third copy of the purchase order, which has been filed, constitutes a check against the vendor for filling the order correctly and as a reminder of unfilled orders that need to be followed up; and, (3) two individuals are watching inventory—the warehouseman and the assistant manager. The warehouseman is a check against improper ordering by the assistant manager, because the warehouseman has a copy of the purchase order for every purchase received or to be received, and will use it to compare with actual incoming shipments.

At this point, documents originating from outside the firm come into the system. A bill of lading or freight receipt usually accompanies the delivery of the order. The warehouseman's responsibility is to determine if the goods delivered are the goods ordered. This is accomplished by comparing the bill of lading, the actual goods, and the third copy of the purchase order. If the orders are incomplete, this will require action outside the warehouseman's purview. He reports to the assistant manager, and files copy no. 3 of the purchase order and bill of lading in an "Incomplete Shipments" file. Goods actually received are noted on the purchase order. Correspondence may be required, or it may simply be a matter of awaiting further shipment.

For complete shipments, copy no. 3 of the purchase order attached to the bill of lading is forwarded to the bookkeeper. In the absence of a receiving report, the warehouseman would indicate the order's correctness by initialing the purchase order. He should also inform the assistant manager of receipt of the goods. This is accomplished by routing the bill of lading and copy no. 3 of the purchase order through the assistant manager for his perusal and initials, and then forwarding it to the bookkeeper. Except for storing the goods, the warehouseman's role in the purchasing function is complete. A flow chart of this operation appears in Figure 1-2.

The operation of receiving goods is a logical one. When the remainder of an incomplete shipment arrives, copy no. 3 of the purchase order and the bill of lading are removed from the incomplete file, and when confirmed by the warehouseman for accuracy, the documents follow the same path as completed orders. The assistant manager is informed of the receipt

Figure 1-2

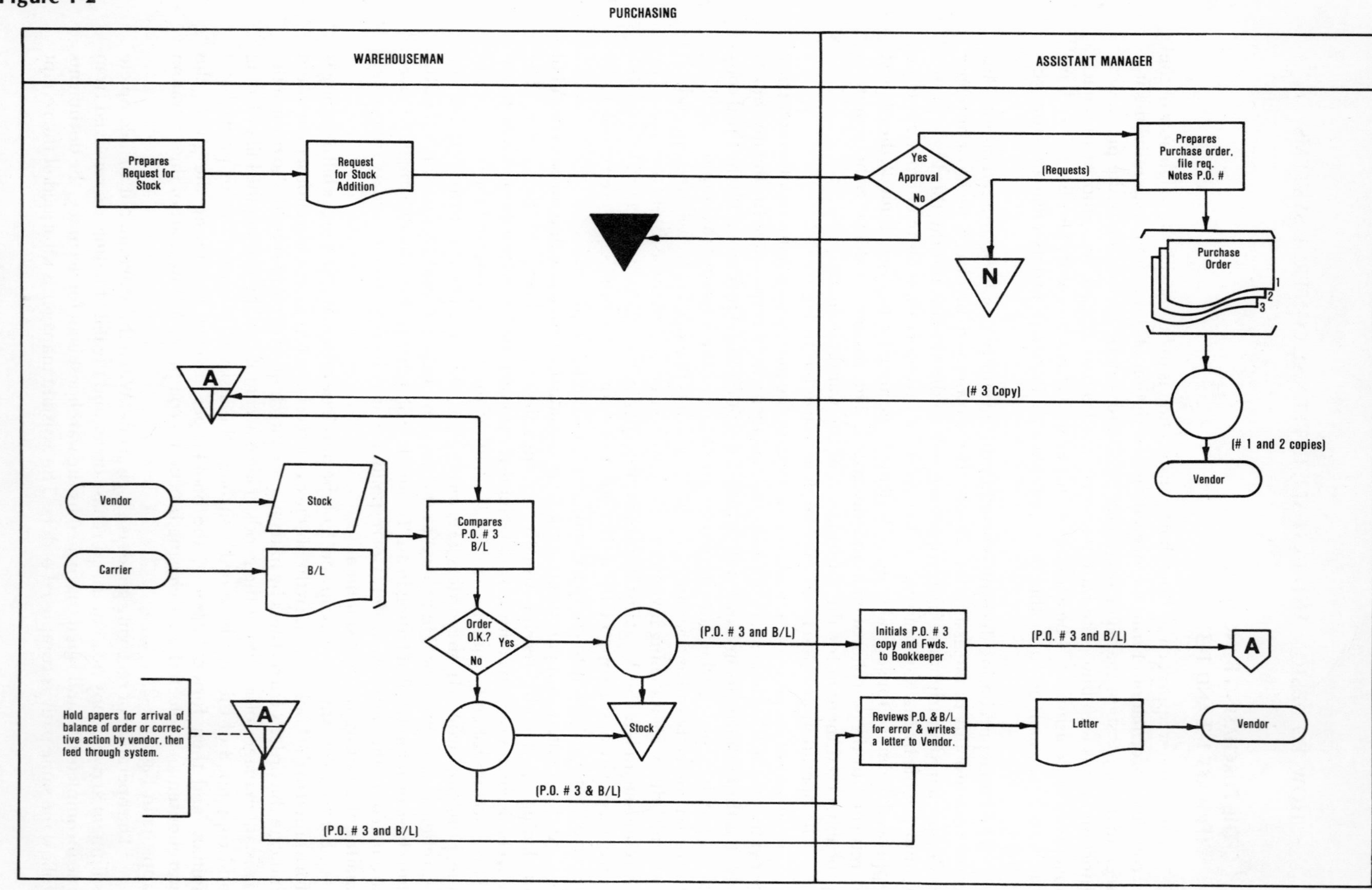
PURCHASING
WAREHOUSEMAN
ASSISTANT MANAGER
Prepares Request for Stock
Request for Stock Addition
Yes
Approval
No
(Requests)
Prepares Purchase order, file req. Notes P.O. #
N
Purchase Order
1
2
3
A
(# 3 Copy)
(# 1 and 2 copies)
Vendor
Vendor
Stock
Carrier
B/L
Compares P.O. # 3 B/L
Order O.K.?
Yes
No
(P.O. # 3 and B/L)
Initials P.O. # 3 copy and Fwds. to Bookkeeper
(P.O. # 3 and B/L)
A
Hold papers for arrival of balance of order or corrective action by vendor, then feed through system.
A
Stock
Reviews P.O. & B/L for error & writes a letter to Vendor.
Letter
Vendor
(P.O. # 3 & B/L)
(P.O. # 3 and B/L)

Figure 1-3

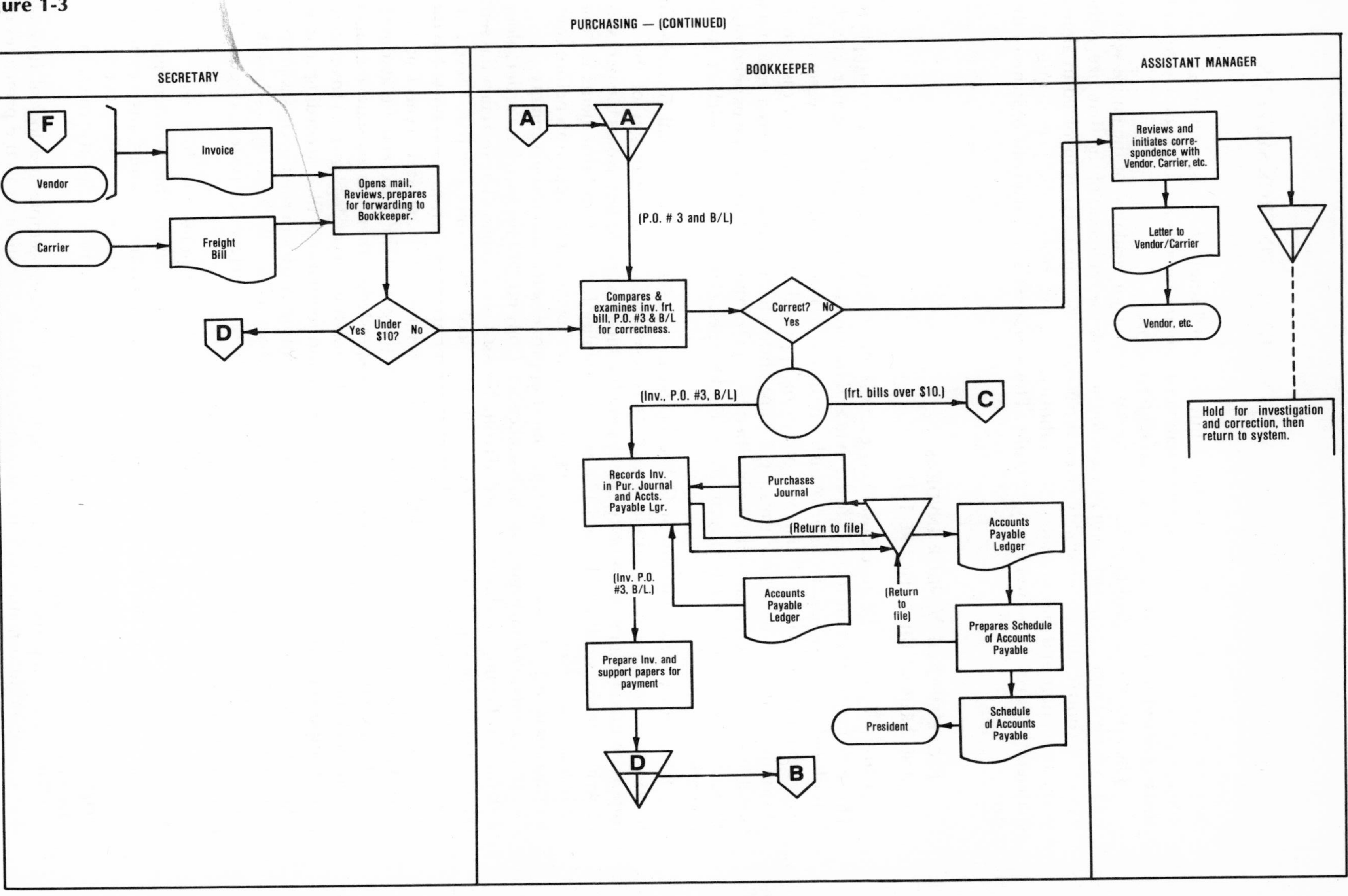
PURCHASING — (CONTINUED)
SECRETARY
BOOKKEEPER
ASSISTANT MANAGER
F
Vendor
Carrier
Invoice
Freight Bill
Opens mail. Reviews, prepares for forwarding to Bookkeeper.
Under $10?
Yes
No
D
A
A
(P.O. # 3 and B/L)
Compares & examines inv. frt. bill, P.O. #3 & B/L for correctness.
Correct?
Yes
No
(Inv., P.O. #3, B/L)
(frt. bills over $10.)
C
Records Inv. in Pur. Journal and Accts. Payable Lgr.
Purchases Journal
(Return to file)
Accounts Payable Ledger
(Inv. P.O. #3, B/L.)
Accounts Payable Ledger
(Return to file)
Prepares Schedule of Accounts Payable
Prepare Inv. and support papers for payment
Schedule of Accounts Payable
President
D
B
Reviews and initiates correspondence with Vendor, Carrier, etc.
Letter to Vendor/Carrier
Vendor, etc.
Hold for investigation and correction, then return to system.

of goods. The purchase order and bill of lading are sent through the assistant manager to the bookkeeper. This provides for independent verification of goods received compared with those ordered by a third party, as will be seen shortly.

The system described here has weaknesses. One major weakness of the entire system, unavoidable from a practical point of view considering the limitation of the firm size, is the extent of control and responsibility given the assistant manager. He is involved in almost every operation and has considerable authority. For this reason, the president/general manager must review his work very carefully. This weakness is characteristic of firms of this size.

Processing of Vendor Invoices and Freight Bills (Figure 1-3)

Chronologically, the next most likely event is the receiving of invoices from suppliers. The secretary receives the invoices in the mail and forwards them to the bookkeeper. Freight bills of under $10 are paid from petty cash. In the interest of expediency, the secretary has been authorized to pay small bills without prior approval. Approval in every case would obviously mean that the assistant manager must always be on hand. There is a risk and a possible weakness here, but it may be justified because of the small size of the expenditure. Freight bills over $10 are sent directly to the bookkeeper. (Figure 1-3 is a flow chart of this operation.)

The positive features of this phase are: (1) having the secretary open mail, provides an important separation of functions as well as relieves the assistant manager of this less important task; (2) an imprest petty cash system for small expenditures avoids the necessity of writing many small checks and places responsibility for small disbursements on one individual, the secretary; and, (3) the system provides for necessary approvals before committing assets, e.g., the assistant manager must approve petty cash disbursements.

Documents are converging on the bookkeeper. Copy no. 3 of the purchase order, along with the bill of lading, has been forwarded from the assistant manager. The secretary has sent the vendor's invoice and freight bill over $10. The bookkeeper must compare these four documents for price and quantity and check them for accuracy. Errors are reported to the assistant manager at once. (It should be noted that if this is more than merely a check of their mathematical accuracy, some degree of expertise on the part of the bookkeeper is assumed. If the bookkeeper does not possess the assumed knowledge, then the assistant manager should check the invoice prices for consistency with quotations or catalog figures.) Invoices of correct shipments are stapled to purchase orders and temporarily filed according to date due. This "package" constitutes the source of accounting entries in the purchases journal, and vendors' accounts in the accounts payable subsidiary ledger. Periodically, a schedule of accounts payable is prepared for the president/general manager for review. (Figure 1-3 indicates how the foregoing may be flow charted.)

The final operation of the purchasing function includes the following sound procedures: (1) a system of review of unpaid vendors' accounts by the president/general manager; (2) review of discrepancies between purchase orders and vendors' invoices by the assistant manager; (3) comparison of vendors' invoice, purchase order, bill of lading and freight bill by bookkeeper for accuracy and correctness; and, (4) filing unpaid invoices by due date to assist in timely payment for discounts, etc.

The purchasing function is now complete. It is a fairly simple and logical flow of documents and information into the accounting records. It conforms to the principles of systems design set out earlier in this chapter and fulfills the purposes of internal control.

Figure 1-4

PAYMENT OF VENDOR'S INVOICES

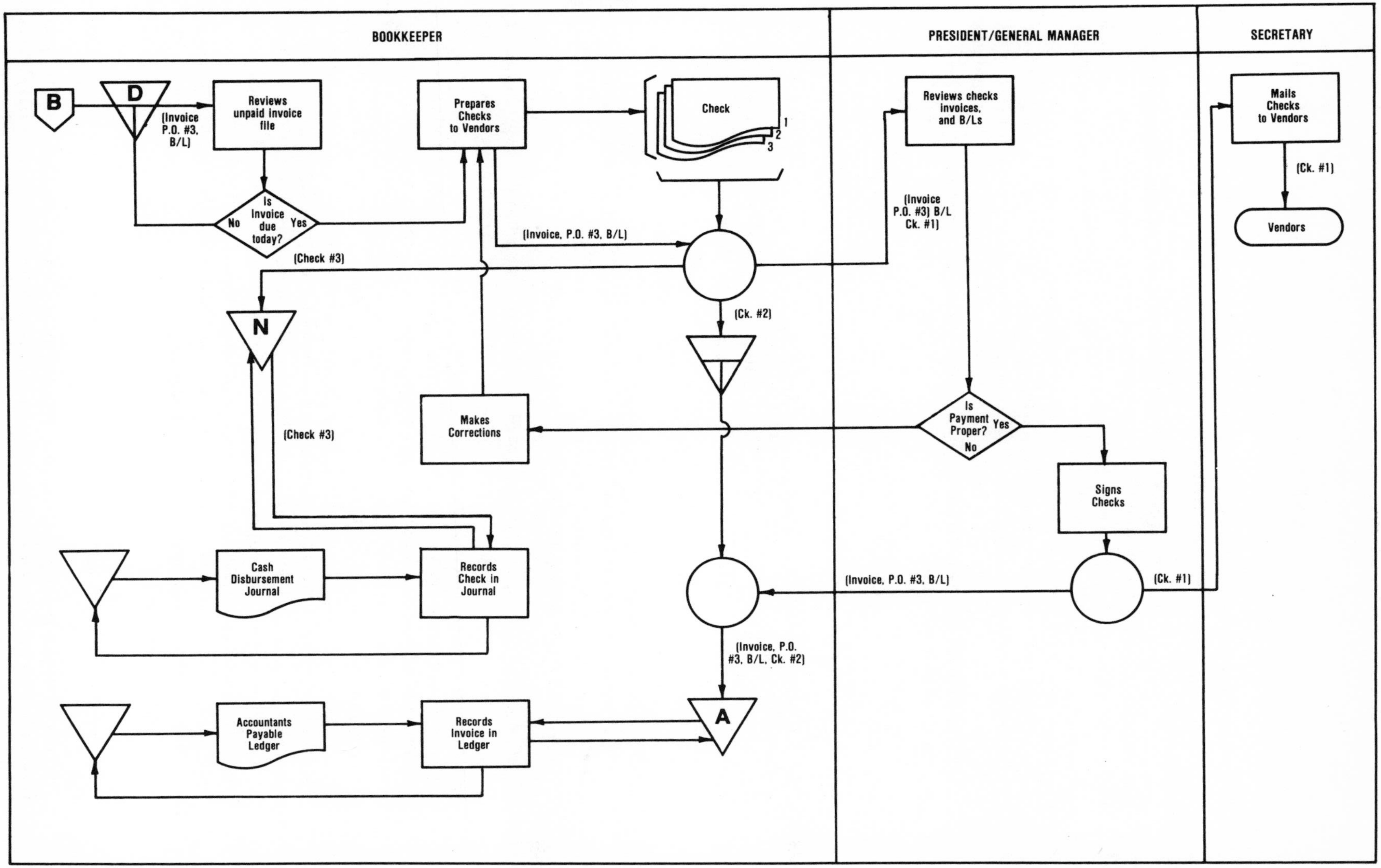

BOOKKEEPER

PRESIDENT/GENERAL MANAGER

SECRETARY

B

D

(Invoice P.O. #3, B/L)

Reviews unpaid invoice file

Is Invoice due today?

No

Yes

Prepares Checks to Vendors

Check

1

2

3

(Invoice, P.O. #3, B/L)

(Check #3)

N

(Ck. #2)

(Check #3)

Makes Corrections

Cash Disbursement Journal

Records Check in Journal

(Invoice, P.O. #3, B/L, Ck. #2)

A

Accountants Payable Ledger

Records Invoice in Ledger

Reviews checks invoices, and B/Ls

(Invoice P.O. #3) B/L Ck. #1)

Is Payment Proper?

Yes

No

Signs Checks

(Invoice, P.O. #3, B/L)

(Ck. #1)

Mails Checks to Vendors

(Ck. #1)

Vendors

The Disbursements Function (Figures 1-4, 1-5, and 1-6)

The process of paying vendors' invoices begins with the bookkeeper, for it is there that the unpaid invoices are stored in a date-due file. Each day it is the bookkeeper's responsibility to remove the stapled "package" of vendors' invoices, copy no. 3 of the purchase orders, and bills of lading due for payment on that day. The bookkeeper must prepare checks in triplicate for payment, taking any discounts allowed, and forward the checks to the president/general manager for approval and signature. Signed checks are forwarded to the secretary for mailing to vendors and the invoice, purchase order copy, and bill of lading are returned to the bookkeeper for filing. The bookkeeper maintains files for paid checks and records such in the cash disbursements journal and vendors' accounts. Figure 1-4 is a graphic portrayal of this operation.

The system of review and approval of checks by the president/general manager is an important feature of this system. It should be noted, in addition, that a separation of duties provides that the bookkeeper, who prepares the checks, does not gain control of them once they are signed. The number of copies and the filing system of these check copies are an important control device. The paid invoice file, by vendor name, supports any query about payment from a vendor. Of course, it also supports entries in the vendor's ledger account. The file of paid checks in check number order is necessary both to record in the cash disbursements journal and to reconcile the bank account. While no mention is made of it in the system described, a spoiled or voided check file must be maintained. Without such control, a weakness in the system exists.

Payment of Freight Bills, Travel and Truck Maintenance (Figures 1-5 and 1-6)

Freight bills over $10 are forwarded from the secretary to the assistant manager for approval, to the bookkeeper for payment, and to the president/general manager for signature. Nearly the same procedure exists for reimbursement for travel expense to the outside salesman and for maintenance and repair expense requests from the deliveryman. The only difference is that the latter do not pass through the secretary's hands except when paid. Instead, requests for travel, and maintenance and repair expenditures come directly to the assistant manager for approval. This is flow charted in Figures 1-5 and 1-6.

As is the case for payment of purchase invoices, a review and approval system exists here. The approval phase covers both approvals to commit funds in excess of a maximum sum and approvals for payment. For example, before travel costing over $100 can be undertaken by the outside salesman, prior approval must be obtained from the assistant manager. Similarly, truck repair exceeding $50 requires authorization. There is good separation of duties. The assistant manager approves invoices for payment, and the bookkeeper prepares checks. Checks are reviewed again and signed by the president/general manager. Finally, the checks are actually disbursed by the secretary.

Petty Cash (Figure 1-7)

The last sub-function under disbursements is petty cash. An impress petty cash fund of $100 is kept by the secretary. The secretary is authorized to make payments directly from petty cash for amounts up to $10. Disbursements for amounts over $10 must be made

Figure 1-5

PAYMENT OF FREIGHT BILLS OVER $10, TRAVEL & TRUCK MAINTENANCE — PART I

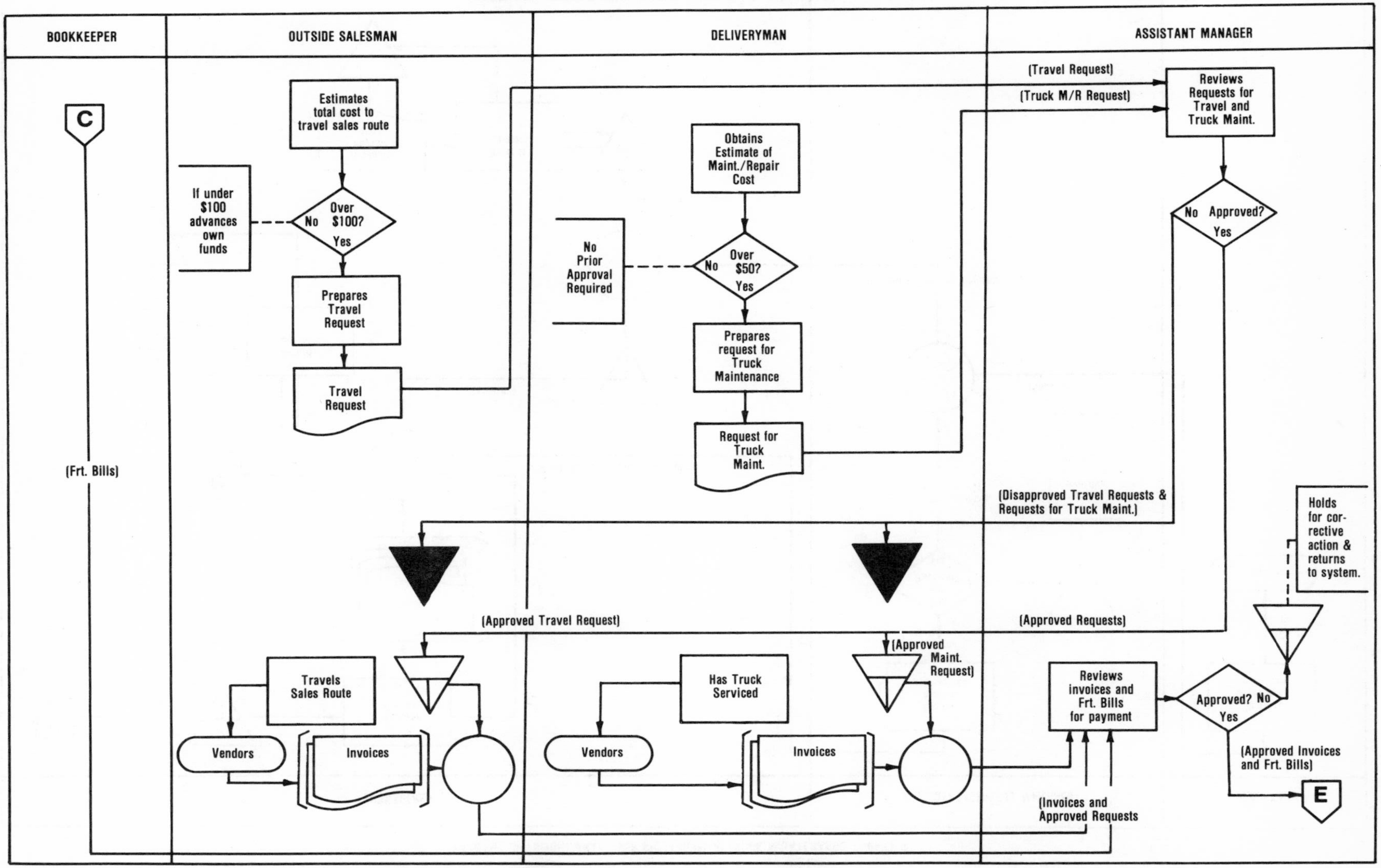

BOOKKEEPER

C

(Frt. Bills)

OUTSIDE SALESMAN

Estimates total cost to travel sales route

Over $100?
No
Yes

If under $100 advances own funds

Prepares Travel Request

Travel Request

Travels Sales Route

Vendors

Invoices

(Approved Travel Request)

DELIVERYMAN

Obtains Estimate of Maint./Repair Cost

Over $50?
No
Yes

No Prior Approval Required

Prepares request for Truck Maintenance

Request for Truck Maint.

Has Truck Serviced

Vendors

Invoices

(Approved Maint. Request)

ASSISTANT MANAGER

(Travel Request)

(Truck M/R Request)

Reviews Requests for Travel and Truck Maint.

Approved?
No
Yes

(Disapproved Travel Requests & Requests for Truck Maint.)

(Approved Requests)

Reviews invoices and Frt. Bills for payment

(Invoices and Approved Requests)

Approved?
No
Yes

Holds for corrective action & returns to system.

(Approved Invoices and Frt. Bills)

E

Figure 1-6

PAYMENT OF FREIGHT BILLS OVER $10, TRAVEL & TRUCK MAINTENANCE — PART II

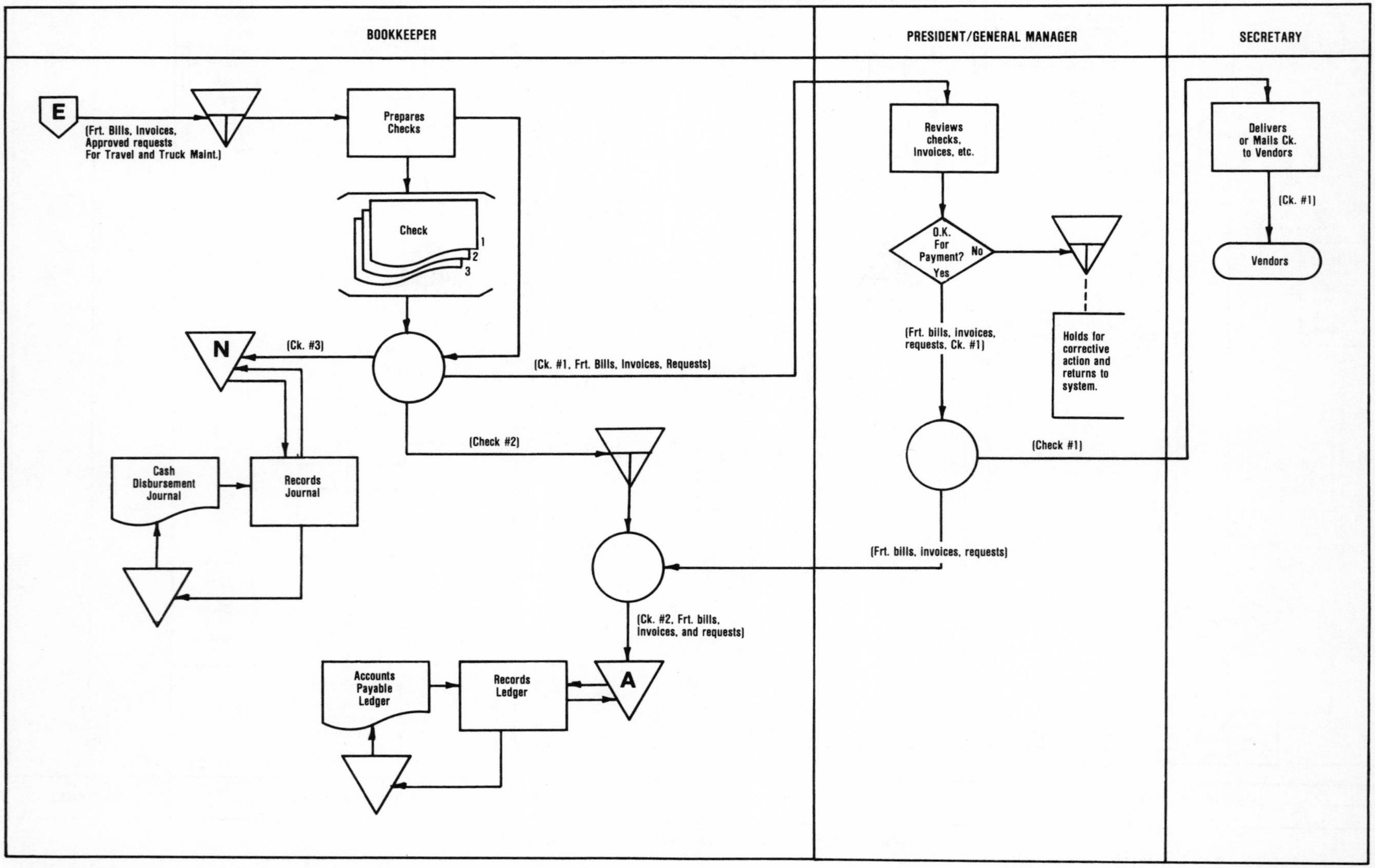

BOOKKEEPER

E

(Frt. Bills, Invoices, Approved requests For Travel and Truck Maint.)

Prepares Checks

Check

1

2

3

N

(Ck. #3)

(Ck. #1, Frt. Bills, Invoices, Requests)

(Check #2)

Cash Disbursement Journal

Records Journal

(Ck. #2, Frt. bills, invoices, and requests)

Accounts Payable Ledger

Records Ledger

A

PRESIDENT/GENERAL MANAGER

Reviews checks, Invoices, etc.

O.K. For Payment?

No

Yes

(Frt. bills, invoices, requests, Ck. #1)

Holds for corrective action and returns to system.

(Check #1)

(Frt. bills, invoices, requests)

SECRETARY

Delivers or Mails Ck. to Vendors

(Ck. #1)

Vendors

Figure 1-7

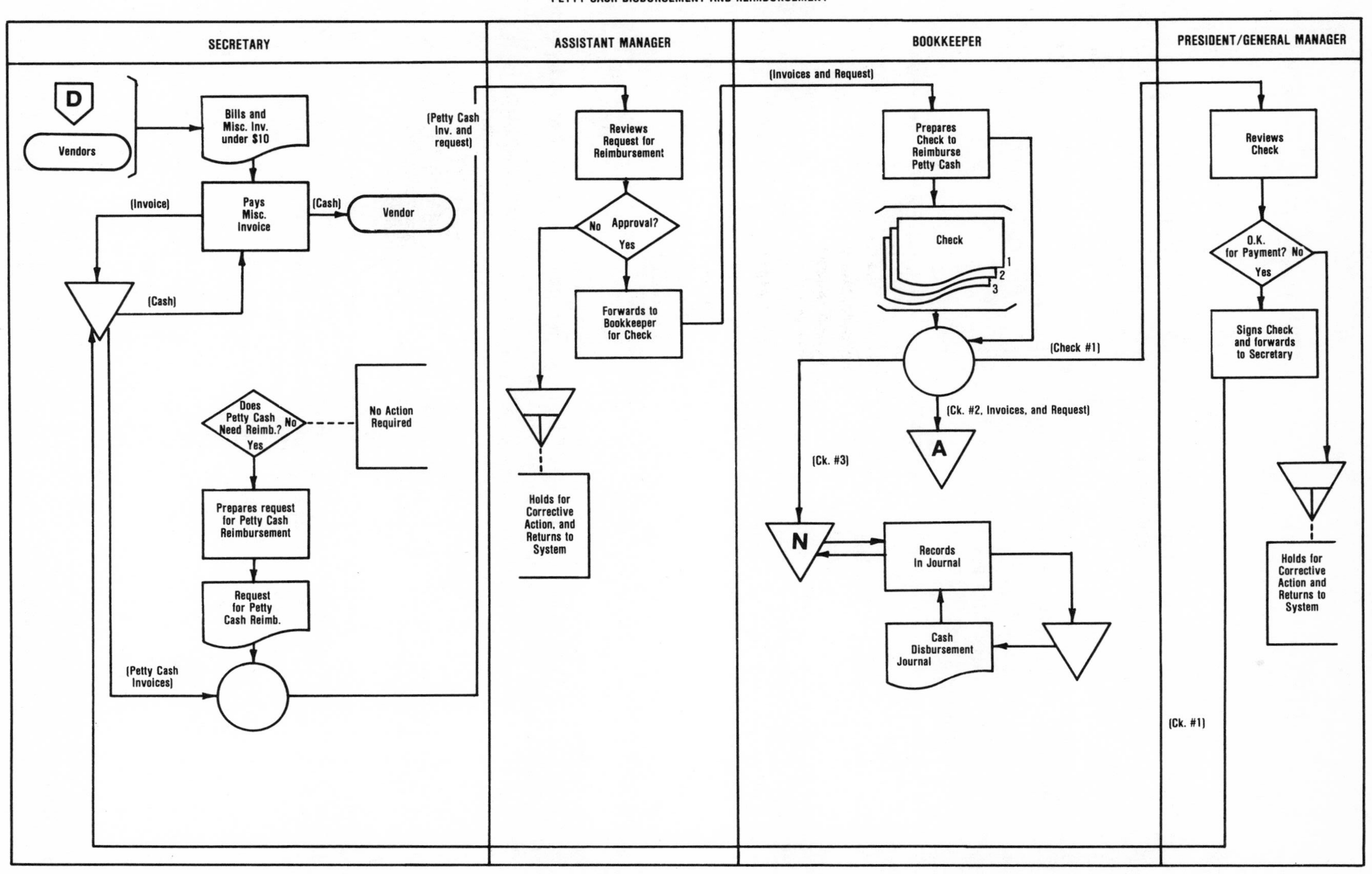
PETTY CASH DISBURSEMENT AND REIMBURSEMENT
SECRETARY
ASSISTANT MANAGER
BOOKKEEPER
PRESIDENT/GENERAL MANAGER
D
Vendors
Bills and Misc. Inv. under $10
Pays Misc. Invoice
(Invoice)
(Cash)
Vendor
(Cash)
Does Petty Cash Need Reimb.?
No
Yes
No Action Required
Prepares request for Petty Cash Reimbursement
Request for Petty Cash Reimb.
(Petty Cash Invoices)
(Petty Cash Inv. and request)
Reviews Request for Reimbursement
No
Approval?
Yes
Forwards to Bookkeeper for Check
Holds for Corrective Action, and Returns to System
(Invoices and Request)
Prepares Check to Reimburse Petty Cash
Check
1
2
3
(Check #1)
(Ck. #2, Invoices, and Request)
A
(Ck. #3)
N
Records In Journal
Cash Disbursement Journal
Reviews Check
O.K. for Payment?
No
Yes
Signs Check and forwards to Secretary
Holds for Corrective Action and Returns to System
(Ck. #1)

by check. Periodic reimbursement is made upon request by the secretary and approval by the assistant manager. Figure 1-7 demonstrates the procedure of petty cash disbursement and reimbursement. The same review and approval system exists here as in the case of a check disbursement, except that expenditures from petty cash are reviewed at the time of reimbursement. One other difference may be noted—the invoices do not accompany the check sent to the president/general manager for signature. This is because the amounts are too small. Moreover, the invoices have already been reviewed by the assistant manager. An imprest petty cash system is itself an important internal control device.

Charge Sales (Figures 1-8 through 1-11)

In the illustrative firm, sales are made both for cash, in which case they are rung-up on a cash register, and on account. Sales on account may originate directly through the inside salesmen and the outside salesman, or orders may come through the mail. Whatever their source, customer orders must be approved for credit. This is the responsibility of the president/general manager. For practical purposes, over-the-counter and other customer orders are routinely approved for regular customers. Salesmen are instructed on handling orders from new customers whose credit is restricted in amount. Figure 1-8 is a flow chart representing incoming customer orders and the system of credit approval. A credit approval system similar to the one depicted is obviously essential to satisfactory control. Again from a practical point of view, sales invoices may be physically typed by the secretary on direction of the salesmen. A three-part sales invoice is used, the purpose of which is described in the next operation.

Customer orders, as approved, must be billed and invoices recorded. It is essential that no goods be delivered without proper billing. Over-the-counter sales are probably delivered simultaneously unless goods are not on hand. Others may be shipped by independent carriers or delivered by the deliveryman. The billing and recording for the over-the-counter sales operation is shown in Figure 1-9. Figure 1-10 is a flow chart of this function for sales to be delivered, and Figure 1-11 shows the flow if shipped by common carrier.

The system of checks, approvals and other controls indicated in Figures 1-9 and 1-10 satisfies all requirements of good internal control. Separation of duties is complete. The salesmen write sales orders (invoices), and the bookkeeper checks them for mathematical accuracy. One sales invoice is kept in a temporary file until notification is received that goods are delivered. The second copy of the sales invoice and the customer order (if there is one) go to the warehouseman who fills the order either for in-store delivery (over-the-counter sales) or for shipment. He compares the customer order with the sales invoice to determine if it is correct in amount, size, etc. After initialing the invoice, he returns it to the bookkeeper.

Receipt of the copy of the sales invoice and customer order by the bookkeeper initiates necessary entries in the sales journal and customer ledger. Copies no. 1 and no. 2 of the sales invoices are filed permanently, copy no. 1 by invoice number and copy no. 2 in the customer file. The over-the-counter customer is given sales invoice copy no. 3 for his records. For customers who order for shipment by common carrier, sales invoice copy no. 3 is mailed directly to them by the bookkeeper when notice is received that goods are shipped or delivered. When goods are delivered by the deliveryman, the third copy of the sales invoice accompanies the goods and the deliveryman obtains the customer's signature on the delivery ticket.

Internal checks here are satisfactory. The sales invoice is checked internally and/or compared with the customer order three times: by the salesman when the invoice is written;

Figure 1-8

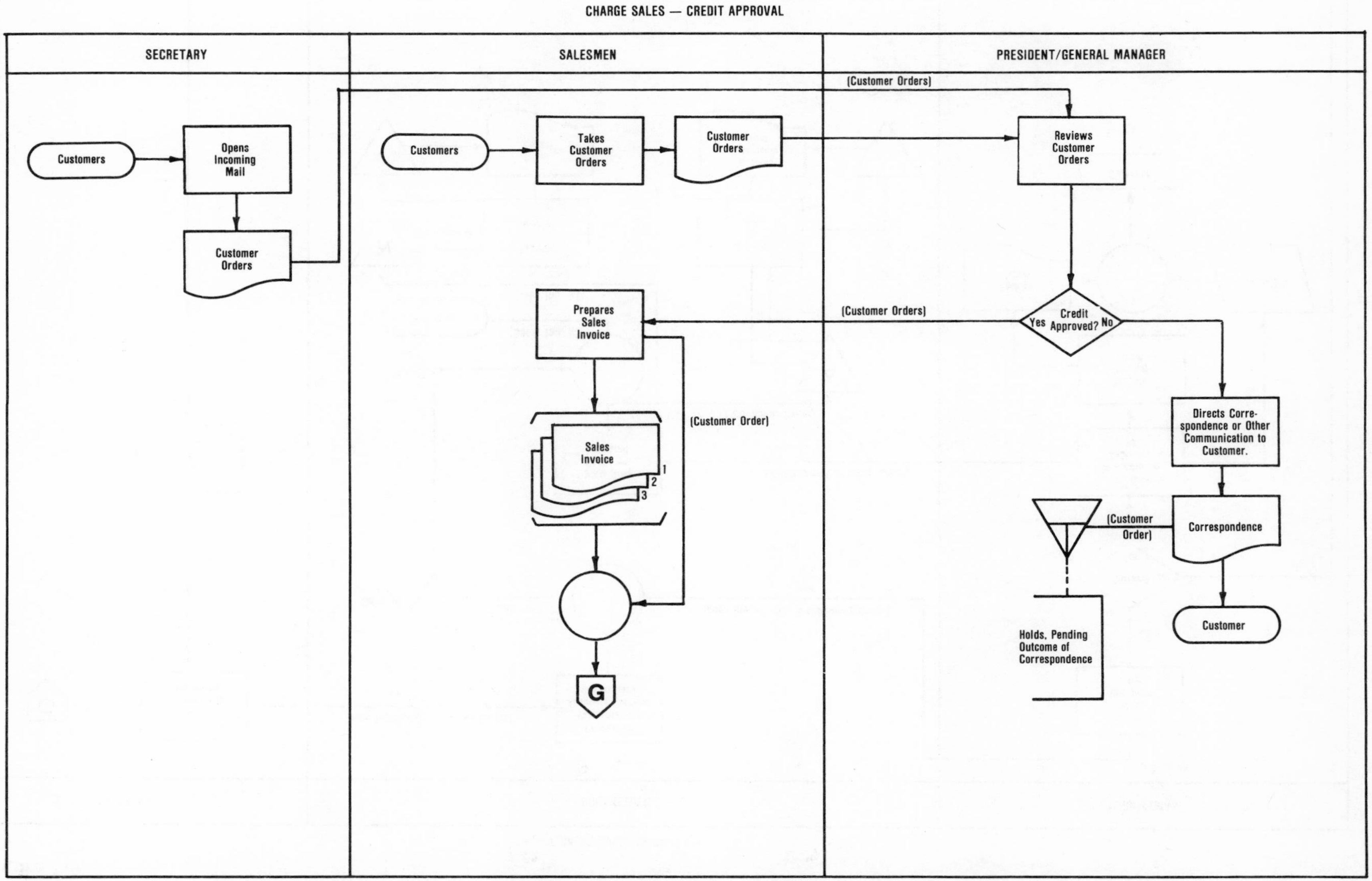

CHARGE SALES — CREDIT APPROVAL

SECRETARY

Customers

Opens Incoming Mail

Customer Orders

SALESMEN

Customers

Takes Customer Orders

Customer Orders

Prepares Sales Invoice

(Customer Order)

Sales Invoice

1

2

3

G

PRESIDENT/GENERAL MANAGER

(Customer Orders)

Reviews Customer Orders

Credit Approved?

Yes

No

(Customer Orders)

Directs Correspondence or Other Communication to Customer.

Correspondence

(Customer Order)

Holds, Pending Outcome of Correspondence

Customer

Figure 1-9

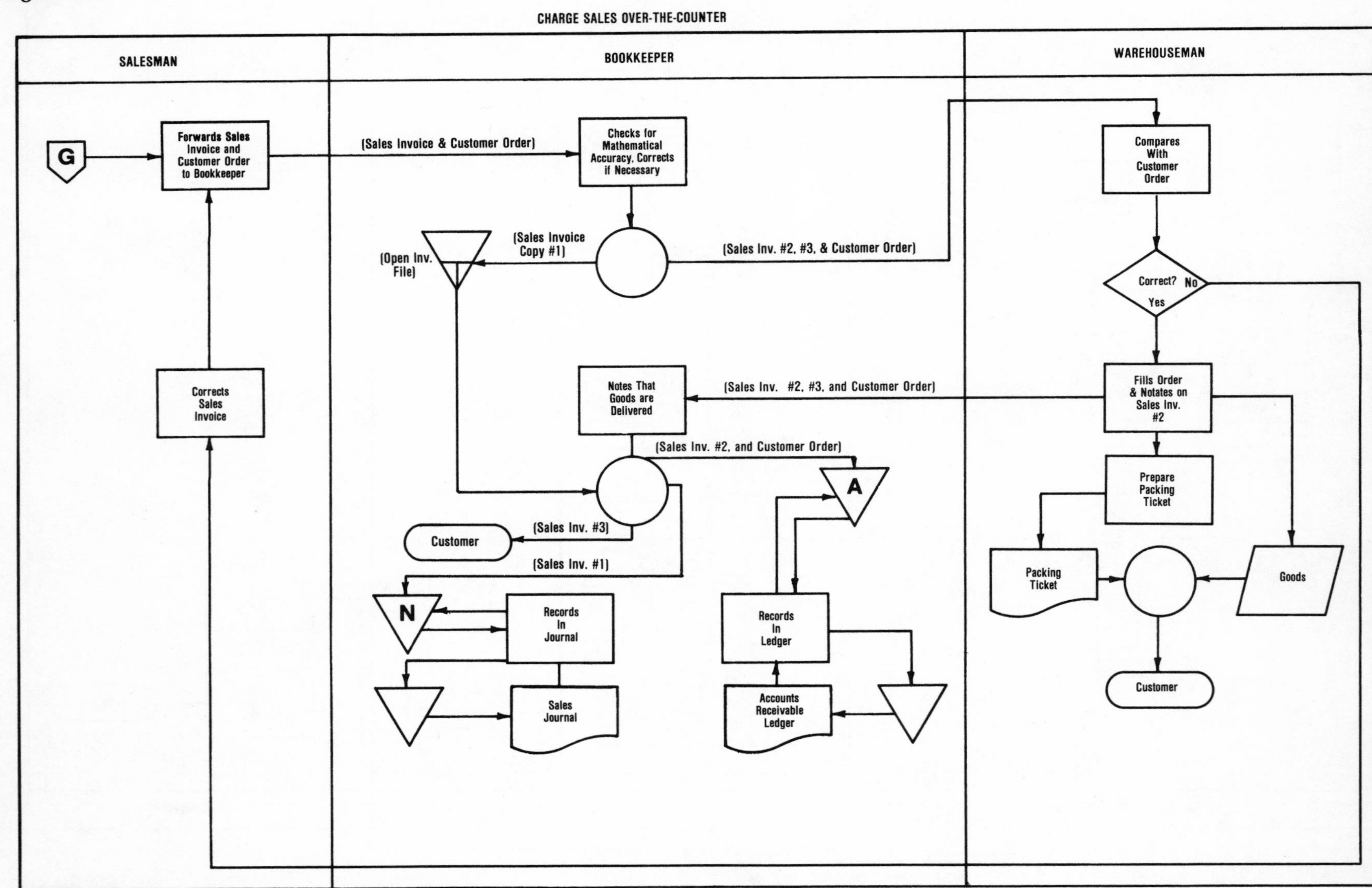
CHARGE SALES OVER-THE-COUNTER
SALESMAN
BOOKKEEPER
WAREHOUSEMAN
G
Forwards Sales Invoice and Customer Order to Bookkeeper
Corrects Sales Invoice
(Sales Invoice & Customer Order)
Checks for Mathematical Accuracy, Corrects if Necessary
(Sales Invoice Copy #1)
(Open Inv. File)
(Sales Inv. #2, #3, & Customer Order)
Compares With Customer Order
Correct?
No
Yes
Fills Order & Notates on Sales Inv. #2
(Sales Inv. #2, #3, and Customer Order)
Notes That Goods are Delivered
(Sales Inv. #2, and Customer Order)
A
(Sales Inv. #3)
Customer
(Sales Inv. #1)
N
Records In Journal
Sales Journal
Records In Ledger
Accounts Receivable Ledger
Prepare Packing Ticket
Packing Ticket
Goods
Customer

Figure 1-10

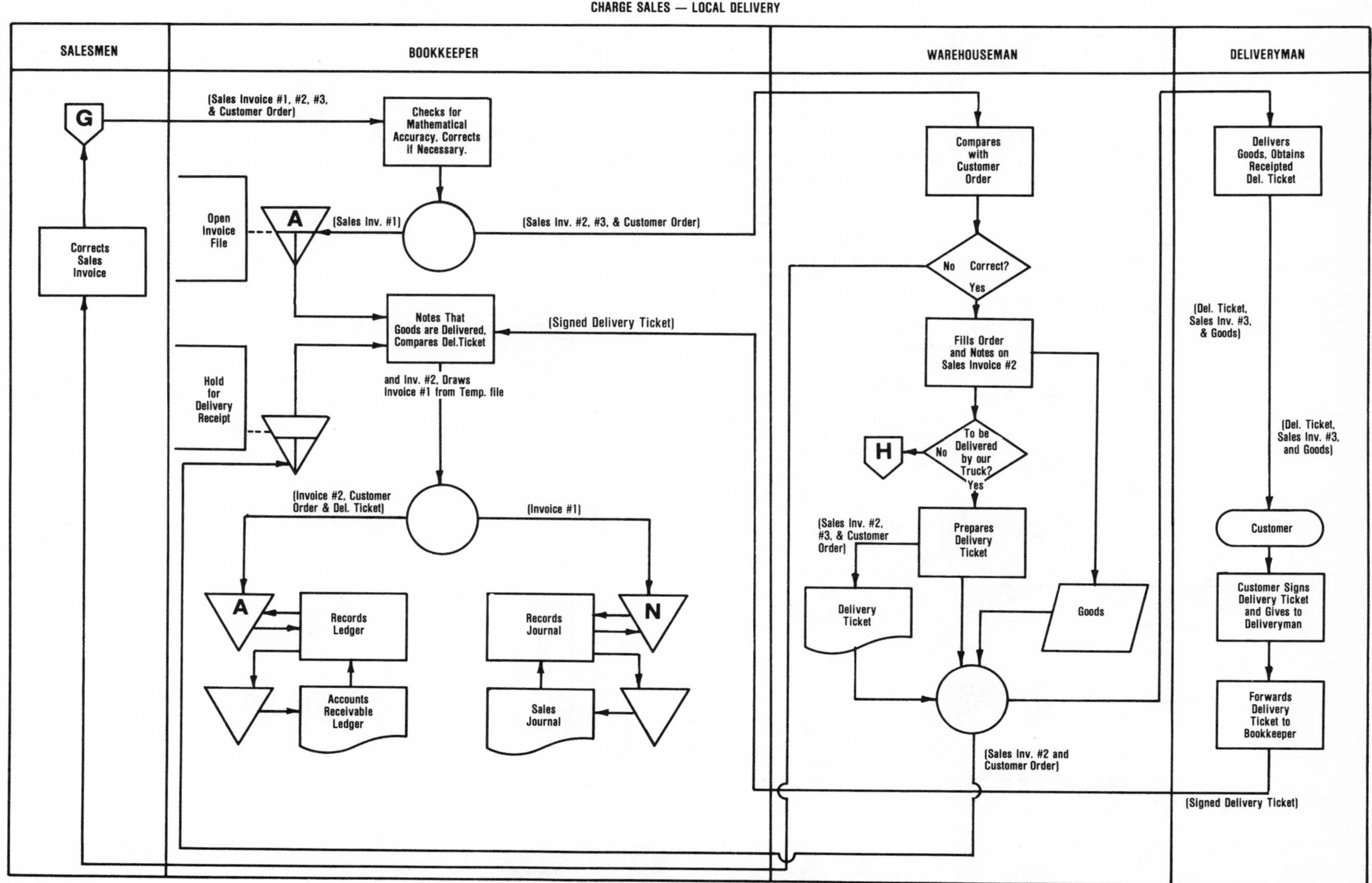
CHARGE SALES — LOCAL DELIVERY
SALESMEN
BOOKKEEPER
WAREHOUSEMAN
DELIVERYMAN
G
Corrects Sales Invoice
(Sales Invoice #1, #2, #3, & Customer Order)
Checks for Mathematical Accuracy, Corrects if Necessary.
Open Invoice File
A
(Sales Inv. #1)
(Sales Inv. #2, #3, & Customer Order)
Notes That Goods are Delivered, Compares Del.Ticket and Inv. #2, Draws Invoice #1 from Temp. file
(Signed Delivery Ticket)
Hold for Delivery Receipt
(Invoice #2, Customer Order & Del. Ticket)
(Invoice #1)
A
Records Ledger
Accounts Receivable Ledger
Records Journal
N
Sales Journal
Compares with Customer Order
No
Correct?
Yes
Fills Order and Notes on Sales Invoice #2
H
No
To be Delivered by our Truck?
Yes
(Sales Inv. #2, #3, & Customer Order)
Prepares Delivery Ticket
Delivery Ticket
Goods
(Sales Inv. #2 and Customer Order)
Delivers Goods, Obtains Receipted Del. Ticket
(Del. Ticket, Sales Inv. #3, & Goods)
(Del. Ticket, Sales Inv. #3, and Goods)
Customer
Customer Signs Delivery Ticket and Gives to Deliveryman
Forwards Delivery Ticket to Bookkeeper
(Signed Delivery Ticket)

Figure 1-11

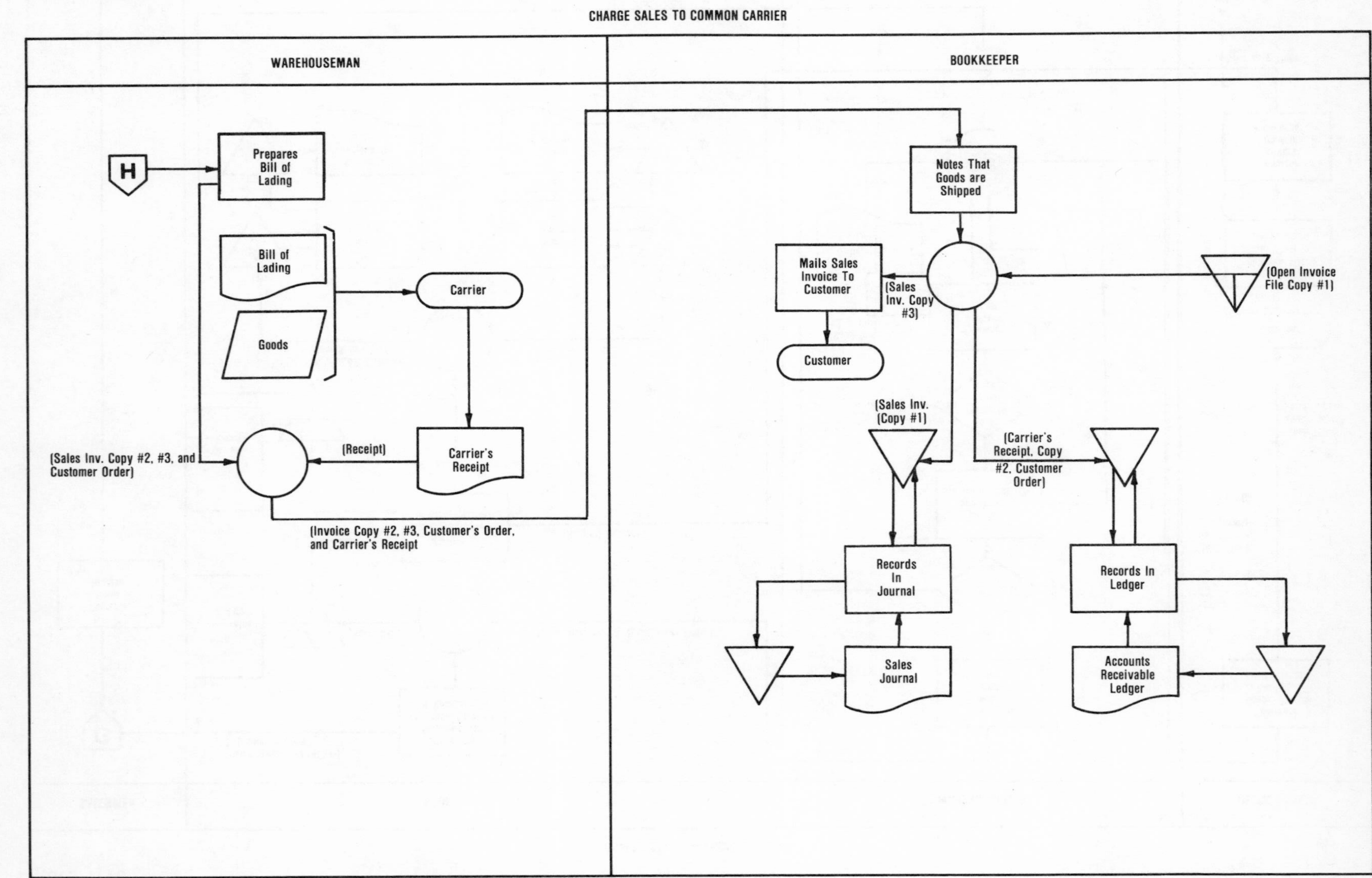
CHARGE SALES TO COMMON CARRIER
WAREHOUSEMAN
BOOKKEEPER
H
Prepares Bill of Lading
Bill of Lading
Goods
Carrier
Carrier's Receipt
(Receipt)
(Sales Inv. Copy #2, #3, and Customer Order)
(Invoice Copy #2, #3, Customer's Order, and Carrier's Receipt
Notes That Goods are Shipped
Mails Sales Invoice To Customer
(Sales Inv. Copy #3)
Customer
(Open Invoice File Copy #1)
(Sales Inv. (Copy #1)
(Carrier's Receipt, Copy #2, Customer Order)
Records In Journal
Records In Ledger
Sales Journal
Accounts Receivable Ledger

by the bookkeeper for mechanical accuracy; and by the warehouseman for comparison of goods invoiced with those ordered. A fourth check occurs when goods are delivered or shipped by the customer who signs a delivery ticket or the receipt from the common carrier.

One weakness of the sales function here is that with several salesmen writing sales invoices, perhaps simultaneously, control could easily be lost unless sales invoices are serially numbered and accounted for. There is no mention of this safeguard. The charge sales function is complete.

Cash Receipts (Figures 1-12, 1-13)

Sources of incoming cash for the illustrative firm are several: over-the-counter sales for cash; collections on account; other receipts mainly originating with the president/general manager, such as the proceeds of loans or additional investments. For ease in reading, cash sales will be flow charted and analyzed first.

Cash Sales (Figure 1-12)

All sales for cash are rung up on the cash register by the salesmen. At the end of the day, the register is totaled and balanced by the assistant manager, who also prepares the day's deposit. The deposit is actually made by the deliveryman. The register balancing done by the assistant manager entails a daily report, summarizing sales by classification, sales tax, collections of cash on account (and also rung-up) and total currency and coin deposited. (The daily report also includes a summary of checks on account received through the mails and made a part of the day's deposit. Because this is not a cash sale, this function is shown on a later flow chart.) Figure 1-12 is a flow chart of the cash sales operation.

A review of Figure 1-12 shows that cash moves directly from the assistant manager to the deliveryman to the depository. The bookkeeper handles no cash, but does perform two important internal checks. One, the bookeeper proves the daily report balance prepared by the assistant manager, and two, the bookkeeper compares the cash shown as collected in the daily report with the duplicate deposit slip given directly to him/her by the deliveryman. Thus, the possibility of error is quite small, as is the possibility of any cash misappropriation. For information purposes, the daily report, duplicate deposit slip, and cash register tape are sent to the president/general manager before filing. This procedure is essential to sound cash management and is shown in Figure 1-12.

Collections on Account (Figure 1-13)

Collections on account through the mails come through the secretary, who opens mail and lists the checks received. The list goes directly to the bookkeeper and the checks are sent to the assistant manager for inclusion in the daily deposit. This is flow charted in Figure 1-13. The listing of incoming checks is important as a device to reduce the chance of errors, lost checks, and possibly misappropriation. The list is compared with the duplicate deposit slip by the bookkeeper and is filed in bookkeeping along with the duplicate deposit slip. Two possible weaknesses exist. First, the secretary should stamp each check with the company's endorsement: "For Deposit Only." This will prevent the checks from being cashed or deposited in another account. Second, the list of checks prepared by the secretary should be made in duplicate, the second copy going to the president/general manager for comparison with the duplicate deposit slip.

Figure 1-12

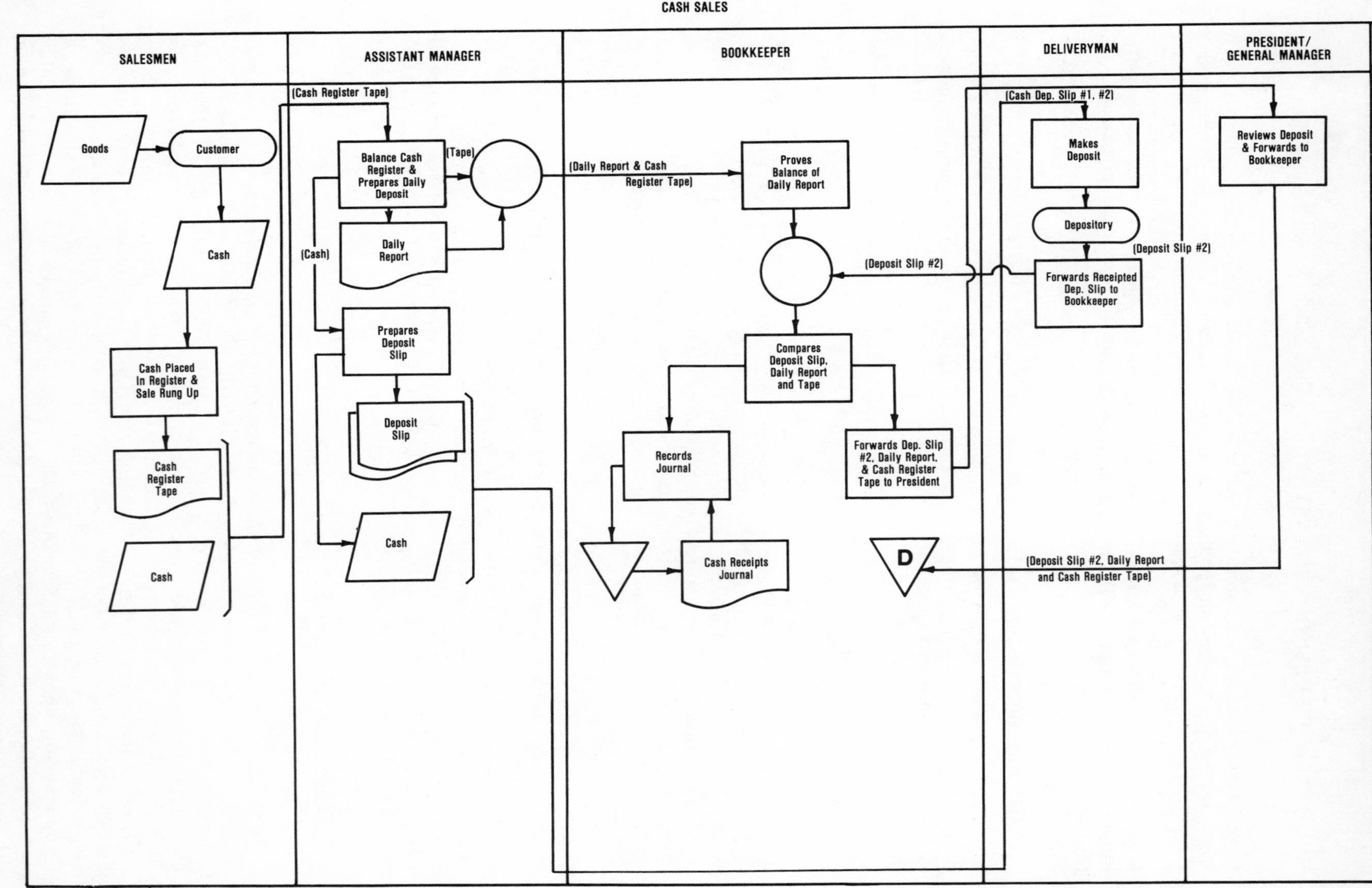
CASH SALES
SALESMEN
ASSISTANT MANAGER
BOOKKEEPER
DELIVERYMAN
PRESIDENT/ GENERAL MANAGER
Goods
Customer
Cash
Cash Placed In Register & Sale Rung Up
Cash Register Tape
Cash
(Cash Register Tape)
Balance Cash Register & Prepares Daily Deposit
(Tape)
Daily Report
(Cash)
Prepares Deposit Slip
Deposit Slip
Cash
(Daily Report & Cash Register Tape)
Proves Balance of Daily Report
(Deposit Slip #2)
Compares Deposit Slip, Daily Report and Tape
Records Journal
Cash Receipts Journal
Forwards Dep. Slip #2, Daily Report, & Cash Register Tape to President
D
(Cash Dep. Slip #1, #2)
Makes Deposit
Depository
(Deposit Slip #2)
Forwards Receipted Dep. Slip to Bookkeeper
Reviews Deposit & Forwards to Bookkeeper
(Deposit Slip #2, Daily Report and Cash Register Tape)

Figure 1-13

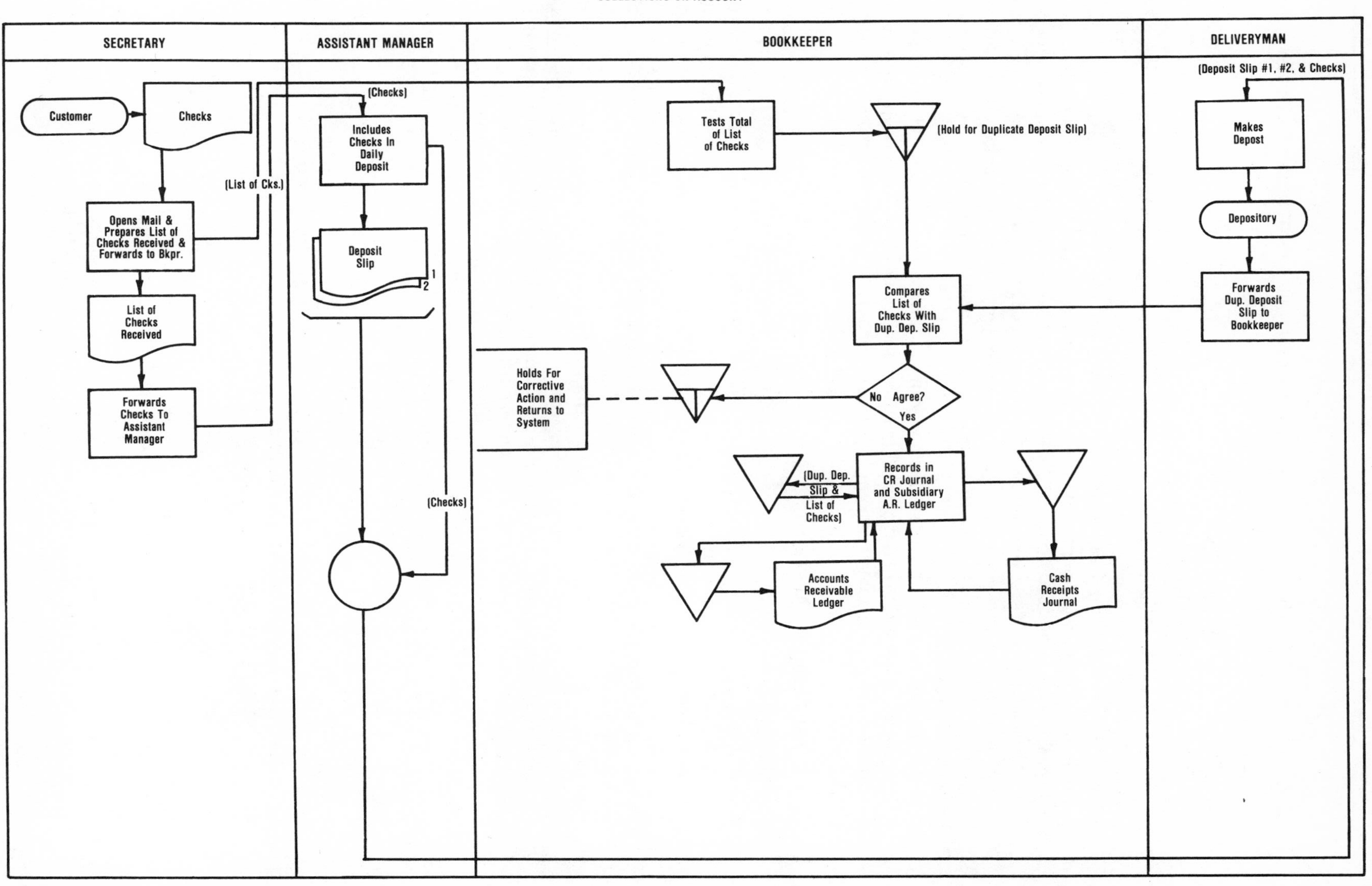
COLLECTIONS ON ACCOUNT
SECRETARY
ASSISTANT MANAGER
BOOKKEEPER
DELIVERYMAN
Customer
Checks
Opens Mail & Prepares List of Checks Received & Forwards to Bkpr.
(List of Cks.)
List of Checks Received
Forwards Checks To Assistant Manager
(Checks)
Includes Checks In Daily Deposit
Deposit Slip
1
2
(Checks)
Tests Total of List of Checks
(Hold for Duplicate Deposit Slip)
Compares List of Checks With Dup. Dep. Slip
No Agree? Yes
Holds For Corrective Action and Returns to System
Records in CR Journal and Subsidiary A.R. Ledger
(Dup. Dep. Slip & List of Checks)
Accounts Receivable Ledger
Cash Receipts Journal
(Deposit Slip #1, #2, & Checks)
Makes Depost
Depository
Forwards Dup. Deposit Slip to Bookkeeper

Other Cash Receipts and Reporting (Figure 1-14)

There are two final operations performed as cash receipts functions. The president/general manager originates incoming cash through borrowing and, possibly, additional investments. In addition, the status of accounts receivable must be reported to him periodically. These two operations are charted in Figure 1-14. The president/general manager's review of unpaid accounts receivable is necessary to fulfill his responsibilities for credit and collection. Moreover, this review serves as a check on the efficiency and accuracy of the bookkeeping function. The system is weak here in that someone other than the bookkeeper should prepare the list of accounts receivable. Possibly the secretary could perform this function.

No mention is made in the system for journal entry authorization. The bookkeeper should not be permitted to make general journal entries unless they have been approved by the president/general manager. A simple journal voucher authorization form may be used.

3. The Chart of Accounts

The final building block of an internal control system is the chart of accounts. This is a listing of the general ledger accounts of the firm.[3] Accounts are more than merely the summarizations of transactions affecting each asset, liability, owner's equity, revenue, and expense. The functions of the accounts are: (1) to provide information necessary to prepare financial statements for third parties; and (2) to yield a variety of information necessary for management to perform its function. Mindful of these functions, and using the firm's organization chart and the flow chart as foundations, a chart of accounts can be drawn up. Most of the general ledger accounts are indicated by and follow directly from the organization chart and flow charts. For example, the accounting information flow makes several cash accounts necessary. Procedures are described for clearing and balancing the cash register; checks are written, necessitating a cash in-bank account; and control over petty cash is given as a responsibility of the president/general manager. The president/general manager is also responsible for cash management and funding, thus accounts are needed for notes payable-banks and notes payable-shareholders. The point is that a chart of accounts follows as the third "overlay," translating the organization chart and flow chart into double entry accounting.

How to Help Management Overcome Staff Resistance to ICS Installation

It is management, not the accountant, who has responsibility for the ICS and its operation, and consequently, it is management who must solve whatever personnel problems that arise. The accountant can help by avoiding creating an atmosphere of resentment or even antagonism, which may arise if certain employees feel that the accountant is a threat in some way, or if his attitude is taken to be demeaning toward the firm's employees.

Some problems that may arise are: first, individuals often feel a sense of ownership in

[3]Actually, the chart of accounts means much more than merely listing the accounts as will be elaborated on in Chapter 2.

Figure 1-14

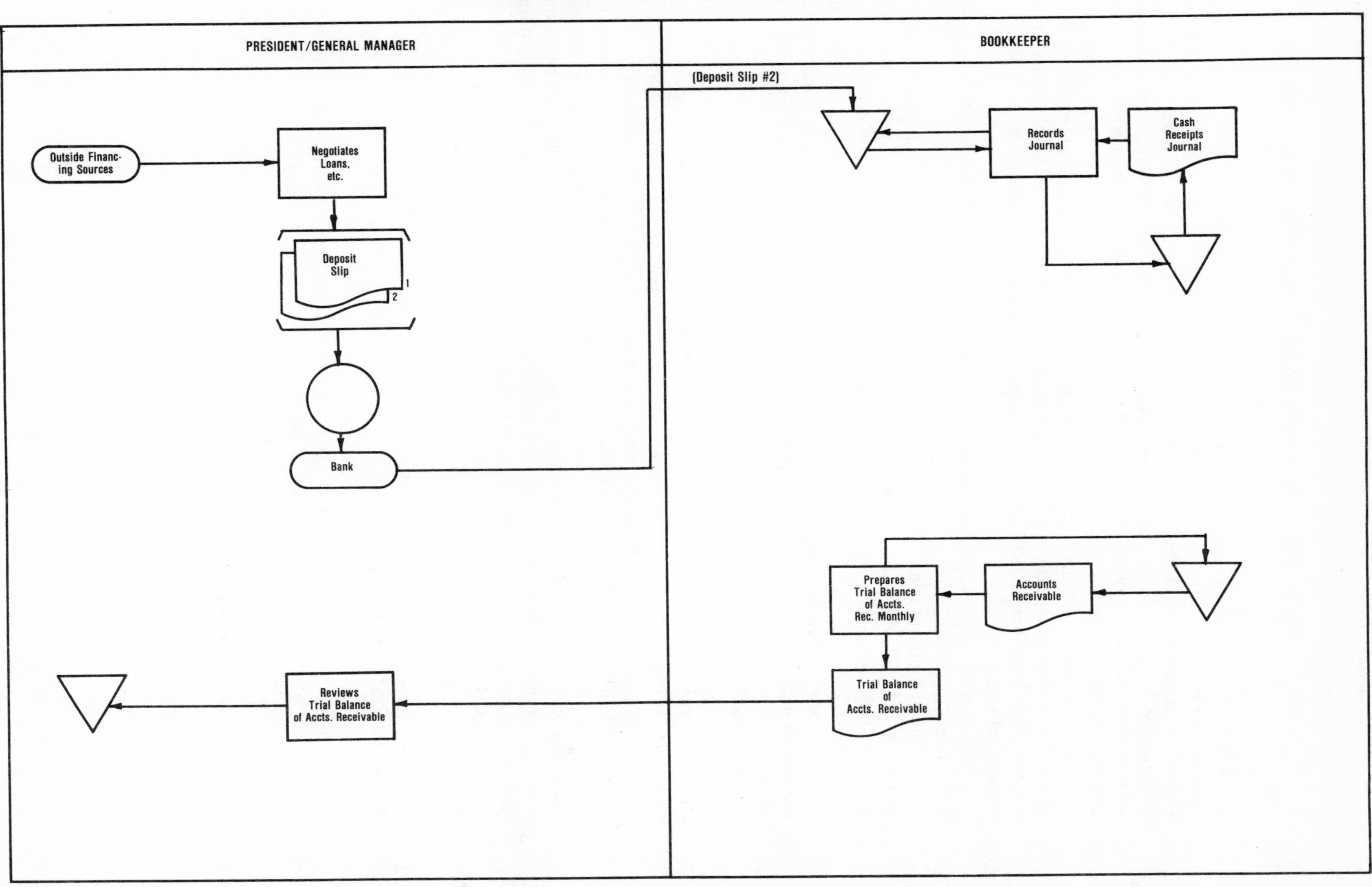

NON-OPERATING CASH RECEIPTS AND REPORTING TO PRESIDENT/GENERAL MANAGER
PRESIDENT/GENERAL MANAGER
BOOKKEEPER
Outside Financ-ing Sources
Negotiates Loans, etc.
Deposit Slip
1
2
Bank
(Deposit Slip #2)
Records Journal
Cash Receipts Journal
Prepares Trial Balance of Accts. Rec. Monthly
Accounts Receivable
Trial Balance of Accts. Receivable
Reviews Trial Balance of Accts. Receivable

procedures or techniques that they themselves may have developed. There may also be a kind of territorial proprietorship—one's desk, chair, papers, etc.; second, once begun, a system or technique however ineffective from a control point of view, tends to be perpetuated because of an aversion to change; third, many people have a strong sense of what ought to be done, not only in their own area of responsibility, but in other areas as well. This may be manifested by giving (or trying to give) directions to peers or by volunteering answers to questions not directed to them. Finally, an individual may feel that he or she has special knowledge of a particular job so that the job cannot be accomplished as efficiently by anyone else. They may be reluctant to communicate their knowledge or to assist in the training of others.

What can the accountant do? There are several ways in which he can assist management in "selling" an ICS:

1. The accountant can take advantage of behavior patterns. For example, the fact that employees take an ownership interest in their work can be of great benefit to the firm if properly directed to support the firm's objectives. Moreover, faithful adherence to a *good* system or technique is quite desirable, and should be encouraged. The point is, rather than trying to alter ingrained behavior patterns or requiring them to be overridden by management fiat, the accountant can help in redirecting the behavior toward the objectives of the ICS.

2. A good working relationship with the firm's staff should be established at the outset. The accountant can maintain a professional attitude and yet be cordial. His work efficiency should not exclude patience and pleasantness. With a minimum of effort, an accountant can easily develop respect for his special knowledge on the part of the firm's employees.

3. A clear explanation of the function and purpose of the system with respect to the individual employee can be of considerable usefulness. The accountant may recommend to management that the accountant himself be allowed to make the explanation, in writing, to each employee. Unless management has reason to object, the accountant may recommend that an overview of the system be given to all employees rather than simply explaining to each, his or her particular role. People often respond favorably when they are familar with how their part fits into the whole.

AFTER THE SYSTEM IS INSTALLED

A final word on designing and installing internal control systems is one of caution. Almost no system can be devised, set in motion, and then left to operate itself. The word "de-bugging," popularly applied to computer program design, is equally applicable here. An ICS, once in operation, must be observed, tested, and amended where necessary. Moreover, the system should be periodically reviewed for required modification due to: (a) changes in the basic operation of the firm, e.g., from retail to wholesale; (b) restructuring of the firm's personnel through expansion, contraction, or changes in the organizational make-up; (c) external forces requiring expanded reporting to governmental agencies; and, (d) other influences, internal or external, exerting pressure on the firm. A change in the physical location of the firm, say to larger quarters, requires a review of the ICS.

APPENDIX

TRADITIONAL SYMBOLS USED IN FLOW CHARTING

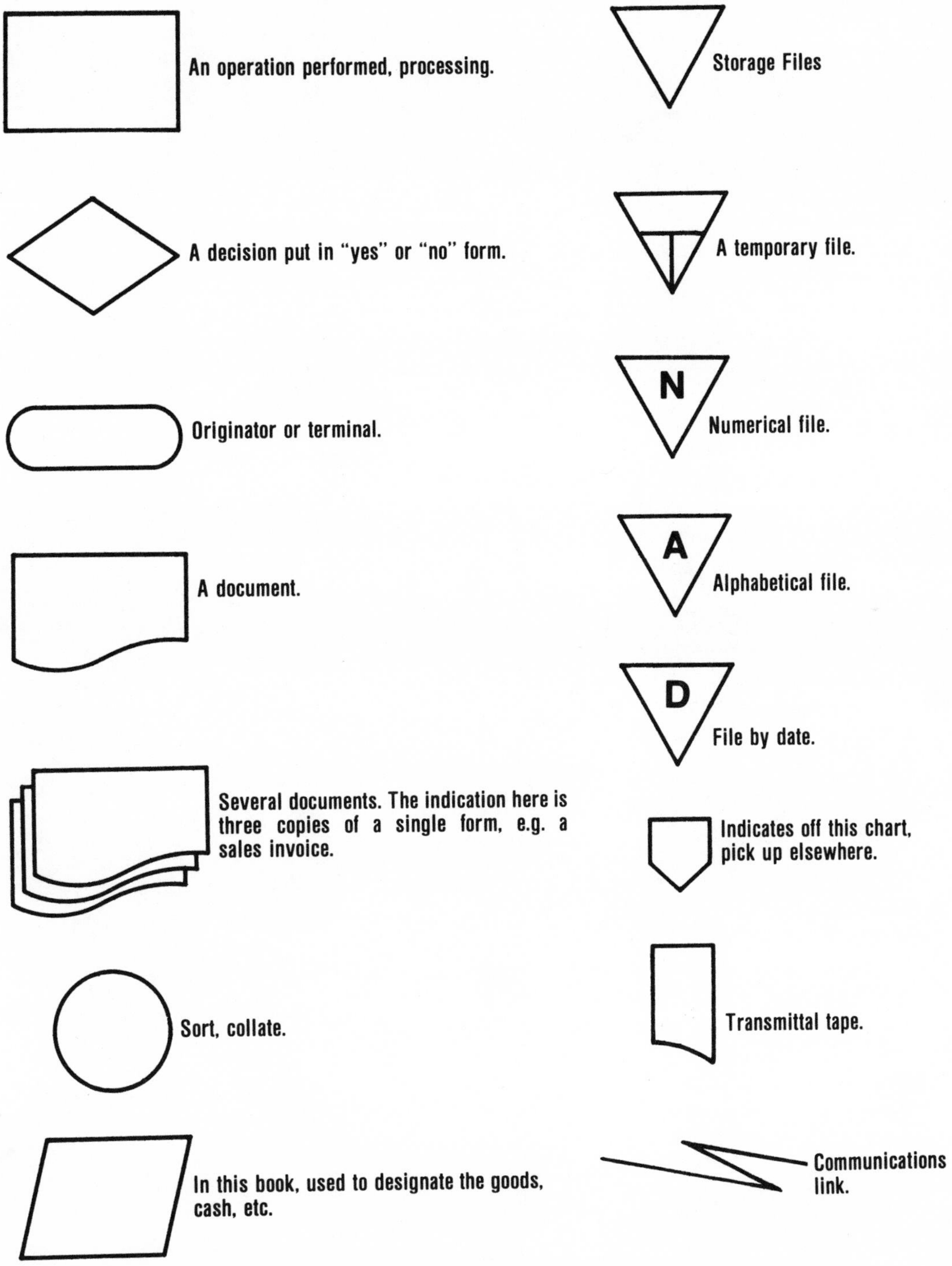

An operation performed, processing.

A decision put in "yes" or "no" form.

Originator or terminal.

A document.

Several documents. The indication here is three copies of a single form, e.g. a sales invoice.

Sort, collate.

In this book, used to designate the goods, cash, etc.

Storage Files

A temporary file.

N

Numerical file.

A

Alphabetical file.

D

File by date.

Indicates off this chart, pick up elsewhere.

Transmittal tape.

Communications link.

CHAPTER 2

EVALUATING AN INTERNAL CONTROL SYSTEM

The purpose of this chapter is twofold: to demonstrate how to evaluate and find weaknesses in each aspect of an ICS, including computer-based accounting systems; and how to assess people as they affect the ICS. Internal control problems inherent in very small firms will also be dealt with.

WHY EVALUATING AN INTERNAL CONTROL SYSTEM IS DIFFICULT

Evaluating an Internal Control System is not only difficult, it is the single most important function an auditor performs during the course of an audit. And today auditors are finding that internal control evaluation is taking on even greater significance.

Evaluating an ICS is difficult for several reasons. First, many firms' accounting systems are computerized. Present-day computers perform more functions than simply that of accumulating voluminous data and printing out journals and ledgers in traditional format. Special sub-routines are often used to: compute and allocate interest on savings accounts; compute depreciation; age accounts receivable; and perform a myriad of other invisible operations that are machine-initiated. For example, some computers have built-in instructions that trigger purchase orders at predetermined inventory levels, pay creditors, or write-off bad accounts. Source documents are separate from data maintained in magnetic tapes or card decks. On-line systems maintain only the current status of an account with no transaction information. In other words, the stored data does not show how an account got to its present balance, thus omitting the accustomed audit trail. The up-to-date auditor does not have to be an expert programmer, but he must comprehend the intricacies of controlling computer-generated accounting information. Some special techniques for evaluating computerized accounting systems are covered later in this chapter.

Second, an Internal Control System (ICS) whether or not computerized, cannot be evaluated as a whole; rather each phase must be independently assessed. The reason for this is probably already clear. A weakness in the cash disbursement process cannot be overcome by even the strongest controls over purchases, sales and cash receipts. If for example, the bookkeeper in the illustrative firm in Chapter 1 is also allowed to handle petty cash, no procedures in the other areas, however well conceived, can eliminate the possibility of error or misappropriation.

Third, a flaw or breakdown in the system can be very subtle. Unfortunately, many auditing firms have improperly evaluated ICS's because of such subtleties. Suppose for example, that the president/general manager wants to temporarily understate accounts payable at the year's end in order to show a higher net income and a larger working capital. Further suppose that he intercepts vendors' invoices before the mail reaches the secretary. Inasmuch as the bookkeeper does not make book entries until the purchase order, bill of lading and vendor's invoice are compared, the liability could be kept temporarily from the accounting records. (It may be noted that an experienced auditor may uncover this sort of omission by careful attention to the year-end cut-off through an examination of open purchase orders. On the other hand, holding invoices for expense items such as advertising, fuel, etc., would be very difficult to catch.)

Fourth, an ICS is difficult to evaluate because the system is a function of the will and intention of the individuals in the firm. Ultimately then, the auditor must assess this will and intention. Moreover, because it is management's system, the auditor needs to determine management's attitude toward making the system work.

The importance of an evaluation of the ICS is found in its effectiveness and in its primary objective. The effectiveness of an ICS is measured by results, that is, the business transactions of the firm must be properly reflected in the financial statements. If this is true, then the ICS is effective. From the auditor's viewpoint, the primary objective of the ICS is its efficacy in providing a basis on which he may rely to restrict or expand the audit function. In other words, the ICS determines how much testing the auditor must do. If the ICS is reliable, then it fulfills its objective.

A Standard for Measuring Internal Control Systems

To evaluate an ICS requires a standard or frame of reference by which existing procedures can be judged. In other words, the auditor must find out what the firm *is* doing and compare this with what it *ought* to be doing. In a special report, the Committee on Auditing Procedure of the American Institute of Certified Public Accountants issued a classic statement on the characteristics of a satisfactory system of internal control. The Committee said that the characteristics should include:

> A plan of organization which provides appropriate segregation of functional responsibilities, a system of authorization and record procedures adequate to provide reasonable accounting control over assets, liabilities, revenues and expenses, sound practices to be followed in performance of duties and functions of each of the organizational departments, and a degree of quality of personnel commensurate with responsibilities.[1]

[1]*Internal Control, Elements of a Coordinated System and Its Importance to Management and the Independent Public Accountant.* Special report by the Committee on Auditing Procedure, (New York: American Institute of Certified Public Accountants, 1949), p. 6.

This is the clearest and most concise statement of a good system of internal control in accounting literature. Consequently, the auditor should measure all ICS's by it.

The First Step in the Evaluation of an Internal Control System

The first step in evaluating any ICS, obviously, is to understand it. This requires a careful scrutiny of the firm's organization plan, the movement of financial information within and among each functional area, and the ultimate resting place of accounting data—the accounts.

Understanding the Organization Plan

Understanding the firm's organization plan is much more than obtaining a pre-printed organization chart; in fact, in many small firms, no such chart exists. Even if a chart exists, the auditor must determine if it is operational. This is done through observation and conversations with key employees. During this process the auditor should sketch the firm's organization according to line and staff functions by level of authority, commencing "at the top." In addition, he should simultaneously write down a description of each position's duties and responsibilities in a manner similar to that illustrated in Chapter 1.

Line function usually refers to the chain of authority and responsibility. Authority is thought of as progressing from the top down, while responsibility flows upward. A "line" chart designation is shown in Figure 2-1.

Figure 2-1: **Line Chart**

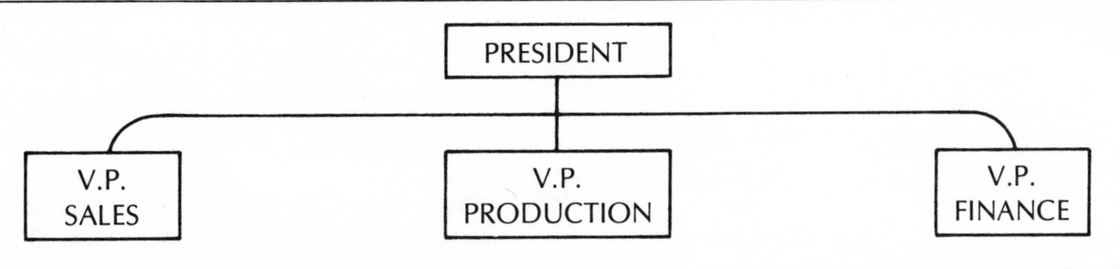

It is clear in Figure 2-1 that each vice president reports to the president, that he has authority over them, and that the vice-presidents are responsible to the President. Staff denotes an advisory or service function and is ordinarily shown as in Figure 2-2.

Figure 2-2: **Staff Designation**

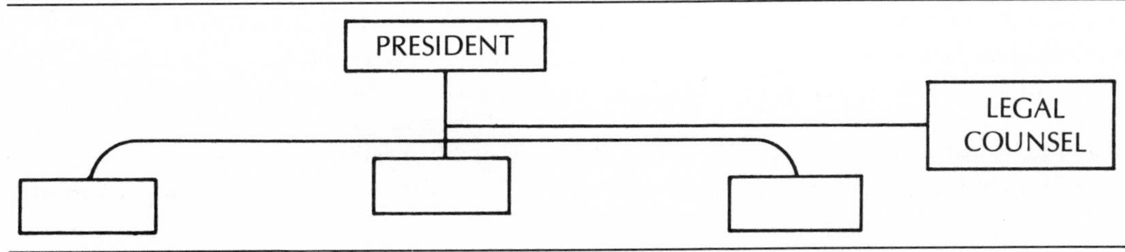

By the position in Figure 2-2, it is equally clear that the legal counsel does not have a line relationship with respect to the vice-presidents. The legal counsel's relationship with the vice-president is mainly advisory. Of course, it is quite likely that line relationships exist within the staff function, for example within the legal department (See Figure 2-3).

Figure 2-3: **Department Organization Chart**

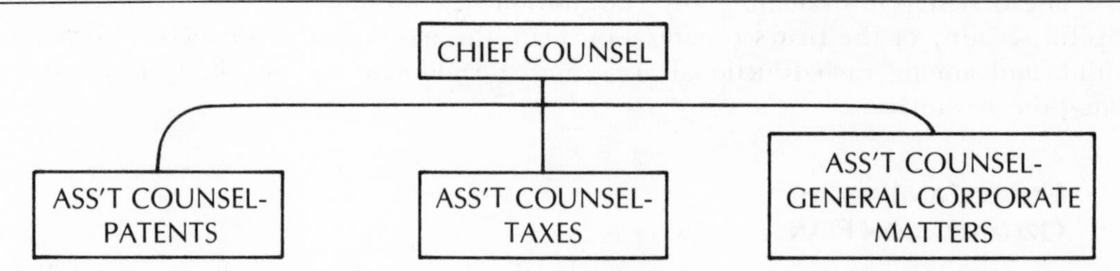

Sketching the firm's organizational arrangement has a twofold purpose: one, it identifies the functional areas of the firm; and, two, it indicates where authority and responsibility lie. Once the functional areas are identified, it can be determined if they are, in fact, independent with respect to each other. Specifying lines of responsibility and authority is essential to ascertaining whether these are clearly defined. It also provides the foundation for the description of duties and responsibilities that is an integral part of understanding the firm's organizational plan.

An example of the description of duties and responsibilities of functional areas of a firm is provided for the illustrative firm in Chapter 1. A reveiw of that section should be undertaken at this point. Remember that one purpose of the description is to identify accounting document originators. Another is to isolate individuals who have the authority to commit the firm's assets.

A Worksheet Example of Describing Duties and Responsibilities

The description of duties and responsibilities may take the following worksheet format. (See Figure 2-4. The assistant manager in the illustrative firm in Chapter 1 is used as an example.)

Understanding the Information Flow

Once the organization is outlined and the positions are described, the auditor should map the movement of financial information within and among the functional areas. It is important that the *actual* data flow be reviewed. This means field observations, discussions with supervisors and employees, study of firm policy and procedure manuals, perhaps preparation of a schematic layout of physical facilities, and a thorough study of documents used.

There are several ways to document the flow of financial data. Two of the ways are: narrative description; and flow charting. Flow charting is the superior technique, primarily

Figure 2-4: **Job Responsibility Worksheet**

Position	Description of Duties and Responsibilities	Accounting Information Originated	Supporting Document	Commits the Firm's Assets? Yes No
Assistant Manager	Supervising all salesmen, warehousemen and deliverymen Training personnel under his supervision. Enforcing personnel policy. Recommending raises, terminations and new employees. Authorizing overtime.	Payroll eliminations, additions & overtime.	Memoranda	Yes
	Purchasing and inventory management.	Purchases	Purchase Orders	Yes
	Requesting display merchandise from warehouse.	Transfers	Memoranda	No
	Approving merchandise returned to supplier.	Purchases returned	Debit Memoranda	No
	Making sales during peak periods. "Substituting" for inside salesmen.	Sales & Cash Receipts	Sales Invoices, Cash Register Tape	No
	Balancing cash register and preparing daily deposit.	Sales & Cash Receipts	Daily sales & cash receipts report, cash register tape, & deposit slip.	No
	Approving petty cash disbursements.	Cash Disbursements	Petty Cash Vouchers	Yes
	Approving travel reimbursement and routine delivery expense.	Cash Disbursements	Invoices	Yes

because it facilitates the evaluation process. It will be recalled from the section on flow charting in Chapter 1 that flow charting is simply a matter of diagramming the movement of documents from their originators into the firm's general ledger accounts. Again, it is important that the *actual* flow be shown, not what some of the firm's employees or managers *think* its movement is, or what it *ought* to be. The standard symbols in Figure 1A-1 should be used. Individual flow charts may be prepared separately for each function, e.g., sales, cash receipts, cash disbursements, purchases, and so forth. The flow charts are part of the auditor's working papers.

UNDERSTANDING THE CHART OF ACCOUNTS

The third phase of understanding the internal control system is to obtain and review the firm's chart of accounts. This includes a brief description of what goes into each of the accounts, identification of controlling accounts and accompanying subsidiary ledgers, and a listing of all books of original entry.

STEP TWO—THE EVALUATION PROCESS

The auditor is now ready to evaluate the system. The evaluation process is a matter of the judgment of the individual auditor. Every practicing accountant knows that "book" solutions seldom comport with reality. For that reason, what follows should be taken merely as a framework within which a great deal of flexibility is necessary. It is not to be construed as a substitute for the judgment of an experienced practitioner, but only as a guide, a refresher.

The evaluation procedure recommended here may be outlined as follows:

1. Study the organization plan for clarity of responsibility and authority, and separation of functional areas.
2. Carefully review the flow charts, noting the system of authorizations and internal checks.
3. Assess both the ability of the documents to support transactions and the flow of transactions into the accounts.

Each of these steps should be consistent with one another. A proven technique for evaluation is to write down the strengths and weaknesses for each step. Weaknesses should be combined with a suggested remedy and a statement of the materiality of the weakness.

An example of the auditor's study of the organization plan may be useful at this point. The reader is referred to the illustration in Chapter 1 for a "good" plan of organization.

The auditor has sketched the organization of an illustrative firm, Summer Hardware, Inc. (See Figure 2-5.)

In this chart the auditor sees that all salesmen and the deliveryman report to and are responsible to the sales manager. The cashier is supervised by the bookkeeper who reports to the warehouse manager. Shipping and receiving are under the purchasing department which also reports to the warehouse manager. The auditor evaluates the organization plan in the worksheet format shown in Figure 2-6.

The auditor's overall evaluation of the organization plan indicates that it is poor. Functional areas are not separate and the likelihood of errors or defalcation is great. (What action the auditor takes as a consequence will depend on a great number of factors. He will certainly have to expand his testing of transactions severalfold.)

This illustration contained several obvious flaws in the firm's organization plan. The auditor must be alert for flaws that are not so obvious.

Figure 2-5: **Summer Hardware Organization Chart**

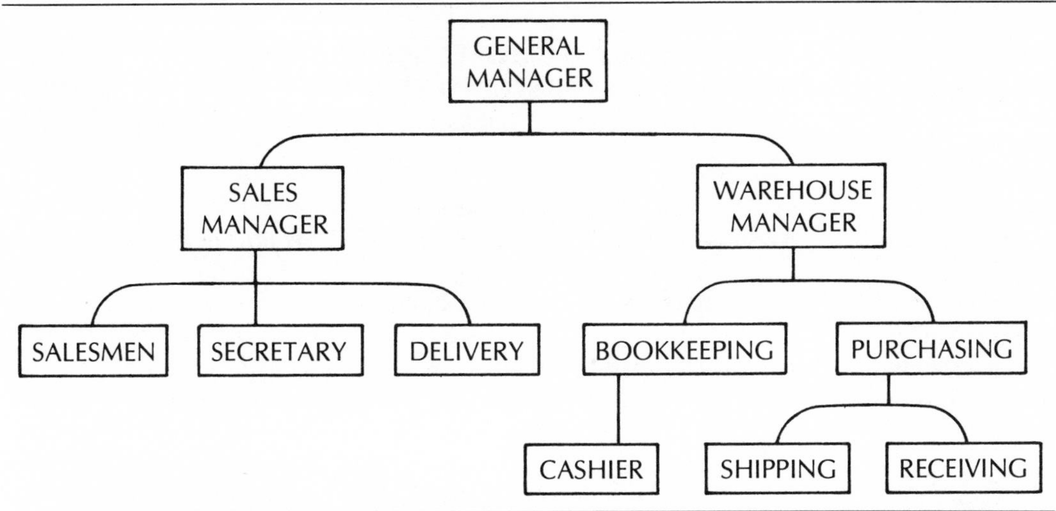

Recognizing Weaknesses in the Organization Plan

How does the auditor learn to recognize weaknesses in a firm's organization plan? The experienced auditor has learned that there are two principles to be followed in the division of responsibilities of personnel and functional areas. He makes certain that the organization plan provides that:

1. No individual or department handles a transaction from its origin until it is recorded.
2. The record-keeping function is totally separate from cash handling. In fact, all asset custodianship should be apart from the accounting for that asset.

Some discussion of these principles may help them to become operational.

To say that no one individual should handle a transaction from beginning to end is a serious generalization. In reality, no one individual should handle two consecutive critical phases of a transaction. For example, a typical cash sale progresses through several phases. First, a cash sale invoice is prepared. The sale is "rung-up" on the cash register. The cash, itself, is part of the day's deposit. The deposit slip is prepared and delivered to the bank. The register tape and invoice support an entry in the sales/cash receipts journal. The journal is the source of posting to general and subsidiary ledger accounts. A graphic portrayal may be as follows:

Phase	Activity
1	Invoice prepared
2	Cash sale "rung-up"
3	Deposit slip prepared
4	Cash (and remaining elements of the deposit) delivered to depository
5	Day's sales recorded in journal
6	Journal posted to ledgers

Figure 2-6: **Evaluating the Organization Plan—A Worksheet Format**

SUMMER HARDWARE, INC.
EVALUATION OF INTERNAL CONTROL
THE ORGANIZATION PLAN

Strengths	Weaknesses	Recommendations for Correction	Significance of Weakness
Line authority of general manager over sales and warehouse is desirable. Sales manager supervises all salesmen. Purchasing is the responsibility of the warehouse manager and reports to him.	General office secretary reports directly to sales manager.	Secretary should be made a staff function under general manager.	Weakness is material due to the assigned duty of the secretary of listing daily mail receipts and giving the lists to sales manager. Sales Manager can not only make sales, but can also handle collections on account. Lapping is a distinct possibility.
	Bookkeeping is under supervision of warehouse manager.	Bookkeeping should be separate from both sales and warehouse functions.	Weakness is material. Having authority over the cashier and bookkeeping function provides opportunities for misappropriations by the warehouse manager of inventory with instruction to bookkeeper for false journal entries.
	Shipping and receiving are in line position under purchasing.	Shipping and receiving should not only be functionally independent of purchasing, but of each other.	Weakness is material. Purchasing agent could direct that goods received be shipped to fictitious customers without any record being made.
	Cashier is subfunction of bookkeeping.	Size of organization indicates that cashier should report to general manager.	Weakness is material. The possibility of false entries and abstraction of cash by bookkeeper exists.

Phases one and two may be accomplished by one individual. Phase three is critical with respect to one and two and should be done by someone who is not permitted to write invoices or "ring-up" sales. Phase four is critical with respect to phase three. To combine phases four and five would violate the separation of cash handling from record-keeping principle. Phases five and six may be done by one individual provided that ledger balances are periodically reviewed by someone else. The point of this is to emphasize the need to review a transaction in its constituent parts for consistency with the two principles of division of responsibility. (This will be elaborated on later in this chapter when the flow chart is evaluated.)

In theory, there are virtually no exceptions to the principle of separation of cash handling and record-keeping. This is fundamental, and a weakness in the system exists whenever division of duties and responsibilities does not provide for this separation. Visualize the simple case where the bookkeeper is charged with the responsibility of maintaining the petty cash fund. Of course the seriousness of the flaw is largely dependent on the amount involved, but this obvious breach in good internal control may indicate a lack of awareness on the part of management of the principle. This lack of awareness in itself, should be recognized as a weakness.

Asset custodianship means more than simply an overseer's function. It encompasses the authority to commit the firm's assets. This includes the purchasing function, committing funds to advertising programs, etc. Thus, one individual should not be given authority to enter into advertising contracts without being required to render reports thereon. In the broad context of the meaning of custodianship, a company truck driver has custody of his truck, but again, he should not be without complete accountability to a higher level of the organization for maintenance programs, operating expenses or utilization. It is not so much that the situation may lead to misuse; rather it may lead to ineffective use of the assets of the firm. In general terms, *every employee should be accountable to someone upward in the firm's hierarchy.* This is a principle of good organization. Anything short of that should be viewed as a weakness.

Evaluating the Information Flow

Before proceeding to evaluate the flow of information within the company's ICS, it is, of course, necessary to construct flow charts. Techniques and procedures found useful in that connection were explained in Chapter 1. It would be helpful to the reader to review the section on how to prepare flow charts at this juncture. It is also important to remember that the objective of information flow is to assure that the financial transactions of the firm are properly reflected in its financial statements. This is a rather broad statement, but it is important as an overview. A useful technique in evaluating a flow chart is to ask the question: How can the system fail?

Detecting Weaknesses in the Information Flow

As is the case in evaluating the organization plan, there are some principles which may be used to detect weaknesses in the information flow. In fact, those principles already enumerated are equally applicable in evaluating the information flow, plus several others. They are:

1. Information should flow only to those who have a need to know: originator-to-user-to-rest.
2. Documents should support every transaction.
3. Documents, whenever feasible, should be sequentially numbered and accountability for spoiled documents should be established.

4. Documents should be prepared in the exact number of copies needed and no more.
5. Responsibility for verifying and reconciling information flowing from different sources should be clearly defined.
6. Documents should be designed to provide for signatures of responsible individuals for approvals or authorizations.

Each of these points needs explaining.

Information should flow only to those who need it for two reasons. First, it is obviously inefficient to burden individuals with useless data. Moreover, it tends to delay the whole process of getting timely information to users. Second, some information is of a confidential nature and should not be made available indiscriminately. Essentially, this principle supports the efficiency and timeliness of accounting information; however, it is conceivable that such delays could aid misappropriations, if not cause them.

That documentation should support every transaction has long been regarded as a truism in internal control. There is nothing new here. It is simply that a word-of-mouth information flow leaves no trail and makes management's evaluation of the discharge of responsibility nearly impossible. Thus, a more or less formal system of memoranda, tapes, invoices, check stubs, correspondence, etc. is an essential element in an ICS. A weakness exists without such documentation. In this connection, the auditor must give some attention to the form and content of documents. More will be said on this subject under the sixth principle.

Using serially numbered documents is not a new concept in a good ICS. Nor is the idea of having one individual assigned responsibility for accounting for spoiled documents novel. The reasons are: one, inasmuch as each transaction has a supporting document, missing documents imply unrecorded transactions; and two, the risk that documents can be misused is minimized. For these reasons, many firms keep documents in locked storage and restrict access thereto. Records of spoiled documents are maintained and unused documents are plainly marked *VOID,* and sometimes destroyed.

The number of copies of a particular document will depend upon its use and upon the number of individuals who need the information. Too many copies are a waste and cause inefficiencies. Company purchase orders, for example, need to be reproduced so that one copy can remain with the vendor, one copy can alert the receiving department of the content of an impending shipment, and one copy can be used as a control device to ascertain that what is ordered is actually received. It is difficult to conceive of a situation where fewer than three copies will suffice. In some systems additional copies may be necessary. Alternatively, a single copy of memoranda authorizing salary increases may be adequate.

The fifth principle, that of having individuals with a clearly defined responsibility for receiving, reviewing and comparing incoming documents from various sources, is fundamental. This means, for example, that one person should be assigned the duty of receiving: the purchase order (or receiving report) from the receiving department; the copy of the purchase order from the control file; the bill of lading and freight bill; and, the vendor's invoice. Each document should be compared to determined if the goods ordered were actually received, freight properly charged, and to determine if billing, terms, date, and condition are consistent with written or verbal agreements.

Document design is the subject of some highly specialized writings and these will not be duplicated here. Certain minimum requirements exist for conveying the proper information to "lubricate" an ICS, however, and the auditor needs to periodically refresh his memory as to what they are. A system in which documents lack one or more features of those presented below may be regarded as weak. Some essential features that a firm's documents should contain are:

a. The company's name and date.
b. A title (e.g. Sales Invoice).
c. Pre-printed serial numbers. (This is, of course, not feasible on some memoranda.)
d. Space for vendor/customer name where appropriate.
e. Space for authorization and/or approval signatures.
f. Data thereon printed or typed and arranged in logical order for easy reference.

An Example of Evaluating a Flow Chart

Recognizing weaknesses in the information flow is a matter of applying the principles elaborated upon above and asking the question of an existing flow: How can it go wrong? The illustration that follows is taken from the information flow of the illustrative firm described in Chapter 1. The general background, description, and personnel are assumed to be identical for this example.

The payroll function of the company described in Chapter 1 will serve as a place to begin the evaluation. It may be recalled that rates of pay and overtime authorization for salesmen, delivery and warehouseman are the responsibility of the assistant manager, that the payroll is made from time cards by the bookkeeper, and that the checks are distributed by the secretary. An illustration of flow charting the payroll functions is shown in Figure 2-7.

The payroll for hourly employees is the responsibility of the assistant manager. He collects time cards from the card rack at the time clock and reviews them for accuracy of both hourly rate and number of hours, initialing those with authorized overtime. Time cards are then sent to the bookkeeper. The bookkeeper uses the approved time cards to prepare the payroll summary, post individual earnings records, and draw up payroll checks in duplicate for hourly employees. Payroll information on monthly employees is kept in a permanent file and this data is used to prepare the payroll summary and checks for this group and to post earning record cards. Entries are made in the journal and checks forwarded for approval. Checks and time cards for hourly employees are sent to the assistant manager, and monthly employees' checks go to the president/general manager. Copies of payroll checks are permanently filed in check number order.

The assistant manager reviews hourly employee checks and compares them with time cards. He returns copies of payroll checks and time cards to the bookkeeper for filing and sends the original checks to the president/general manager for signature. The president/general manager has received payroll checks from two sources: hourly employee checks from the assistant manager and monthly employee checks from the bookkeeper. If they are correct, he signs all checks, and forwards them to the secretary who distributes them to individual employees.

Referring to the illustrative flow chart and description, the question of what could go wrong with the system indicates the following areas of possible concern:

1. No apparent formal method of changing employees' hourly rates exists. Lack of a method could create errors in the payroll and obvious delays and inefficiencies. If the system is informal, that is, word-of-mouth, this is to be construed as a weakness. It should be formalized so that documentation will support the changes. Current federal labor laws make a formal system mandatory.
2. The firm needs a formal system to handle unclaimed payroll checks. In the event unclaimed hourly employees' checks are returned to the assistant manager, a misappropriation could occur. For example, the assistant manager could turn in a card for a fictitious name, and when it is unclaimed, cash the check himself. (It may

Figure 2-7

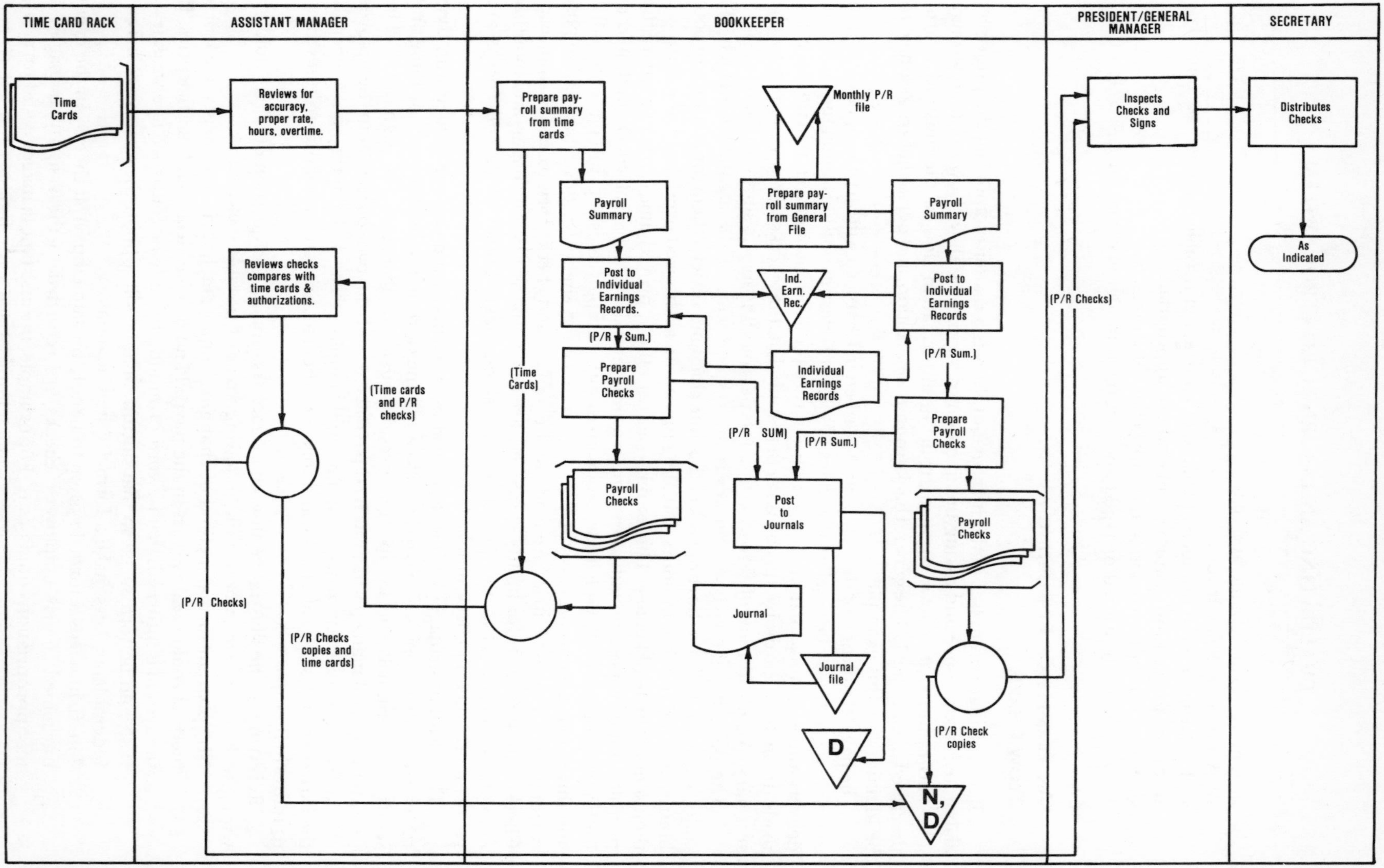

TIME CARD RACK
ASSISTANT MANAGER
BOOKKEEPER
PRESIDENT/GENERAL MANAGER
SECRETARY
Time Cards
Reviews for accuracy, proper rate, hours, overtime.
Prepare payroll summary from time cards
Monthly P/R file
Prepare payroll summary from General File
Payroll Summary
Payroll Summary
Inspects Checks and Signs
Distributes Checks
As Indicated
Reviews checks compares with time cards & authorizations.
Post to Individual Earnings Records.
Ind. Earn. Rec.
Post to Individual Earnings Records
(P/R Checks)
(P/R Sum.)
(P/R Sum.)
(Time Cards)
(Time cards and P/R checks)
Prepare Payroll Checks
Individual Earnings Records
Prepare Payroll Checks
(P/R SUM)
(P/R Sum.)
Payroll Checks
Post to Journals
Payroll Checks
(P/R Checks)
Journal
(P/R Checks copies and time cards)
Journal file
(P/R Check copies
D
N, D

be noted that in a firm of this size such an event does not seem likely. The more likely possibility is that each employee knows every other one.)

3. The bookkeeper could "beat the system" by underwithholding payroll taxes on his/her own payroll check and then creating fictitious entries to show a larger tax withholding at year's end. Controls may be added to prevent this. One is to establish a routine check of the propriety of "gross" versus "net" pay by the president/general manager. Another is to require prior approval of all journal entries by the president/general manager.

In terms of the six "principles" of evaluating information flow presented earlier, the payroll system illustrated will probably be evaluated as satisfactory. Payroll data is restricted to those who are required to have it. Wage rates are often held as confidential, and inasmuch as the assistant manager has no authority over employees on a monthly pay basis, he does not see their checks. Aside from the assistant manager, only the president/general manager, and the bookkeeper and secretary who are responsible only to him, see all the payroll checks. If desirable, the function of distributing checks could be undertaken by the president/general manager, limiting those who see the complete payroll to two. Except as noted, documents, payroll checks, time cards, and payroll memoranda do support the payroll transaction. It is assumed that payroll checks are preprinted and serially numbered, thus fulfilling the third principle. The number of copies of documents is adequate, and it appears that the responsibility for each segment of the payroll function is clearly defined with appropriate checks, comparisons and approvals. Finally, while the forms used for the payroll are not shown, it is assumed that the information they contain meets the requirements enumerated.

Evaluating the Chart of Accounts

To be evaluated as satisfactory, a chart of accounts should have the following characteristics:

1. The chart should provide for subsidiary ledgers supporting controlling accounts where necessary for economy, and efficiency. A feature of a subsidiary ledger is, of course, to yield sufficient detail for management to fulfill its objectives. For example, a satisfactory management credit and collection policy necessitates an accounts receivable subsidiary ledger. In the system described, a policy of taking cash discounts requires an accounts payable ledger.
2. The accounts should be arranged in such a fashion as to aid in the preparation of financial statements for third parties and management. The order of the accounts ordinarily is the same as they appear on the balance sheet and income statement.
3. The accounts should facilitate compliance with any legal statute. Some states have certain requirements for the segregation of corporate capital accounts. Laws levying sales, use and income taxes also often prescribe minimum standards for supporting data of returns filed.
4. The accounts should be adequately supported by books or records of original entry. It should be possible to trace transactions from documents through journals to the ledger, and the reverse with ease.
5. The nature and content of each account should be clearly stated and promulgated to all employees affected. Sometimes this is accomplished by a manual describing the accounts, sources of entries, and content of each account. Personnel should be briefed accordingly.

The use of computerized record-keeping techniques does not diminish the necessity for these characteristics; rather they may simply take on another form.

WHAT TO DO ABOUT EVALUATING PEOPLE

If evaluating an ICS is itself difficult, evaluating personnel is its most difficult phase. The reason is simply this: what the accountant is called upon to do is to assess the *will* and *intent* of the management and the individuals of the firm to make the ICS work. When this will and intent are lacking, no system can function properly. In addition, even though the will may be present, there is a need for certain basic skills on part of the personnel. The evaluation of personnel may be thought of as a four-part maxtrix:

MANAGEMENT	WILL AND INTENT
SKILLS	EMPLOYEES

Thus, both management and the firm's employees must possess the basic skills to operate the ICS as well as the will and intent to cause it to function properly.

EVALUATING SKILLS

What skills does management need? Some fundamental abilities that management should have and that can be perceived by the accountant through conversation and observation during the ordinary course of reviewing an ICS follow:

1. Management should have experience. This means experience in the industry of which the firm is a part, experience in personnel management, experience in the primary activity of the firm, e.g., selling, and experience in whatever technical aspects are involved.
2. Management should have some competency in interpreting financial data. Included here is a need for management to know the kind of information wanted and where to get it, as well as an ability to use the information available.
3. Management should be knowledgeable of the objectives of an ICS and be convinced of its value to management and to the firm.
4. Management should know the capabilities of the employees. There should be a familiarity with the function each performs and the impact of each employee on the objectives of the firm.
5. Finally, management should have clear-cut objectives for the firm, both quantitative and qualitative. Quantitative objectives may be in the form of sales volume or profits or total assets. Qualitative objectives may be satisfactory standards of living for the members of management and for employees.

None of these skills or abilities presupposes a special expertise or a minimum level of education. They are simply characteristics of good management.

Satisfactory employee skills are less general than those needed by management, but no less important to the operation of an ICS. Each employee should:

1. Know his or her job thoroughly *and that of every other employee under him or her in the organization chart.* Job descriptions are useful in this connection. Knowing the job means to know every operation performed and what is expected in terms of performance.
2. Possess whatever technical skill is required by his job. For example, a television repairman should, in fact, be able to repair television sets and a bookkeeper should know the double-entry system.
3. Understand the reasons for the control procedures that they are required to follow. As a general rule, individuals work more effectively if they know why something is to be done.

While the accountant can certainly evaluate each employee's knowledge of the requirements of his or her own job, he alone probably cannot evaluate technical skills, except in the case of the bookkeeping function. The accountant must rely primarily on the judgment of management in this matter. There are some quantitative aids that may be used, however. For example, analysis of the sales returns and allowances account may indicate incompetent or overzealous salesmen. The purchase returns and allowances account can, perhaps, point to poor purchasing techniques. The ability of the purchasing agent can also be measured, at least in part, by the age and condition of inventory. Evaluating even more technical skills may be approached using similar techniques. For example, a television repairman's competency may be partly assessed by a review of the frequency of call backs for the same customer.

A feature of a successful ICS is an awareness by all employees of the purpose of the system and the part each plays in making it a success. This is not merely a deterrent, although such awareness may serve that function, but is a positive encouragement founded on a basic desire by individuals to please management by performing satisfactorily.

Each of these three employee "skills" has a special importance in the case of EDP personnel, requiring that the auditor have more than a cursory understanding of computer-based accounting systems.

EVALUATING WILL AND INTENT

Earlier in this chapter it was stated that no ICS can operate successfully unless this is the will and intent of the firm's personnel, primarily of management. Will and intent imply conscious and positive action rather than passive or permissive endurance. It may be that the only practical way to evaluate will and intent is by considering the result. That is, if the system is in operation and the objectives of the ICS are being fulfilled, it may be inferred that the will and intent exist. Unfortunately, this approach often leads to an erroneous conclusion, because a system may run on its own momentum, temporarily, or perhaps even for a year or two until initial enthusiasm wears thin. Hence, another prerequisite for evaluating for will and intent is that they must be on-going.

One technique for evaluating the will and intent of the company's personnel is for the accountant to ask these questions:

1. Does top management play an active part in making the ICS work?
2. Are internal checks by top management regularly employed?
3. Does management enforce prescribed procedures established by the ICS?
4. Are employees seeking shortcuts or attempting to avoid necessary but unpleasant routine?

5. Do management and employees seem to have an appreciation for the benefits to be derived from the ICS?
6. Is employee morale high?
7. Does management readily accept suggestions from professionals for improvement of the system and implement the suggestions where feasible?
8. Is it management's policy to employ competent individuals and to give training where necessary?

Answers to the foregoing questions will enable the accountant to judge the will and intent of the firm's personnel to have an effective ICS.

DOCUMENTING THE EVALUATION

A word about working papers is in order here. Up to this point, the accountant has studied the ICS, charted its organizational makeup, mapped its information flow, and reviewed the chart of accounts. He has taken the information developed and evaluated each element. This process must be documented in the working papers of the independent accountant. It is important to stress that the working papers must show the progression of the evaluation, from start to finish, including all comments relevant to how the accountant arrived at his overall evaluation. An important next step for the independent accountant is to demonstrate through his working papers just exactly how his evaluation of the ICS affected the amount of testing he did.

Some hints for working paper documentation are included under each heading of this chapter, but a general outline may be of help.

Step	**Working Paper Documentation**
Understanding the firm's organizational plan.	An organization chart of the firm. A description of duties and responsibilities of personnel. A listing of accounting information originating with each individual, and supporting documents. A statement as to each employee who has authority to commit the firm's assets.
Understanding the information flow.	A flow chart of each functional area.
Understanding the chart of accounts.	A list of the accounts used. A description of content of each account. A list of subsidiary ledgers and all books of original entry.
Evaluating the organization plan.	(Follow work sheet format as presented earlier in this chapter.)
	The work sheet setup in the form of a questionnaire is as follows: 1. Does information flow only to those who have a need to know? 2. Is every transaction supported by documentation?

Step	Working Paper Documentation
Evaluating information flow	3. Are documents sequentially numbered? 4. Are documents sufficiently duplicated? 5. Is responsibility for collecting, comparing, etc., documents flowing from different directions clearly defined? 6. Do authorizations and/or approvals appear on all appropriate documents? The questionnaire should be accompanied by a list of weaknesses or possible areas where the system could fail.
Evaluating the chart of accounts.	The questionnaire technique is useful here and may take the following form: 1. Are subsidiary ledgers adequate? 2. Is the arrangement of accounts such as to facilitate statement preparation? 3. Do the accounts provide information for preparation of accurate reports to governmental agencies? 4. Can transactions be easily traced through the journals to the ledger? 5. Are responsible personnel thoroughly familiar with the accounts and their content? Again, a list of weaknesses should accompany the questionnaire.
Evaluating personnel	A questionnaire is useful as part of the working papers to document this evaluation. 1. Does each member of management have a level of experience appropriate to his or her authority and responsibility? 2. Is management competent to interpret financial data? 3. Does management appear to understand the value of the ICS to the firm? 4. Does management know the capabilities of the employees? 5. Does management have specific objectives for the firm? 6. Do employees know their own job and that of every other employee under him or her? 7. Do employees appear to have required technical skills?[2] The question presented in the section "Evaluating Will and Intent" may be set up with yes or no answers similar to those shown above as documentation for work paper purposes.

[2]Support for this judgment may take the form of an analysis of sales returns, purchase returns, etc. This, too, should be made part of the working papers.

INTERNAL CONTROL QUESTIONNAIRES

The questions developed in the preceding section are not ordinarily found in traditional internal control questionnaires, and they may be added if standard questionnaires are used as a tool in the evaluation of an internal control system. Often, an internal control questionnaire can be useful in this role. A comprehensive questionnaire is reproduced in Figure 2A-1.

Three notes of caution are in order here with respect to using so-called "model" internal control questionnaires. One, each questionnaire should be tailored to the firm being audited and modifications should be made where necessary. Two, and this follows from the first caveat, because of their general design and length, the questionnaire is often completed perfunctorily. Therefore, an internal control questionnaire is not to be considered as the whole evaluation process, but merely as an aid. The procedures outlined in this chapter constitute the entire process of evaluating an ICS. Three, most "model" questionnaires when used by or for many small firms indicate results that are quite negative, indicating of course that the questionnaire is unsuited for the size firm.

EVALUATING COMPUTERIZED SYSTEMS

While the principles of evaluating ICS's will be the same, computerized accounting systems may pose special problems for independent accountants. The American Institute of Certified Public Accountants has published much helpful information on this topic and no attempt will be made here to duplicate or substitute for that. The accountant would do well to avail himself of the Institute's literature, and particularily, *Statement on Auditing Standards, No. 3,* issued by the Auditing Standards Executive Committee of the AICPA in December, 1974.

It may be good, from a fairly generalized point of view, to review some of the problems commonly encountered in evaluating ICS's that utilize electronic data processing equipment. These problems may be seen more easily by categorizing firms as either those with in-house computers, computer personnel, etc., or those that use outside computer services to a greater or lesser degree.

Control of fully computerized in-house systems is achieved (or lost) at three points in the process of translating raw data into financial information: the point at which the information is introduced into the computer (input); the point at which the information leaves the computer (output); and, that area in between input and output—processing.

TECHNIQUES FOR TESTING CONTROL OF INPUT DATA

Input data must be verified to determine if it was correctly converted into the language of the computer (coded) and if it was accurately picked up by the computer (punched). Several techniques exist for this kind of control. One method of checking input data is to use edit routines.* Simply put, this is a portion of the computer program itself designed to throw off or reject questionable information. For example, the program contains built-in

*There are proprietary companies that sell or lease edit routines, and the accountant may well avail himself of these.

parameters. Information introduced that falls outside these parameters creates an error situation requiring investigation. One application might be in the case of payroll. The computer may be programmed such that in cases where an individual's total time amounts to more than 48 hours in a week, that individual's payroll is processed and printed-out separately. This "exception" then is investigated. Edit routines may be used to test input data against historical data already stored in the computer, and to test for logical absurdities. An example of the latter might be credit balances in asset accounts, or salaries with no withholding.

Another method of control over input data is to use summary control totals. For example, sales invoices to be processed may be totaled prior to input and this summary control information would follow the sales invoice data throughout the processing function for comparison.

The firm should have a system of review and approval of source documents prior to input, and the forms used to convert data into machine language should be standardized. The purpose of this first input control is to prevent the introduction of unauthorized or duplicate information into the data banks. Use of standardized forms will facilitate punching and help eliminate errors.

Probably the best and most widely used control over input data is a verification of punched information by comparing it with the original document for code numbers, dates, amounts, etc., before punching.

TESTING CONTROL OVER OUTPUT DATA

Output controls are similar in nature to those at the input point, except they are applied at the user end of the computer process. Summary control totals accompanying "runs" should be compared at the user's end. Programming controls, much like edit routines, can be pre-programmed to test the validity of output data. For example, average weekly payroll amounts for certain types of employees may be accumulated and stored in the computer for comparison with current payroll runs. Individual gross pay exceeding 10% of the average may be thrown off and printed out separately. Inasmuch as a possible error situation exists, the user should investigate the error.

An excellent output control device is a simple test of reasonableness. In other words, is the information obtained from the computer reasonable and realistic? Consider the possibility of an error situation in which input personnel punch one month's general ledger information twice. Sales, expenses, etc., will be two times their actual amounts. The test of reasonableness would quickly point out the error.

TESTING CONTROL OVER PROCESSING

Edit routines are used to control computer operations during processing, and to throw off irregular or excess amounts. An example may be a built-in sub-routine whereby the computer is instructed to flag any check written for amount in excess of $999.99. Some sub-routines actually cause the computer to stop processing in the event of predetermined overflows. Other sub-routines cause the computer to bypass excesses and throw them off into separate printouts. Control over such processing intervention should be maintained to prevent misuse. One method of control may take the form of requiring written authorization before processing is interrupted, or before a sub-routine can be used. Some of the controls expanded upon in the next section are effective processing controls.

Testing for Control Over the Program and the Computer

Because much of what occurs in a computer-based accounting system is initiated by the computer itself following the instructions of the program, the auditor must assure himself that the program is delivering the proper instructions and that the machine is carrying them out. Several methods of testing the efficacy of the program follow.

First, there are some fairly simple controls the firm should have over the program and the computer. One of the most commonly used controls is redundancy; that is, certain operations are performed twice and results compared. Coding, for example, may be tested by comparing codes entered into the system to determine if they are consistent with codes authorized and in use. Mathematical computations are done twice and outcomes compared. The machine itself should be consistently maintained and its working order verified by independent technical personnel.

The auditor has means to test the program himself. Two widely used methods are test decks and parallel simulation. Test decks contain a set of real or imaginary transactions anticipating all possible error conditions to determine if the firm's program will reject or otherwise report the errors. An essential requirement for using test decks is a complete understanding on part of the auditor of the logic of the firm's program. The test deck utilizes the firm's own program.

In parallel simulation, the auditor either devises a program that will process real data or he avails himself of a generalized audit program, perhaps through the AICPA. The objective of parallel simulation is to cause the actual processing of real transactions using both the firm's transaction and master files, but with instruction from the auditor's program. The output of the auditor's program is then compared with the output from the firm's program, using the same data. Obviously, parallel simulation ignores the firm's program up to the point of the comparison of the results of processing. The auditor's evaluation of the firm's program and computer will allow him to determine if they can be relied upon as a part of the firm's overall ICS.

Generalized audit programs may be used to perform a variety of other tests, including verification of extensions and footings, comparison of relevant data, selection of random samples for inspection, or selection of accounts receivable for confirmation, just to mention a few applications. This implies, and rightly so, that the computer may be used to perform certain audit functions.

Steps in Evaluating a Computer-Based Accounting System

As an overview of the auditor's review of the firm's computer-based accounting system, the following steps have been shown to be useful:

Step 1. Become familiar with the firm's hardware. Look at the equipment for type, characteristics and capabilities. A sketch of the physical layout of equipment may be useful. The manufacturer's personnel may be very useful at this point as well as later in the auditor's evaluation.

Step 2. Determine the applications to which the firm's computer is put. For example, does it process general ledger data? Does it maintain receivables and payables? Especially important at this stage is to determine what sub-routines are programmed in, particularly those that are automatic or machine-initiated. Earlier reference was made to machine-triggered purchase orders; it is crucial that the "triggering" mechanism is controlled so as not to be misused. Performance of this step will necessitate a review and understanding of the firm's program.

Step 3. Review the flow chart of the computer operation and processing steps (called a block diagram). Of course, if no flow chart exists, the auditor should have one constructed, or else he must extend other audit procedures commensurately. This step includes the following procedures: a) Review instructions to equipment operators, especially with regard to input, processing, and output controls (sometimes contained in an operator's manual)[3]; b) Determine that a system of authorizations and approvals exists for all input data, running of programs (including sub-routines and all program changes); c) Ascertain that computer operation is tightly scheduled and logged. The purpose of tight scheduling of computer operation is to help prevent its unauthorized use. It should be understood that each computer application requires a known processing time.

Step 4. Test the system. This phase includes testing controls over input, processing, output, programs and the equipment. Some techniques for testing each of these were suggested earlier.

Step 5. Evaluate findings. A necessary corollary to this step is to document each previous step (as well as this one) in the working papers. The extent of his reliance on the system will depend on the auditor's evaluation.

Three final points with regard to computer-based accounting systems need to be emphasized. One, it is highly desirable that the auditor be a participant in the initial design and installation of the computer system and subsequent changes in the system. Such participation may be regarded as an essential part of the audit and will render the remainder of the audit manifestly less complex. Two, in the absence of the required degree of technical knowledge on part of the auditor, use of independent computer experts is not only justified, it is necessary. Three, computers can be the best aid the auditor has if properly understood and utilized.

Absence of one or more of these controls at the point of input, during processing, or at the output stage should be regarded as a weakness by the accountant evaluating the ICS.

Some Internal Control Problems of Very Small Firms

Smaller firms are likely to use service centers or other proprietary computer operations for some or all of their accounting function. Input and output controls, as described earlier in this chapter, should be utilized by firm personnel. The auditor's review of processing control is much less critical inasmuch as processing is done by an independent firm, but if such control is desirable, the accountant may use edit routines from software companies that sell or lease them.

[3]Software routines are available that will cause the computer to generate flow charts of programs presently in use. Naturally, the auditor would use such a flow chart for comparison with the existing chart.

The size, in terms of personnel, of some very small firms renders many of the checks and controls discussed here and in Chapter 1 nearly impossible to accomplish. As a result, internal control for these firms is weak or even nonexistent. This means, of course, that auditing procedures must be extended substantially. Inherent weaknesses in these circumstances may be mitigated, in part, by certain procedures or techniques, some of which are shown in the check list following:

A Check List of Internal Control Techniques for Very Small Businesses

1. Use a checking account with;
   a. All disbursements, except very small items, made by check.
   b. All receipts deposited intact daily.
   c. Monthly reconcilement of bank statement with records.
   d. Check writer or check protector.
   e. The owner personally signing all checks.
   f. Checks kept in locked storage.
2. Have a double-entry bookkeeping system, employing:
   a. Periodic trial balances for review by owner.
   b. Controlling accounts and subsidiary ledgers for trade receivables and payables.
   c. Monthly financial statements for the owner's scrutiny.
   d. An approval system for journal entries.
   e. Documents supporting all book entries.
3. Other Internal Checks:
   a. Use pre-printed and sequentially numbered documents—the owner accounting for spoiled forms.
   b. Have employees bonded and insist that each take an annual vacation.
   c. Make small disbursements from an imprest petty cash fund.
   d. Bill customers monthly. The owner should closely oversee this function.
   e. The owner opens incoming mail.
4. Employ an independent accountant for an annual audit and for advice on internal control.

How Much "System" Does a Small Firm Need? What To Do If It Has None

Small firms should not be overwhelmed with recommendations from their accountant for immediate installation of sophisticated internal control systems. Considering costs, a system of procedures such as those described in the check list in the previous section is probably all the very small firm needs. As the firm grows, the accountant can recommend additional controls so that the ICS "grows" with the firm.

Not infrequently, accountants encounter small firms without even the minimum controls suggested above. In these cases, the practitioner has the responsibility to "educate" the owner as to the need for controls and the benefits to be derived. The accountant should dwell on the benefits to the owner, not merely on the benefits to the auditor himself. Of course, testing will have to be extended, but fortunately in firms of this size transactions are relatively few, and financial statements are likely to be less complex than those of larger firms.

APPENDIX

Figure 2A-1:

INTERNAL CONTROL QUESTIONNAIRE

	ANSWER		ANSWER BASED ON		
	YES	NO	INQUIRY	OBSERVATION	TEST
I. General					
1. Does the client have a chart of organization?	___	___	___	___	___
2. Does the client have a chart of accounts?	___	___	___	___	___
3. Is the accounting routine set forth in accounting manuals?	___	___	___	___	___
4. Do we have copies of such charts and manuals in our permanent file for this client?	___	___	___	___	___
5. Does the client have:					
a. A controller?	___	___	___	___	___
b. An internal auditor or audit staff?	___	___	___	___	___
6. If internal auditors are employed:					
a. Do they render written reports on the results of their examinations?	___	___	___	___	___
b. Are they directly responsible to, and do they report to, an executive officer other than the chief accounting officer? Designate:	___	___	___	___	___
c. Have we reviewed their reports?	___	___	___	___	___
7. Is the general accounting department completely separated from:					
a. The purchasing department?	___	___	___	___	___
b. The sales department?	___	___	___	___	___
c. Manufacturing and/or cost departments?	___	___	___	___	___
d. Cash receipts and disbursements?	___	___	___	___	___
8. Are all employees who handle cash, securities, and other valuables bonded?	___	___	___	___	___
9. Are all such employees required to take regular vacations, their regular duties then being assigned to other employees?	___	___	___	___	___

	ANSWER		ANSWER BASED ON		
	YES	NO	INQUIRY	OBSERVATION	TEST
10. Does head office accounting control over branch offices appear to be adequate?	___	___	___	___	___
11. Are expenses and costs under budgetary control?	___	___	___	___	___
12. Is insurance coverage under the supervision of a responsible official or employee?	___	___	___	___	___
13. Are journal entries approved by:					
a. The controller?	___	___	___	___	___
b. Other designated employee?	___	___	___	___	___
14. Does the client use standard journal entries for the regularly recurring monthly closing entries?	___	___	___	___	___
15. Are journal entries adequately explained or supported by vouchers bearing adequate substantiating data?	___	___	___	___	___
16. Are periodic financial statements prepared for submission to the management?	___	___	___	___	___
17. If so, are these sufficiently informative to bring to light abnormal fluctuations in costs, revenues, inventories, etc., and other discrepancies?	___	___	___	___	___

18. a. List names of officials and employees exercising the function noted:

Treasurer ______________________

Secretary ______________________

Controller ______________________

Internal auditor (chief) ______________________

Chief accountant ______________________

General ledger bookkeeper ______________________

Accounts receivable bookkeeper ______________________

Accounts payable bookkeeper ______________________

Cashier ______________________

Department heads:

Purchasing ______________________

Sales ______________________

Credit ______________________

18. a. List names of officials and employees exercising the functions noted—continued:

Cost	________
Receiving	________
Shipping	________
Payroll	________
Personnel	________
Tax	________

b. Is any one of the above, to the best of your information, a relative of any other? ___ ___ ___ ___ ___

c. If so, who? ________

	NAME	DATE	COMMENT
Originally prepared by:	________	________	________
Reviewed in subsequent examination by:	________	________	________
	________	________	________
	________	________	________
	________	________	________

	ANSWER		ANSWER BASED ON		
	YES	NO	INQUIRY	OBSERVATION	TEST
II. Cash Receipts					
A. Mail receipts:					
1. Is the mail opened by someone other than the cashier or accounts receivable bookkeeper?	___	___	___	___	___
2. Does the mail routine prohibit the delivery of unopened mail (other than personal mail) to employees having access to the accounting records?	___	___	___	___	___
3. a. Is a record of the money and checks received prepared by the person opening the mail?	___	___	___	___	___

	ANSWER		ANSWER BASED ON		
	YES	NO	INQUIRY	OBSER-VATION	TEST
b. If so, is this record given to someone other than the cashier for independent verification of the amount recorded?	___	___	___	___	___
c. Is this record compared with the cash receipts book regularly?	___	___	___	___	___
B. Other receipts:					
1. Are the receipts of currency relatively insignificant?	___	___	___	___	___
2. Are receipts recorded by cash registers or other mechanical devices?	___	___	___	___	___
3. If so, are the machine totals checked independently by the accounting department?	___	___	___	___	___
4. Are sales books or receipt books used?	___	___	___	___	___
5. If so:					
a. Are the slips or receipts prenumbered?	___	___	___	___	___
b. Are the daily totals and numerical sequence checked independently by the accounting department?	___	___	___	___	___
c. Are unused books safeguarded?	___	___	___	___	___
6. If none of the above methods are in use, is some other adequate system of control in force?	___	___	___	___	___
If so, explain.					
7. Is there an adequate safeguard against misappropriation of cash through the recording of fictitious discounts or allowances by the cashier?	___	___	___	___	___
8. Are miscellaneous receipts, such as from sale of scrap, salvage, etc., reported to the accounting department by the recipient as well as to the cashier?					
9. Does the accounting department check such reports against the related cash book entries?	___	___	___	___	___
C. General:					
1. Are each day's receipts deposited in the bank intact and without delay?	___	___	___	___	___

	ANSWER		ANSWER BASED ON		
	YES	NO	INQUIRY	OBSER-VATION	TEST
2. Does someone other than the cashier or accounts receivable bookkeeper take the deposits to the bank?	___	___	___	___	___
3. Is a duplicate deposit slip checked and held for the auditors by someone other than the employee making up the deposit?	___	___	___	___	___
4. Are bank debit advices (such as for N.S.F. checks) delivered directly to a responsible employee (other than the cashier) for investigation?	___	___	___	___	___
5. Are the duties of the cashier entirely separate from the recording of notes and accounts receivable?	___	___	___	___	___
6. Is the general ledger posted by an employee who is not from the cashier's department?	___	___	___	___	___
7. Is the office routine so arranged that the cashier is denied access to the accounts receivable ledgers and monthly statements?	___	___	___	___	___
8. Are all other cash funds (i.e., other than cash receipts) and securities handled by someone other than the cashier?	___	___	___	___	___
9. If the cashier handles such funds:					
a. List the items hereunder:					
b. Are such items counted by us during our examination?	___	___	___	___	___
10. Where branch offices make collections, are such collections deposited in a bank account subject to withdrawal only by the head office?	___	___	___	___	___
11. Are rents, dividends, interest, and similar revenues adequately controlled in such manner that their non-receipt would be noted and investigated?	___	___	___	___	___
12. Is the cashier responsible for the cash receipts from the time they are received in his department until they are sent to the bank?	___	___	___	___	___
13. Are proper physical safeguards and facilities employed to protect cash and cash transactions?	___	___	___	___	___

	ANSWER		ANSWER BASED ON		
	YES	NO	INQUIRY	OBSER-VATION	TEST
14. Does any employee having custody of client funds also have custody of non-client funds (e.g., credit union, employee benefit association, etc.)?	___	___	___	___	___

Comment on adequacy of internal control:

	NAME	DATE	COMMENT
Originally prepared by:	___	___	
Reviewed in subsequent examination by:	___	___	___
	___	___	___
	___	___	___
	___	___	___

	ANSWER		ANSWER BASED ON		
	YES	NO	INQUIRY	OBSER-VATION	TEST
III. Cash Disbursements					
1. Are all disbursements, except from petty cash, made by check?	___	___	___	___	___
2. Are all checks prenumbered?	___	___	___	___	___
3. Are voided checks properly defaced or mutilated and held available for subsequent inspection?	___	___	___	___	___
4. Are checks required to be countersigned?	___	___	___	___	___
5. a. Is the signing of checks in advance prohibited?	___	___	___	___	___

	ANSWER		ANSWER BASED ON		
	YES	NO	INQUIRY	OBSER-VATION	TEST
b. Is the countersigning of checks in advance prohibited?					
6. Are authorized signatures limited to officers or employees who have no access to accounting records or to cash?					
7. Is the practice of drawing checks to "cash" or "bearer" prohibited?					
8. If not, are checks so drawn limited to pay rolls and/or petty cash reimbursement?					
9. Are monthly bank statements and paid checks received directly by the accounting department?					
10. Are the bank accounts independently reconciled by someone other than the employees who keep the cash records?					
11. Is the sequence of check numbers accounted for when reconciling the bank accounts?					
12. Is the practice of examining paid checks for date, name, cancellation, and endorsement followed by the employee reconciling the bank accounts?					
13. Are vouchers or other supporting documents presented together with the checks submitted for signature?					
14. Do the signers make adequate investigation before signing checks?					
15. If a check-signing machine is in use, are the machine and signature plates kept under effective control?					
16. Are checks mailed out without allowing them to return to the employee who drew the checks or to the accounts payable bookkeeper?					
17. Are the supporting documents impressed with a "paid" stamp or other mark so as to prevent their use for duplicate payment?					
18. Are payroll checks drawn against a separate payroll bank account?					

	ANSWER		ANSWER BASED ON		
	YES	NO	INQUIRY	OBSER-VATION	TEST
19. Is the payroll bank account on an imprest basis?	___	___	___	___	___
20. Are dividend checks drawn against a separate dividend bank account?	___	___	___	___	___
21. Are transfers from one bank to another under effective accounting control?	___	___	___	___	___

Comment on adequacy of internal control:

	NAME	DATE	COMMENT
Originally prepared by:	___	___	___
Reviewed in subsequent examination by:	___	___	___
	___	___	___
	___	___	___
	___	___	___

IV. Petty Cash Fund

	ANSWER		ANSWER BASED ON		
	YES	NO	INQUIRY	OBSER-VATION	TEST
1. Is imprest fund system in use?	___	___	___	___	___
2. Is the responsibility for each fund vested in one person only?	___	___	___	___	___
3. Is the custodian independent of the cashier or other employees handling remittances from customers and other cash receipts?	___	___	___	___	___
4. Is the amount of the fund restricted so as to require reimbursement at relatively short intervals?	___	___	___	___	___

	ANSWER		ANSWER BASED ON		
	YES	NO	INQUIRY	OBSER-VATION	TEST
5. a. Has a maximum figure for individual payments from the fund been established:	___	___	___	___	___
b. If so, state maximum figure.	___	___	___	___	___
6. Are payees required to sign vouchers for all disbursements?	___	___	___	___	___
7. Is adequate approval required for advances to employees and I.O.U.'s?	___	___	___	___	___
8. a. Is the cashing of personal checks prohibited?	___	___	___	___	___
b. If not, state whether such checks are recashed at bank or are included as vouchers supporting request for reimbursement.	___	___	___	___	___
9. a. Are vouchers and supporting documents checked by a responsible employee at the time of reimbursement?	___	___	___	___	___
b. Does that employee verify the unexpended balance of the fund?	___	___	___	___	___
10. Are the amounts of the vouchers spelled out in words as well as written in numerals?	___	___	___	___	___
11. Are vouchers marked so as to preclude their re-use?	___	___	___	___	___
12. a. Is any part of the fund represented by cash in bank?	___	___	___	___	___
b. Are checks drawn on this account signed by the custodian only?	___	___	___	___	___
13. Are checks for reimbursement made out to the order of the custodian?	___	___	___	___	___
14. Is the fund checked at reasonable intervals by surprise counts made by an internal auditor or other employee independent of the custodian?	___	___	___	___	___
15. Describe the operation of the fund if the same is in part represented by a bank account. (e.g., If an imprest fund, are all reimbursements deposited in the bank and a small working cash balance replenished therefrom, or does the custodian transfer accounts from cash to bank and vice versa in his discretion?)	___	___	___	___	___

Comment on adequacy of internal control:

	NAME	DATE	COMMENT
Originally prepared by:	____	____	
Reviewed in subsequent examination by:	____	____	____
	____	____	____
	____	____	____
	____	____	____

V. SECURITY INVESTMENTS	ANSWER		ANSWER BASED ON		
	YES	NO	INQUIRY	OBSERVATION	TEST
1. Are securities kept in a safe deposit vault in the name of the client?	____	____	____	____	____
2. If so:					
a. Does access thereto require the signatures or presence of two or more designated persons?	____	____	____	____	____
b. Is a record maintained by the client of visits to safe deposit vault?	____	____	____	____	____
3. If not:					
a. Are they kept in safekeeping by an independent person?	____	____	____	____	____
b. Are they kept in a safe place under control of an officer?	____	____	____	____	____
4. Is a record kept by the accounting or the financial department of each security, including certificate numbers?	____	____	____	____	____
5. Are all securities, except "bearer" bonds, in the name of the client?	____	____	____	____	____

	ANSWER		ANSWER BASED ON		
	YES	NO	INQUIRY	OBSER-VATION	TEST
6. Are securities periodically inspected and agreed with the record by internal auditors or other designated officers or employees?	___	___	___	___	___
7. Are purchases and sales of securities authorized by:					
a. The board of directors?	___	___	___	___	___
b. An officer?	___	___	___	___	___
c. The financial department?	___	___	___	___	___
8. Are securities held for others, or as collateral, recorded and safeguarded in similar manner to those owned by the client?	___	___	___	___	___
9. Are security investments which have been written off or fully reserved against followed up as to possible realization?	___	___	___	___	___
10. Are satisfactory records kept to insure the proper and prompt receipt of income on securities owned?	___	___	___	___	___

Comment on adequacy of internal control:

	NAME	DATE	COMMENT
Originally prepared by:	___	___	
Reviewed in subsequent examination by:	___	___	___
	___	___	___
	___	___	___
	___	___	___

	ANSWER		ANSWER BASED ON		
	YES	NO	INQUIRY	OBSER-VATION	TEST
VI. Notes and Accounts Receivable					
1. a. Are notes authorized by a responsible official?	___	___	___	___	___

	ANSWER		ANSWER BASED ON		
	YES	NO	INQUIRY	OBSER-VATION	TEST
b. Are renewals of notes authorized by a responsible official?	___	___	___	___	___
2. a. Is the custodian of notes receivable independent of the cashier or bookkeepers?	___	___	___	___	___
b. Is the custodian of negotiable collateral independent of the cashier or bookkeepers?	___	___	___	___	___
3. Are the customers' ledgers kept by employees who have no access to cash receipts?	___	___	___	___	___
4. Are the customers' ledgers balanced at least monthly and the totals agreed with the general ledger control account?	___	___	___	___	___
5. a. Are statements of open items mailed to all customers monthly? If not, to what extent are they mailed?	___	___	___	___	___
b. If so, is this done by an employee who has no access to cash and who is independent of the accounts receivable bookkeepers and the billing clerks?	___	___	___	___	___
c. Does this employee retain control of the statements until mailed?	___	___	___	___	___
d. Are differences reported by customers routed to this same employee for investigation?	___	___	___	___	___
6. Are delinquent accounts listed periodically for review by an official other than the credit manager?	___	___	___	___	___
7. Are write-offs of bad debts approved by an official other than the credit manager?	___	___	___	___	___
8. Are charged-off accounts kept under memo ledger control and followed up? Explain.	___	___	___	___	___
9. Are credit memos approved by a responsible official?	___	___	___	___	___
10. Are such credit memos under numerical control?	___	___	___	___	___
11. Is approval of a responsible official required for discounts allowed after the discount date or in excess of normal credit terms?	___	___	___	___	___

	ANSWER YES	ANSWER NO	ANSWER BASED ON INQUIRY	ANSWER BASED ON OBSERVATION	ANSWER BASED ON TEST
12. Are credits for returned goods checked against receiving reports?	____	____	____	____	____
13. Are direct confirmations of notes and accounts receivable obtained periodically:					
a. By internal auditors?	____	____	____	____	____
b. By other designated employees?	____	____	____	____	____
14. Is the management of the credit department entirely divorced from the sales department?	____	____	____	____	____
15. Is the cashier denied access to the accounts receivable ledgers?	____	____	____	____	____
16. a. Is merchandise out on consignment recorded in a memorandum accounts receivable ledger?	____	____	____	____	____

b. If consigned merchandise is a material and/or continuing factor, outline the client's procedures in this respect on a separate page, with a cross reference hereto.

17. Are journal entries affecting accounts receivable approved by someone senior to the accounts receivable bookkeeper?

Comment on adequacy of internal control

	NAME	DATE	COMMENT
Originally prepared by:	____________	____________	____________
Reviewed in subsequent examination by:	____________	____________	____________
	____________	____________	____________
	____________	____________	____________

	ANSWER		ANSWER BASED ON		
VII. Inventories	YES	NO	INQUIRY	OBSER-VATION	TEST
A. Physical control:					
1. Are designated stores keepers held responsible for the control of:					
a. Raw materials?					
b. Purchased parts?					
c. Semi-finished merchandise?					
d. Finished merchandise?					
e. Supplies and repair parts?					
2. Do the stores keepers notify the accounting department of all receipts by means of receiving or production reports?					
3. Are issues made only against signed requisitions or shipping orders?					
4. Are the quantities on hand counted:					
a. At the end of the fiscal year?					
b. Periodically during the year?					
5. Are such counts made independent of the stores keepers or other employees responsible for the custody of the items being counted?					
6. Are the following classes of inventories under effective accounting control:					
a. Goods out on consignment?					
b. Materials in hands of processors, suppliers, etc.?					
c. Materials or merchandise in bonded or other outside warehouses?					
d. Returnable containers, pallets, etc.					
7. Is merchandise on hand which is not the property of the client (consignments-in, etc.) physically segregated and under effective accounting control?					
8. With respect to the determination of inventory values:					

	ANSWER		ANSWER BASED ON		
	YES	NO	INQUIRY	OBSERVATION	TEST
a. Are priced inventory sheets double-checked as to:					
i. Cost prices?	___	___	___	___	___
ii. Market prices?	___	___	___	___	___
iii. Extensions, footings, and summarizations?	___	___	___	___	___
b. Is a review made by a responsible official or designated employee as to overstock and as to slow-moving or obsolete items?	___	___	___	___	___
9. Is a reasonable degree of control maintained over stationery and other supplies which are charged directly against operations?	___	___	___	___	___
10. Are scrap, salvaged materials, and "no value" inventories under such accounting control as should assure the proper recording of the sale or re-use of such items?	___	___	___	___	___
11. Are there adequate safeguards to insure that the costs of partial shipments billed to customers are eliminated from inventories at time of billing?	___	___	___	___	___
12. If standard costs are used, is there an established procedure for revising them periodically?	___	___	___	___	___
B. Perpetual inventory records:					
1. Are perpetual inventory records maintained for:					
a. Raw materials?	___	___	___	___	___
b. Supplies and repair parts?	___	___	___	___	___
c. Work in process?	___	___	___	___	___
d. Finished product?	___	___	___	___	___
NOTE: If no perpetual records are maintained, the following six questions (2 to 7 inclusive) are not applicable.					
2. Do such perpetual records show:					
a. Quantities only?	___	___	___	___	___

	ANSWER		ANSWER BASED ON		
	YES	NO	INQUIRY	OBSER-VATION	TEST
b. Quantities and values?	___	___	___	___	___
3. Are such perpetual records kept by employees other than the stores keepers?	___	___	___	___	___
4. Are such records controlled by accounts in the general ledger?	___	___	___	___	___
5. Are perpetual records checked by physical stocktaking at least once annually?	___	___	___	___	___
6. Are the perpetual records regularly adjusted as a result of the physical stocktaking?	___	___	___	___	___
7. Do such adjustments require the approval of a responsible official or employee?	___	___	___	___	___

C. Planning and scheduling:
Outline briefly the client's practices and their effectiveness in controlling inventories.

D. Commitments:
Outline briefly the client's practices and their effectiveness in controlling inventories.

Comments on adequacy of internal control:

	NAME	DATE	COMMENT
Originally prepared by:	___	___	
Reviewed in subsequent examination by:	___	___	___
	___	___	___
	___	___	___
	___	___	___

VIII. Properties and Patents

	ANSWER		ANSWER BASED ON		
	YES	NO	INQUIRY	OBSER-VATION	TEST
1. Are detailed plant ledgers maintained for the various units of property?	___	___	___	___	___

	ANSWER		ANSWER BASED ON		
	YES	NO	INQUIRY	OBSER-VATION	TEST
2. Are such records balanced at least annually with general ledger control accounts?	___	___	___	___	___
3. Does the client:					
a. Take periodic inventory of plant items?	___	___	___	___	___
b. Have periodic appraisals, for insurance or other purpose?	___	___	___	___	___
4. Is a satisfactory system in effect for the control of small tools?	___	___	___	___	___
5. Is a work order system in use:					
a. For capital expenditures?	___	___	___	___	___
b. For major repair jobs?	___	___	___	___	___
c. For research and development projects?	___	___	___	___	___
6. Is prior authorization for capital expenditures required:					
a. From the board of directors?	___	___	___	___	___
b. From officers?	___	___	___	___	___
7. When actual expenditures exceed the amount authorized, is the excess approved as in Question 6 above?	___	___	___	___	___
8. Is there a sound policy in force for the differentiation between capital additions and maintenance and repairs? Explain:	___	___	___	___	___
9. Is the recording and the accounting for capital replacement items so devised as to insure the proper accounting treatment for the removal of items replaced?	___	___	___	___	___
10. Is the approval of a designated official required for the retirement or dismantling of plant items?	___	___	___	___	___
11. Is there an effective procedure to insure that property physically retired is removed from the records and that the proceeds from salvage and sales are accounted for?	___	___	___	___	___
12. Are reserves for depreciation carried by units or groups corresponding with the classifications or grouping of depreciable plant items?	___	___	___	___	___

	ANSWER		ANSWER BASED ON		
	YES	NO	INQUIRY	OBSER-VATION	TEST
13. Is the client assured that patents arising from its research expenditures are issued in its name and not in the name of some individual?	___	___	___	___	___

Comment on adequacy of internal control:

	NAME	DATE	COMMENT
Originally prepared by:	___	___	
Reviewed in subsequent examination by:	___	___	___
	___	___	___
	___	___	___
	___	___	___

IX. Notes and Accounts Payable and Long-Term Debt

	ANSWER		ANSWER BASED ON		
	YES	NO	INQUIRY	OBSER-VATION	TEST
A. Notes and accounts payable:					
1. Are borrowings on notes payable authorized by the board of directors?	___	___	___	___	___
2. Are two or more signatures required on notes payable?	___	___	___	___	___
3. Is a notes payable register kept by an employee who is not authorized to sign checks or notes?	___	___	___	___	___
4. Are paid notes canceled and retained?	___	___	___	___	___
5. Is the voucher register, or accounts payable ledger, regularly reconciled with the general ledger control account?	___	___	___	___	___
6. Are statements from vendors regularly compared with the related ledger accounts (or with open items in voucher register)?	___	___	___	___	___

	ANSWER		ANSWER BASED ON		
	YES	NO	INQUIRY	OBSER-VATION	TEST
7. Are appropriate adjustments made as a result of this comparison?	____	____	____	____	____
8. Are adjustments of accounts payable (including the writing off of debit balances) required to be supported by the approval of a designated official?	____	____	____	____	____
B. Long-term debt:					
1. Are an independent trustee and an independent interest-paying agent employed?	____	____	____	____	____
2. Are redeemed notes, bonds, and interest coupons effectively mutilated?	____	____	____	____	____

Comment on adequacy of internal control:

	NAME	DATE	COMMENT
Originally prepared by:	____________	____________	
Reviewed in subsequent examination by:	____________	____________	____________
	____________	____________	____________
	____________	____________	____________
	____________	____________	____________

	ANSWER		ANSWER BASED ON		
	YES	NO	INQUIRY	OBSER-VATION	TEST
X. Capital Stock					
1. a. Does the client employ an independent registrar?	____	____	____	____	____
b. Transfer agent?	____	____	____	____	____
2. If not:					
a. Are unissued certificates and stock certificate stubs in the custody of an officer?	____	____	____	____	____

	ANSWER		ANSWER BASED ON		
	YES	NO	INQUIRY	OBSER-VATION	TEST
b. Are surrendered certificates effectively canceled?	____	____	____	____	____
c. Are documentary stamps under proper control?	____	____	____	____	____
3. Does the client employ independent dividend-paying agents?	____	____	____	____	____
4. If not, is proper control exercised in preparing and mailing dividends? (i.e., separate bank account, etc.)	____	____	____	____	____
5. Are returned or unclaimed dividend checks promptly redeposited and set up in the accounts as liabilities?	____	____	____	____	____

Comment as to adequacy of internal control:

	NAME	DATE	COMMENT
Originally prepared by:	____________	____________	
Reviewed in subsequent examination by:	____________	____________	____________
	____________	____________	____________
	____________	____________	____________
	____________	____________	____________

	ANSWER		ANSWER BASED ON		
	YES	NO	INQUIRY	OBSER-VATION	TEST
XI. Sales and Shipping					
1. Are sales orders adequately controlled?	____	____	____	____	____
2. Are all orders approved by the credit manager or department before shipment?	____	____	____	____	____

	ANSWER		ANSWER BASED ON		
	YES	NO	INQUIRY	OBSER-VATION	TEST
3. Is the credit department entirely independent of the sales department?	___	___	___	___	___
4. Are sales prices and credit terms based on approved standard price lists?	___	___	___	___	___
5. If so, are any deviations from standard approved:					
a. By an officer?	___	___	___	___	___
b. By another? Explain.	___	___	___	___	___
6. If not, are all sales prices and credit terms approved by the sales manager or in the sales department?	___	___	___	___	___
7. Are prenumbered shipping advices prepared for all goods shipped?	___	___	___	___	___
8. Are the quantities shown on the shipping advices double-checked in the shipping department?	___	___	___	___	___
9. Does the billing clerk or some other designated employee receive the shipping advices directly from the shipping department? (If so, identify this employee.)	___	___	___	___	___
10. Does this employee check the numerical sequence of shipping advices to assure that all are accounted for?	___	___	___	___	___
11. Are sales invoices checked:					
a. As to prices?	___	___	___	___	___
b. As to quantities?	___	___	___	___	___
c. As to credit terms?	___	___	___	___	___
d. As to extensions and footings?	___	___	___	___	___
e. Against customers' orders?	___	___	___	___	___
f. Against shipping advices?	___	___	___	___	___
(Identify the department or individual responsible for the above.)					
12. Are sales invoices prenumbered?	___	___	___	___	___

	ANSWER		ANSWER BASED ON		
	YES	NO	INQUIRY	OBSER-VATION	TEST
13. Is there a check on the arithmetical accuracy of total sales by means of a statistical or product analysis?	___	___	___	___	___
14. Are total sales for the respective accounting periods (e.g., monthly) reported directly to the general ledger bookkeeper independently of the work of the accounts receivable book-keepers?	___	___	___	___	___
15. Are there adequate safeguards against under-statement of sales through the suppression of sales invoices or shipping advices?	___	___	___	___	___
16. Are returned sales cleared through the receiving department (i.e., the department receiving incoming purchased materials and supplies)?	___	___	___	___	___
17. Are credit memos for returned sales supported by adequate data from the receiving depart-ment as to quantity, description, and condi-tion?	___	___	___	___	___
18. Are the following classes of sales accounted for in substantially the same manner as regular credit sales of merchandise:					
a. Sales to employees?	___	___	___	___	___
b. C.O.D. sales?	___	___	___	___	___
c. Sales of property and equipment?	___	___	___	___	___
d. Cash sales of merchandise?	___	___	___	___	___
e. Scrap and waste?	___	___	___	___	___
(If the answers are in any case in the negative, amplify by a concise description of the procedures.)					
19. Is there an adequate check on freight allowances:					
a. By reference to terms of sale?	___	___	___	___	___
b. By checking against freight bills or established and up-to-date schedule of freight rates?	___	___	___	___	___

	ANSWER		ANSWER BASED ON		
	YES	NO	INQUIRY	OBSER-VATION	TEST
c. Other? (If any, explain.)	___	___	___	___	___

Comment on adequacy of internal control:

	NAME	DATE	COMMENT
Originally prepared by:	______	______	
Reviewed in subsequent examination by:	______	______	______
	______	______	______
	______	______	______
	______	______	______

XII. Purchases and Expenses

	ANSWER		ANSWER BASED ON		
	YES	NO	INQUIRY	OBSER-VATION	TEST
1. Is there a purchasing department?	___	___	___	___	___
2. If so, is it entirely independent of:					
a. The accounting department?	___	___	___	___	___
b. The receiving and shipping departments?	___	___	___	___	___
3. Are purchases made only on the basis of purchase requisitions signed by the respective department heads?	___	___	___	___	___
4. Are all purchases (except small items purchased from petty cash) routed through the purchasing department?	___	___	___	___	___
5. Are all purchases made by means of the client's purchase orders sent to the vendors?	___	___	___	___	___
6. Are the purchase order forms prenumbered?	___	___	___	___	___
7. Are certain items required to be purchased subject to competitive bidding?	___	___	___	___	___

	ANSWER		ANSWER BASED ON		
	YES	NO	INQUIRY	OBSER-VATION	TEST
8. If so, does the procedure followed indicate the result of the review of the bids received?	___	___	___	___	___
9. Are purchase prices approved:					
a. By responsible official in purchasing department?	___	___	___	___	___
b. If not, by any other responsible official?	___	___	___	___	___
10. Is the quantity and condition of goods received determined at the time of receipt by someone independent of the purchasing department?	___	___	___	___	___
11. Is the receiving department denied reference to copies of the purchase orders for authority to accept materials, etc.?	___	___	___	___	___
12. Are receiving reports prepared by receiving department?	___	___	___	___	___
a. Are such reports prenumbered?	___	___	___	___	___
13. Are copies of receiving reports:					
a. Filed permanently in the receiving department?	___	___	___	___	___
b. Furnished to the accounting department?	___	___	___	___	___
c. Furnished to the purchasing department?	___	___	___	___	___
14. Is the accounting department notified promptly of purchase goods returned to the vendor?	___	___	___	___	___
15. Are unmatched receiving reports reviewed periodically and investigated for proper recording?	___	___	___	___	___
16. Are purchases returned to the vendor cleared through the shipping department?	___	___	___	___	___
17. Are vendors' invoices registered immediately upon receipt?	___	___	___	___	___
18. Are vendors' invoices delivered in the first instance to the purchasing department?	___	___	___	___	___
19. If so, are the invoices checked in the purchasing department:					
a. Against purchase orders?	___	___	___	___	___

	ANSWER		ANSWER BASED ON		
	YES	NO	INQUIRY	OBSERVATION	TEST
b. Against receiving reports (as to quantity and condition)?	___	___	___	___	___
20. If not, are the invoices checked as above by:					
a. The accounting department?	___	___	___	___	___
b. Others? Explain.	___	___	___	___	___
21. Is there an adequate system for the recording and checking of partial deliveries applicable to a purchase order?	___	___	___	___	___
22. Are invoices approved for payment by a responsible official?	___	___	___	___	___
23. Is there a definite responsibility for the checking of invoices as to:					
a. Prices and credit terms?	___	___	___	___	___
b. Extensions?	___	___	___	___	___
c. Freight charges or allowances?	___	___	___	___	___
24. Is a designated employee made responsible for the determination of the distribution of invoices (pursuant to an established accounting policy) to proper general ledger accounts?	___	___	___	___	___
25. Is the distribution so determined tested or double-checked periodically?	___	___	___	___	___
26. Are invoices not involving materials or supplies (e.g., fees, rentals, power and light bills, taxes, etc.) approved by department heads or executives prior to payment?	___	___	___	___	___
27. Is there a satisfactory check to insure that merchandise purchased for direct delivery to customers is billed to the recipients? Explain.	___	___	___	___	___
28. Are purchases made for employees cleared in regular manner through the receiving, purchasing, and accounting departments?	___	___	___	___	___
29. Are the vouchers, supporting documents, and expense or other distributions reviewed and initialed by an auditor of disbursements or other designated employee before payment is authorized?	___	___	___	___	___

	ANSWER		ANSWER BASED ON		
	YES	NO	INQUIRY	OBSER-VATION	TEST
30. If the answer to Question 29 is in the negative, is the accounts payable clerk or bookkeeper instructed to accept only those invoices which bear complete approval (i.e., rubber stamp endorsement, or equivalent, fully completed)?	___	___	___	___	___
31. Are all purchases (materials, merchandise, services, and expenses) routed through a purchase register or voucher record and not directly through cash disbursements?	___	___	___	___	___
32. If any purchases or expenses are booked originally directly in the cash disbursement records, are adequate vouchers filed therefor? Explain.	___	___	___	___	___
33. Is the accounts payable ledger or voucher register balanced monthly with the general ledger controlling account?	___	___	___	___	___
34. Are statements received from vendors regularly checked by the accounting department with the individual creditors' accounts or against open items in the voucher register?	___	___	___	___	___
35. Is a postage meter used for outgoing mail?	___	___	___	___	___

Comment on adequacy of internal control:

	NAME	DATE	COMMENT
Originally prepared by:	___	___	
Reviewed in subsequent examination by:	___	___	___
	___	___	___
	___	___	___
	___	___	___

	ANSWER		ANSWER BASED ON		
	YES	NO	INQUIRY	OBSER-VATION	TEST
XIII. PAYROLLS					
1. Is a time clock system in use:					
a. For factory workers?	____	____	____	____	____
b. For general office workers?	____	____	____	____	____
2. If so, are the time cards:					
a. Prepared and controlled by the payroll department, independent of foremen?	____	____	____	____	____
b. Punched by the employees in the presence of the foremen or other designated employees?	____	____	____	____	____
c. Signed by the foremen at the close of the pay roll period?	____	____	____	____	____
3. Are piece-work production reports (if any) signed by:					
a. The employees?	____	____	____	____	____
b. The foremen?	____	____	____	____	____
4. Are time cards and piece-work production reports checked to or compared with:					
a. Production schedules:	____	____	____	____	____
b. Payroll distribution:	____	____	____	____	____
5. Does preparation of the payroll require more than one employee?	____	____	____	____	____
6. Are the duties of those preparing the payroll rotated?	____	____	____	____	____
7. Are the names of employees hired reported in writing by the personnel office to the payroll department?	____	____	____	____	____
8. Are the names of employees resigned or discharged reported in writing by the personnel office to the payroll department?	____	____	____	____	____
9. Is the payroll checked at regular intervals against the personnel records?	____	____	____	____	____
10. Are all wage rates fixed by union contract, or authorized in writing by a designated official or employee?	____	____	____	____	____

	ANSWER		ANSWER BASED ON		
	YES	NO	INQUIRY	OBSER-VATION	TEST
11. Are vacation and sick-leave payments similarly fixed or authorized?	___	___	___	___	___
12. Is there adequate check against payments for vacation, etc., in excess of amounts authorized?	___	___	___	___	___
13. Is the payroll double-checked as to:					
a. Hours?	___	___	___	___	___
b. Rates?	___	___	___	___	___
c. Deductions?	___	___	___	___	___
d. Extensions?	___	___	___	___	___
e. Footings?	___	___	___	___	___
14. Are signed authorizations on file for all deductions being made from employees' wages?	___	___	___	___	___
15. Is there a time department independent of the payroll department?	___	___	___	___	___
16. Is the payroll signed prior to payment by:					
a. The employee preparing the payroll?	___	___	___	___	___
b. The employee rechecking the payroll?	___	___	___	___	___
c. The factory manager?	___	___	___	___	___
17. Are salary payrolls approved by a responsible official prior to payment?	___	___	___	___	___
18. Are all employees paid by check?	___	___	___	___	___
19. If paid by check, are the checks pre-numbered?	___	___	___	___	___
20. Are checks drawn and signed by employees who do not:					
a. Prepare the payroll?	___	___	___	___	___
b. Have custody of cash funds?	___	___	___	___	___
c. Keep the accounting records?	___	___	___	___	___
21. Are checks distributed to employees by someone other than the foreman?	___	___	___	___	___
22. Are payroll disbursements made from a special payroll bank account?	___	___	___	___	___

	ANSWER		ANSWER BASED ON		
	YES	NO	INQUIRY	OBSER-VATION	TEST
23. Is the payroll bank account reconciled by employees who do not prepare the payrolls, sign checks, or handle the pay-offs?	___	___	___	___	___
24. If so, does the reconciliation procedure include the comparison of the paid checks with the payroll and the scrutiny of endorsements?	___	___	___	___	___
25. To the extent that wages are paid in cash:					
a. Is an independent pay agent (such as armored car service) employed?	___	___	___	___	___
b. Is the currency placed in pay envelopes by employees who do not prepare the payrolls?	___	___	___	___	___
c. Are payroll receipts obtained from employees?	___	___	___	___	___
d. Are the workers identified by their foremen?	___	___	___	___	___
e. Are different employees assigned to the pay-off from time to time without prior notice?	___	___	___	___	___
26. Are unclaimed wages relatively insignficant?	___	___	___	___	___
27. Is proper control maintained over back pay and unclaimed wages?	___	___	___	___	___
28. Are wages which remain unclaimed for a specified period redeposited in a bank account and liability set up therefor?	___	___	___	___	___
29. Are payrolls audited periodically:					
a. By internal auditors?	___	___	___	___	___
b. By other designated employees?	___	___	___	___	___
30. If so, do the auditors:					
a. Attend occasional pay-offs?	___	___	___	___	___
b. Cover unclaimed wages?	___	___	___	___	___

Comment on adequacy of internal control:

EVALUATING AN INTERNAL CONTROL SYSTEM

	NAME	DATE	COMMENT
Originally prepared by:	__________	__________	
Reviewed in subsequent examination by:	__________	__________	__________
	__________	__________	__________
	__________	__________	__________
	__________	__________	__________

CHAPTER 3

MODERN STATISTICAL SAMPLING APPLICATIONS

USING SAMPLING TECHNIQUES IN PRACTICE

Auditors have been employing sampling techniques for scores of years. Testing is a part of the repertoire of every accountant, and sampling is unquestionably essential in every audit, except uncommonly small ones. To examine every transaction is plainly impossible from a cost viewpoint if from no other. Auditors, both internal and external, use their own judgment to select for scrutiny certain transactions or activities from the year's accumulation. This is called judgment sampling.

Judgment sampling, properly done, is perfectly acceptable under present auditing standards.[1] The sample is based on the auditor's experience, the client, and dozens of other qualitative factors that the auditor considers in selecting his sample. Judgment sampling does have certain limitations, one of which is that the auditor often samples more than he has to for his purposes.

In auditing, an equally acceptable alternative to judgment sampling is statistical sampling. Frequently, an accountant avoids statistical sampling because it is "too complicated," or because the potential user has "forgotten" his statistics. This should not be a deterrent, however, for it is not too complicated and one need know very little about statistical theory to use statistical sampling effectively. This chapter provides simplified illustrations of how the auditor can use statistical sampling, and in what instances, during the course of an audit, it is most appropriate.

THE PURPOSE OF STATISTICAL SAMPLING

The underlying purpose of statistical sampling is to enable the accountant to generalize (make inferences) about the characteristics of the whole from the characteristics of the

[1]*See Statement on Auditing Standards, Number 1,* The Committee on Auditing Standards, American Institute of Certified Public Accountants, New York, N.Y., © 1973, Section 320A, beginning on page 36.

sample. That which distinguishes statistical sampling from judgment sampling is that in statistical sampling the generalization is founded on statistical principles. As a result, both the size of the sample and the interpretation of the results are objectively defensible, that is, the auditor can assess the probability of error. Of course, there is the ever-present risk that the sample is not representative of the whole (the population). The auditor can specify, in selecting the size of the sample, the risk he is willing to assume that the sample is not representative of the whole. In fact, a basic part of the sample selection is establishing the measure of acceptable risk.

Sampling Theory Simplified

There are two aspects to measuring the risk that the sample will differ from the population: the range within which the sample is expected to be reliable (called *precision*); and the likelihood of attaining that degree of reliability (called *confidence*). Precision is usually stated as a percent although it may be in dollar terms. Thus, the auditor may project a 2% error rate in vouchers he wishes to sample. (Error rate simple refers to the percentage of a particular kind of mistake made in the vouchers, such as lacking both required signatures.) While he knows the sample error rate will approximate the population error rate, he also knows the chances of its being identical are slim indeed, but he can place bounds around how far he is willing for the sample error rate to vary from the population error rate. Assume he picks boundaries of + or −1%. What the auditor has said is this: "I expect the sample percentage of errors in signing vouchers that I find in the sample number I inspect to be between 1% and 3% (2% ± 1%), if the percentage of errors that have been made in all the vouchers is 2%." In sampling for errors, the auditor is interested in finding *excessive* rates of error only, and the lower precision limit is not relevant. Obviously, fewer errors than 2% is perfectly acceptable.

One more element in determining sample size is necessary. Although the auditor "expected" the percentage of error in the sample to be about what the percentage is in all the vouchers, that is, ± 1%, he has no certainty that this is the case. Actually, the only way to be *certain* is to inspect every voucher. However, the auditor can choose the degree of confidence he requires that the sample error rate within the precision limits, represents the population error rate.

For example, assume the auditor selects a 95% confidence level. The auditor is saying "that there is a 95% probability that the sample range (2% ± 1%) contains the population error rate."

Steps in Determining Sample Size

Tables can be found for almost any confidence level desired. Tables 3-1 and 3-2 are for confidence levels of 95% and 90%, respectively. The auditor should take the following steps in selecting a sample *size*:

Step 1. Determine the confidence level with which he feels safe. Levels below 90% are not realistic for most audits and auditors. Alternatively, levels above 95% will probably be necessary only rarely. Such a case may be a first-time audit with several weaknesses in internal control. As a rule of thumb, a confidence level of 90% may be satisfactory for repeat audits where controls are good. A 95% confidence level may be desirable for first-time audits or where controls have

Table 3-1

Determination of Sample Size
Percentage of Occurrences in Sample
Reliability (Confidence Level): 95%

Sample Size	1	2	3	4	5	6	7	8	9	10	12	14	16	18	20	25	30	35	40	45	50
50						0	0	0	0	2.0		4.0	6.0	8.0	10.0	14.0	18.0	22.0	26.0	32.0	36.0
60					0	0	0	1.7	1.7		3.3	5.0	6.7	8.3	10.0	15.0	18.3	23.3	28.3	33.3	38.3
70					0	0	1.4		2.9	2.9	4.3	5.7	7.1	10.0	11.4	15.7	20.0	24.3	28.6	34.3	38.6
80				0	0	1.2		2.5		3.8	5.0	6.2	8.8	10.0		16.2	20.0	25.0	30.0	35.0	40.0
90				0	0		2.2		3.3	4.4	5.6	6.7	8.9	10.0	12.2	16.7	21.1	25.6	30.0	35.6	40.0
120			0	.8	.8	1.7	2.5	3.3	4.2	5.0	6.7	8.3	10.0	11.7	13.3	17.5	22.5	27.5	31.7	36.7	41.7
160		0	.6	1.2	1.9	2.5	3.1	3.8	5.0	5.6	7.5	8.8	10.6	12.5	14.4	18.8	23.8	28.1	33.1	38.1	43.1
240		.4	.8	1.7	2.5	3.3	4.2	5.0	5.8	6.7	8.3	10.0	11.7	13.8	15.4	20.0	24.6	29.6	34.6	39.2	44.2
340	0	.6	1.2	2.1	2.9	3.5	4.4	5.3	6.2	7.1	8.8	10.6	12.4	14.4	16.2	20.9	25.6	30.6	35.3	40.3	45.3
460	0	.9	1.5	2.4	3.3	3.9	4.8	5.7	6.7	7.6	9.3	11.1	13.0	14.8	16.7	21.5	26.3	31.1	36.1	40.9	45.9
1000	.4	1.2	2.0	2.9	3.8	4.7	5.6	6.5	7.4	8.4	10.2	12.1	14.0	15.9	17.8	22.7	27.5	32.4	37.4	42.3	47.5

Table 3-2

Determination of Sample Size
Percentage of Occurrences in Sample
Reliability (Confidence Level): 90%

Sample Size	1	2	3	4	5	6	7	8	9	10	12	14	16	18	20	25	30	35	40	45	50
50					0	0	0	2.0	2.0		4.0	6.0	8.0	10.0	10.0	16.0	20.0	24.0	30.0	34.0	38.0
60				0	0	0	1.7		3.3	3.3	5.0	6.7	8.3	10.0	11.7	16.7	21.7	25.0	30.0	35.0	40.0
70				0	0	1.4		2.9		4.3	5.7	7.1	8.6	11.4	12.9	17.1	21.4	25.7	31.4	35.7	41.4
80			0	0	1.2		2.5		3.8	5.0	6.2	7.5	10.0			17.5	22.5	27.5		36.2	
90			0	0		2.2		3.3	4.4		6.7	7.8	10.0	12.2	13.3	17.8	22.2	27.8	32.2	36.7	42.2
120		0	0	.8	1.7	2.5	3.3	4.2	5.0	5.8	7.5	9.2	10.8	12.5	14.2	19.2	24.2	28.3	33.3	38.3	43.3
160		0	.6	1.2	2.5	3.1	3.8	5.0	5.6	6.2	8.1	10.0	11.9	13.8	15.6	20.0	25.0	29.4	34.4	39.4	44.4
240	0	.4	1.2	2.1	2.9	3.8	4.6	5.4	6.2	7.1	8.8	10.8	12.5	14.6	16.2	20.8	25.8	30.8	35.4	40.4	45.4
340	0	.9	1.5	2.4	3.2	4.1	5.0	5.9	6.8	7.6	9.4	11.2	13.2	15.0	17.1	21.8	26.5	31.5	36.2	41.2	46.2
460	.2	.9	1.7	2.6	3.5	4.3	5.2	6.1	7.2	8.0	9.8	11.7	13.7	15.4	17.4	22.2	27.0	32.0	37.0	41.7	46.7
1000	.5	1.3	2.2	3.1	4.0	4.9	5.9	6.8	7.7	8.7	10.6	12.5	14.4	16.4	18.3	23.2	28.0	33.0	37.9	42.9	47.9

been less than satisfactory in the past. From this discussion, it is obvious that the confidence level is a matter of professional judgment on part of the individual auditor. This is equally true for the range of precision. Tables 3-1 and 3-2 are for confidence levels of 95% and 90%. Other statistical tables are sometimes presented according to population size, as well as confidence level. Tables 3-1 and 3-2 are equally applicable to any population size.

Step 2. Establish the required precision. In Tables 3-1 and 3-2 the upper limit of precision is shown across the top of the first row. Precision is a function of materiality, that is, where errors may occur that affect the presentation of expensive inventory items in the balance sheet, much more precision should be required than when the errors are of a procedural nature, such as the voucher signatures referred to earlier. In this latter instance the auditor may be willing to assume a greater risk, hence a wider range of precision.

Step 3. Estimate the expected occurrence rate. This means the auditor must predetermine the rate at which he expects errors to occur in the population. This is not a difficult task; in fact, if the auditor has done this audit in prior years, he will have grounds for such a predetermination. For example, in his test for signatures on vouchers in past years, assume the auditor has found the following:

	Error Rate
19X1	3.1%
19X2	2.8%
19X3	3.0%

It appears that the percentage of errors is fairly consistently around 3.0%. To be especially conservative, the auditor may, in the absence of information to the contrary, estimate that the percentage of errors in the current year will be no higher than the highest of the three years—3.1%. In cases where no prior year experience exists, the auditor may have to take a trial sample. In other words, the auditor may take (at random)[2] 200 vouchers and inspect them, noting the missing second signature. Assume he finds 5 such vouchers, a 2½% occurrence rate. Conservatively, he estimates a 3% occurrence rate.

AN EXAMPLE OF DETERMINING SAMPLE SIZE

Now a sample size can be determined. Using the vouchers mentioned earlier, assume the auditor wishes to sample for the two signatures.[3] He desires a 90% confidence level, an upper precision limit of 6% with an expected occurrence rate of 3.1%. Reading Table 3-2, column 6, for an upper precision limit of 6% to 3.1 the expected occurrence rate, across the row to 160 under "sample size" column, the auditor finds that sampling 160 vouchers will allow him to be 90% confident that the sample represents the population, with an upper limit error rate of 6%. What has just been done is one part of what is called sampling for attributes. In this instance a single attribute (characteristic) has been sampled: proper signatures, of which there must be two. There are two other parts to sampling for attributes: which vouchers to choose, and how to evaluate the results. How to determine *which* 160 vouchers are chosen follows. Evaluating the results of sampling will be considered later.

---

[2]Random sampling will be taken up on page 103.

[3]This is but a single characteristic of the vouchers. Others may be simultaneously sampled, such as proper distribution in the accounts, adequate supporting evidence, and so on. Not to do this would be a significant waste of time. It should be pointed out, however, that the auditor may require a higher confidence level or narrower precision for these other two characteristics, in which case he needs to consider a trade-off of the greater sample size than is necessary for the signature characteristic in order to sample the other characteristics, against the cost of sampling for each characteristic separately.

USING RANDOM NUMBER TABLES

Randomness avoids bias and allows each voucher an equal chance to be selected for inspection for signatures. The best technique for assuring the 160 vouchers are chosen randomly is by use of a random number table.[4] Such a table is reproduced in Table 3-3. Almost any method of using the table is acceptable as long as the auditor is systematic in his method.

For example, it has been determined that 160 vouchers from those consecutively numbered from 1–8,000 are to be selected. The auditor may start in the table at any point. Assume he picks column 6, line 3, number 64809. He may either proceed down the column or across the line. If he goes down column 6, he will pick vouchers numbered 4809 (obviously, he cannot use the whole sequence of numbers, 64809, because no voucher has that number. Alternatively, the auditor may use the *first* four digits in the sequence, 6480, just as long as he continues to do so), 6376, 1782, 3498, 1016, 922, 3488. Notice that he skipped 8103, 9533, 9936, and 9445, because there are no vouchers with these numbers. He must follow this procedure until 160 vouchers have been inspected. Using random number tables assures objectivity and avoids any possible criticism arising from judgment selection.

HOW TO APPLY SYSTEMATIC SAMPLING IN AN AUDIT

What if the vouchers are not pre-numbered? Often it happens that documents to be sampled are not sequentially numbered in which case the auditor has two alternatives. He may number them, actually or by mental count, and then follow the random sampling method just described; or he may use a technique called systematic sampling. The former option is likely too time-consuming, but the latter is a handy tool in this circumstance. Randomness is achieved by introducing a random start, that is, which voucher is examined first? At least two random starts are essential. Assume the same 8,000 vouchers with a desired sample of 160. The interval between vouchers chosen (those "skipped") is determined by dividing the number of vouchers in the population (all of them) by the sample size, and multiplying by the number of random starts, thus:

$$\frac{8{,}000}{160} = 50 \times 2 = 100$$

100 is called the *skip interval,* and it means that every 100th voucher is examined in each *start.* Two starts were assumed. Again, the auditor can begin at any point in the random number table (Table 3-3). Suppose he uses column 6 and specifies for use the two right-hand digits. Obviously, any two digits will fall between 01 and 100, and in column 6, the first two numbers (91646 and 89198) have 46 and 98, both between 01 and 100. Now the auditor had two starting places, the 46th voucher and the 98th voucher, skipping 100 vouchers in each start. Thus, he would examine the 46th, the 146th, the 246th, and so on, and the 98th, 198th, the 298th, etc. If the auditor follows this sequence he will pick for examination 160 vouchers, 80 from each start.

The example used of 8,000 vouchers is, of course, an even number of items from which a sample was chosen. This, obviously, is a rarity and the most likely circumstance is 7,961 or

[4]The auditor's judgment may be introduced here. Out of say, 8,000 vouchers, he may choose to pick every 50th voucher. If they are consecutively numbered, he may pick each voucher ending with the digits 50 or 00. This is not a random sample unless the starting number is randomly determined. See the section on Systematic Sampling.

Table 3-3

	(1)	(2)	(3)	(4)	(5)	(6)	(7)	(8)	(9)	(10)	(11)	(12)	(13)	(14)
1	10480	15011	01536	02011	81647	91646	69179	14194	62590	36207	20969	99570	91291	90700
2	22368	46573	25595	85393	30995	89198	27982	53402	93965	34095	52666	19174	39615	99505
3	24130	48360	22527	97265	76393	64809	15179	24830	49340	32081	30680	19655	63348	58629
4	42167	93093	06243	61680	07856	16376	39440	53537	71341	57004	00849	74917	97758	16379
5	37570	39975	81837	16656	06121	91782	60468	81305	49684	60672	14110	06927	01263	54613
6	77921	06907	11008	42751	27756	53498	18602	70659	90655	15053	21916	81825	44394	42880
7	99562	72905	56420	69994	98872	31016	71194	18738	44013	48840	63213	21069	10634	12952
8	96301	91977	05463	07972	18876	20922	94595	56869	69014	60045	18425	84903	42508	32307
9	89579	14342	63661	10281	17453	18103	57740	84378	25331	12566	58678	44947	05585	56941
10	85475	36857	53342	53988	53060	59533	38867	62300	08158	17983	16439	11458	18593	64952
11	28918	69578	88231	33276	70997	79936	56865	05859	90106	31595	01547	85590	91610	78188
12	63553	40961	48235	03427	49626	69445	18663	72695	52180	20847	12234	90511	33703	90322
13	09429	93969	52636	92737	88974	33488	36320	17617	30015	08272	84115	27156	30613	74952
14	10365	61129	87529	85689	48237	52267	67689	93394	01511	26358	85104	20285	29975	89868
15	07119	97336	71048	08178	77233	13916	47564	81056	97735	85977	29372	74461	28551	90707
16	51085	12765	51821	51259	77452	16308	60756	92144	49442	53900	70960	63990	75601	40719
17	02368	21382	52404	60268	89368	19885	55322	44819	01188	65255	64835	44919	05944	55157
18	01011	54092	33362	94904	31273	04146	18594	29852	71585	85030	51132	01915	92747	64951
19	52162	53916	46369	58586	23216	14513	83149	98736	23495	64350	94738	17752	35156	35749
20	07056	97628	33787	09998	42698	06691	76988	13602	51851	46104	88916	19509	25625	58104
21	48663	91245	85828	14346	09172	30168	90229	04734	59193	22178	30421	61666	99904	32812
22	54164	58492	22421	74103	47070	25306	76468	26384	58151	06646	21524	15227	96909	44592
23	32639	32363	05597	24200	13363	38005	94342	28728	35806	06912	17012	64161	18296	22851
24	29334	27001	87637	87308	58731	00256	45834	15398	46557	41135	10367	07684	36188	18510
25	02488	33062	28834	07351	19731	92420	60952	61280	50001	67658	32586	86679	50720	94953
26	81525	72295	04839	96423	24878	82651	66566	14778	76797	14780	13300	87074	79666	95725
27	29676	20591	68086	26432	46901	20849	89768	81536	86645	12659	92259	57102	80428	25280
28	00742	57392	39064	66432	84673	40027	32832	61362	98947	96067	64760	64584	96096	98253
29	05366	04213	25669	26122	44407	44048	37937	63904	45766	66134	75470	66520	34693	90449
30	91921	26418	64117	94305	26766	25940	39972	22209	71500	64568	91402	42416	07844	69618
31	00582	04711	87917	77341	42206	35126	74087	99547	81817	42607	43808	76655	62028	76630
32	00725	69884	62797	56170	86324	88072	76222	36086	84637	93161	76038	65855	77919	88006
33	69011	65795	95876	55293	18988	27354	26575	08625	40801	59920	29841	80150	12777	48501
34	25976	57948	29888	88604	67917	48708	18912	82271	65424	69774	33611	54262	85963	03547
35	09763	83473	73577	12908	30883	18317	28290	35797	05998	41688	34952	37888	38917	88050
36	91567	42595	27958	30134	04024	86385	29880	99730	55536	84855	29080	09250	79656	73211
37	17955	56349	90999	49127	20044	59931	06115	20542	18059	02008	73708	83517	36103	42791
38	46503	18584	18845	49618	02304	51038	20655	58727	28168	15475	56942	53389	20562	87338
39	92157	89634	94824	78171	84610	82834	09922	25417	44137	48413	25555	21246	35509	20468
40	14577	62765	35605	81263	39667	47358	56873	56307	61607	49518	89656	20103	77490	18062
41	98427	07523	33362	64270	01638	92477	66969	98420	04880	45585	46565	04102	46880	45709
42	34914	63976	88720	82765	34476	17032	87589	40836	32427	70002	70663	88863	77775	69348
43	70060	28277	39475	46473	23219	53416	94970	25832	69975	94884	19661	72828	00102	66794
44	53976	54914	06990	67245	68350	82948	11398	42878	80287	88267	47363	46634	06541	97809
45	76072	29515	40980	07591	58745	25774	22987	80059	39911	96189	41151	14222	60697	59583

Table of 105,000 Decimal Digits, Statement 4914, Interstate Commerce Commission. Reproduced by permission of the Bureau of Economics, Interstate Commerce Commission.

8,098 or some other total number of vouchers. This causes no special problem, and the auditor should simply round his answer, being conservative. For example, assume 8,098 vouchers, of which the auditor wants to examine 160. The "skip interval" is determined:

$$\frac{8{,}098}{160} = 50.61 \times 2 = 101.22, \text{ rounded to } 100.$$

Sampling Items That Have Been Grouped

Before proceeding to the evaluation of the sample result, one more sample selection technique has considerable usefulness for the auditor. It is called *stratified random sampling.* Nothing new need be introduced here except the "stratified" portion of the name. The techniques considered thus far have built-in an implicit assumption that the sequence in which the auditor finds the vouchers came about randomly. In other words, the vouchers are in order of the *event,* not rearranged to the size of dollar amounts, and so forth. Where this is true, or for any other reason the items to be sampled are grouped, it is necessary that the auditor view each group, or strata, independently as a population to be sampled. Inventory is often grouped, and the groupings are of varying dollar values. High priced items, for example, may be in locked storage and, consequently, appear on inventory sheets in a block. Pure random sampling of the entire population will not take into account the materiality of these items, which the auditor may wish to examine more carefully.

The Versatility of Stratified Random Sampling

Stratification allows the auditor to use more than one sampling technique on the inventory. For example, he may group inventory according to dollar value and then proceed to sample as follows:

Items with value of	Sampling Technique
\$1–\$100	Random Sample
\$101–\$500	Systematic Sample
Over \$500	100% Sample

Once the strata, or groups, are determined, the auditor proceeds as previously explained.

Evaluating the Sample Result

To this point discussion has been limited to how to select *size* of the sample, and how to determine *which* items in the population to examine. But the auditor is not finished until he has evaluated the outcome of his sample. It will be recalled that the auditor *estimated* the occurrence of errors or characteristics as a step in determining the sample size. He bounded that rate with an interval percentage within which he was satisfied (the precision limit). There is no assurance that the auditor will uncover exactly the number of errors (missing signature for example), or characteristics, he predicted; in fact, that would indeed be fortuitous. Chances are that the actual number of vouchers with only one signature will be more or less than that expected.

In the example used of the 8,000 vouchers, it was assumed that the auditor expected a 3.1% occurrence rate, that is, he expected 3.1% times 8,000 or 248 vouchers to have a missing signature. Moreover, he was satisfied with an upper precision limit of 6%. Assume that upon examining the 160 sample vouchers, he finds 16 without two signatures. This indicates a rate of occurrence of 10%, or 800 of the 8,000 vouchers are lacking in a signature. The auditor has several alternatives. First, he may reevaluate his upper precision limit and decide that it may be raised. In this case, he would accept the sample as representative of all the vouchers with an upper precision limit of 14%.[5] This means that he can be 90% confident that all the vouchers contain no more than 14% without both signatures. Second, he may expand the size of his sample. This would seem to be the most likely course of action unless the auditor was persuaded that this was a serious situation requiring other auditing procedures, e.g., a complete reevaluation of the internal control system. To determine the degree to which the sample must be expanded, the auditor would use Table 3-4.[6] Using the same upper precision limit of 6%, reading down that column, he finds an occurrence rate of 9% and one of 14%. Being conservative, he picks 14%, then reads across that row to find a sample size of 340. This means that he must sample 180 more (340-160) vouchers. The result of that sample would be evaluated in the same manner. Finally, the auditor may lower his required confidence level. In the case presented, this would result in an inordinately low confidence level and is, therefore, not an acceptable alternative.

Table 3-4

Evaluation of Results
Number of Occurrences in Sample
Reliability (Confidence Level): 90%

Sample Size	Precision (Upper Limit) Percentage																				
	1	2	3	4	5	6	7	8	9	10	12	14	16	18	20	25	30	35	40	45	50
50					0			1			2	3	4	5		8	10	12	15	17	19
60				0			1		2		3	4	5	6	7	10	13	15	18	21	24
70				0		1		2		3	4	5	6	8	9	12	15	18	22	25	29
80			0		1		2		3	4	5	6	8	9	10	14	18	22	25	29	33
90			0		1	2		3	4		6	7	9	11	12	16	20	25	29	33	38
120		0		1	2	3	4	5	6	7	9	11	13	15	17	23	29	34	40	46	52
160		0	1	2	4	5	6	8	9	10	13	16	19	22	25	32	40	47	55	63	71
240	0	1	3	5	7	9	11	13	15	17	21	26	30	35	39	50	62	74	85	97	109
340	0	3	5	8	11	14	17	20	23	26	32	38	45	51	58	74	90	107	123	140	157
460	1	4	8	12	16	20	24	28	33	37	45	54	63	71	80	102	124	147	170	192	215
1000	5	13	22	31	40	49	59	68	77	87	106	125	144	164	183	232	280	330	379	429	479

[5]This is determined by using Table 3-2. For a sample size 160, and an expected occurrence rate of 10%, the upper precision limit is 14%. Read down the "sample size" column to row 160, then across to 10.0, the expected occurrence rate, then up that column to find the new upper precision limit.

[6]As is the case with sample size tables, similar to Tables 3-1 and 3-2, there is an "evaluation of results" table for each confidence level. Inasmuch as the auditor in the example is satisfied with a 90% confidence level, that is the evaluation table he should use.

The Usefulness of Discovery Sampling

There are two special sampling techniques with which the auditor should have familiarity. One, called discovery sampling, is especially useful when fraud is suspected, and the other, called estimation sampling for variables, is valuable for estimating dollar amounts. Estimation sampling is discussed later in this chapter.

In cases where fraud or improprieties are suspected, discovery sampling is an invaluable tool. The idea underlying discovery sampling, as the name implies, is to sample (test) until an

Table 3-5

Probability in Per Cent of Including at Least One Occurrence in a Sample For Populations Between 5,000 and 10,000 If the True Population Rate of Occurrence is:

Sample Size	.1%	.2%	.3%	.4%	.5%	.75%	1%	2%
	The Probability of Including at Least One Occurrence in the Sample is:							
50	5%	10%	14%	18%	22%	31%	40%	64%
60	6	11	17	21	26	36	45	70
70	7	13	19	25	30	41	51	76
80	8	15	21	28	33	45	55	80
90	9	17	24	30	36	49	60	84
100	10	18	26	33	40	53	64	87
120	11	21	30	38	45	60	70	91
140	13	25	35	43	51	65	76	94
160	15	28	38	48	55	70	80	96
200	18	33	45	56	64	78	87	98
240	22	39	52	62	70	84	91	99
300	26	46	60	70	78	90	95	99+
340	29	50	65	75	82	93	97	99+
400	34	56	71	81	87	95	98	99+
460	38	61	76	85	91	97	99	99+
500	40	64	79	87	92	98	99	99+
600	46	71	84	92	96	99	99+	99+
700	52	77	89	95	97	99+	99+	99+
800	57	81	92	96	98	99+	99+	99+
900	61	85	94	98	99	99+	99+	99+
1,000	65	88	96	99	99	99+	99+	99+
1,500	80	96	99	99+	99+	99+	99+	99+
2,000	89	99	99+	99+	99+	99+	99+	99+

Note: 99+ indicates a probability of 99.5% or greater.

Probabilities in these tables are rounded to the nearest 1%.
Differences in rounding techniques may cause a few entries in these tables to differ by one percentage point from comparable entries in other tables.

error or exception is found. Once found, of course, the exception must be weighed for significance by the auditor. Uncovering possible irregularities in an internal control system is an important application of discovery sampling. The auditor can predetermine, within the bounds of probabilities, what sample size is necessary to find one exception. Tables have been constructed to show these probabilities. Table 3-5 is a reproduction of such a table for populations of 5,000 to 10,000.

The auditor needs to know three things to find sample size: the total population (returning to the vouchers—8,000), the rate of occurrence (this he must estimate; assume .4% for this example), and the degree of confidence he wants (for this example, assume the auditor has been forewarned of possible forgeries of signatures on the vouchers and that, as a consequence, he wants a very high degree of likelihood that he will find at least one such forged voucher, say, 99.5%.) Translating this into the table matrix, under the column for "true population rate of occurrence" of, .4%, reading down to 99 + % the auditor finds that he will need to examine at least 1,500 vouchers to be 99 + % sure of finding one occurrence. While this seems a heavy price to pay in terms of time expenditure, it may be justified on the basis of the auditor's forewarning. For less critical exceptions, the auditor may consult the client before incurring the cost.

The table may be used in another way. In the earlier example in which 160 of the 8,000 vouchers were examined, the auditor may estimate his chances of finding an exception. Assuming an occurrence rate of .4% again, reading down column ".4%" to a sample size of 160, he finds that he has only a 48% chance of finding a forged signature. The lesson here seems obvious. Unless the rate of occurrence of the exception is fairly high, discovery sampling can require an inordinate amount of sampling time to reach a high degree of probability of finding an exception. For this reason, discovery sampling needs to be used judiciously.

A Simplified Method of Estimating Totals

Often, it is of value to the auditor to be able to estimate the dollar value of a population. He might find this a convenient way of testing totals in general ledger accounts for, say, work-in-process inventory, or the sum of the classifications on an aging schedule of accounts receivable. Other techniques of sampling introduced previously do not afford the auditor this ability. Estimation sampling for variables, as it is called, does.

The theory of estimation sampling for variables is complex and the mathematical formulations fairly rigorous. Fortunately, it is not necessary to understand all the theory to make use of this tool. A surface understanding of the theory, however, will aid in finding applications.

The total value of a column of figures can be determined by calculating its average and multiplying this by the number of figures in the column. It is obvious that if the auditor goes to this extent he may as well simply add the column. This is not sampling and requires considerable time. The auditor may regard it as a mathematical truism that the average of a *sample* of the figures in the column will approximate the average of the whole. Thus, to estimate the aggregate value, for example, of the 31–60 day column in the accounts receivable aging schedule, the auditor has merely to determine the average of a sample and multiply by the number of figures in the column.

It was learned in sampling for attributes that the sample rarely has qualities identical to that of the population. This is true because of statistical error. The error could be bounded, it was also learned (which was called precision), with a certain degree of probability (called the confidence level). Exactly the same approach is used to estimate the total of the column of the aging schedule. In other words, the auditor can estimate the value of the column at, say, ± $2,000, at a confidence level of 95%. The desired precision interval would depend on the materiality of the population tested, the confidence level on the degree of risk the auditor is willing to assume. Using these two parameters, the auditor can compute the number of figures (the sample) he must select from the population for the purpose of determining the average of the sample.

There are four basic steps to estimating the totals:

1. Establish precision interval and confidence level,
2. Determine the sample size,
3. Examine the sample and compute its mathematical average,
4. Multiply the average of the sample by the total number of accounts 31–60 days old.

Step 1, Criteria for establishing precision and the degree of confidence, has already been suggested. Step 2, the sample size determination, may be developed by using the following sequence of computations:[7]

A. Select a trial sample of at least 30 of the population,[8]
B. Sum the dollar value of the sample,
C. Sum the squares of each of the trial sample in A,
D. Compute the average of the sample, i.e., divide the sum obtained in B by the trial sample, 30,
E. Square the average in D,
F. Multiply the trial sample, 30, by the amount determined in E,
G. Subtract the amount obtained in F from the amount obtained in C,
H. Divide the amount in G by the trial sample minus one (or 30 − 1 = 29),
I. Take the square root of the amount determined in H,
J. Determine the level of confidence necessary (90%, 95%, etc.),
K. Use Table 3-6 and the confidence level in J to find the factor (e.g., at 95% the factor is ± 1.96%),
L. Determine the required precision (e.g., ± $2,000.),
M. Now, multiply the value in I by the value in K and by the total of the population. Then divide this total by the value in L.

This is the sample size.

A numerical example may help. Assume the auditor wishes to verify the 31–60 day column total in his client's aging of accounts receivable. Further assume that the auditor is satisfied with a 95% confidence level that his estimate of the total will be within ± $2,000 of the actual total. The column contains, 1,097 figures and the client's total is $27,088.

---

[7]Those who are mathematically inclined will perceive that the steps are simply an articulation of the equation:

$$\sqrt{n} = \frac{Sxj \cdot Ur \cdot N}{A}$$

where $\sqrt{n}$ = the square root of the sample size. (Thus, squared, it will equal the required sample)
Sxj = the estimated standard deviation of the population,
Ur = the reliability co-efficient, called here the "factor,"
N = total number of population
A = the desired precision

[8]The number 30 is a minimum and has been determined by statisticians.

Table 3-6

Conversion of Reliability Percentages to U Values

Percentage of cases (R) in which $\bar{x} - \bar{\bar{x}}$ will be no more than U standard errors	U
65%	± .93
70%	± 1.04
75%	± 1.15
80%	± 1.28
85%	± 1.44
90%	± 1.64
95%	± 1.96
99%	± 2.58

Conversion of U Values to Reliability Percentages

U	R	U	R	U	R	U	R
± 0.1	7%	± 1.05	70%	± 1.55	87%	± 2.05	95%
± 0.2	15%	± 1.10	72%	± 1.60	89%	± 2.10	96%
± 0.3	23%	± 1.15	74%	± 1.65	90%	± 2.15	96%
± 0.4	31%	± 1.20	76%	± 1.70	91%	± 2.20	97%
± 0.5	38%	± 1.25	78%	± 1.75	91%	± 2.25	97%
± 0.6	45%	± 1.30	80%	± 1.80	92%	± 2.30	97%
± 0.7	51%	± 1.35	82%	± 1.85	93%	± 2.35	98%
± 0.8	56%	± 1.40	83%	± 1.90	94%	± 2.40	98%
± 0.9	63%	± 1.45	86%	± 1.95	94%	± 2.45	98%
± 1.00	68%	± 1.50	86%	± 2.00	95%	± 2.56 or greater	99%

U = number of standard errors of the mean
R = percentage of cases in which $\bar{x} - \bar{\bar{x}}$ will not exceed U
All percentages have been rounded *down*.

Following are the steps to determine sample size:

A. The auditor selects 30 of the figures at random, using the random number tables,
B. The sample totals \$844.50,
C. The sum of the squares of the sample figures = \$33,471,
D. Sample average is \$844.50 ÷ 30 = \$28.15,
E. $(28.15)^2$ = \$792.42,
F. A × E = 30 × \$792.42 = \$23,772.60,
G. C − F = \$33,471 − \$23,772.60 = \$9,699,
H. G ÷ A − 1 = \$9,699 ÷ 29 = \$334.45,
I. $\sqrt{\$334.45}$ = \$18.30,
J. 95% (given),
K. From Table 3-6 at 95%, factor = ± 1.96,
L. ± \$2,000 (given),

M. $\frac{18.30 \times 1.96 \times \$1,097}{\pm \$2,000} = \sqrt{n}$

N. n = 387.

The auditor should sample 387. Of course, 30 have already been sampled; therefore, it is necessary that he randomly pick only 357 more figures. Obviously, requiring less precision would reduce the sample size. For example, doubling the precision interval to ± $4,000 would reduce the required sample size by one-half. In this case such an interval may well be justified, given the non-critical nature of this test.

Step 3, computing the mathematical average of the sample 387 figures, necessitates merely adding the value of the additional 357 figures to the value in step "B," above, ($844.50) and dividing by 387. Assume the total value of the 387 figures to be $9,698.22. The average is $9,698.22 ÷ 387 = $25.06.

Step 4 is the multiplication of the sample average, determined in Step 3 to be $25.06, by the total number of figures in the 31–60 column, 1097, for an estimated total value of $27,490.82. This is sufficiently close to the client's total of $27,088 to be acceptable to the auditor. Thus, he is assured that the total *is* $27,490.82 ± $2,000 with a 95% level of confidence.

Documenting Statistical Sampling Through Working Papers

Both the independent auditor and the internal auditor must document the phases of their audit. This is done by means of the auditor's working papers. Sampling is no exception, and working papers need to be made part of the audit file showing sampling techniques used. Figures 3A-1 to 3A-13 in the appendix to this chapter contain examples of recommended working papers to support the applications described in this chapter. Figures 3A-1 and 3A-2 are the sample working papers to be used in conjunction with the example just presented of estimating the totals on the aging schedule of accounts receivable. Other recommended working papers are shown in the appendix for the examples that follow.

Some Particular Applications of Sampling Techniques

Following are some particular audit areas where statistical sampling is most useful. Of course, sampling techniques are not suitable for use in every phase of an audit. Other audit tools may well be more appropriate.

Applying Sampling Techniques to the Cash Audit

In the audit of cash, three phases readily lend themselves to sampling: testing the firm's bank reconciliations; testing receipts; and testing disbursements.

Testing the firm's bank reconciliations is a good example of joining judgment sampling with random sampling. The *size* of the sample will likely be dependent on the auditor's judgment. For example, he may decide to select two months to be independently reconciled. *Which* two may be a combination of judgment and random sampling. He may want to reconcile the final month of the year (judgment) and one other month at random. Random number tables may be consulted. Assume the auditor selects the first column in Table 3-3, specifying the first number between 1 and 11 in the two left hand figures of the column. From the table it is the first number sequence, 10480, the first two numbers being 10. Thus, he selects the month of October as the second month to reconcile. This assumes, of course, the year began January 1. Should it begin with any other month, the "10" would represent the 10th month of the fiscal year.

Testing receipts and disbursements is an excellent example of the application of random sampling for attributes. The example which follows presupposes a small retail firm, selling mostly on account to its customers. Some cash sales are made, however, to over-the-counter customers. Disbursements are made by check, except for petty cash disbursements from an imprest petty cash fund. The firm makes about 2,200 charge sales per year (all on pre-numbered invoices). Cash sales are also rung-up, making the "daily report" a summary of each day's charge and cash sales from the register tape. Approximately 5,000 checks are written annually, requiring only one signature. These assumptions are made only as points of reference. The procedures described below are applicable in any firm with minor changes.

TESTING CASH DISBURSEMENTS

To test disbursements, the auditor follows the following steps:

Step	Action Required
1. Determine the attributes (characteristics) to be tested.	The auditor decides that he would like to review the following characteristics:[9] a. Signature. The signature of the owner should be present on each check. b. Endorsement. The endorsement should be consistent with the invoice. c. Source Documents. Support in the form of invoices, receipts, etc., should be present. d. Classification. The disbursements should be properly classified in the journals, and the disbursement should be posted to the appropriate general ledger account. e. Agreement of receiving report and invoice.
2. Choose the sample size.	The auditor must: a. Determine the confidence level. This is a "first-time" audit, and the auditor feels a relatively high level of confidence is necessary. He decides on 95%. b. Establish the precision interval. The auditor believes that each of the characteristics to be tested are equally material; therefore, he can have one confidence level and precision interval for all. He is especially conservative, because this is his first time to audit this firm, and because of another reason to be expanded upon later. He sets an upper precision limit of 5%. (It is coincidence that the upper precision limit chosen here when added to the confidence level of 95% equals 100%. There is no such relationship to be inferred.)

[9]It is assumed that purchase orders are not used. In cases where they are, the auditor will probably want to test their agreement with the invoice as a separate characteristic.

c. Estimate the expected rate of occurrence. With no previous experience with this firm, the auditor selects a trial sample at random to estimate the rate of occurrence of "exceptions." Because checks for the year are numbered consecutively from 28,607 to 33,841, he elects to sample the first 100 checks, numbered between 28,607 and 33,841, beginning with column (1), row 1 of the random number table (Table 3-3). The first such number is check #28,918 (column (1), row 11). The next, 32,639, then, 29,334 and so on. The auditor inspects each check for the characteristics desired. Sample working papers in the Appendix to this chapter—Figures 3A-5, through 3A-9—show the outcome of this sample.

3. Select the particular disbursements to to be reviewed.	The auditor decides to continue with the use of random sampling. It is convenient to continue the random technique used in the trial sample, that is, the first 460 random numbers between 28,607 and 33,841. Inasmuch as 100 have already been sampled, only 360 more need to be reviewed. The auditor simply picks up where he left off in the random number table.
4. Evaluate the sample result.	A total of 460 disbursements have been reviewed for the characteristics specified. The auditor must evaluate the outcome. Sample working paper Figure 3A-9 may be used as a guide in evaluating the sample result.

An Example of Using Discovery Sampling in the Audit of Cash Receipts

To continue the example, assume that prior to beginning the audit, the auditor was told that the sole shareholder/operator suspected that a former employee may have diverted certain of the cash receipts. How much may have been taken has not been determined, but the shareholder/operator feels that it was less than $1,000. This is one reason why the auditor was particularly conservative in his sampling of cash disbursements. To sample cash receipts, the auditor elects to use discovery sampling. He follows these steps:

Step	Action Required
1. Determine the total population.	Each receipt and each item on a deposit slip is of significance here because of the possibility of lapping or of simply not adding a collection made to the deposit slip. The auditor estimates approximately 2,300 items on the deposit slips for the year.[10]

[10]Considering the relatively small number of deposit slip entries, it was probably not difficult to estimate the population accurately. In cases where the population is much larger or much less susceptible of judgment estimation, estimation sampling for variables, described earlier in this chapter, is an excellent technique to use. It should be remembered that knowing the population size is necessary to determine which table to use.

2. Estimate the rate of occurrence.	Because he has been informed that it is likely the former employee diverted only a small amount of money, the auditor reasons that the occurrence rate is likely quite small, less than one percent. Thus, he estimates an occurrence rate of .8%, that is, he expects only 1 exception out of every 120 deposit slip entries.
3. Stipulate the degree of confidence wanted.	Following the reasoning above, the auditor desires a high degree of probability that he will find one instance where funds have been diverted. Assume he wants to be 99+% confident of finding an exception.
4. Read the sample size from the table.	In Table 3-7, for populations between 2,000 and 5,000, the auditor reads down column ".8%" to "99+%", then across the row to find the sample size. In this case, at least 700 individual deposit slip entries must be examined to be more than 99% sure of finding an exception. Sample worksheet Figures 3A-10 to 3A-13 may be used to support the sampling of cash receipts.

For purposes of this example, it was assumed in preparing sample worksheets that the first exception occurred upon examination of the 604th deposit slip entry. It was also assumed that examination of receipts was extended to a 100% test and that other procedures were intensified, e.g., a 100% positive confirmation of accounts receivable. It is possible that no exception was found after examining the 700 items. What does the auditor do? He should: 1) stop his examination and consult with management over the cost of continuing versus the chances of finding one exception; 2) consider that the employee was engaged in neither lapping nor failing to record an item on the deposit slip, but rather in some other fraudulent technique such as pocketing over-the-counter cash slips; and 3) evaluate the alternative that management is mistaken in its belief that diversion of monies took place at all. Obviously, the auditor must use his own judgment as to what course to follow after having explored these three areas.

APPLYING SAMPLING TECHNIQUES TO THE AUDIT OF ACCOUNTS RECEIVABLE

Verification of accounts receivable is another audit phase which is readily susceptible to the use of sampling techniques. Earlier in this chapter, an example was presented of using estimation sampling for variables to estimate the dollar value of the column totals of an accounts receivable aging schedule. Also, there is an example of working papers supporting this test. The reader may wish to refer to that example (Figure 3A-2) in connection with this section.

AN EXAMPLE OF SELECTING A CONFIRMATION SAMPLE

Selecting an accounts receivable confirmation sample may be facilitated by the use of several sampling techniques simultaneously: sampling for variables, stratified sampling and systematic sampling. For purposes of this illustration, assume that the firm being audited has

Table 3-7

Probability in Per Cent of Including at Least one Occurrence in a Sample For Populations Between 2,000 and 5,000 If the True Population Rate of Occurrence is:

Sample Size	.3%	.4%	.5%	.6%	.8%	1%	1.5%	2%
	The Probability of Including at Least One Occurrence in the Sample is:							
50	14%	18%	22%	26%	33%	40%	53%	64%
60	17	21	26	30	38	45	60	70
70	19	25	30	35	43	51	66	76
80	22	28	33	38	48	56	70	80
90	24	31	37	42	52	60	75	84
100	26	33	40	46	56	64	78	87
120	31	39	46	52	62	70	84	91
140	35	43	51	57	68	76	88	94
160	39	48	56	62	73	80	91	96
200	46	56	64	71	81	87	95	98
240	52	63	71	77	86	92	98	99
300	61	71	79	84	92	96	99	99+
340	65	76	83	88	94	97	99+	99+
400	71	81	88	92	96	98	99+	99+
460	77	86	91	95	98	99	99+	99+
500	79	88	93	96	99	99	99+	99+
600	85	92	96	98	99	99+	99+	99+
700	90	95	98	99	99+	99+	99+	99+
800	93	97	99	99	99+	99+	99+	99+
900	95	98	99	99+	99+	99+	99+	99+
1,000	97	99	99+	99+	99+	99+	99+	99+

Note: 99+ indicates a probability of 99.5% or greater.

Probabilities in these tables are rounded to the nearest 1%.
Differences in rounding techniques may cause a few entries in these tables to differ by one percentage point from comparable entries in other tables.

1,506 accounts receivable totaling about $375,000. Approximately ¾ of the total number of accounts are "retail" accounts with balances of $1,000 or less. The remaining ¼ are "industrial" accounts with balances ranging upward to $50,000. Further, assume that the auditor arranges all the accounts into groupings or "strata" according to their dollar value as follows:

	Amount	No. of Accounts
Retail and Industrial Accounts	$0 –$ 500	1,118
Retail Accounts	$501 – 1,000	157
Industrial Accounts	$501 – 1,000	208
Industrial Accounts	$1,000– over	23

This is done because the auditor intends to determine a different sample size for each strata. Moreover, he wishes to use more than one sampling technique. Sample working papers (Figures 3A-3 and 3A-4) show how a worksheet may be designed to support a confirmation sample. It may be helpful to follow the worksheet as the procedure is described below. To confirm accounts receivable, the steps are:

Step	Action Required
1. Stratify accounts according to dollar value.	The auditor's judgment must be used in selecting the range of each strata. Many factors must be taken into account including: a) quality of the internal control system; b) the aggregate and relative size of the accounts receivable; and c) prior experience with this audit. The ranges chosen are merely for illustrative purposes here.
2. Determine the confidence level and upper precision limit.	The rationale for selecting both confidence levels and upper precision limits has been mentioned earlier. The reader will notice in the sample working papers (Figures 3A-3 and 3A-4) that the auditor has chosen different confidence levels and precision limits for the various strata. For example, he has required a higher confidence level for industrial accounts from $501 to $1,000 than either smaller industrial accounts or retail accounts of less than $1,000. The reason may be that he feels this is a more critical area than the other strata. In addition, he has elected to confirm each of the 23 larger industrial accounts. The reason for selecting the smaller upper precision limit for retail accounts of from $0–$500 may be because the absolute size of the total of these accounts is quite large relative to the total of the other two strata. Thus, the auditor perceives them as more material. Another reason may be the relatively higher rate of exceptions in the prior year.
3. Estimate the actual occurrence rate.	This was simply a matter of referring to last year's working papers. In the absence of such information, the reader may recall that a trial sample will provide the estimate. Last year's data is better information, however, and should be used when available.
4. Determine the sample size.	From the tables (3-1 and 3-2) for 90% and 95% confidence levels, the auditor reads off the required sample size. For example, the correct table is known from the confidence level. Table 3-2 is for a 90% confidence level. Reading down

the column for upper precision limit of 5% to the estimated occurrence rate of 3.2%, then across the row to the left hand column "sample size," the auditor finds a required sample of 340. The sample procedure would be followed to find the sample size for the other strata.

Once sample size has been determined, the auditor can proceed to determine *which* accounts will be confirmed:

5. Select the random sample.

Random sampling by use of a random number table has been chosen. Inasmuch as the accounts are pre-numbered, stratification removed several accounts from the numbering sequence. For example, the larger industrial accounts, numbered according to their alphabetical arrangement, are now in another strata and their numbers are not sequential. This is equally true for retail accounts $501–$1,000. While the numbering sequence is interrupted for the accounts $0–$500, it is essentially intact. From the sample working papers, Figures 3A-3 and 3A-4, it will be noted that the random path chosen began at column 1, row 1, using the last four digits in the sequence between 0001 and 1506. (1506 is assumed to be the last of the numbered accounts.) It will also be noted that account numbers encountered that, because of stratification, have been removed from the sequence, are simply omitted. The auditor continues until 340 accounts are picked for confirmation.

6. Select the systematic sample.

The auditor is using systematic sampling for both industrial and retail accounts of $501–$1,000. He uses two random starts. For retail accounts of $501–$1,000, he divides the total number of accounts (157) by the number of accounts to be sampled (50) and multiplies by the number of starts (2). From sample working papers, it may be seen that the skip interval is 6. Start number 1 is with the 4th account and start number 2 with the 5th account. Thus, the auditor picks the 4th, 10th, 16th, 22nd, etc., account in the first start and the 5th, 11th, 17th, 23rd, etc., in the second, until 50 accounts are selected. He follows an identical technique in the next strata, selecting 60 accounts.

7. Evaluate the results.

Sample working papers (Figures 3A-3 and 3A-4) reflect the auditor's evaluation of the results of the actual sample. In the confirmation of accounts $0–$500, he found eight occurrences (errors, or differences which needed correction), an actual rate of 2.4%. From Table 3-4, reading row "340" under sample size across to the actual number of occurrences, 8, the auditor read up the column to "4," the actual precision percentage. This is less than his upper precision limit and was therefore accepted. The results of the confirmation of retail accounts in the $501–$1,000 strata were not acceptable. In Table 3-4, the auditor found he had achieved an upper precision limit of 14%, far beyond tolerance. He therefore, elected to confirm 70 more accounts. There were no errors in this sample; thus, from 120 total accounts in this group confirmed, he found 3 exceptions, and in Table 3-4, again, he read across row "120" in the sample size to the actual number of occurrences of 3, and upward in that column to find an upper precision limit of 6%, well within the prescribed limit. Thus, the sample was now accepted. A slightly different situation existed with the group of industrial accounts $501–$1,000. The precision limit achieved of 12% was less precision than specified; however, because the single exception found was of a minor nature and not considered critical, the auditor accepted the higher precision limit of 12%. It may be noted that he had two other options: to lower his confidence level requirement to 90%, in which case he would have achieved an upper precision limit of 9% (from Table 3-4), or he could have sampled 10 more, and assuming no further exceptions, he would have also achieved a precision of 9%. Sampling 20 more without exceptions would yield a precision of 8%.

Table 3-8

Evaluation of Results
Number of Occurrences in Sample
Reliability (Confidence Level): 95%

Sample Size	Precision (Upper Limit) Percentage																				
	1	2	3	4	5	6	7	8	9	10	12	14	16	18	20	25	30	35	40	45	50
50						0				1		2	3	4	5	7	9	11	13	16	18
60					0			1			2	3	4	5	6	9	11	14	17	20	23
70					0		1		2		3	4	5	7	8	11	14	17	20	24	27
80				0		1		2		3	4	5	7	8	9	13	16	20	24	28	32
90				0		1	2		3	4	5	6	8	9	11	15	19	23	27	32	36
120			0	1		2	3	4	5	6	8	10	12	14	16	21	27	33	38	44	50
160		0	1	2	3	4	5	6	8	9	12	14	17	20	23	30	38	45	53	61	69
240		1	2	4	6	8	10	12	14	16	20	24	28	33	37	48	59	71	83	94	106
340	0	2	4	7	10	12	15	18	21	24	30	36	42	49	55	71	87	104	120	137	154
460	0	4	7	11	15	18	22	26	31	35	43	51	60	68	77	99	121	143	166	188	211
1000	4	12	20	29	38	47	56	65	74	84	102	121	140	159	178	227	275	324	374	423	473

One additional observation need be made regarding sample working papers (Figures 3A-3 and 3A-4). The auditor also used the accounts selected for confirmation to sample for two attributes: comparison with ledger account balances and tracing entries to the accounts from books of original entry. The results of these tests should be reflected in the working papers. Inasmuch as the working paper treatment of sampling for variables has been illustrated in sample working papers (Figures 3A-8 and 3A-9), it was not repeated here.

Finally, with respect to the example, it should be pointed out that this is a relatively small number of accounts receivable (1506 were assumed), and it is possible that an auditor would choose to confirm all of them. While this is true, it is also possible that he may select certain accounts to which to send *positive* confirmation, sending *negative* confirmations to the remainder. In this instance, the illustration described here would be useful to select those accounts that are to be positively confirmed.

Applying Statistical Sampling to Auditing Inventory

Statistical sampling applications to inventory testing can be of great usefulness to the auditor. For example, testing extensions, prices, and quantities may all be accomplished through sampling for attributes, illustrated in several earlier examples. Techniques, procedures and supporting working papers for inventories are nearly identical with those described in testing accounts receivable, cash and vouchers.

Other Applications of Statistical Sampling Techniques

The procedures and techniques described above in the audit of vouchers, cash, accounts receivable and inventory are equally applicable to many other phases of the audit. A partial list includes:

1. Accounts and vouchers payable—selecting a confirmation sample, sampling for various attributes, such as: tracing to purchase orders, receiving reports and inventory records, accounts classification, tracing to voucher register and disbursements journal, inventory cut-off, and estimating the total dollar value.
2. Sales—sampling for attributes, such as: cut-off, account classification, proper journalizing, tracing to accounts receivable ledger, customer lists and customer purchase orders, and billing.
3. Expenses—sampling for attributes: account classification, comparisons with prior periods, tracing from vouchers to purchases journal and disbursements journal, authorizations, etc.
4. Internal control—sampling for attributes: authorization signatures on purchase orders and vouchers, location of fixed assets, document flow, tracing recording and posting functions; discovery sampling can be used effectively to uncover weaknesses in the system.

Of course, there are many other uses the auditor can find as he uses statistical sampling and becomes more and more aware of its facility.

Three notes of caution need to be stressed. First, statistical sampling is a powerful tool if used properly with adequate supporting evidence. It should be used judiciously with strict adherence to recommended procedures. It cannot and must not be a substitute for good sense and good judgment, nor should it be regarded as a panacea. Second, the tables reproduced are highly condensed and limited in their use to the particular kinds of sampling illustrated here. Actual applications may require more detailed tables; they are available and should be made a part of the auditor's library. Finally, the auditor *must not interpolate* in the tables. If values other than those in the tables as presented are required, larger tables must be used.

APPENDIX

Figure 3A-1 **Sample Working Paper Preliminary Assumptions**

Sample Working Papers:

The information shown here is merely to refresh the reader's memory on certain aspects of the problem of estimating the aging schedule's column totals. A similarly worded narrative may be made part of the auditor's working papers to establish a foundation for the actual sample technique described in a step-by-step manner in Figure 3A-2.

Preliminary Data

The estimation sampling for variable technique has been selected to estimate the totals of the aging schedule columns prepared by the client. Starr Hardware, Inc. has accounts receivable as follows: accounts 0–30 days old, 31–60 days, 61–90 days, over 90 days. The total of each column will be estimated.

Statistical Assumptions

Establishing the precision interval: a precision interval of ± $2,000 has been selected for accounts 31–60 days (other intervals may be more appropriate for the remaining column totals. They should be stated). Client's total of this 31–60 day column is $27,088. This interval is approximately 7% of the total shown. Due to the relatively small degree of materiality of this column's total to the total value of accounts receivable, ± $2,000 is considered a sufficiently narrow range.

Confidence Level: A confidence level of 95% is required. The degree of risk accepted is not unwarranted considering the satisfactory past experience with this audit. (See last year's working papers.)

Figure 3A-2

STARR HARDWARE, INC.
TESTING OF ACCOUNTS RECEIVABLE AGING SCHEDULE
YEAR ENDED 9/30/XX

Selecting Sample Size

A. A trial sample of 30 figures was chosen at random by systematic sampling as follows:

Number of figures in 31–60 days column $\frac{1{,}097}{30} = 36 \times 2 = 72$

Sample size

Interval of 72

Begin in random number table 3-3, column 1, row 1, first two right hand digits between 00 and 99, the numbers are 80 and 68.

Figures chosen for this sample are 80th, 152nd, 224th, 68th, 140th, 212th, etc. until 30 figures are selected.

B. Sum of this sample of 30 figures = \$844.50.
C. Sum of squares of this sample figures = \$33,471.
D. Sample average $= \frac{844.50}{30} = \$28.15$
E. Square of sample average = $(28.15)^2$ = 792.42
F. A × E = 30 × \$792.42 = \$23,772.60.
G. C − F = \$33,471 − \$23,722.00 = \$9,699.
H. G ÷ A−1 = \$9,699 ÷ 29 = \$334.45
I. Square root of H = $\sqrt{334.45}$ = \$18.30
J. Confidence level is 95%.
K. From Table 3-6, A + 95%, Factor is ± 1.96
L. Precision interval ± \$2,000.
M. $\frac{\$18.30 \times 1.96 \times 1{,}097}{\pm \$2{,}000} = \sqrt{n}$
N. n, sample size, = 387

Additional sample required—357 (387 − 30). Figures were selected by continuing systematic sampling described.

Mathematical Average of Sample

Sum of 387 sample figures $= \frac{\$9{,}689.22}{387}$ = \$25.06 average sample size

Estimate of Column Total

Sample average, \$25.06, times total number of figures: \$25.06 × 1,097 = \$27,490.82.

Results

Client's total of \$27,088 accepted. It falls within ± \$2,000 of estimated value of \$27,490.82.

Figure 3A-3

STARR HARDWARE, INC.
CONFIRMATION OF ACCOUNTS RECEIVABLE
YEAR ENDED 9/30/XX

Preliminary Data

Accounts receivable are to be stratified for confirmation as follows:

Accounts Receivable stratified as follows:	Amount	No. of Accounts	Sampling Technique
Retail & industrial accts.	\$ 0–\$ 500	1,118	Random
Retail Accounts	\$501–\$1,000	157	Systematic
Industrial Accounts	\$501–\$1,000	208	Systematic
Industrial Accounts	over–\$1,000	23	100%

Statistical Assumptions

	Required Confidence Level	Upper Precision Limit	Exceptions Rate based on last year's sample (see worksheet of prior year's audit).
All accounts $0–$500	90%	5%	3.2%
Retail—$501–1,000	90%	8%	2.0%
Industrial—$501–1,000	95%	8%	1.1%
Industrial—over $1,000	100%	-0-	-0-

Random Path:

Accounts 0–$500: Random No. Table 3-3, commence with column 1, row 1 digits sequence between 0001 and 1506, last four digits in sequence. First No. 480, etc. accounts in the sequence moved to another strata are ignored.

Retail Accounts: $501–$1,000

$\frac{157}{50} = 3 \times 2 = 6$. Every 6th account in each start.

Random number Table 3-3, begin with column 3, first digit in right hand column between 01 and 06. Start #1, 52404. Begin with 4th account. Start #2, 35605. Begin with 5th account.

Industrial Accounts: $501–$1,000

$\frac{208}{60} = 3 \times 2 = 6$, every 6th account in each start.

Begin with column 4 same sequence as above. Start #1, 94904, begin with 4th account. Start #2, 74103, begin with 3rd account.

Figure 3A-4

STARR HARDWARE, INC.
CONFIRMATION OF ACCOUNTS RECEIVABLE
YEAR ENDED 9/30/XX

Sample Results and Evaluation

		No. of Exemptions Found*	Actual Occur-rence Rate	Actual** Precision Limit Achieved	Evaluation of Results
All accounts	$ 0–$ 500	8	2.4%	4%	Accepted
Retail	$501–$1,000	3	6%	14%	Not accepted (see below)
Industrial	$501–$1,000	2	3.3%	12%	Accepted***
Industrial	over–$1,000	-0-	-0-	-0-	Accepted

Additional Sample of Retail Accounts $501–$1,000

Additional Sample Size	No. of Exceptions	Revised Actual Occur-rence Rate	Revised Actual Precision Limit Achieved	Evaluation of total Sample
70	0	2.5%	6%	Accepted

*An exception analysis should be made and entered in the working papers.
**From Tables 3-4 and 3-8.
***Because of non-critical nature of the exceptions found in this group, the actual precision limit achieved is accepted as the upper limit. No additional confirmation of these accounts is required.

Figure 3A-5

STARR HARDWARE, INC.
TESTING OF CASH DISBURSEMENTS
YEAR ENDED 9/30/XX

Preliminary Data

The firm writes about 5,000 checks per year, requiring one signature only. Checks are pre-numbered and entered sequentially by month in the check register. The following attributes have to be sampled:

1. Presence of authorized signature
2. An endorsement consistent with vendor shown on purchase order and invoice
3. Agreement with supportive documents
4. Proper classification of the disbursements in the accounts
5. Agreement of vendor's invoice and receiving report

Statistical Assumptions

Upper precision limit, all attributes: 5%

Confidence level required, all attributes: 95%

Trial sample selected to estimate actual occurrence rate—100 checks

Selection technique—Random numbers between 28,607 and 33,841 corresponding to check numbers. Random Path: Begin Column 1, row 1 of Table 3-3

Results of Trial Sample of 100 Checks—See Figure 3A-7.

Figure 3A-6

STARR HARDWARE, INC.
TESTING OF DISBURSEMENTS—TRIAL SAMPLE
YEAR ENDED 9/30/XX

Payee	Random Number/ Check Number	Amount	← ATTRIBUTE → Signature	Endorsement	Supporting Documents	Classification	Agreement: Rec. Dept. with Invoice
Hardware Supplies, Inc.	28,918	$3,782.91	√	√	√	√	√
Bell Tel. Co.	32,639	198.93	√	√	√	E	N.A.
Newspaper, Inc.	29,334	204.00	√	√	√	√	N.A.
A. M. Campbell	33,276	208.66	√	√	√	√	√
Shirley Smith	32,832	91.11	√	√	E	√	N.A.
T. R. Brown	29,880	300.22	√	√	√	E	N.A.
Total Trial Sample			100	100	100	100	100
Number of Sample checks with exceptions			-0-	-0-	2	3	3
Occurrence rate			-0-	-0-	2%	3%	3%

N.A. = Not applicable
√ = O.K.
E = Exception

Trial sample completed with check no. 29880

Figure 3A-7

STARR HARDWARE, INC.
TESTING OF DISBURSEMENTS—TRIAL SAMPLE RESULTS
YEAR ENDED 9/30/XX

	ATTRIBUTE				
	Signature	**Endorsement**	**Agreement with Supporting Documents**	**Proper Account Classification**	**Receiving Report Agree with Invoice**
Sample size indicated by trial sample (from table 3-1)	90	90	240	460	460
Actual sample taken	100*	100*	460**	460	460

*Inasmuch as no exceptions occurred in the trial sample, the trial sample satisfied both the constraints of confidence level and precision. No more checks need be tested for these attributes.

**To be conservative 460 checks will be sampled for each of the remaining three attributes even though the occurrence rate of exception to supporting documents requires a sample of only 240.

Figure 3A-8

STARR HARDWARE, INC.
TESTING OF DISBURSEMENTS—CONTINUATION OF SAMPLE
YEAR ENDED 9/30/XX

			ATTRIBUTE				
Payee	**Random Number/ Check Number**	**Amount**	**Signature**	**Endorsement**	**Supporting Documents**	**Account Classification**	**Invoice Agreement with Receiving Dept.**
ec. Power Co.	32307	$ 77.66	√	√	E	√	√
ıstis Tools, Inc.	32812	962.80	√	√	√	√	√
ɔmax Supplies, Inc.	20975	327.41	√	√	√	E	√
ble Hdwe.	30613	4,189.52	√	√	√	√	E
ɔtal Sample Size (See Figure 3A-7 r first 100 items sampled)			100	100	460	460	460

Total Exceptions	-0-	-0-	5	14	
Results of Sample					
Actual Occurrence Rate	-0-	-0-	1.1%	3.1%	2.
Confidence Level-Constant at 95%					
Actual Precision Limit Achieved (from table 3-8)	less than 1%	less than 1%	3%	5%	
Upper Precision Limit Desired-Constant at 5%					
Result of Sample of Attributes as indicated	accepted	accepted	accepted	accepted	acc

Figure 3A-9 **Exception Analysis**

Exception Analysis:

Check No. 32369—S/B Adv. Exp., chg'd to telephone exp.
Required entry:

Adv. Exp.	$198.93	
Tel. exp.		$198.93

Check No. 32832—Payroll ck., payroll register shows net pay $91.01. No entry required.

Check No. 29880—S/B refund. Chg'd to misc. exp.
Required entry:

Sales-Fencing	$300.22	
Misc. exp.		$300.22

(Note: The exception analysis should be continued to completion).

Figure 3A-10

STARR HARDWARE, INC.
TEST OF CASH RECEIPTS
YEAR ENDED 9/30/XX

We were informed by J. Smith, sole shareholder and manager, that he suspected improper diversion of cash receipts by a former employee. He estimates the amount diverted not to exceed $1,000 during the year.

Statistical Assumptions

Sampling Technique: Discovery Sampling
Computation of sample size:
Estimate of total population—2,300 items on deposit slips for the year

Estimated rate of occurrence—8%*
Degree of confidence stipulated—99+%**
Sample size (from Table 3-7)—700

*The estimate of such a small rate of occurrence is based primarily on management's contention that relatively little money was involved. The total of the sixteen critical exceptions of $900.25, as shown above, bears this contention out.

**The auditor must have a high degree of confidence that his sample will uncover at least one critical exception.

Figure 3A-11

STARR HARDWARE, INC.
TEST OF CASH RECEIPTS
YEAR ENDED 9/30/XX

No. Items	Deposit Slip Date	Amount	Traced to Cash Receipts Journal	Traced to Bank Recon-cilement	Traced to Subsidiary Accts. Rec.	Compare w/ Register tape/ Sales Invoice	Compare w/ Delivery Tickets	Explanation
13	1/3/xx	$2,060.21	√	√	√	√	N.A.	
3	1/4/xx	$1,305.64	√	√	E	√	√	(1 delivery only)—Exception not critical—collection on acct. credited to wrong account.
9	4/8/xx	$1,509.19	√	√	√	E	√	(2 deliveries) Exception critical—See explanation on Figure 3A-12

(The auditor would continue this worksheet to completion)

N.A. = Not applicable
√ = O.K.
E = Exception

Figure 3A-12

STARR HARDWARE, INC.
TEST OF CASH RECEIPTS
YEAR ENDED 9/30/XX

Evaluation of Exceptions

Non-Critical Exceptions:

Results of the test showed the following non-critical exceptions which were corrected as indicated:

(Here would be listed the non-critical exceptions)

Critical Exceptions:

Exception in deposit of 4/8/xx was failure by bookkeeper to show any cash sales on that day. Register tape indicates cash sales of $29.30. Assumption is that these funds diverted to use of bookkeeper. Conference with Mr. Smith concluded with instruction to test all cash receipts.*

Critical exceptions numbered 16. In each case cash sales were either understated as indicated below or no recording of the cash sale was made.

(Here would be listed the critical exceptions along with the total)

*It should be noted that the discovery sampling technique has accomplished its purpose with the critical exception found on the 604th deposit slip entry. The auditor now *knows* that funds were diverted. Thus, the discovery sampling phase is completed and the auditor's interest is in assessing the effect of the funds diversion.

Figure 3A-13 **Results of Cash Receipts Test**

Results:

As a result of these critical exceptions, it is considered desirable to: 1) positively confirm all accounts receivable; 2) test cash receipts for prior years during the term of the bookkeeper; 3) compare two prior year's cash sales with the current year; and 4) to lower precision limits and raise confidence levels in other tests to be performed.

CHAPTER 4

THE FINANCIAL BUDGET—A PRACTICAL APPROACH

The development of a master budget will be illustrated in this chapter. However, before the public accountant or the company accountant begins to construct a budget, certain management decisions have to be made in the way of planning. All the data used, actual or estimated, should be verified by the accountant for accuracy and realism. After the basic guidelines are laid down, it becomes the accountant's responsibility to construct a reliable budget.

PRELIMINARY GROUNDWORK—THE FIRST PHASE

In the case of the preparation of the company's first budget, a certain amount of groundwork needs to be done before the technical aspects of budgeting are begun. Initially the chief executive must be sold on the idea, and he in turn must see to it that the managerial staff at all levels are likewise convinced.

The organization must be reviewed and adjustments made to clarify lines of authority and responsibility. At this point consideration should be given to the types of reports issued in terms of the needs of the recipients. A re-designing of some reports and statements may well be necessary.

Closely related to the organizational structure problem is the need to review the chart of accounts. The proper classification, particularly of the operating accounts, and the need for readily available detail therein, must be determined and appropriate restructuring carried out. As previously indicated, a more detailed breakdown of accounts may be desirable because of the consideration that needs to be given all the revenue and expense items in drawing up a good budget.

Orientation sessions for lower echelon management may be in order. It is absolutely essential that all the staff designated as participants in the preparation of the budget be imbued with the proper budgeting philosophy. The staff must understand that the budget is a quantified plan designed to operate, at least in part, as a control mechanism that will aid them in carrying out their responsibilities and attaining their goals. It is never to be considered or used as a punitive device. It is not designed for the purpose of exercising coercive supervisory pressure to stay within the budget. There are often good reasons for being out of line with the budget. It must never be overlooked that the budget represents a series of financial benchmarks. Peter Drucker labels the late Nicholas Dreystadt, the former head of Cadillac, as one of the wisest managers he ever met and quotes Dreystadt as follows: "Any fool can learn to stay within his budget. But I have seen only a handful of managers in my life who can draw up a budget that is worth staying within."[1]

Basic Planning Information—The Second Phase

Planning can encompass the short-range, the intermediate-range and the long-range. When the planning process by direction effectively incorporates all three ranges, it may justifiably be designated as strategic planning. The short-range future must be successfully covered or there may be no long-range future to worry about. Likewise, the short-range must provide a pathway to the long-range.

The effort put into planning in general will be a function of many factors. These factors include among other elements, a clear understanding and appreciation of the value of planning by management in addition to the willingness to make appropriate sacrifices for it. It is not within the scope of this chapter to make a case for long-range planning though such a case is easily made. Short-range planning is essential, however, if a good budget is to be prepared.

Very early in the planning process, there must be a thorough evaluation of the company's present strategic position—internally and externally. The company must courageously weigh and evaluate its strengths and weaknesses in all financial areas. Any internal weaknesses noted must be corrected or appropriate allowances must be made until correction is possible. The inward look, like confession, is always a bit difficult. It is a task that must be done, however, since the planning effort in the final analysis depends upon the people involved and the resources at their command.

If not already known, the exact competitive position of the company must be determined. This may require a thorough study of competitors, especially from the product and market standpoint. The competitors' products and/or services must be objectively analyzed first in order to avoid misleading management as to the current competitive environment. If at all feasible, a thorough study should be made of the company's market from the standpoint of competitive conditions, selling methods, scope of product/service line, advertising methods and results, sales territories, pricing, credit terms and conditions of sales.

---

[1]Peter N. Drucker, "The Objectives of a Business," *Long-Range Planning for Management.* Edited by David W. Ewing (New York: Harper & Brothers, Publishers, 1958), p. 262.

Forecasting the Environment

Three general environmental forecasts are essential as a major part of sound planning:

a. Economic.
b. Sociological.
c. Technological.

Long-range planning decisions are based primarily on economic trends rather than on the immediate fluctuations above and below the trends. These fluctuations are of more concern in the short-range. The economic forecasts may be treated in two categories, general and industry-related.

Sociological environments of particular interest are apt to be:

a. The demographic structure.
b. Labor conditions.
c. Government roles.
d. International affairs.
e. Shifting consumer expenditures priorities.
f. General education.

Most of these environments are of direct or indirect interest to any operating company.

Technological environments that could influence seriously the status of a company would be the following:

a. The general scientific community.
b. The company's present and prospective customers.
c. The company's competitors.

Research trends in pure science must be considered initially in strategic planning, and these trends are a subject for continuous study and review. The company's strategy will be made according to the environment in which it must operate.

Environmental forecasting is a major concept in the initiation phase or secondary stage in the overall strategic planning process. It is a very critical and important contributor to the whole process. It may be essential to prepare alternate forecasts in some areas because of indeterminate environmental factors; subsequent events may point to more specific choices among the alternate forecasts. Periodic review is essential if these choices are to be made on a timely basis.

The intensity of the environmental study will depend upon the nature of the company and its relative sensitivity to its environment. The forecasts may be made entirely from special studies performed by non-company specialists or firm personnel, or from published materials of general availability, or from some combination of the two. Care must be exercised to avoid unnecessary expenditures for special studies covering topics reviewed elsewhere and to prevent excessive detail in studies and analyses.

The Economic Forecast

Forecasts of the economic environment may be classified into two general groups—the general economic conditions forecast, and the specific industry economic conditions forecast. These may be qualitative or quantitative or in combination. Some companies make and/or purchase more than one type of forecast and cross-check them.

The following institutions were recommended years ago as excellent primary sources of data and remain so to this day for environmental forecasts particularly in the economic segment[2]

[2]"Streamling the Sales Forecast," *Dun's Review,* Vol. 62, No. 2304 (August, 1953), pp. 42–45.

1. U.S. Government
   Bureau of the Budget
   Department of Labor, Bureau of Labor Statistics
   Securities and Exchange Commission
   Federal Reserve Board "Bulletin"
   Bureau of the Census (Population trends, manufacturing data)
   Department of Defense (Obligations)
   Bureau of Mines (Basic production data)
   Department of Commerce ("Survey of Current Business")
   Bureau of Agricultural Economics
   Federal Power Commission
2. Private Research Organizations
   Brookings Institution
   Twentieth Century Fund
   National Bureau of Economic Research
   National Industrial Conference Board
   Research Institute of America
3. Trade Associations
   Important industry data available in various publications.
   Many associations actively cooperate with members in assembling special information.
4. Trade Publications
   Many of the so-called vertical industry magazines publish valuable production and price data. *Iron Age,* for example, prints extensive price, operating and marketing information. Regional analyses published by the Federal Reserve District Banks, and monthly letters printed by private banks provide valuable interpretation.
5. Professional Associations
   American Marketing Association
   American Economic Association
   American Statistical Association

THE SOCIOLOGICAL FORECAST

Not so common as economic and technological forecasting, sociological forecasting is receiving increasing emphasis in larger companies. This type of forecasting is concerned with the ways in which various key social factors and institutions will affect a company's future. According to one writer (who is considered by the authors to have outlined a universally applicable set of factors) the following represent the most important sociological environments to forecast:[3]

1. The demographic structure—the size, location, age, ethnic structure, sex, and economic distribution of future populations.
2. Shifting expenditure priorities—public versus private consumption; preference shifts within product groups; the acceptability of substitute and synthetic products; relative emphasis on personal needs, home, transportation,

[3]James B. Quinn, "Long-Range Planning of Industrial Research," *Harvard Business Review,* Vol. 39, No. 4 (July/August, 1961), pp. 88–102. Copyright © 1961 by the president and fellows of Harvard College; all rights reserved.

communication, entertainment, health, community, education, foreign versus domestic products, and so on.

3. The role of the government—the activities of state, local and federal governments as customers, investors, competitors, quasi-judicial controllers, coordinators of activities, and sources of information.
4. Public and legal attitudes toward business—attitudes toward bigness; toward patent sanctity; toward what constitutes monopoly, interstate commerce, and restraint of trade; toward public control of prices, profits, labor and materials costs, and so forth.
5. International affairs—the general political atmosphere, foreign markets, overseas resources, tariff barriers, continuation of foreign aid programs, international monetary stability, possible military involvements, or the political recognition of certain nations.
6. Labor conditions—labor back-pressures against automation and the introduction of new products, the available skilled labor pool, the union-management bargaining balance, domestic versus foreign labor costs, management flexibility in hiring and layoffs, and so on.
7. Education—the number of trained scientific and skilled personnel, the sophistication levels of consumers, and the output of university research programs.

The impact of these factors on any organization, irrespective of size, cannot be overlooked. More information in this segment is becoming generally available through the medium of research organizations of various types. Some companies use the consulting services of educators or professional groups. Many utilize published services such as the *Long-Range Planning Service* of Stanford Research Institute. A few companies have organized internal sociological forecasting groups.[4]

The Technological Forecast

The technological forecast is concerned with three major sources of new technical developments:[5]

1. The scientific community generally
2. The company's present and prospective customers
3. The company's competitors

The first task is to study technological sources beyond the company's control, i.e., the scientific community generally and the company's competitors particularly. The starting point is current development programs. From such sources as government contract announcements, publicity releases, trade talk, professional papers, and so on, knowledgeable forecasters can predict with reasonable accuracy the technology which will certainly be available three to five years ahead. The real problem is to digest the information and sift the wheat from the chaff.[6]

Of all possible technology flows, the company is most interested in those which will impinge on the needs of its present and potential customers. Projecting technology to support present lines is not uncommon. As a matter of routine some marketing research groups look ahead to customers' needs three to five years in the future.[7]

---

[4] *Ibid.*, p. 92.
[5] *Ibid.*, p. 92.
[6] *Ibid.*, pp. 92–93.
[7] *Ibid.*, pp. 93–94.

The opinion has been expressed that forecasting (with particular reference to sales estimates or projections) is the weak spot in blueprinting the future of the enterprise. One writer feels that in a well-designed planning operation, the controller should really play the control role.[8]

THE CONTROLLER'S/PUBLIC ACCOUNTANT'S ROLE

James Dowd has offered an excellent series of questions (classics in the forecasting field) the controller might ask in his "control role"; the executive charged with the planning responsibility in the forecasting phase should be most interested in the answers to these questions.[9] It must be emphasized here that management has the fundamental responsibility for all the forecasting and planning that provide the foundation for the budget. The accountant should perform what amounts to an internal audit of the forecasts and the operating plans in order to determine fiscal feasibility and insure coordination of all plan elements.

---

1. Who prepares the forecasts?
2. How are the forecasts prepared?
3. How are they used?
4. Is the organizational location of the forecasting responsibility logical?
5. Does it appear to work well, personalities and functions considered?

Having located the man or department doing the forecasting:

6. What duties does the man (department) perform in addition to forecasting?
7. Are these duties logically related?
8. Do they take too much time away from the forecasting activity?
9. What is the forecaster's education and experience?
10. In what professional activities is he engaged?
11. How does he keep himself informed?
12. Can I learn something broad-gage about the business from this man?
13. Has the sales forecast been prepared with reference to explicit anticipations in the general economy, in the industry of which the company is a part and in the markets to which the company sells? And if so, how were these anticipations arrived at? (Controller should expect to find some specific information on the outlook for the general economy: gross national product, industrial production, personal income, retail sales, employment, capital expenditures, corporate profits, etc. Forecast should be broken down into market segments.)

Where field sales forecast is used:

14. Is the field sales force setting its own goals or is headquarters setting the goals for the field?
15. What are management's objectives in employing quotas, and on what basis are they set?

---

[8]James Dowd, "The Controller's Responsibility for Forecasting," *The Controller*, Vol. XXIX, No. 6 (June, 1961), pp. 267–273, 302–305.

[9]*Ibid.*, pp. 267–273.

Technical Considerations:

16. Has good judgment been used in specifying the amount of product and geographic and customer class and other breakdowns? (Avoid unnecessary details which are costly—don't make it a numbers game.)
17. How detailed should the forecast be? (There is a point of diminishing return.)
18. How many figures can management digest?
19. How significant are the seasonal factors apart from the number of working days in the month?
20. Can the forecasting schedule be improved?
21. How far ahead should we be forecasting?
22. What are our needs for longer-range operating and cost flow statements, capital budgets and balance sheets?

Having considered the who and how of forecast preparation:

23. Are all the individuals who are charged with decision-making, planning or supervisory cost-control responsibilities on the distribution list for sales forecasts and related budgetary documents?
24. Are the forecasts being used intelligently?
25. What happens when the forecast has to be changed?
26. How much improvisation goes on? (A scheduled periodic opportunity to submit changes in estimates—say semi-annually—is essential to an orderly budgeting operation. All forecasts need fire escapes.)
27. Are significant deviations between forecasts and actuals appraised and explained as a standard procedure?
28. Why the optimism originally? Why are sales off?

As previously indicated, the depth and quality of the studies and analyses to be made as a foundation for the budget are naturally subject to managerial discretion.

The Budgeting Program—The Third Phase

A good budgeting program must be designed to meet the specific needs and requirements of the company for which it is being prepared. One author has outlined a comprehensive budget program that can be used as a model in developing a program for a specific company.[10] It is detailed enough to be suitable for use in very large companies.

If the budgeting exercise is the first for the company, it would be wise to outline a program for the development process. A conceptual model is presented in Figure 4-1 to aid in visualizing the processional order of the budgeting exercise. The solid lines represent the flow of essential information to develop the master budget. The broken lines represent major coordinative information flows essential to the completion of the master budget. There are, of course, continuing information flows between all participants during the

[10]Glenn A. Welsch, *Budgeting: Profit Planning and Control,* Fourth Edition (Englewood Cliffs, New Jersey: Prentice-Hall, Inc., 1976).

Figure 4-1 **Budget Preparation Program Conceptual Model**

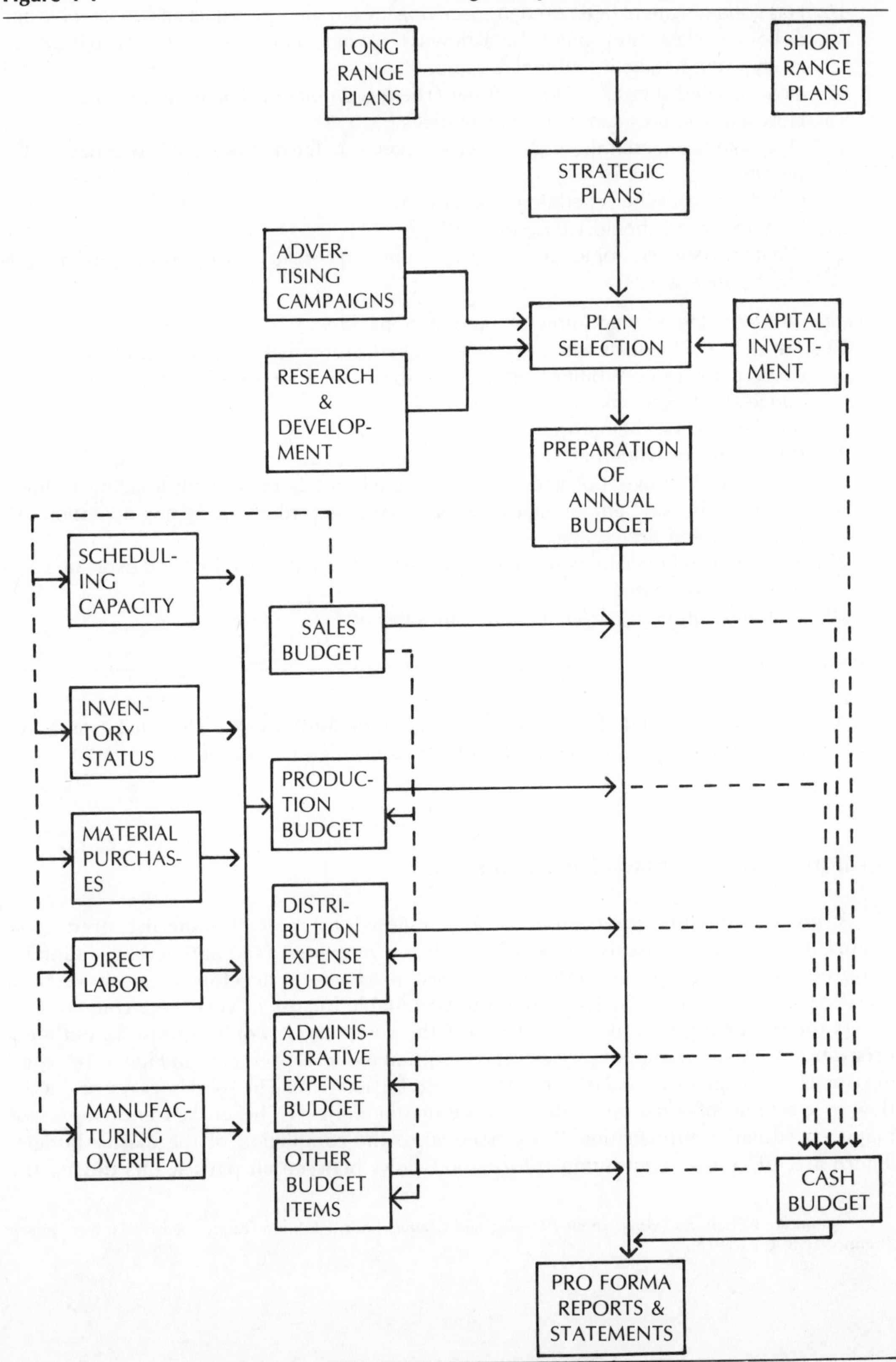

budget process that are not shown in Figure 4-1. It is not feasible to attempt to present graphically the maze of lines designating all possible communication lines, available and used, between participants in developing a budget.

The Sales Budget

In light of forecasts available to the company, a realistic sales budget should be developed in considerable detail. Basically, the projections will be founded on historical data from the company's sales records. Company plans with respect to new products, new territories, increased sales staff, new selling methods, changes in pricing policies, and knowledge of competitors' plans will be incorporated in the projections.

It may be appropriate to classify the projected sales as follows:

1. Sales by products (and/or product lines)
2. Sales by territories (company designated)
3. Sales by sales personnel (groups, divisions)
4. Sales by reporting periods (days, weeks, months, etc.)
5. Sales by customer class (type: business organization; individual by sex, age, race, married, wife, etc.)

Not all classifications may be pertinent in each case. Conceivably, other classifications or sub-classifications may be helpful; for example, sales by products within territories. The various classifications will tend to strengthen each other in terms of realism. When measured against historical data, unrealistic projections may be identified.

Sooner or later, and preferably sooner, the matter of the physical capacity of the company facilities must be taken into account. Should a realistic sales budget be developed only to discover that plant capacity is insufficient, alternative plans must be considered to resolve the problem. These plans could include expanding facilities, extra shifts, overtime, or even tempering the sales effort. This budgeting problem occurs only when the company is presently operating at or near capacity.

The Production Budget

As may be seen in Figure 4-1, the production budget is really a summary derived from several satellite budgets which in turn have taken their dimensions from the sales budget. Without consideration of inventory levels, the production budget parallels the sales budget. Decisions regarding changes in inventory levels will, of necessity, affect the production budget. The matters of inventory control and related problems are the subject of Chapter 7. It is assumed here that specific physical volumes have been provided for use in developing the production budget.

Closely related to the inventory change problem is the scheduling of production throughout the year. This must be measured against periodic sales volume, plant capacity, availability of labor and materials, and storage space for both materials and finished goods. The length of the production period may also be a complicating factor requiring consideration in scheduling. These factors may add up to a group of elements representing adverse interests. Complete reconciliation may not be possible. If the decision is made to maintain stable production, the inventories may fluctuate sharply and inversely with the periodic sales pattern. If the inventory must be maintained within narrow parameters, seasonal sales patterns may cause production to fluctuate sharply, a generally undesirable situation.

The materials purchases budget preparation may involve some scheduling problems of its own. Meeting requirements for projected inventory levels and scheduled production with limitations on storage space, avoidance of shortages, and consideration of price changes, represent scheduling (and budgeting) problems of no small dimensions. This budget must be developed so as to realistically provide for the product configuration that was developed in the sales budget.

The same general principles apply in the case of wholesale and retail companies in the matter of inventory changes and material purchases. In this case the "material" purchases represent the goods for resale and are accordingly related to sales from either a unit standpoint or a gross margin (planned) relationship. If a retailing company is involved, there is a good probability that the retail method of inventory and record-keeping is being used. The purchases budget will be determined as a derivation from the sales plans and target gross margins on a departmental basis. In order to allocate funds between the variety of goods in a given department, the buyer will have to keep, or cause to be kept, open-to-buy records to avoid unplanned and uncontrolled overspending.

In the case of wholesaling companies, the warehouse operation may require a budget somewhat comparable to the manufacturing overhead budget. The general breakdown of expenses and the requirements of reports and statements will determine the expense account structure. There is normally no allocation of expenses to operating departments, as in the case of manufacturing operations.

The direct labor budget can be drawn up when the nature and volume of the planned production are known. Care must be taken to budget manpower training if additional personnel will be needed. Hourly rates may have to be estimated if union negotiations are up-coming. Labor costs are usually a large item in production costs, and if the rate changes are larger than anticipated, the budget may have to be revised to be meaningful. The labor costs must include payroll taxes and fringe benefits. The exact place of these items in the budget will depend upon the cost accounting system in use. With the volume of production and the manpower requirements for the direct labor force known, all the manufacturing support elements can be determined and a budget for manufacturing overhead can be developed. The plant layout, organization, and type of cost accounting system will largely determine the method of assembly of costs for the manufacturing overhead budget. If the plant identifies producing departments and service departments as cost accumulation centers, the service department budgets may have to be developed first in order to allocate the costs to the producing departments. Again, this will depend upon the nature of the cost accounting system in use.

The Administrative Expense Budget

Many of the expense items in the administrative expense budget tend to be of a fixed nature. The sales budget benchmarks provided will determine a sort of relevant range for estimating administrative work loads. While it is true that the administrative areas have a minimum level of personnel, equipment usage, and supply consumption necessary for even low sales volume, and can absorb activity resulting from increased volume, there are variables to be considered.

The various departments in the administrative category will have different responses to a new level of activity and will have varying needs as a result. These budgets should be developed departmentally and coordinated in conference. If there are to be organizational changes, the introduction of new equipment and/or major information system changes, new manpower training programs, or expanded areas of administrative activity, the budgeting process will be somewhat more complex. Since these factors represent the breaking of new ground, historical operating patterns will not be available for reference.

The Distribution Expense Budget

The very nature of the expenses included in this phase of management's activities make the distribution expense budget more responsive to changes in sales volume. Development of this budget from the standpoint of overall fixed and variable expenses as well as by departments or divisions, with a final reconciliation, might be very helpful in avoiding unrealistic estimates. Historical operating patterns are helpful here, also, as with administrative estimations. Likewise, the types of operating changes indicated in connection with the administrative budget will increase budgeting complexities.

There are likely to be a greater number of expense items responding more or less proportionately to the sales volume in the distribution expense category. The degree of the relationship can alter, however, with significant sales volume changes. This factor must be taken into consideration when reviewing historical operating data and patterns. If the possibility exists that a variety of budgeted sales volumes are up for reconsideration, it may be necessary to prepare several distribution expense budgets (not to mention production expense budgets) to match the possible relevant ranges of the sales volumes. Short-term cost-volume relationships within rather narrow relevant ranges of volume can be indicated if alternate budgets or variable budgets are prepared. The variable budget has as its objective the determination of how the various expenses should change with volume changes.[11]

Other Income and Expense Items

Consideration must be given financial income and expense items, as well as a plethora of other non-operating transaction possibilities, in developing a master budget. Some items may arise in the course of budgeting such as the interest expense on short term loans, the need for which is determined in finalizing the cash budget. Plans to dispose of some plant and equipment and/or investments will also affect the budget.

There are budgets of the appropriation type that are usually developed in the planning process. These budgets are more apt to affect the sales forecast and resulting budget than to be a function thereof. Budgets of this type are represented by the advertising, research and capital additions budgets. Mention of these at this point in the chapter is not to be construed as indicating that their consideration can be deferred until late in the budgeting process. Reference to the chart (Figure 4-1) of the conceptual budget model will place them in proper perspective. The point is, they must be finalized along with all other related budgets.

The Cash Budget

This particular phase of the budget is treated more extensively in a later chapter. At this point, the major consideration is the final assembly of data regarding all sources of receipts

[11]For a more extensive treatment of variable budgets and the controlling of costs, see: Glenn A. Welsch, *Budgeting: Profit Planning And Control,* Fourth Edition (Englewood Cliffs, New Jersey: Prentice-Hall, Inc., 1976).

and all planned disbursements of cash. Obviously, the master budget cannot be finalized until a satisfactory solution is reached with respect to the cash position. In reaching such a solution, the matter of investment of surplus funds and the need for short-and/or long-term loans must be considered, and appropriate steps must be taken to incorporate them in the master budget. The chronological refinement at this stage usually extends no further than the smallest accounting period (usually one month) adopted in segmenting the budget for managerial use.

Conceivably, it may be discovered at this stage that revisions in one or more of the various budget components are necessary to finalize a realistic cash budget. This could involve re-scheduling of some planned expenditures or disposition of assets as well as a re-studying of both short-term and long-term financing plans.

The Master Budget

Upon the completion of all segments of the budget, the master budget literally appears in final form as pro-forma reports and statements, identical to those prepared for management covering actual operations. Distribution of the appropriate parts of the budget at the proper time to the proper individuals completes the *preparatory* process, however, the budgeting exercise is not complete until full and effective use is made of it throughout the respective time period covered.

Actual operating results will agree with the budget only coincidentally. The budget should not be changed, even for sharp variations, unless it is determined that one or more major premises were faulty, for whatever reason, in developing the benchmarks for the budget. This will have to be a matter of judgment and any unique facts in each case will affect such judgment.

Illustrative Budget Working Papers

The possible variations in budgetary working papers are, of course, infinite. Only the most general classifications can be developed for them. One classification might follow the conceptual model of the budget preparation program shown earlier (Figure 4-1); another simpler classification might be as follows:

1. Preliminary working papers to assemble basic data.
2. Assembly of summary working papers (Figures 4-2 to 4-17, inclusive) for major operating divisions.
3. Final assembly working papers (Figures 4-18 and 4-19). (Budget journal entries and work sheet.)
4. Financial and operating reports and statements.

This illustrative set of papers includes only summary working papers and final assembly working papers. Since no uniform design is possible or necessary for preliminary working papers, and since financial statements and operating reports would be patterned after the historical reports and statements of the respective company, none are included here.

The working papers illustrated here are simplified and are presented with a small manufacturing company in mind. Many supporting and supplementary papers of greater sophistication would obviously be required for larger companies. Retailers, wholesalers, and service companies can dispense with some of the papers since they would not be applicable. Some others may need to be adapted to particular operating circumstances. The general detail and depth of the working papers will be a function of the managerial planning and of the amount of information necessary to both develop a good budget and provide the additional operating and financial information needed by management.

SALES BUDGET FORMS

Figures 4-2 and 4-3 are representative of working papers for finalizing the sales budget development. The sales working papers set forth sales by months, products, and districts

Figure 4-2

SALES DISTRICT I—ALL PRODUCTS

Budget—19X2

Product	Jan.	Feb.	Mar.	Apr.	May	June	July	Aug.	Sept.	Oct.	Nov.	Dec.		Total
A														
B														
C														
ETC.														

(Prepared in dollars and units)

Figure 4-3

ALL DISTRICT SUMMARY—ALL PRODUCTS

Budget—19X2

Product	Jan.	Feb.	Mar.	Apr.	May	June	July	Aug.	Sept.	Oct.	Nov.	Dec.		Total
A														
B														
C														

(Prepared in dollars and units)

with a summary schedule combining all districts. Other breakdowns of sales may be more important in a different set of circumstances. The types of sales reports to be provided for management may also influence the sales assembly working papers. In the case of some companies, it may not be feasible to prepare working papers showing physical units. Product lines may constitute a sufficient breakdown of sales from the product standpoint.

PRODUCTION BUDGET FORMS

The production budget is a summary budget built up from inventory change plans, the material purchases budget, direct labor budget, and manufacturing overhead budget. No working paper is presented here for developing planned changes in inventories. Figure 4-4 is prepared from the planned inventory changes and the sales budget (physical units). Figure 4-5 picks up the units to be produced from Figure 4-4 for translation into raw material requirements. With planned inventory changes in mind and raw material requirements determined, Figure 4-6, which provides physical units and dollar amounts for material purchases to be made, can be prepared.

These figures represent a considerable amount of detail with respect to material purchases. It is quite possible that the nature of the manufacturing operation will be such that a more simplified method may be used to assemble material purchases information. Figure 4-4 develops the cost of production by use of a unit cost. No working paper is presented for the unit cost (by product) development. The methods of computation are many in number and short cuts might be taken in developing cost of production by using standard costs and/or approximating material and labor costs for the working papers.

Figures 4-7, 4-8, 4-9 and 4-10 provide for assembly of direct labor costs under standard costing and job order and process cost situations. Short cuts may be found here, also. If the operating processes and the product cost configuration cannot be refined, or have not been refined to the extent indicated by these figures, then the best possible estimates will have to be made. No doubt fewer worksheets will be required to arrive at the budgeted labor costs.

Figure 4-4

UNITS OF PRODUCTION—ALL PRODUCTS

Month of: Budget—19X2

Product	Sales	+	End Inv.	=	Total Need	–	Beg. Inv.	=	Units to be prod.	×	Unit Cost	=	Cost of Prod.
A		Time Periods: Monthly, Quarterly, Annually as required											
B				(Sub-total by product lines)									
C													

Figure 4-5

MATERIAL REQUIREMENTS—UNITS

All Products ☐ (Check Type)

Month of: Product Lines ☐ Budget—19X2

Product	Units to be Prod.	MATERIALS #1	#2	#3	#4	#5	#6	#7	#8	#9	#10	#11	#12	#Etc.
A														
B		Time periods: Monthly, Quarterly, Annually as required												
C														
ETC. (or product line designation)														

Figure 4-6

MATERIAL PURCHASES

Month Of: Budget—19X2

Materials	For Production Units	Amt.	+	Ending Inventory Units	Amt.	=	Total Requirement Units	Amt.	–	Beginning Inventory Units	Amt.	=	To Be Purchased Units	Amt.
		Time periods: Monthly, Quarterly, Annually as required												
#1														
#2														
#3														

Figure 4-7

DIRECT LABOR HOURS		
Month Of:	(STANDARD COST SYSTEM)	Budget—19X2

		Units		(STANDARD TIME—BY OPERATION)											
	Products	to be	#1	#2	#3	#4	#5	#6	#7	#8	#9	#10	#Etc.		
		prod.	per U	per U	per U	per U	per U	per U	per U	per U	per U	per U	per U		
	A		Time periods: Monthly, Quarterly, Annually as required												
	B (Standard time per product obtained by multiplying standard per unit by units to be produced)														
	C														

Figure 4-8

DIRECT LABOR COST		
Month Of:	(STANDARD COST SYSTEM)	Budget—19X2

					Standard Cost—Operations										
	Product	#1	#2	#3	#4	#5	#6	#7	#8	#9	#10	#Etc.			Total
		Rate	Rate	Rate	Rate	Rate	Rate	Rate	Rate	Rate	Rate	Rate			Cost
	A		Time periods: Monthly, Quarterly, Annually as required												
	B		(Standard costs per operation obtained by multiplying standard												
	C			hourly rate by direct labor hours scheduled)											
	ETC.														

Figure 4-9

DIRECT LABOR HOURS

(JOB ORDER, PROCESS COST SYSTEM)

Month Of: Budget—19X2

Products	Units to be Prod.	Producing Departments #1 (*)	#2 (*)	#3 (*)	#4 (*)	#5 (*)	#6 (*)	#7 (*)	#8 (*)	#9 (*)	#10 (*)	#Etc. (*)		Total Hours
A														
B	*(Estimated number of men in each department classified as direct labor)													
C		Time periods: Monthly, Quarterly, Annually as required												
ETC.		(Obtained by multiplying estimated per unit (or multiples thereof) hours												
		required in each department by number of men in each department.)												

Figure 4-10

DIRECT LABOR COST

(JOB ORDER, PROCESS COST SYSTEM)

Month Of: Budget—19X2

Products	#1 Rate	#2 Rate	#3 Rate	#4 Rate	#5 Rate	#6 Rate	#7 Rate	#8 Rate	#9 Rate	#10 Rate	#Etc. Rate			Total Cost
A		Time Periods: Monthly, Quarterly, Annually as required												
B	(Obtained by multiplying average hourly rate in the department by the													
C			estimated direct labor hours scheduled.)											
ETC.														

In this case, manufacturing expense has been assumed to be developed by service and producing departments on a fixed and variable basis. For control purposes it may be helpful to recast the expense budget by functional types across all departments (see Figure 4-11). The breakdown into fixed and variable expenses is essential if expense application rates are to be developed for several different volumes of production. Better control can be maintained over manufacturing expenses if this type of breakdown is used. Figure 4-12 is a working paper for allocating service department expenses to the producing departments for the determination of overhead application rates. Refinements of the allocation process should be used with discretion in consideration of cost and the relative value of the derived cost figures.

Figure 4-13 may or may not be useful, depending upon the manner of assembly of the budget elements and the types of cost reports to be prepared. The worksheet for assembling the budget will pick up the budgeted manufacturing overhead, so there will obviously be no over-applied or under-applied overhead to consider. At this stage budgeted overhead and applied overhead are identical.

Figure 4-11

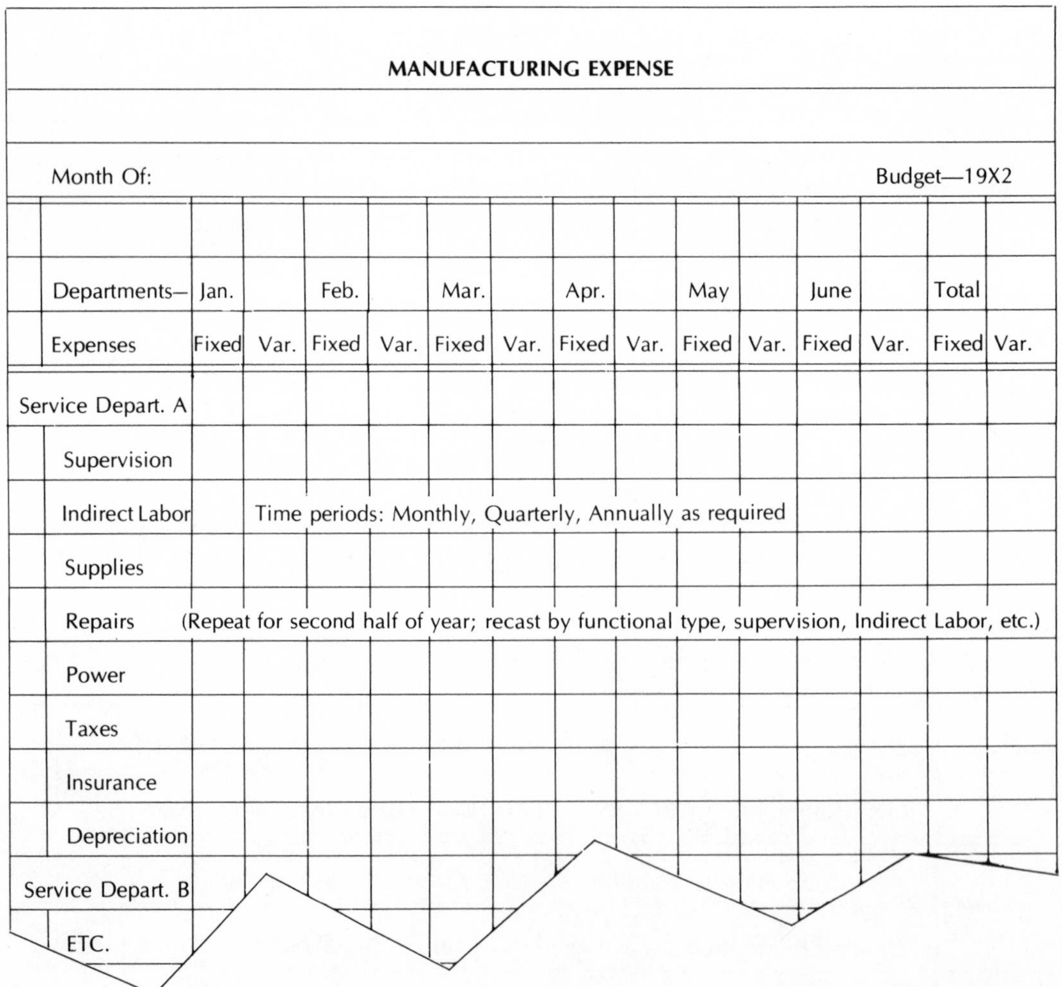

MANUFACTURING EXPENSE

Month Of: Budget—19X2

Departments—	Jan.		Feb.		Mar.		Apr.		May		June		Total	
Expenses	Fixed	Var.	Fixed	Var.	Fixed	Var.	Fixed	Var.	Fixed	Var.	Fixed	Var.	Fixed	Var.
Service Depart. A														
Supervision														
Indirect Labor		Time periods: Monthly, Quarterly, Annually as required												
Supplies														
Repairs	(Repeat for second half of year; recast by functional type, supervision, Indirect Labor, etc.)													
Power														
Taxes														
Insurance														
Depreciation														
Service Depart. B														
ETC.														

Figure 4-12

MANUFACTURING EXPENSE DISTRIBUTION WORKSHEET															
Annual														Budget—19X2	
			Service Departments						Producing Departments						
	Totals		A		B		C		1		2		3		
	Fixed	Var.	Fixed	Var.	Fixed	Var.	Fixed	Var.	Fixed	Var.	Fixed	Var.	Fixed	Var.	
Direct Expense	xxx	xxx	xx	xx	xx	xx	xx	xx	xx	xx	xx	xx	xx	xx	
Distribute															
Ser. Dept. A			→	→	x	x	x	x	x	x	x	x	x	x	
Ser. Dept. B					→	→	x	x	x	x	x	x	x	x	
Ser. Dept. C							→	→	x	x	x	x	x	x	
Totals	xxx	xxx							xx	xx	xx	xx	xx	xx	

(Calculate direct labor hour, direct labor cost or machine hour rates for application of fixed and variable overhead)

Figure 4-13

APPLIED MANUFACTURING EXPENSE														
	Fixed ☐ (Check Type)													
Annual	Variable ☐											Budget—19X2		
Products	Direct Labor Hours	Jan.	Feb.	March	April	May	June	July	Aug.	Sept.	Oct.	Nov.	Dec.	Total
A	(Can use direct labor cost or machine hours as a basis for application)													
B														
C														

Distribution and Administrative Expense Budget Forms

The forms illustrated in Figures 4-14 and 4-15 for developing distribution and administrative expenses for the budget are basically interchangeable. Depending upon the operating configuration and the control needs of management, the forms can be used in each area and recast as indicated where appropriate and useful. While these forms provide for a development of expenses in the fixed and variable categories, it may not be worthwhile to do so in many situations. If such is the case, the working papers are accordingly simplified. Working papers of this type are generally suitable for use in developing appropriation-type budgets such as advertising, research and development, capital additions, and miscellaneous accounts in the other income and expense categories.

Cash Budget Forms

Forms used in cash flow planning, budgeting, and control can be as extensive and sophisticated as the processes are thorough. The subject is treated in greater depth in Chapter 6. At this point, the treatment involves only the budgeting aspect with time periods no shorter than a month. Figure 4-16 is designed to schedule cash collections of receivables

Figure 4-14

DISTRIBUTION EXPENSE

Budget—19X2

Districts–	January		February		March		April		May		June		Totals	
Functions	Fixed	Var.	Fixed	Var.	Fixed	Var.	Fixed	Var.	Fixed	Var.	Fixed	Var.	Fixed	Var.
District #1														
Sales Salaries														
Supervision														
Travel	(Repeat for second half of year; can be set up on a department basis if appropriate,													
Etc.	recast by functional type sales salaries, supervision, etc.)													
Total														
District#2														
ETC.														

Figure 4-15

ADMINISTRATIVE EXPENSE														
													Budget—19X2	
Function	January		February		March		April		May		June		Totals	
	Fixed	Var.	Fixed	Var.	Fixed	Var.	Fixed	Var.	Fixed	Var.	Fixed	Var.	Fixed	Var.
Officers Salaries														
Supervisory Salaries														
Other Salaries														
Supplies														
Telephone														
Professional Fees														
Travel														
Entertainment														
Taxes														
Insurance														
Depreciation														
ETC.														

(This form applicable for advertising, research and development, and other special items to be included in the budget.)
(Repeat for second half of year; can also be set up on a departmental basis, then by function if desired.)

with consideration of uncollectible accounts. It is assumed that the estimated uncollectibles have been developed in connection with the sales budget. No special form is illustrated since infinite variety is possible and will most likely involve using a simple percentage calculation.

The final figures from Figure 4-16 are carried forward to Figure 4-17, which is a summary form to finalize the cash budget. It may be as condensed or as detailed as is required in developing the master budget. The operating environment and the nature of the company's business will have a bearing on the cash budget development detail.

If loans are to be sought for financing company operations in part, supporting working papers may be required for scheduling repayment and interest on the loans. A distribution type working paper is normally satisfactory for this type of budget development.

Figure 4-16

SCHEDULE OF COLLECTIONS ON ACCOUNT RECEIVABLE

Budget - 19 x

Collection Period	Amt.	Est. Uncol.	Net To Be Col.	Jan.	Feb.	Mar.	Apr.	May	June	Etc.				Rec. Bal. EO Y
Prior Year Accounts														
All prior to Sept.														
September														
October														
November														
December														
Sales (Estimated)														
January														
February														
Etc.														
Totals														
Less Ending Receivables														
Est. Collections														
Less Discounts														
Net Estimated														
Collections on Receivables														

Figure 4-17

SCHEDULE OF CASH RECEIPTS AND DISBURSEMENTS

Budget—19X2

Items	Jan.	Feb.	Mar.	Apr.	May	June	July	Aug.	Sept.	Oct.	Nov.	Dec.		Total
Receipts														
Coll. on Rec.														
Dividends														
Interest														
Misc. Income														
Loans														
Total Receipts														
Disbursements														
Purchases														
Direct Labor														
Mfg. Expense														
Dist. Expense														
Admin. Expense														
Advertising														
Research & Devel.														
Taxes														
Insurance														
Dividends														
Mtge. Pmts.														
Notes Payable														
Income Taxes														

Figure 4-17 continued

	Items	Jan.	Feb.	Mar.	Apr.	May	June	July	Aug.	Sept.	Oct.	Nov.	Dec.		Total
	Other														
	Total Disb.														
Excess (Deficit) of															
	Receipts over Disb.														
	Cash Bal.— Beginning														
	Cash Bal.— Ending														

BUDGET ASSEMBLY FORMS

The budget may be assembled by the traditional worksheet technique. Figure 4-18 illustrates the type of budget worksheet used for the assembly in company with the journal entries developed to complete the process. The trial balance may be the actual fiscal year end trial balance if the budgeting exercise is running behind schedule. It should be far enough in advance of the fiscal year concerned so that the opening trial balance will be an estimated one. When the journal entries have been prepared and entered and the accounts extended, any oversights, other than minor ones, in developing the budget should be detected. The formal financial statements can then be prepared. If journal entries and a worksheet are not to be used in assembling budget detail, the working papers used will then be in the nature of working financial statements of the conventional type.

When fully completed, the master budget should be used comparatively with all reports and financial statements prepared covering actual operating results for each budget period. Variances from management's operating plans are readily determinable, and appropriate action can be taken. While comparisons with prior period operating results may be interesting and helpful, the budget represents the current environment and the plans that have been made to deal with that environment.

Figure 4-18

BUDGET WORKSHEET

Accounts	Trial Bal.	Budget Entries	Mfg. Summary	Income Summary	Balance Sheets
	12-31-19X1	19X2	19X2	19X2	12-31-19X2
Cash					
Accts. Rec.					
ETC.					

JOURNAL ENTRIES TO DEVELOP BUDGET FOR 19X2

	Debit	Credit
(1)		
Accounts Receivable		
Sales		
From Figure 4-3		
(2)		
Cash		
Sales Discounts		
Accounts Receivable		
From Figure 4-16		
(3)		
Allowance for Uncollectible Accounts		
Accounts Receivable		
From Figure 4-16		
(4)		
Raw Material Purchases (Inventory)		
Cash		
From Figure 4-6		
(5)		
Direct Labor		
Accrued Payroll		
Cash		
From Figures 4-8 or 4-10, 4-11, 4-14, 4-15		
(6)		
Manufacturing Expense Control		
Cash		
Accrued Payroll		
Manufacturing Supplies on Hand		
Prepaid Insurance		
Accrued Taxes		
Allowance for Depreciation		
From Figure 4-11 and Supporting Exhibits		
(7)		
Raw Material Inventory		
Raw Material		
From Figure 4-6, purchases inventory difference, (may be in reverse) to adjust for inventory change.		

	Debit	Credit
(8)		
Finished Goods Inventory		
Work in process inventory		
From Supplementary exhibit, planned inventory difference, (may be in reverse) to adjust for inventory change.		
(9)		
Distribution Expense Control		
Cash		
Accrued Payroll		
Supplies on Hand		
Prepaid Insurance		
Accrued Taxes		
Allowance for Depreciation		
From Figure 4-14 and Supporting Exhibits.		
(10)		
Administrative Expense Control		
Cash		
Accrued Payroll		
Supplies on Hand		
Prepaid Insurance		
Accrued Taxes		
Allowance for Depreciation		
From Figure 4-15 and Supporting Exhibits.		
(11)		
Advertising		
Research and Development		
Plant and Equipment		
Dividends		
Supplies on Hand		
Manufacturing Supplies		
Prepaid Insurance		
Accrued Taxes		
Cash		
Accounts Payable (change only)		
Mortgage Payable		
Notes Payable		
From Figure 4-17 and supplementary exhibits developing budget for each account.		

	Debit	Credit
(12)		
Mortgages Payable		
Notes Payable		
Interest Expense		
Income Taxes		
Cash		
Accrued Interest		
Accrued Taxes		
From Figure 4-17 and supplementary exhibits developing budget for each account.		
(13)		
Other Accounts		
Cash		
From Figure 4-17 and supplementary exhibits developing budget for each account.		
(14)		
Cash		
Dividends		
Interest		
Miscellaneous		
Notes Payable		
From Figure 4-17 and supplementary exhibits developing budget for each account.		

CHAPTER 5

PLANNING AND CONTROLLING CAPITAL ADDITIONS

INTRODUCTION

In the preceding chapter, the matter of capital additions was considered only from the cash outlay standpoint. It was assumed that the proper capital investment planning had been carried out and that this included all necessary calculations to determine the feasibility of various capital additions alternatives. This chapter presents the latest techniques, currently in use, of planning capital additions and the related methods for determining the most advantageous investment in capital assets.

The public accountant must be alert to contemplated capital additions by clients. Unless there is a fairly continuous contact throughout the year, the client may make some large commitment and then consult his accountant-advisor when a financial problem arises. This limits the choices the accountant has available in trying to resolve the matter for the client in the financial environment.

PLANNING RELATIONSHIPS

Capital additions planning must be integrated with long-range master planning. The use of these larger capital items extends well into the time frame of long-range plans. The ever-present circular characteristic of planning is particularly noticeable here. Financing large capital items affects the cash flow as does the use of these same capital items in the short-range and long-range. Operational and financial budgeting cannot be complete unless the capital additions plans are complete.

PLANNING FOR FACILITIES

Consideration must be given to company objectives in the framework of the company's operating environment, both present and projected. Will raw materials be available in the required quality and quantity? Will human resources be available in the necessary quantity and types of skills? Another consideration involves sufficient and timely community services and facilities. Primary costs are, of course, of major importance. Still another matter to be thought of is transportation facilities, i.e., accessibility to materials and markets. Operating and maintenance costs must be researched and taken into account. To the extent possible, the plans must take into account foreseeable changes in technology. Other factors influencing capital additions plans include present plant expansion, new facilities, diversification, new production methods, own/lease policies, and development of raw material sources.

The management planners must reconcile all of these elements by sifting out those pieces that will fit in with the overall company objectives—long-range and short-range. This requires a variety of cost and revenue projections based on the various alternatives available. The accountant will usually provide these projections for management.

Facilities planning will involve either the replacement of obsolete and/or worn out facilities or the development of new expanded facilities. The facilities may be further classified as productive or supportive (all support elements to the actual production process).

The Capital Expenditure Management Process

The following steps provide an outline of the capital expenditure management process:

1. Develop long-range plans covering company growth and direction which will require consideration of capital expenditures.
2. Develop short-range plans covering the financing and integration of the capital improvements so as to match the company's current operating situation.
3. Evaluate carefully the various addition proposals that are available to the company. (These are illustrated in a later part of this chapter.)
4. Assign responsibility for managing the development of capital additions projects.
5. Install project cost controls and report on the progress of the projects.
6. Carry out a post-completion audit of the additions as to actual cost and operating performance.
7. Analyze the rate of return on the capital additions for comparison with the return initially estimated.

Financing problems in terms of both the short-range and long-range cash flow projections may affect the final choice among the capital additions projects considered feasible. This may require two projections of cash flows under the different circumstances. When the final choice is made, a detailed budget must be prepared for control purposes to be used by the project manager or the cost controller. The extent of detail of the project budget and the size of the project management staff will depend upon the size and complexity of the project(s).

Controlling Capital Additions

The more formal and complex the company organization, the more formal the final approval of the capital additions project(s) should be. This could mean obtaining stockholder approval before the company president authorizes the project manager to start the project(s). Once approval has been obtained, the project manager or controller can be assigned, and the capital budget set up in the accounts that will be used to gather the expenditures in the budget framework. This can be done on a memorandum basis or as a budgeted appropriation as in fund accounting. If a computer is available, this control procedure is more easily accomplished in that the budget can be used as a control device to measure actual expenditures and report balances still available as well as the rate of spending. Special account codes can be assigned and distributed to concerned offices to aid in identification of all project cost elements as incurred throughout the company.

If the project(s) is complex and/or numerous it may be that special requisitions and purchase orders are called for as well as readily identifiable time-keeping records, segregated bank accounts and special disbursement procedures. The extent of accounting system changes to accommodate capital projects should be limited to actual need. Identification of project expenditures, collections in the proper control and subsidiary accounts under fixed assets, detailed in reporting of progress expenditures, and projected over/under runs constitute the heart of capital project control. All this may be accomplished in most cases without mechanical changes in the accounting system.

The project manager must be alert for the possibility of cost overruns. Unless a reasonably liberal budget (normally rare) has been authorized, there is a good possibility that the project will cost more than anticipated. The careful and timely recording of expenditures will aid in the control process but of itself will not be effective in identifying imminent cost overruns. Technical supervision and inspection are necessary in most cases. Unless the project manager is technically qualified personally, such technical assistance should be provided so that regular and timely technical review and accounting review together can point up impending cost overruns.

Detailed reporting of actual and budgeted expenditures, percentage of completion, project modifications implemented and/or proposed and projected cost over/under runs should be made at appropriate intervals to all concerned managerial levels. Authorizations from the proper authorizing management level should be obtained for cost overruns before the expenditures are made.

THE POST-COMPLETION AUDIT

Management needs to know the results of its investment decisions. The completion of the project is not the end of the story. One reason for performing a post-completion audit is to assign responsibility for mistakes in project development and implementation as well as to give credit for good performance. Some additional reasons for the post-completion audit are listed below: The list is not all-inclusive, of course.

1. To review the operation of the project and make whatever adjustments are necessary and feasible so initial goals may be achieved or to recommend abandonment if unprofitability is indicated.
2. To derive experience in project implementation for future use.
3. To take a measure of the aptitudes and abilities of those involved in the project development.
4. To refine and improve post audit procedures.
5. To establish and maintain an effective control system over the whole capital additions procedure in terms of planning, evaluation and implementation.

One of the major aspects of the audit will be a comparison of actual with estimated earnings of the capital project. Consideration must be given to the "start up" or "getting on line" problems in the first operating time frame. Finding a representative operating period in these first years may be difficult. The financial accounting pattern followed by the company probably will not match the pattern of the estimates developed in the evaluation process. Cost and revenues will have to be carefully separated and assigned to the project by a "worksheet" analysis of the accounts. The accounting system will more than likely not provide highly selective account groupings to match capital project operations. It may not be possible to make such groupings. In some cases where a computer is in use, a complex coding system may make it possible to recast costs and revenues so as to identify them to specific additions or projects. Certain elements of the individual account codes will be keyed to the specific projects.

A comparative analysis of actual versus estimated earnings by projects should be carried out in later periods after the project is well-established and integrated into the operating system. This will insure a fair evaluation and avoid the possibility of a project not carrying its weight while being "covered up" in accounts of a complex operation. If the accounting system can be designed to identify specific capital additions, then there is less need for the more or less continuous post audit.

Financing Capital Additions

When considering the possible sources of funds for financing capital additions, it's essential to have a clear picture of company funds expected to become available for such additions. Here the circular characteristic of budgeting makes itself felt again. Financial and operating budgets will have to be prepared in more or less detail for future periods in relation to the type of financing to be used. The type of financing will, in turn, have some bearing on the master budget. If various financing alternatives are available, alternate budgets may have to be prepared in order to develop the best plan.

Cash flow statements setting forth projections as far ahead as feasible and necessary are essential to the process of capital budgeting. For the short-range, the cash budget prepared as a part of the master budget provides cash flow information needed. For the long-range, cash flow projections will be based on less detailed operating budgets and will, accordingly, be less precise in measurement.

Over and above internally generated funds, there are three sources of funds. These are institutional lenders (banks, commercial finance companies, etc.), manufacturer's financing, and leasing. In the classification used here, internally generated funds include the sale of stock and bonds and mortgaging of existing assets. The most advantageous method of financing capital additions may not always be available to the company for one reason or another. The manufacturer may not sell on the installment basis; no lessor may be found; or bank credit may already be stretched to the limit. Managerial judgment will determine whether the less attractive methods of financing additions should be considered.

The lending agent will be very interested in reviewing financial plans for handling additions. A realistic master budget and cash flow projection can help smooth the way in obtaining requisite funds. The use of these budgetary working papers is not ended when a choice among alternatives has been made by the company. Put in appropriate form they may be included in the loan application.

Evaluating Investment Alternatives

If there should be no investment alternatives available to management, then there is no evaluation problem in making capital additions. The only problem to be studied is that of going out of business if the essential addition cannot be financed by the one available method. This is rarely the case, so some type of evaluative process will be called for in almost every situation.

There are many factors affecting the choice of capital additions that are not based on mathematical calculations. In the first place, the choice between alternatives may be very narrow from a mathematical standpoint. Qualitative factors play a larger role in this case. The board of directors, certain major creditors and employees represent groups that may need or require a justification for the planned choice. Each group could have some input into the evaluation. Business relations with equipment suppliers may affect the decision. There is always a risk factor in capital additions decisions which is usually impossible to quantify. Quite possibly, long-range considerations, which cannot be measured at the time of decision-making, will play a major role in making the choice, especially if the choice is narrow.

In the examples presented here, no attempt is made to consider any judgment factors. It is assumed that they have been, or will be, resolved one way or another, and it is now a matter of financial computation only. Obviously, the wide range of possibilities makes it impossible to attempt any classification or clear-cut series of examples. However, the examples do illustrate the latest practices and analytical techniques used to evaluate proposed capital additions.

Basic Evaluation Approaches

The three most commonly used approaches to evaluation of alternative capital additions plans are:

1. Pay-back.
2. Return on investment (arithmetic basis).
3. Return on investment (discounted basis).

Pay-Back Approach

The pay-back approach does not provide any real measure of the worth of an investment; it merely gives a measure of how long it will take to recover the investment in the form of additional earnings or reduced operating expenses. Pay-back is also weak from the standpoint of failing to set forth the total economic benefits over the life of a productive asset, i.e., savings in costs or increases in income. However, information provided by the pay-back method may be of some importance in certain situations and, if so, should not be ignored in the evaluation process.

A firm considering the use of an asset for a very short term, say one year, would not be concerned with the life-long capabilities of the asset in question. Instead, the investment that would most likely be selected would be the one in which the greatest benefit could be derived in the one year period and at the lowest cost. This is especially true where rapid technological change plays a major part. It is really a qualitative type of evaluation even though numbers are involved in the sense that it does not measure rate of return on investment.

The following example will illustrate the pay-back method of computation.

Net delivered cost of tugboat				$97,500
Estimated useful life (no salvage)				25 years
Estimated earnings before taxes and depreciation				$12,000
Income tax rate				48%
Annual depreciation (S.Y.D.)	$7,500	$7,200	$6,900	etc.
Annual depreciation (straight-line)				$3,900

Applying the formula for the pay-back computation, and using straight-line depreciation, the following results are obtained:

Formula:

$$\frac{\text{Net Cost of Addition}}{\text{Net Annual earnings before depreciation, after taxes (or net expense reduction)}} = \text{Years to pay back}$$

Computation:

$$\frac{\$97{,}500}{\$12{,}000 - \$3{,}888^*} = \frac{\$97{,}500}{\$\ 8{,}112} = 12.02 \text{ years to pay back}$$

*($12,000 – $3,900) × 48% = $3,888 annual income tax.

Using the sum-of-years-digits depreciation method, the following results are obtained:

1	2	3	4	5	6	7	8
Year	**Annual Earnings**	**Annual S.Y.D. Deprecia-tion**	**Net Earn-ings (before taxes)**	**Annual Income Tax @ 48%**	**Net Earn-ings (after taxes)**	**Add back Annual Deprecia-tion**	**Cumulative Earnings after taxes before Depreciation**
			2 – 3	**4 × 48%**	**4 – 5**	**3**	**6 + 7 + 8**
1	$12,000	$7,500	$4,500	$2,160	$2,340	$7,500	$9,840
2	12,000	7,200	4,800	2,304	2,496	7,200	19,536
3	12,000	6,900	5,100	2,448	2,652	6,900	29,088
4	12,000	6,600	5,400	2,592	2,808	6,600	38,496
5	12,000	6,300	5,700	2,736	2,964	6,300	47,760
6	12,000	6,000	6,000	2,880	3,120	6,000	56,880
7	12,000	5,700	6,300	3,024	3,276	5,700	65,856
8	12,000	5,400	6,600	3,168	3,432	5,400	74,688
9	12,000	5,100	6,900	3,312	3,588	5,100	83,376
10	12,000	4,800	7,200	3,456	3,744	4,800	91,920
11	12,000	4,500	7,500	3,600	3,900	4,500	100,320*

*Interpolation here indicates pay-back period amounts to 10.66 years.

It will be noticed there is not a substantial difference in the pay-back periods between the use of straight-line depreciation and an accelerated method. Unless a fairly exact computation can be made which in turn would be very helpful in the decision-making, it is questionable as to whether the computations in the above table are worthwhile. The difference between the methods narrows as shorter asset lives are encountered.

Return on Investment (Arithmetic Basis) Approach

This evaluation method provides management with an approximate average rate of return on the investment in the capital addition proposed. Since this method does not consider the time value of money, the word "approximate" is appropriate. If large amounts are involved over a considerable period of time, the rate of return developed could be actually misleading when compared to that rate developed using the discounted basis. The following example, using the data in the pay-back example, will illustrate the method of computation.

Using the formula for this method set forth below, the following results are obtained:

Formula:

$$\frac{\text{Net annual earnings before depreciation, after taxes (or net expense reduction)}}{\text{Average Life Investment*}} = \text{Approximate average rate of return}$$

*Cost of addition divided by two.

Computation:

$$\frac{\$12{,}000 - \$3{,}888^*}{\$97{,}500 \div 2} = 16.64\% \text{ average rate of return}$$

*($12,000 − $3,900) × 48% = $3,888 annual income tax

If an accelerated depreciation method is used for determining the annual income tax, obviously the rate of return in the first years would be greater than average and, in the later years less than average. No particular purpose seems to be served in calculating a rate of return in this situation. The general crudeness of the method itself makes detailed computations redundant.

There are variations of the arithmetic approach to return on investment method, but none seem to be of any particular importance. No one seems to offer any special advantages over another.

Return on Investment (Discounted Basis) Approach

Provision for discounting the cash flow in the formula gives consideration to the time value of money. Where relatively large amounts are involved and the time period is of substantial length, the discounted rate of return basis is the superior approach. Management is concerned with the rate of return on the investment to be made in a given situation. The question asked is: Will the rate of return on the proposed capital addition equal or exceed the rate of return that could be obtained in other feasible investments? Also, will the rate of return equal or exceed the company's minimum acceptable rate? To illustrate the time value of the money factor, a simple example will be presented and a table converting the entire life of the capital addition will be developed to show the action of time on the money involved.

Assume an investment of $19,963.55 is expected to produce earnings of $5,000.00 per year for five years. A return of 8% is desired on the investment. If $5,000.00 can be withdrawn (realized) each year from the investment and no funds are left invested at the end of five years, exactly 8% will have been earned on the investment.

The following table shows the time value action of the funds:

1	2	3	4	5
Year	**Beginning of Year Investment**	**Yearly Interest Earned**	**Earnings to be Withdrawn**	**End of Year Investment**
1	$19,963.55	$1,597.08	$5,000.00	$16,560.63
2	16,560.63	1,324.85	5,000.00	12,885.48
3	12,885.48	1,030.84	5,000.00	8,916.32
4	8,916.32	713.31	5,000.00	4,629.63
5	4,629.63	370.37	5,000.00	-0-

Col. 3 = Col. 2 × 8%
Col. 5 = Col. 2 + Col. 3 − Col. 4

In this illustration, the investment returned exactly 8% because of predetermined amounts used. The multiplier (present value factor) for a period of five years at 8% was taken from a present value of an annuity of 1 (ordinary) table: 3.99271. This amount multiplied by the annual earnings figure of $5,000.00 yields the present value of the earnings annuity, $19,963.55. The next illustration will present the procedure for determining the rate of return when some factors are not known.

Using the same data from the pay-back example, the rate of return on the proposed investment is not known and must be determined. The following steps are suggested:

Step 1. Set up and work out the formula to determine the annuity table factor.

Formula:

$$\frac{\text{Net Cost of Addition}}{\text{Net annual earnings before depreciation, after taxes (or net expense reduction)}} = \text{Table Factor}$$

Computation:

$$\frac{\$97{,}500}{\$12{,}000 - \$3{,}888^{*}} = \frac{\$97{,}500}{\$\ 8{,}112} = 12.01923 \text{ (Table Factor)}$$

*($12,000 – $3,900) × 48% = $3,888 annual income tax

Step II. Locate a number corresponding to the table factor determined above in a present value of an annuity of 1 (ordinary) by searching the row of numbers opposite twenty-five periods.

In this illustration the table factor of 12.01823 will be found to fall between the 6% and 8% columns, representing the approximate rate of return.

Step III. Interpolation between the 6% and 8% rates will yield a more mathematically exact rate of return.

%	Table Factor		
6%	12.783	.764	2.108
Unknown	12.019		
8%	10.675		

$$6\% + \left(\frac{.764}{2.108}\right) \times 2 = 6.725\% \text{ Rate of Return}$$

	P.V. Factor	P.V.
Initial Investment of Cash Outlay	\$97,500 × 1.00	(\$97,500)
Annual Savings or Addition to Cash from the Investment	\$8,112 × 12.01923	\$97,500
	NET PRESENT VALUE	-0-

The time adjusted rate of return (or internal rate of return) is the rate (in this case 6.725%) that equates the present value of expected future inflows with the present value of expected future outflows.

The investment of \$97,500 in the tugboat is expected to return \$8,112 (after taxes, before depreciation) per year for twenty-five years. This will amount to \$202,800. The difference between \$202,800 and \$97,500 represents a uniform return of 6.725% on the investment over the period of twenty-five years. Measured against any standard that the company feels is appropriate, the rate of return computed will determine whether or not the investment is made. For example, if the company requires an 8% return, then the likelihood is that the investment will not be made. Alternatively, if a 6% return is satisfactory, the firm will probably seek other similar investment opportunities. It is, perhaps, worthwhile repeating here that qualitative factors may seriously affect the final decision, especially if the expected rate of return is close to the company standard.

EQUIPMENT ALTERNATIVES—AN ILLUSTRATION

Assume that a company is planning to buy a fleet of heavy dump trucks. Two different sizes have been suggested that will incur varying operating expenses. Because of these differences and variations in initial cost, a detailed analysis is necessary in order to determine which truck size would represent the most advantageous investment. A tabulation of estimated revenues and operating expenses follows:

	TRUCK SIZE	
	12 cubic yards	17 cubic yards
Number of Units to be Purchased	10	7
Estimated Life	6 years	8 years
Delivered Cost Each	$19,500	$34,000
Estimated Salvage Value Each	$ 1,500	$ 2,000
Estimated Annual Gas & Oil Cost for Fleet.	$8,000	$12,000
Estimated Annual Taxes, Insurance, Repairs, etc. Cost for Fleet.	$20,000	$26,800
Estimated Annual Drivers' Wages and Fringe Benefits Cost for Fleet.	$90,000	$ 78,000
Estimated Annual Fleet Gross Revenue.	$190,000	$188,000

Using the above data the estimated annual net revenues are scheduled below:

	TRUCK SIZE	
	12 cubic yards	17 cubic yards
Gross Revenue	$190,000	$188,000
Operating Expense		
Wages and Benefits	90,000	78,000
Taxes, Insurance, Repairs, etc.	20,000	26,800
Gas and Oil	8,000	12,000
Total Operating Expense	$118,000	$116,800
Net Revenue (before depreciation & taxes)	$72,000	$71,200
Depreciation	30,000	28,000
Net Revenue (before taxes)	$42,000	$43,200
Income Taxes (48%)	$20,160	$20,736
Net Revenue	$21,840	$22,464

To determine the rate of return on the proposed investment in order to aid in making a choice, it is necessary to carry out the steps previously outlined for the discounted rate of return method.

Step I: Set up and work out the formula to determine the annuity table factor:

Formula:

$$\frac{\text{Net Cost of Addition}}{\text{Net annual earnings before depreciation, after taxes (or net expense reduction)}} = \text{Table Factor}$$

Computations:

12 Cubic Yard Trucks

$$\frac{\$195{,}000 - \$\ 7{,}605^{*}}{\$\ 72{,}000 - \$20{,}160^{**}} = \frac{\$187{,}395}{\$\ 51{,}840} = 3.615 \text{ (Table Factor)}$$

*Present value of fleet salvage value of $15,000 ($1,500 × 10 units), using a company target return on its investment of 12% for a six-year period, times a multiplier of .507. See present value of 1 table, 6 periods at 12% for the multiplier of .507.

**($72,000 –$30,000 annual depreciation) × 48% = $20,160 annual income tax

17 Cubic Yard Trucks

$$\frac{\$238{,}000 - \$\ 5{,}656^{*}}{\$\ 71{,}200 - \$20{,}736^{**}} = \frac{\$232{,}344}{\$\ 50{,}464} = 4.604 \text{ (Table Factor)}$$

*Present value of fleet salvage value of $14,000 ($2,000 × 7 units), using a company target return on its investment of 12% for an eight-year period, times a multiplier of .404. See present value of 1 table, 8 periods at 12% for the multiplier of .404.

**($71,200 – $28,000) × 48% = $20,736 annual income tax

Step II: Locate numbers corresponding to the table factors determined above in a present value of an annuity of 1 (ordinary) by searching the row of numbers opposite 6 periods in the case of the 12 cubic yard trucks and opposite 8 periods in the case of the 17 cubic yard trucks.

In this illustration, the table factor of 3.615 will be found to fall between the 16% and 18% columns (6 period line), representing the approximate rate of return on the 12 cubic yard trucks. The table factor of 4.604 will be found to fall between the 14% and 16% columns (8 period line), representing the approximate rate of return on the 17 cubic yard trucks.

Step III: Interpolation between the approximate percentages in each case will yield a more mathematically exact rate of return.

12 Cubic Yard Trucks

16%	3.685 }		
Unknown	3.615 }	.070 }	.187
18%	3.498		

$$16\% + \left(\frac{.070}{.187} \times 2\right) = 16.749\% \text{ Rate of Return}$$

17 Cubic Yard Trucks

14%	4.639	.035	.295
Unknown	4.604		
16%	4.344		

$$14\% + \left(\frac{.035}{.295} \times 2\right) = 14.237\% \text{ Rate of Return}$$

It is obvious from the rates of return calculated here that the 12 cubic yard trucks represent the better investment, assuming there are no other factors bearing on the analysis that would outweigh the difference in rates of return. The difference of 2.512% (16.749 – 14.237) is a fairly substantial one and represents a reasonably comfortable hedge against fluctuation in the actual performance of the trucks as well in the expected revenue. *It must never be overlooked that the validity of the results is strictly a function of the accuracy of the estimations, revenues and expenses used in the computations.*

Equipment Alternatives—A Second Illustration

Alternate investment possibilities require the determination of the present value of net cash flows. It is based on a company-determined target rate of return. It would be an easier method to use where the analysis must deal with variable annual revenues instead of a presumed uniform flow of revenue as in the preceding illustration.

In this illustration the same facts as above are used except for the estimated annual net revenues (before depreciation, after taxes) which are listed below:

Year	12 Cubic Yard Trucks	17 Cubic Yard Trucks
1	$45,250	$44,300
2	51,000	49,500
3	57,090	57,000
4	56,000	59,500
5	52,700	58,080
6	49,000	51,508
7	-0-	46,000
8	-0-	40,000
	$311,040	$405,888

Unless an average annual revenue was determined and used as in the previous illustration, a much more complex analysis would have to be made in order to determine the rate of return overall. The irregular revenue flow, forced to an average, would contribute some inaccuracy to the final results.

The target rate of return will be assumed to be 15%. The return on the alternate investments will be measured from this rate. The calculation of the present values of the cash inflows to be measured against the initial investment is set forth in the table below.

12 CUBIC YARD TRUCKS

Year	Estimated Revenue*	Present Value of 1 Factor at 15% for the respective year	Present Value of Estimated Revenue
1	$45,250	.870	$39,368
2	51,000	.756	38,556
3	57,090	.658	37,565
4	56,000	.572	32,032
5	52,700	.497	26,192
6	49,000	.432	21,168
		TOTAL	$194,881
Add: Present Value of Total Fleet Salvage Value ($15,000 × .432)			6,480
			$201,361
Deduct: Initial investment			$195,000
Net present value (excess of inflows over outgo)			$6,361

*Before depreciation, after taxes.

17 CUBIC YARD TRUCKS

Year	Estimated Revenue*	Present Value of 1 Factor at 15% for the respective year	Present Value of Estimated Revenue
1	$44,300	.870	$38,541
2	49,500	.756	37,422
3	57,000	.658	37,506
4	59,500	.572	34,034
5	58,080	.497	28,866
6	51,508	.432	22,251
7	46,000	.376	17,296
8	40,000	.327	13,080
		TOTAL	$228,996
Add: Present Value of Total Fleet Salvage Value ($14,000 × .327)			$4,578
			$233,574
Deduct: Initial investment			$238,000
Net present value (excess of outgo over inflows)			($4,426)

*Before depreciation, after taxes

Since there is an excess of cash inflow over outgo in the case of the 12 cubic yard trucks, the estimated rate of return exceeds the company target of 15%. In the case of the 17 cubic yard trucks, the cash outgo exceeds the inflow. The estimated rate of return, therefore, does not come up to the company target.

While the indicated choice of investments here followed the same pattern in each case, it will not necessarily do so in all cases. The timing of the different amounts of cash inflows could change the pattern, especially where the difference in rates of return, as determined in the first illustration, is relatively small. In each of the illustrations, the time value of money can be seen to seriously affect the results of the analyses.

Illustration—Determining the Lowest Cost Method of Financing

A situation is presented here wherein it is essential to replace some machinery; the choice of type and manufacturer has already been made. The choice as to type could have been made by an analytical procedure similar to that illustrated in the previous case. This illustration is concerned only with the procedures for determining the lowest cost method of financing the capital addition needed. Four different methods will be considered.

In the case of the first method, the machinery to be purchased is offered at a cash price of $250,000.00 by the manufacturer. As a second method, the manufacturer has offered to sell the machinery on the installment basis under a conditional sales contract for five annual payments of $60,000.00 each. The third method makes use of a bank loan. The company's bank has offered an eight-year loan at 8% interest, payable on a monthly basis, with the interest calculated on the unpaid balance. Principal payments are to be uniform; as a result, the total monthly interest and principal payment will be reducing each month. The fourth method involves an equipment leasing concern which will purchase the machinery and lease it to the company for $3,500 per month for the eight-year period. No subsequent purchasing arrangement was offered.

The company plans to depreciate the machinery, if purchased, over an eight-year period. It is expected that technological advances will make the machinery obsolete in eight years. The double-declining balance method of depreciation is to be used. The estimated net scrap value is expected to be $2,500. A 48% income tax rate will be used in the computations. It is felt that the scrap value of the present machinery will be offset by the cost of removal and site preparation for the new machinery. Any financial gain or loss resulting from the disposition is considered to be negligible.

Figure 5-1 sets forth the schedule of proposed principal and interest payments on the bank loan for the eight-year period. Since the monthly principal payments are uniform, the interest on the principal amount payable each month during each year will be uniform, also. That schedule is not reproduced here because of its simplicity. The benefit of the tax shield is included in the calculations so as to reduce the interest cost.

The calculation of the tax shield from the depreciation to be taken is set forth in Figure 5-2. This information is needed for determining the total cost under the installment plan.

Figure 5-1

HALEY EQUIPMENT MANUFACTURERS, INC.
SCHEDULE OF PRINCIPAL AND INTEREST PAYMENTS
BANK LOAN FOR EQUIPMENT

	19 × 1	19 × 2	19 × 3	19 × 4	19 × 5	19 × 6	19 × 7	19 × 8
Beginning Loan Balance	$250,000	218,750	187,500	156,250	125,000	93,750	62,500	31,250
Annual Principal Payments Paid Monthly	31,250	31,250	31,250	31,250	31,250	31,250	31,250	31,250
Ending Loan Balance	218,750	187,500	156,250	125,000	93,750	62,500	31,250	-0-
Interest Cost—8%								
On Ending Balance	17,500*	15,000	12,500	10,000	7,500	5,000	2,500	-0-
On Monthly Payments	1,355	1,355	1,355	1,355	1,355	1,355	1,355	1,355
Total	18,855	16,355	13,855	11,355	8,855	6,355	3,855	1,355
Less 48% Tax Shield	9,050**	7,850	6,650	5,450	4,250	3,050	1,850	650
Net Cost of Interest	9,805	8,505	7,205	5,905	4,605	3,305	2,005	705
Total Cost Outflow—Annual Payments & Net Cost of Interest	$41,055***	39,755	38,455	37,155	35,855	34,555	33,255	31,955
Grand Total Cash Flow	$292,040							

*$218,750 × 8% = $17,500.
**$18,855 × 48% = $9,050.
***$31,250 + $9,805 = $41,055.

Figure 5-2

HALEY EQUIPMENT MANUFACTURERS, INC.
SCHEDULE OF DEPRECIATION—TAX SHIELD

Year	Beginning Balance	Depreciation 25% D.D.B.	Tax Shield 48% × Depreciation
1	$250,000	$62,500	$30,000
2	187,500	46,875	22,500
3	140,625	35,156	16,875
4	105,469	26,367	12,656
5	79,102	19,776	9,492
6	59,326	14,832	7,119
7	44,494	11,124	5,340
8	33,370	8,343	4,005
9	25,027*		
		$224,973	$107,987

*Assumed Salvage Value.

In Figure 5-3 the installment payments are scheduled so as to determine the "interest" cost element in the payments and reduce that element by the amount of the tax shield.

Figure 5-3

HALEY EQUIPMENT MANUFACTURERS, INC.
SCHEDULE OF INSTALLMENT PAYMENTS—MANUFACTURER FINANCING

	Annual	Total
Payments (5 Years)	$60,000	$300,000
Cash Price of Machinery		250,000
Difference Treated as Interest	10,000	50,000
Less: 48% Tax Shield	(4,800)	(24,000)
Net Cash Outflow	$55,200	$276,000

Information on the leasing plan is outlined in Figure 5-4. Here again the tax shield has been taken into consideration and a net cost developed for comparative purposes.

Figure 5-4

HALEY EQUIPMENT MANUFACTURERS, INC.
SCHEDULE OF LEASING COSTS

Rental of $3,500 per month for 8 years amounts to total rent of	$336,000
Less: Tax Shield of 48%	161,280
Net Cost	$174,720
Annual Rental	
Net Cost—$174,720 ÷ 8 years	$21,840

A schedule of comparative costs of the three methods of financing is presented in Figure 5-5 without consideration of the time value of money. In the computation the depreciation tax shield is included as well as the tax shield from the disposition of the machinery. The comparison is continued in Figure 5-6 in order to derive the net cash flow difference between the bank loan plan and the installment plan. Figure 5-7 develops the net cash flow difference between the bank loan plan and the leasing plan. The differences can be subjected to a discounting to determine a true cost of financing.

Figure 5-5

HALEY EQUIPMENT MANUFACTURERS, INC.
SCHEDULE OF COMPARATIVE COSTS

	Bank Loan	Manufacturer's Loan	8-Year Lease
Total Cost, before depreciation, after Taxes	$292,040 (Figure 5-1)	$276,000 (Figure 5-3)	$174,720 (Figure 5-4)
Less: Depreciation Tax Shield (from Figure 2)	107,987	107,987	-0-
	184,053	163,013	174,720
Deduct: Tax Shield On Unrecovered Cost*	10,813	10,813	-0-
Net Cost	$173,240	$157,200	$174,720
*Book value, end of 8th year	$25,027		
Less Proceeds as Scrap	2,500		
Loss on Disposal (unrecovered cost)	22,527		
Tax @ 48%	$10,813		

Figure 5-6

HALEY EQUIPMENT MANUFACTURERS, INC.
FINANCING BY BANK LOAN VS. MANUFACTURER'S INSTALLMENT PLAN

	Cash Flow		
Year	**Bank Loan**	**Installment Plan**	**Bank (Over)/Under**
19 × 1	$ 41,055	$ 55,200	$14,145
19 × 2	39,755	55,200	15,445
19 × 3	38,455	55,200	16,745
19 × 4	37,155	55,200	18,045
19 × 5	35,855	55,200	19,345
19 × 6	34,555	-0-	(34,555)
19 × 7	33,255	-0-	(33,255)
19 × 8	31,955	-0-	(31,955)
TOTALS	$292,040	$276,000	($16,040)

Figure 5-7

HALEY EQUIPMENT MANUFACTURERS, INC.
SCHEDULE OF COMPARATIVE CASH FLOWS—
FINANCING BY BANK LOAN VS. LEASING

Year	Cash Outflow Bank Loan	Depreciation Tax Shield	Net Outflow	Cash Outflow Leasing	Bank (Over)/Under
19 × 1	$ 41,055	$ 30,000	$ 11,055	$ 21,840	$ 10,785
19 × 2	39,755	22,500	17,255	21,840	4,585
19 × 3	38,455	16,875	21,580	21,840	260
19 × 4	37,155	12,656	24,499	21,840	(2,659)
19 × 5	35,855	9,492	26,363	21,840	(4,523)
19 × 6	34,555	7,119	27,436	21,840	(5,596)
19 × 7	33,255	5,340	27,915	21,840	(6,075)
19 × 8	31,955	14,818*	17,137	21,840	4,703
TOTAL	$292,040	$118,800	$173,240	$174,720	$1,480

*Includes tax shield from write-off of unrecovered cost—$10,813.

Figure 5-8

HALEY EQUIPMENT MANUFACTURERS, INC.
SCHEDULE FOR DETERMINING RATE OF RETURN—
BANK LOAN VS. MANUFACTURER'S INSTALLMENT PLAN

Year	Bank (Over)/Under Installment Plan	Trial Discount Factors 4½%	5%	Present Value 4½%	5%
19 × 1	$14,145	.957	.952	$13,537	$13,466
19 × 2	15,445	.916	.907	14,148	14,009
19 × 3	16,745	.876	.864	14,669	14,468
19 × 4	18,045	.839	.823	15,140	14,851
19 × 5	19,345	.802	.784	15,515	15,166
19 × 6	(34,555)	.768	.746	(26,538)	(25,778)
19 × 7	(33,255)	.735	.711	(24,442)	(23,644)
19 × 8	(31,955)	.703	.677	(22,464)	(21,634)
TOTAL	($16,040)			($435)	$904

(Rough interpolation indicates 4.67%)

The bank loan vs. installment plan differences are discounted on a trial basis as set forth in Figure 5-8 to determine the present values. As can be seen from Figure 5-8, a return of approximately 4.67% would yield a zero present value on the total differences. This is a rough interpolation between the trial discount rates of 4½% and 5%. This means that if the funds not required for the cash flow under the bank plan in years 1 to 5 as compared with the installment plan, can be invested at a rate in excess of 4.67%, the bank plan is the most economical of the two. Not only will the excess cash flow under the bank plan have been recovered, but additional earnings will be realized to the extent of the rate of return above 4.67%.

With reference to Figure 5-7 it will be noted that the bank plan net cash outflow is less than that under the leasing plan in terms of absolute amounts. Since the disposition of the machinery has also been considered in making the comparison, no further financial analysis is required.

The differences in the financing plans in this illustration are not so great as to preclude a choice being made as a result of other considerations, including those of a non-financial character. The larger cash outflow in the early years under the installment plan could be a problem. The advantages of ownership, in terms of possible continued use of the machinery after eight years, could be a factor in the decision. Unless definitely ruled out by the leasing company, a lease-purchase arrangement might be found to be advantageous. In this illustration, the time value of money changed what appeared to be a clear-cut result that indicated a considerable advantage for the installment plan to an advantage in favor of the bank loan plan.

ILLUSTRATION—KEEP OR REPLACE EQUIPMENT

It is not at all unusual for management to be faced with the temptation to buy new equipment to replace the present equipment because of technological advances. When faced with this situation, an analysis should be made considering the time value of money. A present value can be determined for the cash flows involved in both the "keep" and "replace" choices. As in all capital additions studies, there are judgmental factors that must be considered here. For example, in the illustration at hand, a six-year period is used for comparative purposes, but the replacement machine will have an estimated two-year life beyond the six-year period. The estimated sales price is taken into account as of that time, but it could be determined that it would be to the company's advantage to continue the use of the equipment instead of selling it. It should not be overlooked that the validity of the comparison is also a function of the accuracy of the estimates used.

In this example, a company has a milling machine that cost $60,000 four years ago, and it has a remaining life of six years. A major overhaul, expected to cost $7,500, is due in one year. The following tabulation gives the facts for each choice:

	Old Machine	New Machine
Cash Price	$60,000	$72,000
Estimated Life	10 years	8 years
Depreciation Basis	S. Y. D.	S. Y. D.
Residual Book Value—End of 10 years	5,000	-0-

	Old Machine	New Machine
Estimated Salvage Value—in 6 years	7,500	18,000
Now	22,500	N. A.
Estimated Annual Operating Expenses	36,000	25,000
Accumulated Depreciation to Date	34,000	N. A.
Income Tax Rate	48%	48%
Expected Rate of Return After Taxes	8%	8%

No major overhaul is expected during the life of the new milling machine. The calculations for determining the present values of the cash flows are set forth below:

Keep Present Machine

1. Annual Operating Costs:

Remaining Years	Operating Cost*	Tax Shield @ 48%	Net (Cost) Savings	Discount** Factor—8%	Present Value
1st	$36,000	$17,280	$(18,720)	.925925	($17,333)
2nd	36,000	17,280	(18,720)	.857338	(16,049)
3rd	36,000	17,280	(18,720)	.793832	(14,861)
4th	36,000	17,280	(18,720)	.735029	(13,760)
5th	36,000	17,280	(18,720)	.680583	(12,741)
6th	36,000	17,280	(18,720)	.630169	(11,797)
					($86,541)

*No depreciation included

**See alternate calculation in replacement example. Use present value of annuity multiplier (8% for 6 periods) of 4.6229 times annual net cost of $18,720 = $86,541. In this example, present value of 1 multipliers are used.

2. Overhaul Costs:

Remaining Years	Overhaul Cost*	Tax Shield @ 48%	Net (Cost) Savings	Discount Factor—8%	Present Value
1st	$7,500	$3,600	$(3,900)	.925925	($3,611)

*Presumed to be fully deductible in year of overhaul.

3. Depreciation Tax Shield:

Remaining Years	Depreciation (S.Y.D.)	Tax Shield @ 48%	Net (Cost) Savings	Discount Factor—8%	Present Value
1st	$6,000	$2,880	$2,880	.925925	$2,667
2nd	5,000	2,400	2,400	.857338	2,058
3rd	4,000	1,920	1,920	.793832	1,524
4th	3,000	1,440	1,440	.735029	1,058
5th	2,000	960	960	.680583	653
6th	1,000	480	480	.630169	302
					$8,262

4. Residual Value:

Remaining Years	Sale Profit	Income Tax @ 48%	Net (Cost) Savings	Discount Factor—8%	Present Value
6th	$2,500	$1,200	$1,300	.630169	$ 819
	Total cash flows at present value (Items 1-4)				($81,071)

Replace Present Machine

1. Annual Operating Costs:

Remaining Years	Operating Cost	Tax Shield @ 48%	Net (Cost) Savings	Discount Factor—8%	Present Value
1–6 each	$25,000	$12,000	($13,000)	4.6229*	($60,098)

*Present value of an annuity multiplier @ 8% for 6 periods.

2. Initial Capital Addition:
Actual Cash Outflow*—$(72,000) 1.000 ($72,000)

*If purchased by loan or installment plan, add interest cost less tax shield @ 48%

3. Disposition of Old Equipment:

Original Cost	$60,000	
Less: S.Y.D. Depreciation to date (10 years)	34,000	
Book Value	26,000	
Current Disposition Price	22,500	
Net Loss	$ 3,500	
Tax Shield from loss @ 48%	$ 1,680	
Current Disposition Price	22,500	
Net Cash Effect	$24,180 × 1.000 =	$24,180

4. Depreciation Tax Shield:

Remaining Years	Depreciation (S.Y.D.)	Tax Shield @ 48%	Net (Cost) Savings	Discount Factor—8%	Present Value
19 × 1	$16,000	$7,680	$7,680	.925925	$ 7,111
19 × 2	14,000	6,720	6,720	.857338	5,761
19 × 3	12,000	5,760	5,760	.793832	4,572
19 × 4	10,000	4,800	4,800	.735029	3,528
19 × 5	8,000	3,840	3,840	.680583	2,613
19 × 6	6,000	2,880	2,880	.630169	1,815
					$25,400

5. Residual Value:

Remaining Years	Salvage Profit	Income Tax @ 48%	Net (Cost) Savings	Discount Factor—8%	Present Value
6th	$12,000	$5,760	$6,240	.630169	$ 3,932
	Total Cash Flow at present value (Items 1-5)				($78,586)

Summary of Above

Annual Operating Costs	($60,098)
Initial Capital Addition	(72,000)
Disposition of Old Equipment	24,180
Depreciation Tax Shield	25,400
Residual Value	3,932
	($78,586)

It will be noted that different methods of calculating the present value of the annual operating cost cash flows were used in the two examples. The more detailed calculation in the first case treats each year's cost as a separate item. This method is necessary in situations where the annual operating costs are not expected to be uniform. Where the costs are expected to be uniform, the treatment as an annuity represents a saving in calculation time.

In this illustration, the negative cash flow total is the smallest by $2,485 in the replacement choice; therefore the present milling machine could be replaced to advantage. This assumes that other factors, non-quantitative in nature, do not outweigh this relatively small difference.

Unfortunately, many textbook examples suggest spectacular differences in capital additions options of various types. In a highly competitive business environment, this is not apt to be the usual situation. Because absolute dollar amounts may be close together in options, it is essential to consider the time value of money. If tight control is not exercised over cash balances, the whole matter of measuring the time value of money in capital additions analyses becomes more or less academic. Idle money will, in effect, absorb the gain projected so the expected advantage in the choice made will not be realized. Realistic rates of return expected should be used; others could result in seriously misleading figures.

This example of capital addition evaluation also represents Step 3 in the overall process of managing capital expenditure.

CHAPTER 6

CASH PLANNING AND CONTROL

Of necessity, cash planning and control go hand-in-hand. Each activity requires information and in turn develops information needed by the other. The preceding chapter treated these two activities as one with a view to developing an overall satisfactory cash budget for a year. Other than to determine monthly balances of cash, no attention was paid to size of cash balances, to day-to-day changes in volume, or to possible long-range problems.

This chapter considers the development of the cash budget for inclusion in the master budget as well as deals with the problems of day-to-day cash control, the periodic updating of the cash budget, and cash planning for the long-range. The illustration used in this chapter is based on the assumption that little or nothing has been done in the way of cash planning and control in the model company. This will not always be the case in practice, of course, so adaptations will have to be made. Use the illustrations as references or models.

Another assumption made here is that the company has done all it can to speed up collections from customers by instituting effective credit and collection policies. If this has not already been done in many companies, the processing time of customers' checks can be reduced by better mailing procedures and use of area banks for deposit of checks. Arrangements can be made with these banks in respect to timely advice as to deposits. The whole matter of cash forecasting, planning and control can be readily described in two words: *cash management.*

SELLING CASH MANAGEMENT TO MANAGERS

It is in the best financial interest of a company to reduce its cash funds used in operations to the absolute minimum necessary. Checking account balances do not provide a return on capital. A tight cash position makes careful management essential. In our opinion, the following list of objectives represents sufficient support for improved management of cash:

1. To increase the rate of return on assets employed in the company.
2. To get the company out of a "tight" cash position.
3. To provide assistance in securing additional working capital when needed.
4. To help provide additional funds for company growth.
5. To facilitate the scheduling of payments to creditors and stockholders.
6. To provide for temporary investment of surplus cash.

The above list is not necessarily exhaustive but indicative of some of the benefits to be reaped from skillful cash management. Keep in mind that it is quite possible to over-manage cash to the extent that it costs more to manage it than the total of the benefits derived therefrom.

Preparation for Cash Management

Where to Start

Before effective cash planning can be carried out, the historical patterns of cash receipts and disbursements need to be uncovered and reviewed in the light of past business activity and then used as benchmarks for the future. Normally, one year's historical records will be sufficient to get a fair pattern. Any abnormalities can be identified and excluded from the worksheets.

It is recommended that the budget form for the scheduling of cash receipts and disbursements be used as a worksheet in tabulating the actual figures for the pattern year. Refer to Figure 6-1 for an example of developing historical cash receipts and disbursement figures. On this worksheet, some significant proportions will probably be indicated in the relationship of each month to the year as a whole. These may be of special significance with respect to collections of accounts receivable of various types. The sources of the figures for the worksheet such as that used in Figure 6-1 could be the cash receipts and disbursement journals (summaries) and the ledger accounts. The various books of original entry and ledger structure will dictate to some extent the procedure for developing the figures for the worksheet. In some cases it will be necessary to prepare preliminary summaries before entering items.

Analyzing Collections of Receivables

In the first step, in the process of analysis of collections of receivables, the receivables should be set forth separately by types, such as thirty-day accounts, ninety-day budget accounts, lay aways (if significant), and installment accounts. The collection pattern may indicate seasonal differences by types of accounts. The percentages of each month's collections by types of accounts to the year's total should be calculated. This calculation has been made and entered in Figure 6-1.

The next step will require the tabulating of daily collections of accounts in each month. This tabulation will show how collections vary throughout the month. The daily collection patterns by months may be quite similar; however, there could be some variations related to the time of the year. The percentage of each day's collections by type of accounts to the month's total should be calculated. Refer to Figure 6-2 for an example. Only the months of

Figure 6-1

SCHEDULE OF CASH RECEIPTS AND DISBURSEMENTS

(000 Omitted) Actual—19X1

Items	January	February	March	April	May	June	July	August	September	October	November	December		Total
Receipts														
Cash Sales	42	41	53	65	57	48	45	59	68	54	71	89		692
Coll. on Rec.—30 Day	814	707	693	724	715	671	659	702	796	732	761	784		8758
(% to Year Total)	(9.29)	(8.07)	(7.91)	(8.27)	(8.16)	(7.66)	(7.53)	(8.02)	(9.09)	(8.36)	(8.69)	(8.95)		(100.00)
Interest (Temporary Investments)	24						35							59
Misc. Income	5	3	2	4	6	3	4	2	4	4	5	5		47
Loans—Bank		95	120			40								255
Sale of Assets								17						17
Total	885	846	868	793	778	762	743	780	868	790	837	878		9828
Disbursements														
Purchases	342	300	221	175	165	180	150	171	195	194	204	208		2505
Direct Labor	240	260	265	280	270	230	245	250	276	262	239	256		3073
Mfg. Expense	125	130	130	146	161	145	127	120	125	128	119	137		1593
Distrib. Expense	80	82	76	91	68	71	70	74	89	91	88	89		969
Admin. Expense	85	86	85	80	84	83	84	85	81	84	86	95		1018
Advertising	3	2	2		4	2	3	2			6	4		28
Research & Devel.	5	5	6	5	5	6	6	5	5	5	5	5		63
Taxes—Property										10				10
Insurance			24			24			25			25		98
Dividends			15			15			15			15		60
Mtge. Payments					4	4	4	4	4	4	4	4		32
Loans—Bank				10	10		50	50	50		85			255
Temp. Investments												40		40
Income Taxes			15			11			11			11		48
Purchase—Equipment			30											30
Total	880	865	869	787	771	771	739	761	876	778	836	889		9822
Excess Receipts Over Disbursements	5	(19)	(1)	6	7	(9)	4	19	(8)	12	1	(11)		6
Beginning Balance	20	25	6	5	11	18	9	13	32	24	36	37		
Ending Balance	25	6	5	11	18	9	13	32	24	36	37	26		

January and February are used in the example set forth in Figure 6-2. It is to be noted that the percentages are fairly uniform between months. This may not be the case where smaller companies are concerned. There could be sharp variations on what might be described as "off days," that is, days of normally light collections. In this example, the collections tended to cluster around the ninth to the eleventh working days. In the event of those sharp variations, assumptions will have to be made regarding the future in the light of past experience. If cycle billing is used, collections may present a somewhat more uniform pattern throughout the month. This pattern will be affected by the company's credit terms with regard to billings in the latter part of the month. The assumption here, of course, is that cash management on a daily basis is planned.

The collection percentages determined, as indicated above, may be applied to the budgeted net sales after allowing for estimated write-offs of customer accounts and for any

Figure 6-2

SCHEDULE OF COLLECTIONS OF RECEIVABLES—30-DAY ACCOUNTS

(000 Omitted) Actual—19X1

Business Day	January $	% to Total	February $	% to Total	etc.	etc.
1	5	.61	5	.62		
2	7	.86	5	.75		
3	17	2.09	15	2.15		
4	20	2.46	18	2.51		
5	21	2.58	18	2.60		
6	30	3.69	27	3.80		
7	42	5.16	37	5.24		
8	60	7.37	51	7.19		
9	115	14.13	105	14.69		
10	128	15.72	111	15.58		
11	159	19.53	135	19.16		
12	81	9.95	71	10.07		
13	38	4.67	34	4.80		
14	16	1.97	14	2.01		
15	14	1.72	12	1.65		
16	15	1.84	14	2.00		
17	14	1.72	13	1.84		
18	16	1.97	12	1.73		
19	4	.49	4	.60		
20	4	.49	0	.00		
21	3	.37	3	.48		
22	0	.00	1	.21		
23	2	.25	2	.26		
24	1	.12	0	.06		
25	1	.12	—	—		
26	1	.12	—	—		
27	—	—	—	—		
Total	814	100.00	707	100.00		
	(See Figure 6-1)					

planned increase (or decrease) in receivable balances to be carried forward (change in credit terms). These percentages will aid materially in the development of daily and monthly cash receipts from collections of accounts by type for the budget year.

Another method of determining the collection pattern of receivables involves the analysis of a randomly selected group of accounts by receivable type. The objective here is to determine the percentage of each account collected in the month of sale and each subsequent month until paid out (Figure 6-3). Add-on sales should be treated individually as though they were separate accounts. In Chapter 4, use of this method was implied by the layout of Figure 4-16, Schedule of Collections on Accounts Receivable.

If the group of accounts analyzed is selected with reference to a single month's sales, it is assumed the collection pattern for that month's sales is representative of all months' sales. If such is not the case, perhaps a sample should be taken from each month in the past year. This type of analysis may not be feasible because of the volume of accounts needed for good

Figure 6-3

SCHEDULE OF COLLECTIONS OF RECEIVABLES—30-DAY ACCOUNTS

Month of March, 19X1

	Amount	Collections on Account				
Customers #	of	Current	Month After Sale			Uncol-
	Sale	Month	1st.	2nd.	3rd.	lectible
142	140		140			
197	250	75	175			
243	95			95		
276	84	84				
331	120			40	40	40
357	165		165			
389	50		50			
421	75			75		
444	240		160		80	
479	150	50	100			
510	90			30		60
543	175	75	50	50		
589	265		265			
etc.	etc.					
Totals	22,780	2,893	12,848	4,829	1,731	479
%	100.0	12.7	56.4	21.2	7.6	2.1

samples. In that case, the previously outlined procedure should be used and will probably provide a fair degree of reliability. The percentages developed in Figure 6-3 would be applied to each month's net sales of the budget year.

Other Receipts and Disbursements

While the analysis of collections of receivables and development of daily and monthly collection percentages may be troublesome and time-consuming, the other receipt and disbursement items still need careful attention. Quite often, some disbursements can be made to coincide with available cash without irritating the vendors. Disbursements in connection with appropriation type budget items may be subject to a more convenient placement in the cash budget. Items of this type should be entered after other disbursements of a more or less fixed nature with regularly scheduled due dates are entered in the schedules.

If cash sales are of any significance, care should be taken to review past patterns in order to derive the best possible daily and monthly percentages for allocation of the budgeted cash sales to the respective periods. In some companies, there will be seasonal differences in cash sales of considerable magnitude.

Interest from temporary investments may be one of the last items to schedule in that the interest will be a function of the amount of cash finally determined to be available for temporary investment. Depending upon their source and nature, miscellaneous income items will present varying degrees of difficulty in scheduling. Unless really immaterial, income items should be considered.

The sale of assets other than temporary investments will occasionally be a significant source of cash and should be identified with the proper time frame if at all possible. All cash items that cannot be accurately placed in the proper time frame naturally become candidates for adjustment in the cash budget working papers at a later date. Obviously, the fewer changes there are to be made, the smoother will be the cash management process and the more precise will be the measurements of cash availability. If bonds or stocks are to be sold for cash, the receipts can usually be placed according to date with a fair degree of accuracy.

While the illustration used here covers a calendar year of historical expenditures, it will normally be necessary to take a pattern from September 1 to August 31, since the coming calendar year's budget will be developed in advance of the period budgeted. The starting point of September 1 is simply a suggested date.

If the number of business days in the budget month is different from the pattern month, adjustments will have to be made in the day-to-day percentages of the receivable collections. Company experience will dictate how and where adjustment should be made. Normally the percentage(s) to be absorbed (or extended) will be relatively small and can be allocated to the days expected to pick up the collections. Cash sales percentages can be moved from one month to the other as required since the number of business days tends to be the controlling factor here rather than the scheduled payment dates for monthly collections on receivables. For example, based on the pattern year's percentages, the budget year's percentages of cash sales for, say March and April, might be 97.5% and 102.4%, respectively. This situation occurs because in the budget year (19X2) the month of April has one more business day than the pattern year.

Cash Management Illustrated

Basic Cash Budget

In this illustration, the pattern year, 19X1 (Figure 6-1), is used as the basis for developing the schedule of cash receipts and disbursements for the budget year, 19X2 (Figure 6-4). The collections of receivables percentages from Figure 6-1 were used to allocate the budgeted credit sale collections as set forth in Figure 6-4. The cash sales on Figure 6-4 were allocated on a pattern similar to that indicated on Figure 6-1 with consideration of planned changes in sales strategy. Other items were placed according to past experience and future plans, i.e., the sale of equipment, the purchase of equipment and the investment of surplus funds. Bank loans and their repayment were of necessity the last items placed.

The Investments-Savings balance is set forth in Figure 6-4 as a memorandum reference since the savings account will be drawn upon to cover the indicated cash deficits as needed. The amount of cushion needed depends upon the cash balance fluctuation from day-to-day and month-to-month. The balance of the investments can be placed so as to earn a larger return until permanently invested. No significance should be attached to the amount of temporary investments used in this illustration. It will be noted that there is a disbursement item for Investments-Savings which increases the memorandum balances of Investments Savings set forth at the bottom of Figure 6-4.

The breakdown of disbursements in Figure 6-4 is different from that used in the pattern year. This would not be an unusal situation because cash budgeting is being carried out for the first time. The particular breakdown used in a given case will depend upon the nature of the company expenditures, relative timing and their controllability (or lack of it). In the illustration at hand, the disbursement breakdown is limited to a relatively few items in order

Figure 6-4

SCHEDULE OF CASH RECEIPTS AND DISBURSEMENTS

(000 Omitted) Budget—19X2

Items	January	February	March	April	May	June	July	August	September	October	November	December		Total
Receipts														
Cash Sales	46	46	59	70	64	54	50	65	75	60	78	100		767
Collections on Receivables 30-day	901	783	767	802	792	743	730	778	882	811	843	868		9,700
Misc. Income	5	4	3	4	5	4	4	3	4	5	5	6		52
Sale of Equipment	65									40				105
Interest—Temp. Investments					24									24
Bank Loans		100	100		40									240
Total	1017	933	929	876	925	801	784	846	961	916	926	974		10,888
Disbursements														
Salaries and Wages	340	365	365	370	368	320	330	330	320	310	270	332		4,020
Payroll Taxes	68	73	73	74	74	64	66	66	64	62	54	66		804
Fringe Benefits	20	22	22	22	22	19	20	20	19	19	16	20		241
Taxes and Licenses	3									12				15
Insurance			25			25			26			26		102
Dividends			15			15			15			15		60
Bank Loans								80	80	80				240
Interest on Loans								8	6	4				18
Mortgage Payments	4	4	4	4	4	4	4	4	4	4	4	4		48
Equip. Purchases	90													90
Income Taxes			17			12			12			12		53
Accounts Payable	500	480	438	385	480	315	333	357	400	425	517	508		5,138
Investments—Savings, etc.				5		6		4	17		28			60
Total	1025	944	959	860	948	780	753	869	963	916	889	983		10,889
Excess (Deficit) of Receipts Over Disbursements	(8)	(11)	(30)	16	(23)	21	31	(23)	(2)	0	37	(9)		(1)
Cash Bal.—Beginning	26	18	7	(23)	(7)	(30)	(9)	22	(1)	(3)	(3)	34		
Cash Bal.—Ending	18	7	(23)	(7)	(30)	(9)	22	(1)	(3)	(3)	34	25		
Investments—Savings, etc. Balance	40	40	40	45	45	51	51	55	72	72	100	100		

to keep the example manageable. The major costs and expenses are treated as accounts payable.

In order to arrive at a single figure, it is necessary to prepare summary sheets for the various categories of costs and expenses not otherwise set forth separately. Inventory policy with regard to merchandise or raw materials and supply items and credit terms of vendors will have a great effect on the disbursement schedule. In this illustration, it is assumed that in addition to planned order placement there is some "push and pull" possible in the timing of accounts payable settlements. This should not be too difficult to work out on a month-to-month basis; the day-to-day basis within a given month may be quite different, however.

Figure 6-5

CASH CONTROL SCHEDULE														
														(page 1)
(000 Omitted)						Month of January 19X2							Business Days (1-6)	
													Cumulative	
Items	**1**		**2**		**3**		**4**		**5**		**6**		**Totals**	
	Budget	**Actual**	**Budget**	**Actual**	**Budget**	**Actual**	**Budget**	**Actual**	**Budget**	**Actual**	**Budget**	**Actual**	**Budget**	**Actual**
Receipts														
Cash Sales	3	3	1	2	2	1	2	2	2	2	2	1	12	11
Collection on Rec. 30-Day	5	4	8	6	19	16	22	15	23	27	33	35	110	103
Misc. Income											1	0	1	0
Sale of Equipment													—	—
Interest—Temporary Investments													—	—
Total	8	7	9	8	21	17	24	17	25	29	36	36	123	114
Disbursements														
Salaries and Wages							180	185					180	185
Payroll Taxes														
Fringe Benefits											10	10	10	10
Taxes and Licenses													—	—
Insurance													—	—
Dividends													—	—
Interest on Debt													—	—
Mortgage Payments													—	—
Equipment Purchases													—	—
Income Taxes													—	—
Accounts Payable									25	0	25	25	50	25
Accounts Payable (fwd)											(25)			(25)
Total	0	0	0	0	0	0	180	185	25	0	35	35	240	220
Excess (Deficit) of Receipts Over Disbursements	8	7	9	8	21	17	(156)	(168)	0	29	1	1	(117)	(106)
Additions														
From Savings Acct.														
From Other Invest.														
From Bank Loans							100	100					100	100
Reductions														
To Savings Acct.														
To Other Invest.														
To Bank Loans														
Cash Bal.—Beginning	26	26	34	33	43	41	64	58	8	(10)	8	19	26	26
Cash Bal.—Ending	34	33	43	41	64	58	8	(10)	8	19	9	20	9	20

USING THE CASH CONTROL SCHEDULE

The month of January is used in this case to illustrate a cash control schedule for day-to-day control. The receipts and disbursements for January are taken from Figure 6-4 and recorded in Figure 6-5, Cash Control Schedule, Month of January, 19X2, on a daily basis in the budget columns. The basis for allocation to specific business days is derived from past

Figure 6-5 continued

CASH CONTROL SCHEDULE														
													(page 2)	
				Month of January 19X2					Business Days (7-12)					
													Cumulative	
Items	7		8		9		10		11		12		**Totals**	
	Budget	**Actual**	**Budget**	**Actual**	**Budget**	**Actual**	**Budget**	**Actual**	**Budget**	**Actual**	**Budget**	**Actual**	**Budget**	**Actual**
Receipts														
Cash Sales	3	3	1	2	1	1	2	2	2		2		11	
Collections on Rec. (30-Day)	46	50	66	72	127	128	142	139	176		90		647	
Misc. Income											1		1	
Sale of Equipment													—	
Interest—Temporary Investments													—	
Total	49	53	67	74	128	129	144	141	178		93		659	
Disbursements														
Salaries and Wages													—	
Payroll Taxes	36	37											36	
Fringe Benefits									5				5	
Taxes and Licenses													—	
Insurance													—	
Dividends													—	
Interest on Debt													—	
Mortgage Payments			4	4									4	
Equipment Purchases													—	
Income Taxes													—	
Accounts Payable	25	25	50	50	125	125	50	50			100		350	
Accounts Payable (fwd)	(25)		(25)	25										
Total	61	62	54	79	125	125	50	50	5		100		395	
Excess (Deficit) of Receipts Over Disbursements	(12)	(9)	13	(5)	3	4	94	91	173		(7)		264	
Additions														
From Savings Acct.														
From Other Invest.														
From Bank Loans														
Reductions														
To Savings Acct.							(100)	(100)	(100)				(100)	
To Other Invest.													(100)	
To Bank Loans														
Cash Bal.—Beginning	9	20	(3)	11	10	6	13	10	7	1	80		9	
Cash Bal.—Ending	(3)	11	10	6	13	10	7	1	80		73		73	

patterns and plans for future operations. The allocation of collections of receivables is based on the percentages developed in Figure 6-2 for the month of January. The date of disbursement is fixed in the case of disbursements for salaries, fringe benefits, payroll taxes, mortgage and note payments and other fixed schedule items. Accounts payable disbursements were scheduled to match available cash to some extent on the assumption that credit terms (and possible discount terms) permitted some options in scheduling the payments.

Figure 6-5 continued

CASH CONTROL SCHEDULE														
													(page 3)	
				Month of January 19X2						Business Days (13-18)				
													Cumulative	
Items	13		14		15		16		17		18		Totals	
	Budget	Actual	Budget	Actual	Budget	Actual	Budget	Actual	Budget	Actual	Budget	Actual	Budget	Actual
Receipts														
Cash Sales	3		1		1		2		2		2		11	
Collection on Rec. (30-Day)	42		18		16		18		16		18		128	
Misc. Income											1		1	
Sale of Equipment					65								65	
Interest—Temporary Investments													—	
Total	45		19		82		20		18		21		205	
Disbursements														
Salaries and Wages							160						160	
Payroll Taxes													—	
Fringe Benefits													—	
Taxes and Licenses													—	
Insurance													—	
Dividends													—	
Interest on Debt													—	
Mortgage Payments													—	
Equipment Purchases													—	
Income Taxes													—	
Accounts Payable	50		25								25		100	
Total	50		25		0		160		0		25		260	
Excess (Deficit) of Receipts Over Disbursements	(5)		(6)		82		(140)		18		(4)		(55)	
Additions														
From Savings Acct.														
From Other Invest.														
From Bank Loans														
Reductions														
To Savings Acct.														
To Other Invest.														
To Bank Loans														
Cash Bal.—Beginning	73		68		62		144		4		22		73	
Cash Bal.—Ending	68		62		144		4		22		18		18	

It can be readily seen from Figure 6-5 that daily cash balance fluctuations can create problems. Cash overdrafts appear four days in January. If the "float" in the cash account will not cover these overdrafts it will be necessary to draw on the savings account. Because of the timing of cash receipts in relation to payrolls, accounts payable and other items, it is necessary to borrow $100,000 from the bank for a few days. Later in the month it is possible to transfer a like amount to the savings account for a few days. This situation does not show up on the schedule of cash receipts and disbursements for the year 19X2, and illustrates emphatically the need for the daily cash control schedule. Past experience, including the carrying of large

Figure 6-5 continued

CASH CONTROL SCHEDULE														
													(page 4)	
			Month of January 19X2							Business Days (19-24)				
													Cumulative	
Items	19		20		21		22		23		24		Totals	
	Budget	Actual	Budget	Actual	Budget	Actual	Budget	Actual	Budget	Actual	Budget	Actual	Budget	Actual
Receipts														
Cash Sales	3		1		1		1		1		2		9	
Collections on Rec.—(30-Day)	4		4		3		0		2		1		14	
Misc. Income											1		1	
Sale of Equipment													—	
Interest—Temporary Investments													—	
Total	7		5		4		1		3		4		24	
Disbursements														
Salaries and Wages													—	
Payroll Taxes	32												32	
Fringe Benefits														
Taxes and Licenses													—	
Insurance													—	
Dividends													—	
Interest on Debt													—	
Mortgage Payments													—	
Equipment Purchases													—	
Income Taxes											90		90	
Accounts Payable													—	
Total	32		0		0		0		0		90		122	
Excess (Deficit) of Receipts Over Disbursements	(25)		5		4		1		3		(86)		(98)	
Additions														
From Savings Acct.											100		100	
From Other Invest.														
From Bank Loans														
Reductions														
To Savings Acct.														
To Other Invest.														
To Bank Loans														
Cash Bal.—Beginning	18		(7)		(2)		2		3		6		18	
Cash Bal.Ending	(7)		(2)		2		3		6		20		20	

cash balances, should have already alerted management to the probability of this type of short-term difficulty in respect to normal expenditures. It is also quite possible that planned or required expenditures for the future could create a similar situation not otherwise foreseen.

A schedule such as shown in Figure 6-5 makes provision for recording actual cash receipts and disbursements in a framework exactly like the budget. In a more detailed cash budget, a more sensitive measure can be taken of the actual cash situation. If it is noted that actual operating results are straying too far from the plan, appropriate adjustments can be

Figure 6-5 continued

CASH CONTROL SCHEDULE

(page 5)

Month of January 19X2 Business Days (25-26)

Items	25		26										Cumulative Totals	
	Budget	Actual	Budget	Actual	Budget	Actual	Budget	Actual	Budget	Actual	Budget	Actual	Budget	Actual
Receipts														
Cash Sales	2		1										46	
Collection on Rec.- (30-Day)	1		1										901	
Misc. Income			1										5	
Sale of Equipment													65	
Interest—Temporary Investments													—	
Total	3		3										1017	
Disbursements														
Salaries and Wages													340	
Payroll Taxes													68	
Fringe Benefits			5										20	
Taxes and Licenses			3										3	
Insurance													—	
Dividends													—	
Interest on Debt													—	
Mortgage Payments													4	
Equipment Purchases													90	
Income Taxes													—	
Accounts Payable													500	
Total	0		8										1025	
Excess (Deficit) of Receipts Over Disbursements	3		(5)										(8)	
Additions														
From Savings Acct.														
From Other Invest.														
From Bank Loans														
Reductions														
To Savings Acct.														
From Other Invest.														
To Bank Loans														
Cash Bal.—Beginning	20		23										26	
Cash Bal.—Ending	23		18										18	

made. In this illustration, actual receipts and disbursements have been entered daily for a few working days. The reader's attention is directed to the fifth, sixth and eighth business days. Because collections of receivables did not come up to expectations, it was necessary to defer payment of a portion of the accounts payable from the fifth day to the eighth day. Provision is made in the schedule to carrying forward unliquidated accounts as indicated. If liquidation could not be deferred, it would be necessary to draw on the savings account.

The format of Figure 6-5 is designed to facilitate the day-to-day control of cash in relation to the cash plan. In this illustration, budgeted and actual figures are sub-totaled by six-day weeks. This may be useless to some companies. Cumulative totals throughout the month could be more helpful in some cases. Since a daily cash balance is determined, sub-totaling and/or cumulative totaling may provide no worthwhile information.

This daily schedule is subject to considerable variety in design. Even greater variety will be found in the supporting working papers on schedules used to develop the essential item totals for each day. In this connection some procedural and/or accounting system changes may be necessary in order to gather information on cash receipts promptly and to maintain control over disbursements. This schedule can act as the control device for releasing company checks.

The Usefulness of Long-Range Projections

There is not much enthusiasm for making long-range cash projections in terms of receipts, disbursements and balances. In the case of cash projections, long-range will be considered to be two or more years. In the example at hand, the projections are carried forward six years. The primary reason for the lack of enthusiasm is that it is very difficult to project cash movement and balances very far in advance with any degree of accuracy.

Even though the task of projecting cash balances is difficult, the attempt should be made if there are planned major changes in the financial structure and/or in the composition of the inventories, plant, property and equipment of the company. Normally these changes will have too great an impact to be ignored. Even if some fairly "raw estimates" have to be made in the planning process, the projections should be carried out as far as feasible.

Long-Range Projections—An Illustration

Figure 6-6 sets forth a six-year projection of cash and marketable securities to be derived from operations. This type of figure cannot be prepared with the refinements indicated unless master budgets are first prepared for the periods in question. A good deal of abridgement of the items may be necessary if these budgets are not available; for example, the net change in the working capital items might be presented as one amount. In any case, some type of estimate of the funds to be derived from operations will have to be made in order to effect a worthwhile long-range projection involving major cash flow changes.

The detailed long-range projection illustrated here is set forth in Figure 6-7. In addition to the cash and marketable securities derived from operations, the projected receipts include cash derived from the sale of plant and equipment and the issuance of bonds. Cash from short-term bank loans is not included in the total receipts but is treated as a balancing item near the end of the figure. Likewise, the repayment of the short-term loans is deducted in the last section.

Certain items have been set forth separately in the disbursement section because of their uncertain impact on the cash picture in developing the projections. Income taxes, debt reduction and dividends are cases in point. When trying to reconcile the receipts and disbursements of large sums with debt retirement, interest charges, dividend payments, and the maintenance of appropriate bank balances, obviously, some flexibility may be required.

Such a projection as this, even though lacking the refinement and general accuracy of the current annual budget, will serve to point up problem areas in the financial plans being

Figure 6-6

LONG-RANGE PROJECTIONS

(000 omitted) Cash and Marketable Securities Derived From Operations Supporting Schedule 1

	Budget Year	19X3		19X4		19X5		19X6		19X7		19X8	
	19X2	Budget	Revised	Budget	Revised	Budget	Revised	Budget	Revised	Budget	Revised	Budget	Revised
Net Income per budgets (or estimates) before extraordinary items, income taxes, and interest on indebtedness	175	187		178		257		300		363		369	
Add (deduct) items neither requiring nor generating cash in the fiscal year:													
Depreciation	35	30		45		100		110		110		110	
Amortization—Goodwill	5	5		5		5		5		5		5	
Increase (Decrease) in:													
Accounts and Trade Notes Payable	(3)	0		4		5		6		3		1	
Accrued Taxes and Expenses	(1)	0		0		0		2		1		1	
Etc. (current liabilities)	—	—		—		—		—		—		—	
Decrease (Increase) in:													
Accounts and Trade Notes Receivable	4	2		0		(10)		(15)		(25)		(25)	
Inventories	9	1		0		(20)		(25)		(35)		(35)	
Prepaid Expenses	(1)	0		0		(2)		(3)		0		0	
Etc. (current assets)	—	—		—		—		—		—		—	
Total Cash and Marketable Securities Derived from Operations	223	225		232		335		380		422		426	

developed. This is particularly true in the case of large borrowings such as the issuance of bonds or long-term notes. Terms of repayment may have to be changed from the original plans because of the projected cash flow inward. In Figure 6-7, it will be noted that the bonds are being retired on a serial basis and the cash and marketable securities balances are being reduced annually in the process. It might be well worth the effort to carry the overall projection further than the six years illustrated in view of the fact that the annual cash balance is dropping rather rapidly. After all, one of the major objectives of cash management is to avoid unpleasant surprises of a financial nature.

The Importance of Good Bank Relations

Bank officers are generally quite sympathetic to the idea of sound cash management by their customers. It indicates to them that the odds for serious financial problems on the part of their customers will be greatly reduced. It will certainly facilitate the obtaining of loans when loans are needed. A variety of arrangements can be made with banks, by negotiation, to handle checking accounts on a minimum balance basis. Service charges for checks and deposits handled can be weighed against the interest that could be earned on maintained balances that may be suggested by the bank. A study of outstanding checks from day-to-day

Figure 6-7

LONG-RANGE PROJECTIONS Of Cash Receipts and Disbursements (000 Omitted)	Support Schedule #	Budget Year 19X2	19X3 Budget	19X3 Revised	19X4 Budget	19X4 Revised	19X5 Budget	19X5 Revised	19X6 Budget	19X6 Revised	19X7 Budget	19X7 Revised	19X8 Budget	19X8 Revised
Receipts														
Cash and Marketable Securities from Operations (Supporting Schedule # 1)		223	225		232		335		380		422		426	
Sale of Assets (detail)		105					300							
Sale of Capital Stock (detail)														
Sale of Bonds					2,000									
Issuance of Mortgages														
Other														
Total Receipts		328	225		2,232		635		380		422		426	
Disbursements														
Income Taxes		53	54		26		47		100		120		122	
Principal Reduction—Long-term debts (detail)		48	48		48		48		48		200		200	
Interest on Long-term Debt (detail)					80		160		160		152		128	
Dividends		60	60		60		60		60		64		64	
Acquisition of Plant and Equipment (detail)		90			1,850		100		10					
Other														
Total Disbursements		251	162		2,064		415		378		536		514	
Excess (Deficit) of Receipts Over Disbursements		77	63		168		220		2		(114)		(88)	
Cash and Marketable Securities—Beginning of Period		66	125		178		336		556		558		444	
Sub-Total		143	188		346		556		558		444		356	
Bank Loans (Add)		240	250		250									
Bank Loans Plus Interest Deduct)		(258)	(260)		(260)		—		—		—		—	
Cash and Marketable Securities—End of Period		125	178		336		556		558		444		356	

and/or measurement of bank balances with cash book balances will provide a measure of the size of the "float" in the account. Quite often considerable advantage may be taken of the "float" factor in "smoothing out" the effect of cash balance fluctuations. It will be noted in Figure 6-5 that a cash deficit was tolerated for four days, assuming the "float" would prevent an actual overdraft.

Summary

When the cash management process is to be attempted on a day-to-day (or week-to-week) basis for the first time, the amount of preparatory work involved may seem to outweigh the expected advantages. It may, indeed, in the first year. Once the cash flow patterns have been mapped out and inefficiencies in collections and payments rectified, it becomes simply a matter of updating the respective budgets and projections.

Certain changes in the accounting system may be worthwhile in order to obtain essential information on a timely basis for the cash management process. These changes will call for very prompt reporting of cash collections from the various cashiers' stations, branch offices and/or collecting agencies of whatever type. Also, the accounts payable operation will possibly have to be redesigned, in some respects, so as to provide reports on disbursements made daily. In turn, the accounts payable operation may have to make disbursements under guidelines received from the cash management office. Specific disbursements may be held up temporarily or rescheduled for early or later payment.

These system changes should subsequently facilitate the cash management process in such a way as to more than cover any additional operating cost and any one-time redesign costs. Once the cash management process becomes "built-in" as far as the whole administrative structure is concerned, full benefits will be received and, no doubt, be adjudged to be well worthwhile.

CHAPTER 7

EFFECTIVE INVENTORY CONTROL

Inventory control encompasses the activities undertaken to achieve and maintain both physical and accounting control including record-keeping, reporting, ordering, storing, manufacturing, and delivering inventory. Viewed from this standpoint, much of the effort of retailing, wholesaling and manufacturing companies is consumed with inventory, not a surprising circumstance considering the size of investment in inventory that firms of this type usually have.

Often, many smaller firms lack an adequate inventory policy, and as a consequence, their controls are lax or based on out-dated premises or circumstances. For example, some firms utilize inventory control techniques which may have been suitable for inventories at levels a fraction of the size now required. Other firms simply fail to adopt a sound inventory policy from the outset. As a result perhaps, firms of both types have built-in inefficiencies or cost excesses impairing their profitability. Because the practitioner servicing the smaller client or the firm's accountant will likely be called on to recommend an inventory control system, he or she will want a "refresher" in up-to-date inventory control techniques.

This chapter presents several inventory control techniques most commonly used that have been proven effective, and indicates how these control devices may be evaluated to determine if they have, in fact, been effective in a particular firm. The emphasis, then, is on accounting control as opposed to physical control. Obviously, there must be both, and physical control cannot be ignored, so problems peculiar to physical control are also presented in a later section of this chapter.

HOW CAN INVENTORY CONTROL SAVE MONEY?

Simply put, inventory control saves money (and adds to profit) by making certain that the firm has neither too much inventory nor too little, and that the inventory was acquired at the best possible price. Holding inventory carries a cost to the firm which is an aggregate of the following factors:

1. Lost opportunities to invest the equivalent of the cost of the inventory in another income-producing asset. At a very minimum this would equal the average inventory investment times the going rate of interest in low-risk bonds.
2. Storage costs, including rent (or depreciation), insurance, security, etc.
3. Property taxes.
4. Handling costs, including record-keeping and other clerical costs.
5. The risk that, while being held, the inventory will become obsolete.

For these reasons, the firm should not carry an overabundance of inventory.

There is also a cost of having too little inventory, called the cost of stock outs. This cost includes:

1. Lost profit on sales not made because inventory was not on hand. This cost may be minimized if the customer accepts a substitute; however, there may be an overall impact on customer confidence and goodwill, and consequently, further lost sales.
2. For manufacturing firms, production may be halted or disrupted.
3. Foregone volume discounts or special prices.
4. Added costs of special or rush orders.

From this it seems obvious that a firm produces the greatest profit by having an investment in inventory that is optimum, neither too great nor too small. Another fact is similarily obvious: not all of these costs are susceptible to ready measurement. The measurement issue and the problem of finding the optimum inventory will be dealt with in a later section of this chapter.

Finally, inventory control saves money by promoting the buying of inventory at the lowest possible prices. Buying at favorable prices is not simply a fortuitous event; rather it is the result of a carefully planned and judicious program aggressively pursued by the firm. Some principles or practices to be followed to obtain inventory at favorable prices probably will include the following:

1. Management must develop expertise in the purchasing function. Many larger firms have purchasing departments consisting of skilled professionals who have been trained primarily in purchasing. Smaller firms do not have individuals with such specialities. The expertise can be developed, however, by experience and study. One important point to be remembered by the management of smaller firms is that the purchasing function is not to be looked upon as a menial chore to be delegated to unmotivated or clerical personnel. The decisons made are management ones.

2. Management must have knowledge of the available markets. This may be a part of point one, but it is so critical as to deserve individual comment. Specialists, as described above, know the markets. How can small business management become knowledgeable? They can: (a) read trade and professional magazines; (b) attend industry trade fairs; and, (c) use the knowledge of friendly competitors and major suppliers.

3. Some specialized practices may be: (a) to develop and issue specifications and take bids or quotations; (b) to "shop" for suppliers and prices; and, (c) to take full advantage of volume, seasonal and cash discounts.

A comprehensive discussion of when and how much inventory to order will be found later in this chapter in the sections on Economic Order Quantity and Economic Order Point. Of course, no decision on inventory prices and quantities is complete without also considering quality.

Inventory Control Systems—Perpetual Inventories

Perhaps the best method of controlling inventory, once on hand, is a perpetual inventory system. The decision to install a perpetual system must be tempered by its cost. The decision includes not only whether records are to be kept as to quantities but also as to price. Records of quantities and/or prices are maintained either manually or through electronic data processing equipment. Manual systems require that individual record cards be maintained for each classification of inventory. Purchases are added to existing quantities and sales are shown as reductions. A typical perpetual inventory record card may take the form shown in Figure 7-1.

Figure 7.1: **Perpetual Inventory Record Card**

DESCRIPTION: Carburetors **LOCATION:** Warehouse

MODEL NO.: MP 3861 **ROW:** 8 **BIN:** 13

DATE	**IN**		**OUT**		**BALANCE**	
	QUANTITY	UNIT COST	QUANTITY	UNIT COST	QUANTITY	UNIT COST

It may be noted that a full description and the location of the item are shown as well as a record of units purchased and sold. A column for units on order and one for units reserved may be used. When included, unit cost of the balance will depend on the inventory costing method used by the firm. If desired, a total cost column can be provided beside the unit cost column.

Some perpetual inventory record cards contain information on temporary stock relocations. For example, a high degree of efficiency in keeping the cards posted and up-to-date probably requires that they be physically located near the inventory, say in a central warehouse location or office area. Showroom areas and branch locations often do not lend themselves to this kind of proximity, and the card may be designed to show items on hand in warehouse and those on display. Of course, if a sale is made from display merchandise, this information must promptly find its way to the card. This is sometimes accomplished by supplemental records kept in the sales area, perhaps by the cash register, or by use of a sophisticated cash register capable of accepting inventory code numbers and units, as well as prices. In the former instance, the supplemental record is transmitted to the warehouse daily for posting. In the latter case, the cash register tape is used, and inventory cards are maintained and posted by code numbers rather than by descriptive designation.

The mechanics of perpetual inventory record-keeping are greatly reduced by use of computerized systems. In some automated systems, electronic cash registers are on-line with computer storage discs. An entry into the cash register provides instantaneous inventory reduction, and in some cases, with pre-programmed order points also stored, triggers purchase order data for stock replenishment. Some industries, notably the retail grocery industry, have established universal product identifier codes. The sensitized codes are imprinted on the packaging materials.

Electronic scanners "read" the code, and in on-line systems, accomplish inventory reduction and purchase order data. While this approach may not be applicable to smaller firms, the equipment is available and inventory can be entered manually by code number into cash registers to achieve the same end. The decision to computerize a perpetual inventory system and avoid the cost of a manually-operated one is a capital budgeting decision and may be approached using techniques described in Chapter 5.

As an inventory control device, a properly maintained perpetual system has two principal advantages:

1. A perpetual system provides ready information on the quantity of inventory on hand, its location, costs, etc.
2. Inventory shrinkage can be easily computed by comparing actual counts with perpetual cards.

Perpetual systems also yield inventory data for interim financial statements without the necessity of monthly physical inventories. In addition, perpetual records assist in the actual inventory taking in two ways. First of course, when written unit cost data is available on the perpetual card, it is unnecessary to mark the cost on inventory items individually or to cost inventory sheets. Second, the annual inventory taking and its concomitant cost can be partly avoided by a policy of routine physical counts of classes of inventory and correction of perpetual cards on a staggered basis throughout the year. Naturally, computerized systems are even more efficient.

There are obvious disadvantages with perpetual systems. When items of inventory are numerous, the cost of the record-keeping may be prohibitive. Computer-based systems are usually quite expensive and therefore not feasible for smaller firms. Low value items are probably not worth the cost of controlling through perpetual record-keeping. A perpetual system can easily fail unless management has made a vigorous commitment to maintain it. The problem of keeping perpetual records for inventory of low or moderate value may be solved by what has come to be known as the ABC System.

Using the Control

The ABC Method

The ABC method is a method of establishing the portions of the inventory worthy of extraordinary control measures, those over which ordinary controls will be exercised, and that part of inventory requiring minimal control. The ABC method is not based on the cost of the inventory item alone, but also takes into account its usage. For example, a moderately priced, but high usage item may be more carefully controlled than an expensive but rarely used one. The degree of control, then, is based on the *total* value of a category of inventory rather than on unit costs. An illustration of the application of the ABC method of classifying inventory may be of help.

The annual dollar usage of each item of inventory must be determined by multiplying the unit cost of the item by the number of those units used (or sold) in a year. Once the dollar usage is known, the amounts are arranged in tabular form in descending order, highest total dollar usage first, and so on. The tabulation should provide a cumulative dollar usage column. A sample tabulation follows:

Dollar Value Usage of Inventory

Classification of Inventory	Number of Units	% of Total Units	Unit Cost	Dollar Value of Usage	% of Total Value
(Code or	93	1%	$116.30	$10,816	21%
Description)	120	3%	85.10	21,028	41%
	318	7%	30.30	30,663	60%
	924	20%	10.10	39,996	78%
	1,620	41%	4.15	46,719	92%
	2,117	70%	1.18	49,217	97%
	2,236	100%	.73	50,849	100%

The impact of certain items of the inventory on the total dollar value usage may be easily seen. Seven percent of the units account for 60% of the value. Only 20% of the units make-up 78% of the total value. From this tabulation, the inventory may be grouped into three general categories: "A," which may consist of the first three kinds of inventory; "B," consisting of the 924 units; and "C," which is all remaining classifications, accounting for only 8% of total dollar value of usage.

Controls for each category may now be implemented. For example, category "A" may be controlled by a perpetual inventory system. Less precise methods may be used for "B" items, while "C" items may get only periodic attention. Of course, the necessity of keeping high value items in locked storage or segregated in some way is not eliminated, but the most precise accounting controls are exercised over the inventory items that contribute the greatest amount to sales.

Some Other Tools for Controlling Inventory Effectively

In addition to full or partial inventory systems, such as a perpetual system or estimation techniques, other tools of inventory control are available. Analysis of certain general ledger accounts is one control method. Although additional record-keeping may be required, maintaining separate accounts for categories of sales can provide useful information.

Changes in the volume of sales of a particular class of inventory may appear to signal a need to carry more or less of that item; however, close analysis of the volume change may indicate that increase in the sales of a particular item, for example, was a large, one-time sale, not requiring a build-up in that inventory, but simply replacement. Analysis of sales accounts over time can indicate trends of shifts in customer buying habits. A proper course of action may be to reduce stocks in particular categories to avoid obsolescence.

Sales returns can show customer dissatisfaction with certain inventory items. If analysis shows that the basis for the dissatisfaction is the nature of the item, perhaps because of poor quality or unsuitability, the firm may seek substitutes or corrective action on the part of the supplier. Difficulties of this type with suppliers over the quality of a product can be uncovered through an analysis of purchase returns. The purchase returns account can also indicate over-buying and poor judgment, as well as poor product quality.

While the sales and sales returns accounts can point to possible obsolescence, visual control is often very valuable in avoiding or anticipating obsolescence and shop wear. Goods should be continually rotated with new items to the rear of old. In most industries, a FIFO goods flow is essential. Responsible personnel should be alert to dated goods and evidence of spoilage, soiling, or discoloration. Boxes, cans, etc. need to be kept dust free, dry, and so forth.

Adequacy of storage is an inventory control device. Crowded or poorly laid out inventory storage areas are contributors to loss of both physical and accounting control. Often inventory is actually lost and not found until its sales potential is substantially diminished. Warehouse and showroom layout is a fairly complex problem which cannot be adequately dealt with here, but at a minimum the storage area should provide:

1. Adequate space for each category of goods.
2. Appropriate storage conditions, i.e., refrigeration, darkness, off-the-floor, locked vaults, ventilation, etc.
3. A schematic or some other centrally located indication of the location of each type of inventory.
4. An individual charged with the responsibility of the physical location and care of the inventory.
5. Separate receiving and shipping areas.
6. A plenitude of safety devices such as, fire extinguishers, ladders, guardrails, and such personal safety items as are needed to comply with governmental regulations at least minimally.

A discussion of inventory storage would be incomplete without mention of inventory insurance. Insurance is an important corollary to good inventory management. Few firms can afford to be self-insured, and stock insurance is available through a variety of carriers and in almost infinite form. The monthly reporting form is a popular type of insurance that has the advantage of keeping premium outlay proportionate to the inventory on hand. Under this method the inventory value is reported and the premium is paid monthly. The premium rate is established by the carrier. Physical inventories on a monthly basis or perpetual systems are not required; rather, the inventory may be estimated using the gross profit or retail method. The insurance usually covers both fire and theft risk and may contain co-insurance provisions. Often, the policy has a dollar risk limit which can be raised or lowered without premium penalty. Recent trends have been toward broader coverages such as blanket or "umbrella" policies wherein a single, and often large, amount of risk is assumed by the carrier on property, including inventory, for a single premium. It is common for these policies to cover peripheral risks such as business interruption. The premium rate is in large measure predicated on the quality of control over inventory; thus, good inventory control can lower premium cost.

WHAT RECORD-KEEPING IS REQUIRED?

The more precise the inventory control, the more record-keeping is required. Information needed to support perpetual inventory has been shown and explained. Other documentation is needed aside from these records. A list of some typical records, or forms, maintained by some firms and a brief explanation of the function of each may be of help. It would be good to remember that there is a trade-off between the cost of record-keeping and the benefit to be derived. Some commonly used forms are:

Purchase Request—This form is used most frequently in fairly large firms when a purchasing department exists apart from the warehousing function. The purchase request is used to prompt the purchasing department to order goods and is usually prepared by a stock clerk. It contains precise information on type and quantity of goods needed. Sometimes the form includes a date on which the items are needed.

Purchase Order—Purchase orders are formal documents sent to vendors. They are offers to buy and usually include price as well as type and quantity of goods and date wanted. In nonprofit organizations, purchase orders are often recorded in the accounting records as encumbrances. Purchase orders are invaluable for controlling purchases and are used to compare with shipments received for correctness and so forth.

Receiving Report—This is the official record of the receipt of goods. It may include a notation of where the goods are stored, besides information as to what, how much, and from whom received. Aside from its informational content, receiving reports document the physical receipt of goods prior to payment. In a good system of internal control, no invoice can be paid until it is compared with the purchase request, purchase order, and receiving report. Entries in perpetual records, if used, are made at that point.

Material Requisition—Many firms use a material requisition as authority to move inventory from its warehouse location. It originates within departments such as production, if the goods are to be placed in process; sales, if to go on display; branches, if to be transferred internally; or service, if to be used for maintenance.

Debit Memorandum—Debit memoranda are prepared to support goods returned to vendors. A typical form includes data on quantities and description of goods being returned and a notation of the authorization of the selling firm to do so. Proper inventory control requires documentary evidence of returned goods in order to: (a) assure proper payment of invoices; and, (b) prevent misappropriation of inventory.

Freight bills and vendors' invoices are also essential, and of course, they originate outside the firm.

Reports necessary for control of inventory include: a periodic (at the very least, annual) physical inventory report showing prices and quantities; reports of lost or stolen goods; obsolete, damaged and worn goods reports; and, of course, reports showing the amount of various kinds of inventory on hand as required by management for planning orders, etc. In fully computerized systems, some of these reports, and especially the latter, are automatic.

Some Special Problems of Controlling Manufacturing Inventories and What to do About Them

The problems of physical control of inventories in a manufacturing operation are nearly the same as those for trading concerns. Differences are found in the need to control waste and spoilage during manufacture and product quality.

Perpetual records are an excellent means of identifying waste and spoilage. Some waste may be expected, of course, but extraordinary waste or spoilage deserves attention and correction and could be the result of:

1. Sub-standard material.
2. Careless or ill-trained employees.
3. Production line inefficiencies.

Quality control is a broad subject, too broad in fact to be treated satisfactorily here. Suffice it to say that the objective of quality control is to assure that the final product conforms to the proper specifications, for example, size, shape, weight, color, consistency, etc., and that neither too much nor too little of any ingredient goes into the product. Various methods of quality control, of which physical inspection is the most common, are used in practice. The selection of units to be inspected lends itself readily to the application of random sampling for variables as is described in Chapter 3. The point is that both materials and labor need to be controlled during all phases of production. The degree of success obtained often determines the profitability and, indeed, the continued existence of the firm.

Accounting control of manufactured inventories, as opposed to physical control, is somewhat more complex than control of inventories of trading concerns, mainly because of the characteristics of the manufacturing process. In the first instance, there are three inventories to be controlled: raw materials, work-in-progress and finished goods inventories. Second, there are three elements to work-in-progress and finished goods: materials, labor and overhead. Some techniques of accounting for manufacturing processes are described in detail in Chapters 11, 12, and 13.

EOQ—A Simplified Model for Controlling the Number of Inventory Orders

Earlier it was stated that a firm can produce the greatest profit, all other things equal, by maintaining an "optimum" inventory, one which is neither too large nor too small. Finding the "optimum" amount of inventory is a matter of determining how much inventory to order and when to order it. How much to order, economic order quantity (EOQ), will be considered here. When to order is the subject of the next section.

How much inventory to order is contingent on many factors, including the reliability of suppliers and the perishability of the product. Within these limits, it is possible to compute an economic order quantity which is a combination of the least costs of ordering inventory and the costs of carrying it. Obviously, these costs are competing. For example, larger orders are more economical than smaller orders; however, larger orders result in more inventory on hand. Continuing this line of thought, if a firm desires to order 5,000 units in a year's time, it can make 5,000 orders of one unit each, one order of 5,000 units, or some number of orders in quantities between these two extremes. Obviously, the first alternative minimizes carrying costs while the second minimizes ordering costs. Neither alternative may be desirable, however, because the alternate cost in both instances will be a maximum.

To use the EOQ formulation, the firm must quantify its order and carrying costs. Order costs consist of salaries of purchasing and clerical personnel, telephone and mailing costs and any other costs directly associated with placing orders. Usually, only direct costs are considered, and such indirect costs as rent, president's salary, etc. are not prorated. Proration may be required, however. In cases where the firm has a purchasing department, all its costs must be considered. Alternatively, smaller firms may have an individual who has purchasing as only one of his duties. In the later instance, the salary must be apportioned between the purchase and other functions. Salaries include directly attributable fringe benefits such as pension contributions, and payroll costs such as matching social security. Next, the ordering costs must be expressed on a per-purchase-order basis. This is ordinarily simply a matter of dividing the accumulated costs by the average annual output of purchase orders.

Some costs of carrying inventory were listed early in this chapter. This list is repeated here, along with a discussion of how each element may be measured.

A dollar investment in inventory means that the funds cannot simultaneously be invested in another income-producing activity. There are a range of possibilities for estimating the rate of return lost on the investment, from a minimum rate equal to that yielded by low risk government securities to the highest rate of return desired by the company. Many firms find neither of these realistic; rather, the firm may estimate its cost of capital, and use that as the alternative return on the inventory investment. An example of estimating cost of capital may help.

Assume a firm earns $60,000 before interest and taxes.[1] Further assume that the annual interest is $9,500 (based on an average debt of $100,000), and that income is taxed at an effective rate of 31%. The income is distributed as follows:

Earnings Before Interest And Taxes	$60,000
Interest (Return on Debt)	9,500
Net Before Taxes	$50,500
Income Taxes (Times 31%)	15,655
Net Income (Return on Equity)	$34,845

It is also assumed that debt totals $100,000 and that owners' equity is $200,000.[2] The cost of capital may be approximated by the following formula:

$$C = CD\left(\frac{D}{D + E}\right) + CE\left(\frac{E}{D + E}\right)$$

where C = the overall cost of capital[3], CD = Cost of Debt, CE = Cost of Equity, D = Amount of Debt, and E = Amount of Equity.

[1]This is usually *expected* earnings, but may be based on historical performance.

[2]Ideally these figures are market values. For smaller firms estimates of market value for either debt or equity may be impossible. A possible substitute for market value is book value.

[3]A weighted average, weighted between the cost of debt and the cost of equity.

Solving for C:

$$C = .095\left(\frac{\$100{,}000}{\$300{,}000}\right) + .1742\left(\frac{\$200{,}000}{\$300{,}000}\right),\ C = .0317 + .1161,\ C = .1478$$

$$\left(\text{CE was determined: } \frac{\$34{,}845}{\$200{,}000} = .1742;\ \text{CD} = \frac{\$9{,}500}{\$100{,}000} = .095\right)$$

As an alternative to this computation, the firm may adopt a "target" rate of return for use. The illustrative firm, for example, may establish 20% as its target rate. The rate, however determined, is applied to the inventory investment per unit as a part of carrying costs. Assume that the average cost of a unit of inventory is $6.00, and using the cost of capital as computed above, then the lost investment income per unit is $.89 (.1478 × $6.00).

Another element in the cost of carrying inventory is storage cost, which ordinarily consists of rent (or warehouse depreciation), insurance and security. As an example, if the annual rent attributable to inventory storage is $12,000, insurance on inventory is $2,000 and a security guard costs $6,000, then the total storage cost equals $20,000. Assuming an average of 40,000 units of inventory on hand, the unit cost is $.50 ($20,000 ÷ 40,000).

A third factor contributing to the cost of carrying inventory is property tax. If the millage is 146 per 1,000 of inventory, then on an average inventory investment of $240,000, property taxes amount to $350. On a per unit basis, taxes are $.009 ($350 ÷ 40,000 units).

Handling and other costs associated with holding the inventory need to be estimated. In the example, suppose a per unit cost of $.01.

Finally, there is the cost of the risk of obsolescence while the inventory is on hand. One approach to measurement may be to compare the cost of inventory with current replacement costs. Another may be to periodically estimate any obsolete inventory on hand, related to some time period. This is a difficult cost to quantify, and from a practical point of view, is often ignored. In the example here, it is assumed that the risk is minimal.

A summary of the carrying costs is as follows:

	Per Unit Of Inventory
Cost of Lost Investment Income On Investment in Inventory – $6.00 × .1478	$ .89
Cost of Storage	.50
Cost of Taxes	.009
Cost of Handling, etc.	.01
Total Carrying Costs	$1.409
Rounded To	$1.41

To continue the example, ordering costs are estimated as follows:

Salaries:

Personnel	Percentage of Time Devoted to Purchasing	Annual Salary Plus Fringes	
Clerical	10%	7,000	700
Assistant Manager	33⅓%	18,000	$6,000
Warehouseman	15%	10,000	1,500
		Total Salaries	$8,200
Telephone			800
Postage			200
Stationery and Other			200
	Estimated Total Ordering Costs		$9,400
	Estimated Number of Purchase Orders per Year		1,880
	Average Cost Per Order		$5.00

The traditional formula for EOQ is:

$$EOQ = \sqrt{\frac{2 \times S \times C}{I}}$$

Where: S = The Annual Sales in Units
C = Cost Per Purchase Order
I = Carrying Cost Per Unit

Assuming that 300,000 units are sold per year, the EOQ is computed as follows:

$$EOQ = \sqrt{\frac{2 \times 300{,}000 \times \$5}{\$1.41}}$$

$$EOQ = \sqrt{\frac{3{,}000{,}000}{\$1.41}} = \sqrt{2{,}127{,}660}$$

$$EOQ = 1{,}459$$

Thus, the most economical order size is 1,459 units. This is convenient inasmuch as it approximates 120 dozen. Realistically, the standard order quantity may be designated as dozens or hundreds. In either case, judgment must be exercised. A tool to assist in comparing the cost of ordering varying quantities is a tabulation similar to the one that follows:

Table for Approximating Ordering Costs by Size of Order

Size of Order	500	1,000	1,500	2,000	3,000
Average Inventory (Units)[4]	250	500	750	1,000	1,500
Number of Orders $\left(\frac{300{,}000}{\text{order size}}\right)$	600	300	200	150	100
Annual Carrying Cost ($1.41 × Avg. Inventory)	$353	$705	$1,058	$1,410	$2,115
Annual Ordering Cost (No. of Orders × $5.00)	$3,000	$1,500	$1,000	750	500
Total Annual Cost	$3,353	$2,205	$2,058	$2,160	$2,615

Comparing the EOQ computed by use of the formula with the tabular presentation indicates that the two costs, the cost of carrying inventory and the cost of ordering it, are minimized at about 1,500 units per order. Two points need to be made from the example. First, the illustrative firm appears to be placing far too many orders, about 1,880, and far too few units per order, about 160 (300,000 ÷ 1,880). Second, all the costs used in the EOQ formula are variable costs; thus, it is an implicit assumption that per-order ordering costs will remain at $5.00 each. This, of course, assumes that all the elements used in determining ordering costs: salaries, telephone, postage, stationery, etc., will cease except to the extent of $5.00 per order.[5] The total ordering costs, then, will decrease from $9,400 to $1,000 (200 orders of 1,500 units each at $5.00 per order.) This is, certainly, a desirable consequence.

Another assumption implicit in the EOQ formula is that the inventory has a high degree of homogeneity. In firms with one or a few different types of inventory, the assumption may be valid. This is especially true in cases where the inventory in each of the classes may well be homogeneous. Alternatively, firms with a variety of kinds of inventory obtained from a variety of suppliers will find it difficult to either establish an "average" inventory price or to allocate costs so that an economic order quantity for a particular type of inventory is practical. It seems obvious that low cost inventory, because it requires a small investment, may be purchased in great quantity and infrequently, whereas an inventory of high value perhaps ought to be purchased more frequently, and in smaller quantities.

The point of this discussion is this: Perhaps the best use to which EOQ can be put in firms whose inventory is heterogeneous is to find an approximation of the number of orders which is most economical for the firm to make. In the illustrative firm, it was fairly obvious that too much effort and cost was being expended in ordering. This alone, is valuable information and is worth the effort of accumulating data to place into the formula.

Finally, there is the problem of the necessary use of estimates in the EOQ equation. How much impact is there on the outcome of an error in the estimates? Is the firm likely to get bad or even false information if it "misestimates" by a substantial margin? An example will

[4]Average inventory is assumed to be one-half of the order. The basis for this assumption seems sound, for the inventory will diminish to zero and another order will arrive. (Of course, the inventory may diminish to a safety level only, but this will not change the outcome.)

[5]Plainly, the costs of salaries and the other costs will not literally *cease;* rather they will be directed toward other productive areas. The point is that there is an assumption of perfect variability of costs in the EOQ Equation.

provide answers to both these questions. Returning to the EOQ equation in the example for the illustrative firm, it may be remembered that ordering costs were estimated at $5.00 per order, average unit cost of inventory was $6.00, carrying costs per unit were $1.41 and that 300,000 units were expected to be sold. The EOQ was determined as:

$$EOQ = \sqrt{\frac{2 \times 300{,}000 \times \$5}{\$1.41}} = 1{,}459$$

Suppose that an error was made in estimating ordering costs, and that they were estimated at $10 per order. The EOQ is:

$$EOQ = \sqrt{\frac{2 \times 300{,}000 \times \$10}{\$1.41}} = 2{,}063$$

Notice that a 100% error in the ordering cost resulted in only about 40% error in the quantity ordered. Of course, 40% is significant; however, the effect on total cost is much less. For example, the cost of ordering 1,500 units from the table is $2,058. The cost of ordering quantities of 2,063 is as follows:

Size of Order	2,063
Average Inventory	1,031
Number of Orders $\left(\frac{300{,}000}{2{,}063}\right)$	145
Annual Carrying Cost ($1.41 × 1,031)	$1,454
Annual Order Cost (145 × $5)[6]	725
	$2,179

Thus, a 100% error in ordering cost results in a cost differential of less than 6% $\frac{(\$2{,}179 - \$2{,}058),}{\$2{,}058}$

and even if the firm orders in quantities of 2,063 units, the additional cost over what is considered "optimum" is minimal.

[6]It should be noted that the *actual* order cost is $5.00 per order, not $10.00.

Four Methods of Determining When to Order Inventory

Knowing the quantity to order is only one-half of the problem of acquiring inventory. The companion issue is when to order, that is, at what point in the diminishing quantity of inventory left on hand is an order placed? There are several possible answers to this question; one is found in the calculation of the economic order point (EOP). Other systems of when to order inventory are in use and will be discussed first.

The Visual Inspection Method

The least sophisticated of the "other" methods in use for determining when to order is simply a visual review of the status of each inventory item. This means that whoever is responsible for inventory (or someone assigned to the task) visually inspects inventory and orders items believed to need replenishment. Visual inspection has limited usefulness for obvious reasons, and should be confined to low value, low usage items where shortages are not critical. A variation of this technique often used by small firms is to allow vendor's representatives to call periodically. At that time, inventory supplied by their company is reviewed and orders are placed if appropriate. Again, this is a highly unscientific and subjective approach, not to mention the cost of lost time dealing with the myriad of representatives who call. A not uncommon additional variation is to allow the vendor's representative himself to order (or furnish on the spot) inventory, subject to constraints imposed by management. An application of this latter technique is often found in smaller grocery stores where the bakery vendor is permitted to "fill a counter" with his products. It has the advantage of saving management's time and the serious disadvantage of the possible loss of control by management over this inventory.

Reserve Stock System

The reserve stock method, sometimes called the two-bin system, is one in which each category of inventory is stored in two bins, or two physically separated areas. The second bin contains inventory equal to the reorder point and is not used until items in the first bin are exhausted. At that time an order is placed. During the time lapse between when the order is placed, and when it is received, the second or reserve bin is being depleted. This technique presupposes a determination of what the reorder point is, considering lead times and other variables. Methods of establishing reorder points and lead times are discussed fully later in this chapter. The reserve stock system minimizes record-keeping costs in that once the reorder point is established, a visual inspection is all that is needed to trigger a requisition. Whether the system is satisfactory or not depends on the attention and reliability of warehouse personnel, and this is, of course, its chief disadvantage.

Minimum—Maximum System

Abbreviated as "mini-max," the minimum-maximum system is predicated on a minimum quantity of inventory equal to the reorder point. The maximum is the minimum quantity plus the EOQ calculated as described earlier. A reorder occurs when inventory is depleted to the minimum or below, and the quantity ordered equals the maximum less inventory on hand at the time of reorder. An example may help. From the illustration of computing EOQ, the firm's EOQ was about 1,500 units. Assume that a minimum quantity on hand has been determined to be 300 units. Thus, the maximum is 1800 (1,500 + 300) and the minimum 300 (the reorder point.) Further assume that the last sale depletes inventory to 240 units. The quantity to be ordered is 1,560 (the maximum, 1,800, less the quantity on hand, 240). As is true in the two-bin method, minimum record-keeping is necessary, and satisfactory results can be obtained provided the maximum and minimum quantities are accurately determined and personnel are efficient.

The Economic Order Point Method

Large inventories necessitating perpetual inventory systems do not lend themselves to visual systems of determining when to reorder. Rather, periodic inventory status reports, perhaps manually prepared if not automated, are issued and reviewed and the decision is made to order. The decision needs to be made on a rational basis using objective data. This does not mean that non-perpetual systems can be based on irrational grounds or on purely subjective judgments. In fact, the opposite is true. Knowledge of reorder points and economic order quantities is necessary in any effective system. It is simply that the larger the inventory the greater is the need for automatic reordering and the less feasible is personalized attention to reordering, quantities to order, etc. Consider the time expenditure necessary for the purchasing agent (or other responsible individual) to personally review records of several hundred types of inventory to determine when to reorder each type.

An alternative to a personal review of each inventory type for the quantity to be ordered was discussed in the section on EOQ. An alternative for determining at what point to order is the economic order point (EOP). The EOP equation can be as complex or as simple as the firm desires, but in any case it must incorporate the following:

1. The EOQ.
2. Lead Time.
3. Average Usage (Sales).

A complication which will be discussed is the need for safety stock to minimize the cost of stockouts.

Lead time is the lag between when an order is made and when it is received. Average usage is the average number of units placed in production or sold in a given time period. Lead time can be estimated by knowing the habits and customs of vendors and shippers, and production departments. Domestic goods will likely have shorter lead times than imported items. Local suppliers will probably deliver inventory more quickly than out-of-town suppliers. With a little experience, management can estimate lead time with considerable accuracy. In some cases, the terms of the sale provide shipment or delivery dates.

Average usage is more difficult to quantify. In the simple case where sales (or production) are uniform through time, average usage is simply a matter of dividing annual sales in units by the time segment desired, usually a week. For example, if sales per year are 100,000 units, then the average weekly usage is 1,923 units. Unfortunately, the simple case rarely appears in practice, that is, sales are not made uniformly each week. Thus, in one week, 600 units may be sold and in the next week, 2,500 units. Because of the lack of uniformity of sales in a given time period, many firms hold a safety stock.

Safety stock is a hedge against the cost of stockouts and is necessitated because usage of inventory is not uniform. Some of the costs of being out of inventory were listed early in this chapter. Obviously, these costs are quite difficult to measure for several reasons, but primarily because customers may take substitutes for out-of-stock inventory, or they may simply wait until new inventory is received. Whether it is because of this predicted customer behavior, or because management shies away from attempting to quantify its cost and consequently is ignorant of its full impact, many firms are tolerant of a certain amount of the risk of stockouts. Thus, they are willing to be out-of-stock on occasions to offset the more readily measurable costs of carrying inventory.

Once the factors of lead time, average usage and safety stock are established, the economic order point can be determined. The computation is as follows: EOP = L (U) + S When:

L = lead time in weeks. (It could be days or months. If so, the usage must also be stated in the same time frame.)
U = Average number of units used per week.
S = Safety Stock

Determining Lead Time

Estimating lead time poses one special problem; that is, while experience will yield good information on shipping policies, transit times, etc., for trading concerns, often there are many suppliers to the firm, few of which will deliver on identical schedules. Two approaches to the problem may be taken. One, an *average* lead time for all suppliers may be computed. Naturally, this introduces an error factor to be tolerated. Two, lead times may be determined for individual larger suppliers. This, of course, means that the EOP will be different for each of several types of inventory according to the supplier. The latter approach is preferred because of the additional accuracy achieved. The time delay between ordering and delivery should be watched carefully and recorded. In a relatively short time, a definite trend will appear. (Actually, this procedure should be done by the firm anyway as an indicator of efficiency of the order process and to optimize distribution channels. For example, the firm may find more efficient carriers or modes of transportation as well as finding shippers who can deliver more quickly.)

Determining Average Usage and Safety Stock

When sales (or production) are not uniform in a given time period, an average weekly usage computation may be the only practical one, but even assuming that refinement, the firm is left with some weeks where many more than the "average" are used, thus risking frequent stockouts. One approach is to develop a frequency distribution table for each item of inventory.

As an example, assume the sale of 12,000 units of product annually. The mathematical average per week is 231 units. A study of the frequency of sales made each week for a year reveals the following:

SALES FREQUENCY DISTRIBUTION

Number of Units Sold	Number of Weeks
75	2
100	2
125	2
150	1

Number of Units Sold	Number of Weeks
175	5
200	5
225	12
250	10
275	3
300	3
325	4
350	0
375	2
400	1

Analysis of the distribution indicates that sales of units are clustered around the average of 231; in fact, in 22 of the 52 weeks, 225 or 250 units per week were sold. However, there were 4 weeks in each of which 325 units were sold, two weeks when 375 units were sold and one week of sales of 400 units. Obviously, because of these weeks of much higher than average sales volume, ordering based on the mean usage of 231 will result in stockouts. The company may be willing to take a minimum risk of being out-of-stock. For example, in only 3 of the 52 weeks were more than 325 units sold; thus, the firm may not anticipate the extremes of selling 375 or 400 in a week.

EOQ and EOP—A Comprehensive Example

A numerical example incorporating the frequency distribution just presented may clarify some points and facilitate application of EOQ and EOP equations. Assume the following data:

Annual Sales (Units)	12,000
Average Weekly Usage (Units)	231
Cost Per Purchase Order	$4.00
Carrying Cost Per Unit	$.50
Lead Time	1 Week

$$\text{EOQ} = \sqrt{\frac{2 \times 12{,}000 \times \$4}{.50}}$$

$$\text{EOQ} = \sqrt{192{,}000}$$

$$\text{EOQ} = 438 \text{ Units (Rounded)}$$

$$\text{EOP} = 1\,(231) + 94$$

$$\text{EOP} = 325$$

A safety stock of 94 units is determined as follows: The firm has elected to tolerate stockouts under the extraordinary conditions of selling 375 units two weeks of the year and 400 units once. It wishes to be protected for the occasions on which 325 units are sold in a

Figure 7-2

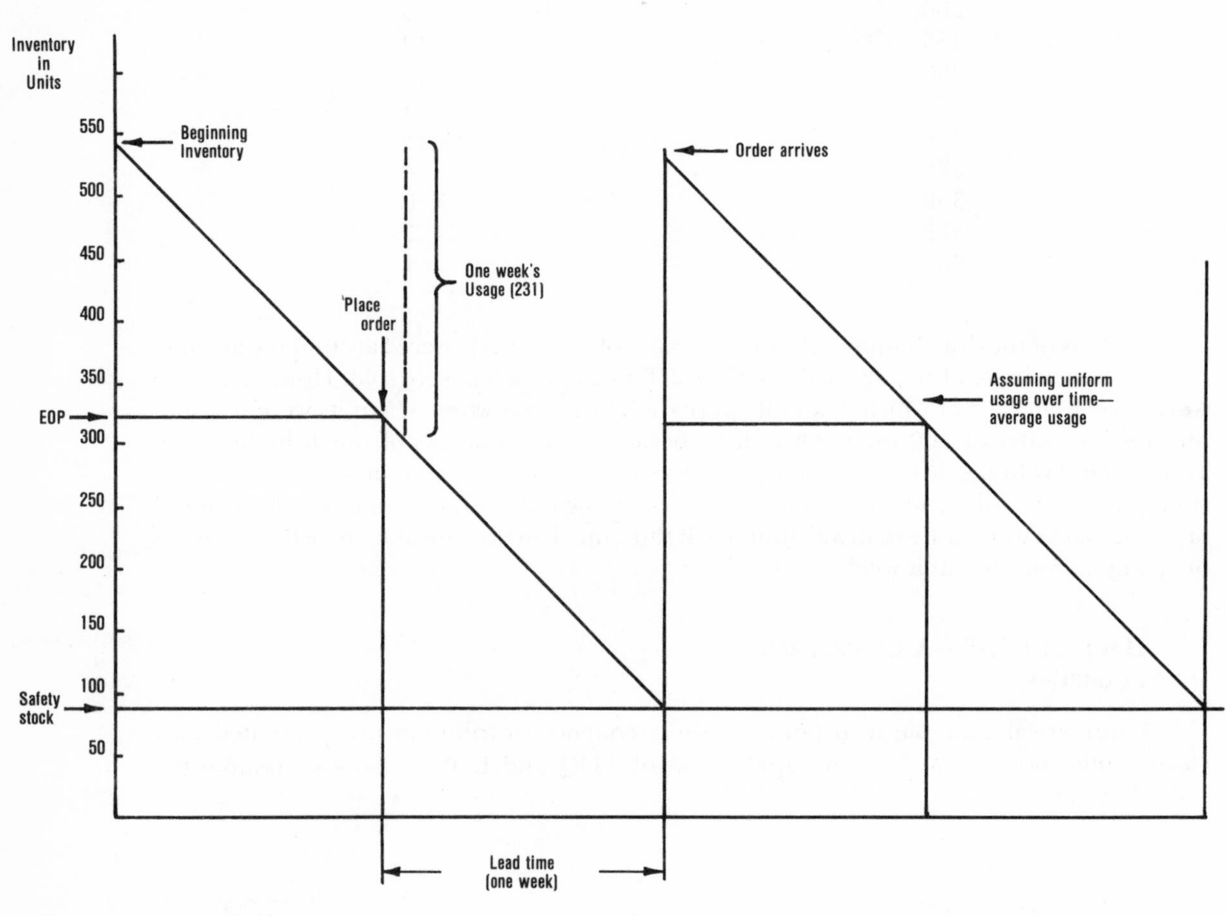

week's time. Thus, a safety stock of 94 units (325 − 231, the weekly average) is indicated. If the firm can tolerate no stockouts, it should maintain a safety stock of 169 (400 − 231). A graphic illustration of the inventory movement with a safety stock of 94 is presented in Figure 7-2 assuming a beginning inventory of the EOQ plus safety stock.

From a practical point of view, the principal disadvantage of EOQ and EOP for smaller companies with a wide variety of inventory items is the need to compute EOQ and EOP for each type of inventory. Clothing stores, for example, may find a need to develop sales frequency distributions by *size* as well as by category.

Perhaps a practical solution is to use the ABC system, using the EOQ and EOP equations for type "A" inventory items only and less sophisticated approaches to types "B" and "C". There are approaches to aggregating sales frequency distributions, rather than by individual item, which are statistically sound. An excellent coverage of some of these may be found in *Scientific Inventory Management,* by Joseph Buchan and Ernest Koenigsberg.

Some Techniques for Evaluating the Firm's Inventory Control System

Once installed, how effective is the inventory control system in operation? Assume that the firm applies some of the control techniques described in this chapter. How can its success be measured? Several ways are available. One method, of course, is to measure and compare the costs the inventory system is supposed to minimize. These costs include inventory carrying and ordering costs. If objective data exists to measure the cost of stockouts, this cost, too, may be compared on a "before and after" basis. Returning to an earlier example in this chapter, it may be recalled that the illustrative firm measured its carrying and ordering costs. Ordering costs were estimated to be a total of $9,400 per year. By reducing the number of annual orders from 1,880 per year to 200, the firm reduced its ordering costs to $1,000. While this is a dramatic reduction used here for illustrative purposes, it does demonstrate the potential for savings and provides a measure of the amount saved. Similar comparison may be made of inventory carrying costs.

A change from a periodic system to a perpetual system may not be so susceptible to comparison of relative cost. However, such indirect methods as comparison of inventory turnover may provide an indicator of effectiveness. Inventory turnovers, unfortunately, are suspect when used alone because they are, by definition, averages. A well-managed perpetual system will probably reduce carrying and ordering costs, however, and these costs can be measured.

Some other tools of measuring the effectiveness of the system are: comparison of the total *number* of stockouts, comparison of the *amount* of obsolete inventory and of shrinkage, and comparison of gross profit percentages (being careful to account for changes in selling price and relative sales mix.) Other more complex methods of evaluating the effectiveness of inventory control systems exist. Two of these methods, determining acceptable inventory investment and developing an "index" of inventory effectiveness, may have applicability to a particular firm. These two methods are described in NAA Research Report, No. 4, *Techniques In Inventory Management,* published by the National Association of Accountants at 505 Park Avenue, New York, New York, in 1964.

What Inventory Control Measures Should the Accountant Recommend?

Good judgment on part of both the accountant and management is a prerequisite to deciding the degree of control over inventory to be used. As is true in internal control system installation, too much inventory control is not only a needless expense, but cumbersome and inefficient.

The following guidelines are provided for recommending an inventory control system to management:

1. A large investment in inventory, relative to the firm's other assets, establishes the need for a high degree of control and justifies its cost.
2. Expanding firms should have a system which "looks forward" five to ten years. In other words, whatever system is recommended should have the ability to grow with the firm.

3. The system recommended should be consistent with sound management principles, insofar as possible. It is incumbent upon the accountant to render advice as to what the firm "ought to do," not necessarily what management wants to do (or not do).
4. Management's capabilities must be considered. It is pointless to recommend a system not understood by management. Management must be convinced that this is the "best" system for the firm, now, and in the immediate future, and that it will "work."

Applying the principles and practical applications described in this chapter judiciously and with great attention to the individual situation will yield considerable benefits.

Chapter 8

Preparation of Bankruptcy and Receivership Statements

When the Business Runs Into Financial Difficulty

Bankruptcy and insolvency are major considerations today in every accountant's practice. A business life cycle progresses from inception and organization through growth to maturity and, often finally, to decline. Decline, when it occurs, leads either to a financial readjustment or to liquidation and dissolution. Obviously it is managements' and owners' objective to perpetuate the growth and maturity phases and to avoid decline. How to avoid a decline is not at issue here; rather, it is assumed that decline has reached a critical stage for whatever reason, and the unhappy state of insolvency exists.

Insolvency has two meanings. The traditional definition is an inability to pay debts as they mature. Technically, then, insolvency can exist even if assets exceed liabilities. The Federal Bankruptcy Act defines insolvency as an insufficiency of assets at their fair market value to pay debts. Thus, under the bankruptcy definition, liabilities exceed assets. It is important to note that a debtor cannot be forced into involuntary bankruptcy unless the debtor is insolvent in the bankruptcy sense.

Remedies for the Insolvent Short of Bankruptcy

Difficulty in meeting currently maturing debts will likely cause an adverse reaction of creditors. Under common law, an agreement between the debtor and his creditors can be made in an attempt to forestall drastic measures. One such agreement is an *extension* whereby creditors simply agree to a postponement of payment. Another is a *composition.* Here, creditors concede to a reduction in the amount owed to them. Usually, this is accomplished by an "across-the-board" percentage reduction in the debtor's obligations. The objective of both these agreements is to continue the business, if possible, with the hope that a sound firm will emerge, and this is their obvious advantage. The chief disadvantage is that such an agreement is not binding on non-assenting creditors, and any one of this group may upset the agreement by filing a petition in bankruptcy.

One step removed from extensions and compositions is the formation of a *creditors' committee.* This also is a voluntary act and usually grants creditors (ordinarily one of them as a representative) control to operate the debtor firm, to hire and fire, and to actually manage the firm.

The next remedy short of bankruptcy is for the debtor to grant a *general assignment for the benefit of creditors.* Under this arrangement, title to the debtor firm's assets is usually transferred to the assignee, the objective being to protect the assets. From a practical viewpoint, assent, or at the very least acquiescence, on the part of all creditors is necessary; otherwise, as will be seen very shortly, because an assignment is an "act of bankruptcy," it can easily be overturned by one recalcitrant creditor. The essence of an assignment, contrary to that of extension, composition, and the formation of a creditors' committee, is that it is looking toward liquidation. Assignments are regulated by state courts.

A final remedy prior to bankruptcy is a legal one. Under equity court, creditors can request a court appointed receiver, called a *General Equity Receiver.* The receiver's responsibility is to administer the debtor's assets for the benefit of the parties. The proceeding is instituted by "general creditors' bill" filed with the court. The receiver takes title to assets and attempts to rehabilitate the firm. Inasmuch as all creditors must approve, chances of one of them filing a bankruptcy petition are minimal.

The Protection of Bankruptcy

Ultimately the recourse of the firm may be to seek protection under federal bankruptcy laws. Alternatively, a debtor firm may be forced into bankruptcy by creditors. The latter course, known as involuntary bankruptcy, is applicable, with few exceptions, to most commercial corporations. Proceedings in a voluntary bankruptcy may begin by filing a petition in a District Court. A voluntary bankrupt may plead under Chapters X, XI, or XIII. Chapter X provides for corporate reorganization. Chapter XIII allows for wage earners to make installment settlement of claims. Chapter XI is available to both individuals and corporations (with a few exceptions) and expands and elaborates on the common law composition or extension. Under Chapter XI, once it is accepted by a majority of creditors and is confirmed by the District Court, the minority creditors are bound by its provisions. A creditor's petition in involuntary cases cannot be entered under Chapter XI, but must come under Chapter X.

Involuntary Bankruptcies and Acts of Bankruptcy

In order to support a petition in involuntary bankruptcy, creditors must show two circumstances to exist: one, that the debtor is insolvent in the bankruptcy sense; and two, that the debtor has committed an act of bankruptcy. An act of bankruptcy is assumed to have been committed if the debtor:

1. Transfers or conceals assets with the intent to delay or defraud creditors.

2. Makes a preferential transfer to a creditor within four months prior to the filing of the petition.
3. Fails to discharge a lien by legal proceedings or distraint.
4. Makes a general assignment for the benefit of creditors.
5. Allows the appointment of a receiver while insolvent either in the traditional or bankruptcy sense.
6. Admits his inability to pay his debts and indicates a willingness to be adjudged a bankrupt.

The burden of proof is on the bankrupt to show that he is solvent.

Steps Taken to Obtain Relief under Chapter XI

As was mentioned earlier, Chapter XI is available to both business firms and individuals on a voluntary basis, and its operation is confined to unsecured debts. Secured claimants may be temporarily stayed from action, however. Because of its rather broad application, a brief description of the steps to be taken by the firm to obtain relief under Chapter XI of the Act follows as an illustration. Some of the requirements under a Chapter X proceeding differ in important ways, and those interested should avail themselves of the Act or explanations of it. Two points need to be made here. First, and most importantly, the firm must obtain the services of an attorney when bankruptcy is contemplated. This is a *legal* proceeding and advice from an expert is essential. Second, while the accountant cannot advise on the legal ramifications of bankruptcy, an accountant's services are also essential, as will be shown shortly. Accountants need to be familiar with bankruptcy proceedings because they will likely be intimate with the firm's financial status, and will be called upon to render advice. Also, the accountant will have to work closely with the firm's attorney.

The steps under Chapter XI are:

Step 1—File bankruptcy petition with Federal District Court. Because this is a voluntary procedure, the petition is filed by the bankrupt. The petition must be accompanied by: (a) schedules of all assets and liabilities; (b) any property claimed exempt; and (c) a statement of affairs. (The statement of affairs will be discussed in detail later in this chapter.) The schedule of liabilities must list: (a) claims entitled to priority; (b) secured claims; (c) unsecured claims. These, also, will be discussed later.

Step 2—The court responds at this point. Literally, the "court" probably means a referee in bankruptcy. Referees are appointed by a federal judge for a six-year term. The referee is answerable to the judge, with powers essentially equivalent to those of the court. The referee's duties are mainly administrative and include appointing the receiver and overseeing the receiver and the trustee. Whether a receiver is appointed or not rests on the judgment of the referee. Often, creditors will move for the appointment of a receiver in the interim between the filing of a petition and the appointment of a trustee. The objective of the receiver is to preserve the properties of the bankrupt for the general protection of creditors. The receiver is a court appointed office while the trustee is chosen by creditors and supervised by the court. The duties of both these fiduciaries are essentially identical. Receivers and trustees must maintain complete and detailed records of their receivership.

The response of the court is very likely to be to call a meeting of creditors. Based on the schedules of assets and liabilities, the statement of affairs, and the attitudes of creditors, the referee determines if the company is to be rehabilitated or liquidated. If liquidation is necessary, the referee may accept a trustee appointed by creditors who acts for them and takes title to the firm's assets. It should be noted here that the trustee (and the receiver, if appointed) must keep detailed records of his custodianship, report periodically to the referee, and make a final accounting to the court prior to the final meeting of creditors.

Step 3—It may be recalled that the essence of Chapter XI is to save the business. To this end, the referee will entertain a proposal from the debtor for an arrangement. Assuming that the proposal is viewed favorably, the referee may hold hearings, at which time creditors or their trustee will be heard.

Step 4—An arrangement is adopted. This usually entails a scaling down of claims of unsecured creditors (a composition) or a postponing of the time of payment (an extension), or both. Once the plan is adopted and approved by a majority of creditors (majority both in number of creditors and the amount of claims) it is binding on all non-assenting claimants.

Step 5—The direction of this step depends on prior judgments of the referee and the ability to get a majority of the creditors to agree. If adoption of the arrangement fails or if the plan is approved and implemented and then fails, recourse may be toward asset liquidation. If the arrangement meets with success, the trustee will execute the arrangement.

Step 6—In the event liquidation is necessary, assets are sold, and creditors are paid according to their priority. Ultimately the debtor is discharged. This means that the debtor is relieved of the legal obligations to pay creditors, except for certain debts from which the debtor cannot be discharged. The most important of these are:

(a) Taxes Due.
(b) Unscheduled claims (that is, those not filed within statutory time because of lack of notice).
(c) Debts created by fraud, etc.
(d) Wages earned within three months of the commencement of bankruptcy proceedings.

THE ROLE OF THE ACCOUNTANT

The process just described emphasizes the several stages during which the accountant has a significant role. It may be of help to set out the points at which the accountant's special expertise is needed and the nature of his service to the debtor and the trustee or receiver. According to the six steps just enumerated, the accountant's role related to each is as follows:

Step 1—Accompanying the petition are schedules (lists) of assets and liabilities and a statement of affairs. Obviously, the accountant is the logical one to prepare these schedules and statements. The schedule of assets is a listing of all properties of the firm, tangible, and intangible, real and personal. The list should include the assets' locations, account numbers (for bank accounts), descriptions and a statement as to whether or not each is security on a liability of the firm. The liability schedule should set out separately (a) claims with priority; (b) secured claims; and, (c) unsecured claims, showing the amount of each. Claims with priority are established by the Act and are as follows:

1. Costs and expenses of administering the bankrupt's estate.
2. Up to $600 per claimant for wages earned within three months prior to the filing of the petition.
3. Expenses of creditors incurred in successful opposition to discharge, and expenses of obtaining a conviction for an offense under the Act.
4. Federal, state and local taxes rightfully due.
5. Claims of the U.S. Government (other than taxes) and the landlord's priority under existing state law.

Secured claims are those for which certain assets have been pledged. They include pledged receivables, mortgaged property and the like. Unsecured claims, as is implied, include all others.

Another of the accountant's roles at this step is the preparation of the statement of affairs. The primary function of the statement is to assist in administering the bankrupt's estate for the creditors. In this connection, the statement reflects the financial position of the creditor on a liquidating basis and the status of the creditors with respect to the creditors' position. A comprehensive example of the statement appears later in this chapter.

Steps 2–5—When the firm is to be rehabilitated, the trustee or receiver is required to account for his custodianship by rendering financial statements to the referee. The accountant will probably be called upon to assist in their preparation. An illustration of accounting for a receiver will be presented shortly.

Step 6—During the course of the administration of the trustee or receiver, periodic financial reports must be submitted to creditors and the referee. One such special report prepared by the accountant, is the statement of realization and liquidation. Of course, as the name implies, these statements have their greatest usefulness in cases where rehabilitation is not possible and assets are being "realized" and liabilities liquidated. Often, the statement of realization and liquidation is accompanied by a traditional balance sheet and income statement. This statement is also illustrated at a later point in this chapter.

Preparing the Statement of Affairs

From this point to the conclusion of this chapter, Summer Hardware, Inc., will be used to illustrate the entire process of accounting for a firm in financial difficulty.

Summer Hardware, Inc. has experienced increasingly larger losses in the last few years, such that it has had great difficulty paying creditors. Lines of credit have been exhausted and management has had no success in getting agreement among creditors on a course of action. Obligations due by April 10, 19XX, simply cannot be paid, and on April 1, the firm's attorney files a petition under Chapter XI of the National Bankruptcy Act. A balance sheet prepared as of March 31, 19XX, is as follows:

SUMMER HARDWARE, INC.
BALANCE SHEET
MARCH 31, 19XX

ASSETS

Current Assets			
Cash		$10,000	
Receivables	$60,000		
Less: Allowance for Bad Debts	8,000	52,000	
Inventory		70,000	
Prepaid Expense		3,000	
Total Current Assets			$135,000
Property, Plant and Equipment (Net of Accumulated Depreciation)			
Building**		$66,000	
Furniture, Fixtures and Equipment*		9,000	
Land**		17,000	92,000
Other Assets			
Goodwill			8,000
Total Assets			$235,000

LIABILITIES AND CAPITAL

Current Liabilities			
Notes Payable*		$61,000	
Mortgage Payable-Current**		12,000	
Accounts Payable		77,000	
Taxes Payable		8,500	
Accrued Expenses:			
Interest on Notes	$2,050		
Interest on Mortgage	850		
Salaries	3,700	6,600	
Total Current Liabilities			$165,100
Non-Current Liabilities			
Mortgage Payable-less Current Portion**			70,000
Total Liabilities			$235,100
Capital			
Common Stock		$25,000	
Additional Paid In Capital		9,900	
Retained Earnings (Deficit)		(35,000)	(100)
Total Liabilities And Capital			$235,000

*Receivables are pledged as security on notes payable of $50,000. Remaining notes payable are secured by furniture, fixtures and equipment.

**The building and land are pledged as security on the mortgage payable.

From the balance sheet, the firm's accountant prepares a statement of affairs. A convenient form of the statement shows liabilities arrayed under four headings: those with priority, creditors fully secured, creditors partly secured and unsecured debts. Fully secured creditors are those to whom assets with a fair market value equal to or exceeding the amount of the debt have been pledged. Any amount in excess of the debt is available to unsecured creditors. Partly secured creditors, as the name implies, are those to whom assets with a value which is inadequate to cover the amount of the debt have been pledged. To the extent that the asset's value fails to satisfy the debt, that creditor is classified among the unsecured creditors.

Before completing the statement, the accountant must obtain fair market values for all assets. This may be accomplished by appraisal (requiring the services of an independent appraiser). In addition, estimated expenses of the administration of the firm's assets must be shown among the liabilities. Assume the administration expenses are estimated to be $10,000. A statement of affairs would appear as in Figure 8-1.

UNDERSTANDING THE STATEMENT OF AFFAIRS

Referring to Figure 8-1, several observations can be made. The headings on the statement seem fairly straightforward. The "adjusted" column in the liabilities section must include liabilities not on the books. As an example, estimated administrative expenses are not recorded, but must be shown as a liability with priority. Other unrecorded liabilities that must appear in the "adjusted" column are estimates of losses in pending legal suits or product warranties and estimates of losses from contingencies such as guaranteed or discounted notes and endorsements. In the asset section, adjusted figures are estimates of the salable or appraised value of each asset. It may be noted that the land and building are expected to bring $84,850 rather than the $83,000 book value. Alternatively, receivables, inventory and equipment are estimated to have a lesser realizable value than their book value. Prepaid insurance premiums may result in rebates from the insurer upon cancellation. Goodwill has no value which can be realized upon liquidation.

Interest accrued on notes and mortgages accompanies the note or mortgage. For that reason, interest payable has been associated with the debt on the statement, and the mortgage interest accrued is fully secured inasmuch as the estimated value of the security (land and building) exceeds the mortgage and its interest.

As stated earlier, the portion of a debt for which its security at realizable value is less than the debt is considered as unsecured. Thus, the notes payable of $50,000 and interest of $1,800 accrued are only partly secured inasmuch as the net realizable value of the security (receivables) is $48,000, or $3,800 less than the amount of the debt. The same situation exists with respect to the remaining notes payable, only partly secured by the equipment.

Priority debts shown are federal and state payroll taxes of $8,500, wages not exceeding $600 per employee and having been earned within three months of April 1, 19XX, totaling $3,700, and an estimated $10,000 of expenses for administering the estate of the petitioner. The total amount of priority obligations is shown in the asset section of the statement as a deduction from assets available to unsecured creditors.

Finally, and this is of considerable importance to the creditors and the referee in determining the course of action to take, an estimate is made of the deficiency to unsecured creditors and of what each unsecured creditor could expect to receive per dollar of liability. In the example, each unsecured creditor can expect 66 cents on the dollar.

THE PURPOSE OF THE DEFICIENCY STATEMENT

A special statement, called a deficiency statement, is often prepared to accompany the

Figure 8-1

SUMMER HARDWARE, INC.
STATEMENT OF AFFAIRS
March 31, 19XX

Liabilities and Owners Equity	Book Value	Adjusted	Creditors: With Priority	Fully Secured	Partly Secured	Unsecured
Notes Payable—Partly Secured by Receivables	$ 50,000	$ 50,000			$ 48,000	$ 3,800
Interest Payable on Above Notes	1,800	1,800				
Notes Payable—Partly Secured by Equipment	11,000	11,000			6,000	5,250
Interest Payable on Above	250	250				
Accounts Payable	77,000	77,000				77,000
Taxes Payable	8,500	8,500	$ 8,500			
Salaries Payable	3,700	3,700	3,700			
Mortgage Payable	82,000	82,000		$ 82,850		
Interest Payable on Mortgage	850	850				
Estimated Administration Expenses	-0-	10,000	10,000			
Common Stock	25,000	25,000				
Additional Paid-In Capital	9,900	9,900				
Deficit	(35,000)	(35,000)				
Totals	$235,000	$245,000	$ 22,200	$ 82,850	$ 54,000	$ 86,050

Assets	Book Value	Estimated Realizable Value	Assets Available to Creditors: With Priority	Fully Secured	Partly Secured	Unsecured
Cash	$ 10,000	$ 10,000				$ 10,000
Receivables (Net)	52,000	48,000			$ 48,000	
Inventory	70,000	67,000				67,000
Prepaid Expense	3,000	150*				150
Building (Net)	66,000	84,850 (Building and Land)		$ 82,850		2,000
Land	17,000					
Equipment (Net)	9,000	6,000			6,000	
Goodwill	8,000	-0-				
	$235,000	$216,000		82,850	54,000	79,150
Creditors with Priority			$ 22,200			(22,200)
Totals	$235,000	$216,000	$ 22,200	$ 82,850	$ 54,000	$ 56,950

Liability to Unsecured Creditors	$ 86,050
Estimated Amount Available	56,950
Estimated Deficiency To Unsecured Creditors	29,100

Per \$1 of Liability $\frac{\$56,950}{86,050} = 66¢$

*Estimated Rebate on Insurance Premium.

Figure 8-2

SUMMER HARDWARE, INC.
DEFICIENCY STATEMENT
March 31, 19XX

Estimated Gains and Losses on Realization of Assets		
Gains:		
Land and Buildings		$ 1,850
Losses:		
Receivables	$ 4,000	
Inventory	3,000	
Prepayments	2,850	
Equipment	3,000	
Goodwill	8,000	20,850
Estimated Net Loss on Realization		$19,000
Additional Liabilities:		
Estimated Expenses of Administration		10,000
Total Estimated Loss		$29,000
Loss to be Borne as Follows:		
By Owners		
Common Stock	$25,000	
Additional Paid-In Capital	9,900	
Less: Deficit	(35,000)	100
By Unsecured Creditors		$29,100

statement of affairs. Its purpose is to explain the source of the deficiency to unsecured creditors. The statement of affairs and the balance sheet are used to prepare the deficiency statement. An example of the deficiency statement for Summer Hardware, Inc., is presented in Figure 8-2.

ACCOUNTING FOR THE TRUSTEE

Trustees and receivers, it may be recalled, take title to the firm's assets and function under the supervision of the referee. For this illustration, assume that the referee in the Summer Hardware, Inc. case has determined that an attempt should be made to rehabilitate the firm and has agreed to the appointment of Amos Adams as trustee by the creditors.

The trustee has a fiduciary relationship and, consequently, must keep careful and detailed records of his custodianship. Some points to be remembered in accounting for a trustee or receiver in bankruptcy are:

1. A distinction must be made between assets assumed at the beginning of the trustee's receivership and assets generated or acquired during the trustee's term. One reason is that the trustee's responsibility is to administer the assets of the debtor, and gains and losses that were incurred prior to the trustee's tenure, even if not recognized until the trusteeship has begun, are identified with the debtor firm. Moreover, the trustee's administration cannot be burdened with pre-existing conditions which may

have arisen from poor asset management, or obviously, the trustee's effectiveness will be reduced. Finally, the assets must be separated, because the trustee could not render an accounting of his custodianship if assets, and gains and losses thereon, are commingled. He has full responsibility for assets he acquires, while his responsibility for existing assets is limited to their realization.

2. Liabilities arising prior to the trustee's term must be separated from those existing on the day the petition is filed. Essentially the same reasons apply here as are applied to the separation of assets. In addition, liabilities incurred by the trustee may have legal preference over debts of the firm, and the trustee satisfies old claims only upon the authority of the referee.[1]

Entries at the Beginning of the Trustee's Term

To be consistent with the requirements of points one and two above, the accounting entries at the time the trusteeship commences, for Summer Hardware, Inc., follow as they would appear on Amos Adams' book and on those of the company.

TRUSTEE'S BOOKS

Cash	$10,000	
Receivables—Debtor	60,000	
Inventory—Debtor	70,000	
Prepaid Expense—Debtor	3,000	
Building—Debtor	76,000	
Land—Debtor	17,000	
Furniture, Fixtures and Equipment—Debtor	12,000	
Goodwill—Debtor	8,000	
Allowance for Bad Debts—Debtor		$8,000
Accumulated Depreciation-Building—Debtor		10,000
Accumulated Depreciation-Fixtures—Debtor		3,000
Summer Hardware, Inc.		235,000
To record assets transferred per court order.		

[1]Interpretation No. 2 of the Financial Accounting Standards Board issued in June, 1974, makes Opinion No. 21 of the Accounting Principles Board applicable to notes issued under provisions of the Federal Bankruptcy Act. Briefly, APB 21 requires recognition of a discount or premium when a note is issued for property, goods, or service when: (a) interest is not stated in the face of the note; (b) the stated interest is unreasonable; or (c) the amount of the note differs materially from the fair value of the property, good or service.

An example of the application of FASB Interpretation No. 2 occurs in an arrangement or composition where the trustee, under instructions from the referee, issues notes in exchange for the debtor's notes for an amount less than the face of the original note. Assume a debtor firm has interest bearing notes outstanding with a present value of $100,000 in exchange for which the trustee issues notes with a present value of a lesser amount (or for that matter at an interest rate less than the going market rate), say $75,000. The indicated entry on the trustee's books is:

Notes Payable Paid—Old	$100,000	
Notes Payable—Trustee		$75,000
Premium on Notes Payable		25,000

The premium account is to be amortized over the life of the note on what is described as the "scientific" basis, yielding a constant rate when applied to the amount outstanding. Unamortized premium is added to the face of the note for balance sheet presentation.

SUMMER HARDWARE, INC.'S BOOKS

Amos Adams, Trustee	$235,000	
Allowance for Bad Debts	8,000	
Accumulated Depreciation—Building	10,000	
Accumulated Depreciation—Fixtures	3,000	
Cash		$10,000
Receivables		60,000
Inventory		70,000
Prepaid Expense		3,000
Building		76,000
Land		17,000
Furniture, Fixtures and Equipment		12,000
Goodwill		8,000
To transfer assets to trustee		

From the preceding entries it may be noted that assets, except cash, transferred from the firm are identified as "debtor" and that all liabilities are left on the company's books. This approach is a convenient method of satisfying the need for separation of assets and liabilities. Because the decision has been reached to attempt to operate the company, prepayments and goodwill need not be written off at this time, and as a consequence, these accounts come forward to the trustee's books.

RECORDING TRANSACTIONS OF THE TRUSTEE

The action taken by the trustee at this point will, of course, be contingent on many factors, chief among which is the need to raise cash to liquidate the tax liability, a priority item, and to finance current operations. There is no way to predict the trustee's course, but in an attempt to make this illustration as realistic as possible, assume that the trustee's transactions take the direction described below and are recorded as shown on his books from April 1 to June 30, 19XX.

SUMMER HARDWARE, INC., AMOS ADAMS TRUSTEE
TRANSACTIONS
APRIL 1, XX–JUNE 30, XX

Transaction			
(a) Merchandise sold	Cash	$16,000	
	Accounts Receivable —Trustee	2,000	
	Sales		$18,000
(b) Partial Payment of tax liability* (as directed by the referee)	Tax Payable—Debtor —Paid	3,000	
	Cash		3,000

*Inasmuch as this transaction affects an account on the firm's books, the company will make the following entry:

Taxes Payable	$ 3,000	
Amos Adams—Trustee		$ 3,000

(c) Operating expenses paid	Expenses	9,000	
	Cash		9,000
(d) Merchandise Purchased	Purchases	6,000	
	Cash		2,000
	Accounts Payable—Trustee		4,000
(e) Fees and Administrative Expenses Paid	Trustee's Fees and Administrative Expense	1,800	
	Cash		1,800
(f) Collections on Old Accounts Receivable	Cash	20,000	
	Accounts Receivable—Debtor		20,000
(g) Payment of Secured Notes and Interest Thereon (as directed by the referee)*	Notes Payable—Debtor—Paid	18,200	
	Interest Payable—Debtor	1,800	
	Cash		20,000
(h) Collection of New Accounts Receivable	Cash	1,000	
	Accounts Receivable—Trustee		1,000
(i) Old Accounts Receivable Determined Worthless	Allowance for Bad Debts	4,000	
	Accounts Receivable—Debtor		4,000
(j) New Accounts Receivable Possibly Bad	Bad Debts Expense	200	
	Allowance for Bad Debts		200
(k) Remainder of Tax Liability Paid (as directed by the referee)*	Taxes Payable—Debtor—Paid	5,500	
	Cash		5,500
(l) Partial Payment of Accounts Payable—New	Accounts Payable—Trustee	2,000	
	Cash		2,000
(m) Payment of Interest Accrued to April 1, on Mortgage Payable (as directed by the referee)*	Interest Payable—Debtor—Paid	850	
	Cash		850

*The company's entries are:

Notes Payable	$18,200	
Interest Payable	1,800	
Amos Adams, trustee		$20,000
Tax Payable	5,500	
Amos Adams, Trustee		5,500
Interest Payable		
Amos Adams, Trustee	850	850

Figure 8-3

SUMMER HARDWARE, INC., AND AMOS ADAMS, TRUSTEE
Worksheet
4/1/XX — 6/30/XX

	Trial Balance 4/1/XX		Transactions 4/1 — 6/30/XX		Adjustments		Eliminations		Balance Sheet		Income Statement	
	Dr.	Cr.	Dr.	Cr.	Dr.	Cr.	Dr.	Cr.	Dr.	Cr.	Dr.	Cr.
Amos Adams, Trustee												
Cash	10,000		(a) 16,000	9,000 (c)					2,850			
			(f) 20,000	850 (m)								
			(h) 1,000	2,000 (l)								
				3,000 (b)								
				2,000 (d)								
				1,800 (e)								
				20,000 (g)								
				5,500 (k)								
Receivables—Debtor	60,000			4,000 (i)					36,000			
				20,000 (f)								
Receivables—Trustee			(a) 2,000	1,000 (h)					1,000			
Inventory—Debtor	70,000					70,000 (4)						
Allowance for Bad Debts—Debtor		8,000	(i) 4,000			3,000 (1)				7,000		
Allowance for Bad Debts—Trustee				200 (j)						200		
Prepaid Expense—Debtor	3,000					300 (2)			2,700			
Building—Debtor	76,000								76,000			
Accumulated Depr-Bldg-Debtor		10,000				190 (3)				10,190		
Land—Debtor	17,000								17,000			
Furn., Fixt. & Equip.—Debtor	12,000								12,000			
Acc. Depr-Equip-Debtor		3,000				60 (3)				3,060		
Goodwill—Debtor	8,000								8,000			
Summer Hardware, Inc.		235,000					235,000					
	256,000	256,000										
Accounts Payable—Trustee			(l) 2,000	4,000 (d)						2,000		
Sales				18,000 (a)								18,000
Purchases			(d) 6,000								6,000	
Bad Debts Expense			(j) 200								200	
Expenses			(c) 9,000		(2) 300						9,300	
Fees and Admin. Expense			(e) 1,800								1,800	
Depr. Expense					(3) 250						250	
Taxes Payable—Debtor—Paid			(b) 3,000									
			(k) 5,500					8,500				
Notes Payable—Debtor—Paid			(g) 18,200					18,200				
Interest Payable—Debtor—Paid			(g) 1,800					1,800				
			(m) 850					850				

Figure 8-3 continued

SUMMER HARDWARE, INC., AND
AMOS ADAMS, TRUSTEE
Worksheet
4/1/XX—6/30/XX

	Trial Balance 4/1/XX		Transactions 4/1/—6/30/XX		Adjustments		Eliminations		Balance Sheet		Income Statement	
Summer Hardware, Inc.	**Dr.**	**Cr.**	**Dr.**	**Cr.**	**Dr.**	**Cr.**	**Dr.**	**Cr.**	**Dr.**	**Cr.**	**Dr.**	**Cr.**
Inventory					(4) 65,000				65,000			
Bad Debts Expense—Debtor					(1) 3,000						3,000	
Interest Expense—Debtor					(5) 1,400						1,400	
Income Summary					(4) 70,000	65,000 (4)					70,000	65,000
Interest Payable—Notes						550 (5)						
Interest Payable—Mortgage						850 (5)				1,400		
Amos Adams, Trustee	235,000			850 (m–m)				205,650				
				5,500 (k–k)								
				3,000 (b–b)								
				20,000 (g–g)								
Notes Payable		61,000	(g–g) 18,200							42,800		
Interest Payable—Notes		2,050	(g–g) 1,800							250		
Mortgage Payable		82,000								82,000		
Interest Payable—Mort.		850	(m-m) 850									
Accounts Payable		77,000								77,000		
Taxes Payable		8,500	(b–b) 3,000									
			(k–k) 5,500									
Salaries Payable		3,700								3,700		
Common Stock		25,000								25,000		
Additional Paid-In Capital		9,900								9,900		
Retained Earnings	35,000								35,000			
	270,000	270,000	120,700	120,700	139,950	139,950	235,000	235,000	255,550	264,500	91,950	83,000
Decrease In Retained Earnings									8,950			8,950
									264,500	264,500	91,950	91,950

USING A WORKSHEET

The worksheet, Figure 8-3, is a summary of the trial balances of the trustee's and the firm's books, giving effect to the foregoing transactions. It is a convenient device for consolidation and for preparation of traditional financial statements. The "adjustments" column contains typical accrual and deferral entries and they are shown below. The "transactions" column summarizes the transactions entries just shown above.

SUMMER HARDWARE, INC., AMOS ADAMS TRUSTEE
ADJUSTING ENTRIES
JUNE 30, 19XX

	Debit	Credit
(1) Bad Debts Expense—Debtor	$3,000	
Allowance for Bad Debts—Debtor		$3,000
Estimated additional uncollectibles on old accounts receivable		
(2) Expenses	300	
Prepaid Expenses—Debtor		300
To record expiration of prepaid expense		
(3) Depreciation Expense	250	
Accumulated Depreciation—Building—Debtor		190
Accumulated Depreciation—Equipment—Debtor		60
Depreciation from April 1—June 30, 19XX		
(4) Income Summary	70,000	
Inventory—Debtor		70,000
Inventory—Trustee	65,000	
Income Summary		65,000
To adjust inventory accounts		
(5) Interest Expense—Debtor	1,400	
Interest Payable—Mortgage		850
Interest Payable—Notes		550
Interest accrued to June 30, 19XX		

Referring again to the worksheet, one eliminating entry was required to eliminate the reciprocal accounts, Summer Hardware, Inc., on the trustee's books and Amos Adams, Trustee, on the firm's books. Because the company made concurrent entries when old liabilities were paid thus reducing the liabilities balances, the accounts on the trustee's books for the debtor's liabilities paid, which are nominal accounts there, must also be eliminated. It may be recalled that the trustee's account on the firm's books was reduced when the liabilities were paid.

PREPARING FINANCIAL STATEMENTS FROM THE WORKSHEET

Figures 8-4 and 8-5 are the balance sheet and income statements prepared from the

Figure 8-4 **Balance Sheet Prepared on "Going Concern" Basis**

AMOS ADAMS, TRUSTEE FOR
SUMMER HARDWARE, INC.
BALANCE SHEET
JUNE 30, 19XX

Assets

Current Assets:			
Cash		$ 2,850	
Receivables (Net)[1]		29,800	
Inventory		65,000	
Prepaid Expenses		2,700	
Total Current Assets			$100,350
Property, Plant and Equipment (Net of Depreciation):			
Buildings[2]		$ 65,810	
Land[2]		17,000	
Furniture, Fixtures, and Equipment		8,940	
Total Property, Plant, and Equipment			91,750
Intangibles			
Goodwill			8,000
Total Assets			$200,100

Liabilities and Capital

Current Liabilities			
Notes Payable[1]		$ 42,800	
Mortgage Payable—Current[2]		15,000	
Accounts Payable		79,000	
Accrued Expenses:			
Salaries Payable	$ 3,700		
Interest on Notes	800		
Interest on Mortgage	850	5,350	
Total Current Liabilities			$142,150
Non-Current Liabilities			
Mortgage Payable—Less Current Portion			67,000
Total Liabilities			$209,150
Capital			
Common Stock		$ 25,000	
Additional Paid-In Capital		9,900	
Retained Earnings (Deficit)		(43,950)	
Total Capital (Deficit)			(9,050)
Total Liabilities and Capital			$200,100

[1]Receivables with an estimated net realizable value of $29,000 are pledged as security on notes payable of $31,800. Remaining notes payable are secured by furniture, fixtures, & equipment.

[2]The building and land are pledged as security on the mortgage payable.

Figure 8-5 **Income Statement Prepared On "Going Concern" Basis**

AMOS ADAMS, TRUSTEE FOR
SUMMER HARDWARE, INC.
INCOME STATEMENT
For the Period 4/1/XX to 6/30/XX

Sales		$ 18,000
Cost of Sales:		
Beginning Inventory	$ 70,000	
Purchases	6,000	
Goods Available for Sale	$ 76,000	
Less: Ending Inventory	65,000	
Cost of Sales		$ 11,000
Gross Profit		$ 7,000
Trustee's Expenses:		
General Expense	$ 9,300	
Bad Debts Expense	200	
Fees and Administration Expenses	1,800	
Depreciation	250	
Total Trustee's Expenses		11,550
Net Loss from Trustee's Operation		$ (4,550)
Corporation's Expenses:		
Bad Debts Expense	$ 3,000	
Interest on Corporation's Debt	1,400	
Total Corporation's Expenses		(4,400)
Total Net Loss		$ (8,950)

worksheet. Some comments on the financial statements are in order. The statements are prepared on a traditional "going concern" basis, because that is the intention of the parties. Nonetheless, a question may be raised as to the advisability of continuing to carry goodwill on the balance sheet. Apparently, the trustee has chosen to do so, at least temporarily. It may be recalled that the amount of the receivables collected was used to pay accrued interest and a portion of the principal on the notes on which the receivables are security. Thus, the remaining uncollected old receivables of $36,000, less the current allowance for bad debts on those receivables of $7,000, equals the net realizable value of $29,000, shown in Footnote No. 1, remaining as security on unpaid notes. One further observation concerning the balance sheet is that inasmuch as no principal payments have been made on the mortgage payable, an additional three months at $1,000 per month has been added to the portion currently due.

INTERPRETING THE TRUSTEE'S INCOME STATEMENT

The income statement is in two parts, the first of which shows the trustee's operations only, unencumbered by any past commitments of the firm. For example, bad debts of $200 is that portion expected to be uncollectible on the trustee's receivables. Moreover, interest expense is attributable to the firm's debt, not debt created by the trustee. The second part of the income statement reflects all expenses and losses attributable to the old management. The worth of this dichotomy of the statement seems obvious. If the firm is to be rehabilitated, the decision should be based on current and expected future operations—not on what has happened in the past. Past events have obviously been unsuccessful and cannot be used as a measure of future potential. It is equally obvious, from a review of the income statement, that in three months the trustee has not been able to operate profitably, even if the trustee's fees and other expenses of administrations were not deducted. This is exactly the information needed by the trustee, the referee and the creditors. Because of the inability to show a profit, assume that the referee directs the trustee to liquidate.

Liquidating the Firm—The Statement of Realization and Liquidation

Liquidation means that assets must be converted into cash and liabilities paid according to their legal priorities. The course of liquidation does not necessarily mean an immediate cessation of normal operations; in fact, the trustee may require several months, or more, to obtain the "best" prices available for assets. Meanwhile, plans are laid and arrangements are begun to find buyers for the various assets and to settle claims. This whole process involves realizing assets (converting to cash) and liquidating (paying claims). The statement designed to reflect this activity is the Statement of Realization and Liquidation.

The form of the statement shown in Figure 8-6, if somewhat unwieldy, is simple to understand and combines transaction analysis with statement format. In other words, an analysis of the trustee's transactions in the form illustrated *is* the statement of realization and liquidation. Nothing else is required.

The statement itself consists of three parts, and there are "supplemental" schedules accompanying the statement. Part I of the statement is assets, set out in the following format:

FORMAT OF THE STATEMENT OF REALIZATION AND LIQUIDATION

Part I—Assets

Assets to be Realized	Assets Realized
Assets Acquired	Assets not Realized

There is a mathematical realtionship here (as well as a debit/credit one). Assets to be realized plus assets acquired minus assets realized equal assets not realized. Thus, this part, as is Part II, is self-balancing. Part II is the liabilities section as follows:

Part II—Liabilities

Liabilities Liquidated	Liabilities to be Liquidated
Liabilities not Liquidated	Liabilities Assumed

The same relationship exists as in the assets part, that is, liabilities to be liquidated plus liabilities assumed minus liabilities liquidated equal liabilities not liquidated. The third part shows all transactions affecting nominal accounts as:

Part III—Revenue and Expense

Charges	Credits

Obviously, income or loss for the period is determined by these amounts and the balancing figure (income or loss) is transferred to retained earnings, which is one of the supplemental schedules as are common stock, additional paid-in capital, and cash, which of course, is already realized.

Working with the Statement of Realization and Liquidation

While Figure 8-6 is necessarily already in completed form, the procedure used in its preparation follows the pattern described below:

Step 1—Place headings on the statement as shown earlier, that is, under the asset section (Part I); at top left show the subheading "Assets to be Realized." Items listed there are obtained directly from the balance sheet filed with the original petition, except cash. Summer Hardware, Inc.'s balance sheet at March 31, 19XX, was presented earlier. Complete the headings in the asset section, showing "Assets Acquired" under "Assets to be Realized," "Assets Realized" at top on the right hand side, with "Assets Not Realized" below. Leave sufficient space under each heading to accommodate the transactions. The liabilities section (Part II) is headed next with "Liabilities Liquidated" top left and "Liabilities not Liquidated" underneath, "Liabilities to be Liquidated" top right and "Liabilities Assumed" below, again leaving adequate space. "Liabilities to be Liquidated" are listed directly from the March 31, 19XX, balance sheet. Provide headings for Part III, the revenue and expense section, showing "charges" at left and "credits" right.

Step 2—Establish a supplemental schedule for cash and enter the balance of $10,000 as a debit. Schedules of retained earnings, common stock and additional paid-in capital, and any other capital accounts should likewise be established and balances entered.

Step 3—The trustee's transactions may now be "posted" directly on the statement and supplemental schedules. Transactions from 3/31/XX to 6/30/XX have been shown previously in general journal form. Both those transactions and remaining transactions of the trustee during the course of his administration must be translated into the language of the statement and recorded thereon. An illustration of this will be forthcoming shortly.

Step 4—Deduct "Assets Realized" from "Assets to be Realized" and "Assets Acquired" to obtain "Assets Not Realized" and list them under that heading. Follow this procedure in the liabilities section to obtain "Liabilities Not Liquidated."

Figure 8-6

SUMMER HARDWARE, INC.
STATEMENT OF REALIZATION AND LIQUIDATION
APRIL 1, 19XX — October 15, 19XX

Assets (Part I)

Trans-action			
	Assets to be Realized: (From 3/31/XX Balance Sheet)		
	Receivables	$60,000	
	Less: Allowance for Bad Debts	8,000	$ 52,000
	Inventory		70,000
	Prepaid Expense		3,000
	Building	$76,000	
	Less: Accumulated Depr.	10,000	66,000
	Land		17,000
	Furniture, Fixtures & Equipment	$12,000	
	Less: Accumulated Depr.	3,000	9,000
	Goodwill		8,000
			$225,000
	Assets Acquired		
a)	Accounts Receivable		2,000
			$227,000

Trans-action		
	Assets Realized:	
f)	Accounts Receivable—Debtor	$ 20,000
h)	Accounts Receivable—Trustee	1,000
i)	Accounts Receivable—Debtor	4,000
i)	Allowance for Bad Debts—Debtor	4,000 DR.
j)	Allowance for Bad Debts—Trustee	200
o)	Prepaid Expense	3,000
q)	Accounts Receivable—Debtor	19,200
q)	Accounts Receivable—Trustee	800
q)	Allowance for Bad Debts—Debtor	4,000 DR.
q)	Accounts Receivable—Debtor	16,800
q)	Allowance for Bad Debts—Trustee	200 DR.
q)	Accounts Receivable—Trustee	200
r)	Goodwill	8,000
s)	Accumulated Depr.—Bldg.	10,000 DR.
s)	Land	17,000
s)	Building	76,000
t)	Accumulated Depr.—Furniture, Fixtures, & Equip.	3,000 DR.
t)	Furniture, Fixtures, and Equipment	12,000
u)	Inventory	70,000
		$227,000
	Assets to be Realized:	
	None	0
		$227,000

Figure 8-6 continued

SUMMER HARDWARE, INC.
STATEMENT OF
REALIZATION AND LIQUIDATION
APRIL 1, 19XX — OCTOBER 15, 19XX

Liabilities (Part II)

Trans-action		
	Liabilities Liquidated	
b)	Taxes Payable—Debtor	$ 3,000
g)	Notes Payable—Debtor	18,200
g)	Interest Payable—Notes—Debtor	1,800
k)	Taxes Payable—Debtor	5,500
l)	Accounts Payable—Trustee	2,000
m)	Interest Payable—Debtor	850
v)	Notes Payable—Debtor	18,950
v)	Interest Payable on Notes—Debtor	250
w)	Mortgage Payable—Debtor	82,000
x)	Notes Payable—Debtor	5,800
y)	Wages Payable—Debtor	3,700
y)	Accounts Payable—Trustee	2,000
z)	Notes Payable—Debtor	10,772
z)	Accounts Payable—Debtor	45,948
a–a)	Notes Payable—Debtor	7,278
a–a)	Accounts Payable—Debtor	31,052
		$239,100
	Liabilities Not Liquidated	-0-
		$239,100

Trans-action		
	Liabilities to be Liquidated: (From 3/31/XX Balance Sheet)	
	Notes Payable	$ 61,000
	Accrued Interest	2,050
	Mortgage Payable	82,000
	Accrued Interest	850
	Accounts Payable	77,000
	Taxes Payable	8,500
	Salaries Payable	3,700
		$235,100
	Liabilities Assumed:	
d)	Accounts Payable	4,000
		$ 239,100

Figure 8-6 continued **Statement of Realization And Liquidation**

SUMMER HARDWARE, INC.
STATEMENT OF REALIZATION AND LIQUIDATION
APRIL 1, 19XX — OCTOBER 15, 19XX

REVENUE AND EXPENSE (PART III)

Transaction		Charges	Credits	Balance
a)	Sales of Merchandise		18,000	
c)	Operating Expenses Paid	9,000		
d)	Merchandise Purchased	6,000		
e)	Trustee's Fees and Administrative Expense Paid	1,800		
j)	Provision for Bad Debts	200		
n)	Sales of Merchandise		21,000	
o)	Write-off of Prepayments	2,880		
p)	Sales of Merchandise		41,000	
q)	Loss on Bad Accounts	12,800		
r)	Write-Off of Goodwill	8,000		
s)	Gain on Sale of Land and Building		1,850	
t)	Loss on Sale of Furn., Fixt., & Equip.	3,200		
u)	Merchandise Inventory—Beginning	70,000		
w)	Interest on Mortgage	200		
y)	Trustee's Fees	6,000		
a–a)	Final Discharge in Bankruptcy—Income From Discharge of Indebtedness		38,330	
	Sub-Total	120,080	120,180	100 Cr.
b–b)	To Close	100		-0-

Step 5—Determine the income or loss from the revenue and expense section and transfer the balance to retained earnings.

Step 6—Determine the balance in the supplemental schedule of cash.

The procedure just described, once completed, will yield a finished Statement of Realization and Liquidation and accompanying schedules. Ultimately, of course, there will be no further assets not realized, for they will all be converted into cash and disbursed. The total of any remaining liabilities not liquidated, because cash was inadequate, will equal debit balances in capital accounts and may be offset by one final entry. At this time, having met all legal requirements, the debtor is discharged.

TRANSLATING TRANSACTIONS INTO STATEMENT LANGUAGE

Continuing the illustration of Summer Hardware, Inc., and following the steps above, the following transactions were completed by the trustee subsequent to June 30, 19XX, in

Figure 8-6 continued

SUMMER HARDWARE, INC.
SCHEDULES TO ACCOMPANY THE
STATEMENT OF REALIZATION AND LIQUIDATION
APRIL 1, 19XX — OCTOBER 15, 19XX

Cash Schedule

Trans-action		Debit	Credit	Balance
	Balance 4/1/XX (From 3/31/XX Balance Sheet)			10,000
a)		16,000		
b)			3,000	
c)			9,000	
d)			2,000	
e)			1,800	
f)		20,000		
g)			20,000	
h)		1,000		
k)			5,500	
l)			2,000	
m)			850	
n)		21,000		
o)		120		
p)		41,000		
q)		20,000		
s)		84,850		
t)		5,800		
v)			19,200	
w)			82,200	
x)			5,800	
y)			11,700	56,720
z)			56,720	-0-
	Common Stock			
	Balance 4/1/XX			25,000
c–c)	Dissolution	25,000		-0-
	Additional Paid-In Capital			
	Balance 4/1/XX			9,900
c–c)	Dissolution	9,900		-0-
	Retained Earnings			
	Balance 4/1/XX			35,000 Dr.
b–b)	To Close		100	34,900 Dr.
c–c)	Dissolution		34,900	-0-

final liquidation of the company. It is assumed that the corporate shell in not retained; rather its charter is abandoned by its owners, and the corporation ceases to exist. It should be remembered that the earlier transactions (those from 3/31/XX to 6/30/XX) must also be recorded. To that end, they are reproduced here and are translated into statement language for the reader's convenience in following the whole process.[2]

AMOS ADAMS, TRUSTEE TRANSACTIONS
MARCH 31, 19XX TO OCTOBER 14, 19XX

March 31, 19XX to June 30, 19XX

Transaction	Entry on Statement Of Realization and Liquidation		
(a) Sold merchandise	Cash (Cash Schedule)	$16,000	
	Accounts Receivable (Assets Acquired)	2,000	
	Sales (Revenue & Expense-Credits)		$18,000
(b) Partial payment of taxes	Taxes Payable (Liabilities Liquidated)	3,000	
	Cash (Cash Schedule)		3,000
(c) Operating expenses	Expenses (Revenue & Expense—Charges)	9,000	
	Cash (Cash Schedule)		9,000
(d) Merchandise purchased	Purchases (Revenue & Expense—Charges)	6,000	
	Accounts Payable (Liabilities Assumed)		4,000
	Cash (Cash Schedule)		2,000
(e) Fees and administrative expense paid	Trustee's Fees and Administrative Expense (Revenue and Expense—Charges)	1,800	
	Cash (Cash Schedule)		1,800
(f) Collections on old accounts receivable	Cash (Cash Schedule)	20,000	
	Accounts Receivable (Assets Realized)		20,000
(g) Payment of notes and interest	Notes Payable (Liabilities Liquidated)	18,200	
	Interest Payable (Liabilities Liquidated)	1,800	
	Cash (Cash Schedule)		20,000
(h) Collection of new accounts receivable	Cash (Cash Schedule)	1,000	
	Accounts Receivable (Assets Realized)		1,000

[2]The adjusting entries at June 30, 19XX, made and shown on the worksheet, Figure 8-3, are assumed to have been interim entries for statement purposes only, and not recorded in the accounts.

(i) Write-off of old accounts receivable	Allowance for Bad Debts (Assets Realized)	4,000	
	Accounts Receivable —Debtor (Assets Realized)		4,000
(j) Provision for bad debts —new accounts receivable	Bad Debts Expense (Revenue and Expense—Charges)	200	
	Allowance for Bad Debts (Assets Realized)		200
(k) Remainder of liability paid	Taxes Payable—Debtor (Liabilities Liquidated)	5,500	
	Cash (Cash Schedule)		5,500
(l) Partial payment of new accounts payable	Accounts Payable (Liabilities Liquidated)	2,000	
	Cash (Cash Schedule)		2,000
(m) Payment of mortgage interest	Interest Payable—Debtor (Liabilities Liquidated)	850	
	Cash (Cash Schedule)		850

The trustee completed the following additional transactions which are put in the Statement of Realization and Liquidation format:

July 1, 19XX, to October 15, 19XX:

Transaction	Entry on the Statement of Realization and Liquidation		
(n) Made sales for cash	Cash (Cash Schedule)	$21,000	
	Sales (Revenues & Expenses-Credits)		$21,000
(o) Received cash from claim with insurance company for rebate on prepaid insurance and wrote off the remainder	Cash (Cash Schedule)	120	
	Insurance Expenses (Revenues and Expenses—Charges)	2,880	
	Prepaid Expense (Assets Realized)		3,000
(p) Sold remainder of inventory for cash	Cash (Cash Schedule)	41,000	
	Sales (Revenues and Expenses-Credits)		41,000
(q) Collected accounts receivable, remainder written off as uncollectible	Cash (Cash Schedule)	20,000	
	Accounts Receivable —Debtor (Assets Realized)		19,200
	Accounts Receivable —Trustee (Assets Realized)		800

	Loss on Bad Debts (Revenues) and Expenses-Charges)	12,800	
	Allowance for Bad Debts —Debtor (Assets Realized)	4,000	
	Accounts Receivable —Debtor (Assets Realized)		16,800
	Allowance for Bad Debts —Trustee (Assets Realized)	200	
	Accounts Receivable —Trustee (Assets Realized)		200
(r) Wrote off Goodwill	Loss on write-off of Goodwill (Revenues and Expenses—Charges)	8,000	
	Goodwill (Assets Realized)		8,000
(s) Sale of land and building for cash	Cash (Cash Schedule)	84,850	
	Accumulated Depreciation (Assets Realized)	10,000	
	Land (Assets Realized)		17,000
	Building (Assets Realized)		76,000
	Gain on sale of Land and Building (Revenues and Expenses-Credits)		1,850
(t) Sale of furniture, fixtures and equipment	Loss on sale of Furniture (Revenues and Expenses -Charges)	3,200	
	Cash (Cash Schedule)	5,800	
	Accumulated Depreciation —Furniture (Assets Realized)	3,000	
	Furniture, Fixture and Equipment (Assets Realized)		12,000

At this point in "posting" the above transactions to the statement, it will be observed that all the assets, including those acquired by the trustee, have been realized either as cash or written off as losses. All that remains as far as the assets section is concerned is to make and record the inventory adjustment. The beginning inventory of $70,000 must be shown as realized and charged to the revenue and expense schedule. When this is accomplished, the assets section "balances"; there are no more assets to be realized, and assets to be realized plus assets acquired equal assets realized. The trustee's next transactions must be the liquidation of liabilities insofar as is possible. The inventory adjustment appears next, followed by the payment of the firm's debts.

Transaction	**Entry on Statement of Realization and Liquidation**		
(u) Adjust for beginning inventory sold (no ending inventory)	Merchandise Inventory (Revenues and Expenses -Charges)	$70,000	
	Inventory (Assets Realized)		$70,000

Transaction	Entry	Debit	Credit
(v) Proceeds of remainder of receivables collected paid on notes payable and interest accrued thereon on which the receivables are security.	Notes Payable—Debtor (Liabilities Liquidated)	18,950	
	Interest Payable—Debtor (Liabilities Liquidated)	250	
	Cash (Cash Schedule)		19,200
(w) Proceeds of sale of land and building applied to payment of mortgage and interest accrued since date of last payment.	Mortgage Payable—Debtor (Liabilities Liquidated)	82,000	
	Interest Expense (Revenues and Expenses-charges)	200	
	Cash (Cash Schedule)		82,200
(x) Proceeds of sale of furniture, fixture and equipment applied to notes payable on which they are security.	Notes Payable—Debtor (Liabilities Liquidated)	5,800	
	Cash (Cash Schedule)		5,800
(y) Priority Claims Paid: Trustee's Accounts Payable $2,000	Accounts Payable -Trustee (Liabilities Liquidated)	2,000	
Wages Payable 3,700	Wages Payable—Debtor (Liabilities Liquidated)	3,700	
Trustee's Fees 6,000			
$11,700	Trustee's Fees (Revenues and Expenses—Charges)	6,000	
	Cash (Cash Schedule)		11,700

An important observation here is that the trustee has paid secured debt (notes and mortgage payable) to the extent of the cash received from assets pledged as security. A recapitulation of the cash received and payments made follows:

Notes Payable and Interest thereon (secured by receivables)	$52,050
Collected on Receivables:	
(transaction "f" and paid in transaction "g")	(20,000)
(transaction "q" and paid in transaction "v")	(19,200)
Balance Owing—Unsecured	$12,850
Notes Payable (Secured by furniture, fixture and equipment)	$11,000
Collected from sale of furniture, fixture and equipment (transaction "t" and paid in transaction "x")	(5,800)
Balance Owing—Unsecured	$5,200

Mortgage Payable and Interest Accrued thereon to (10/15/XX)	$83,050
Collected from sale of land and building (transaction "s" and paid in transactions "m" and "w")	(83,050)
Balance Owing	-0-

Computation of Payments to Unsecured Creditors

The trustee has only unsecured debt remaining as unpaid as follows:

Unsecured portion of notes payable secured by receivables (above)	$12,850
Unsecured portion of notes payable secured by furniture, fixture and equipment (above)	5,200
Accounts payable—old (from liabilities to be liquidated)	77,000
Total Remaining Debt	$95,050
Cash remaining (balance as of transaction "y")	56,720
Actual Deficiency to Unsecured Creditors	$38,330

Unsecured creditors will be paid on a pro-rata basis determined as follows:

Amount to unsecured creditors per $1 of liability = $.5967 (56,720 ÷ $95,050) allocated to:

		AMOUNT OF CASH TO CREDITORS
Unpaid balance on note payable partly secured by receivables	$12,850 × 59.67%	$ 7,668
Unpaid balance on note payable partly secured by furniture, fixtures and equipment	5,200 × 59.67%	3,104
Accounts payable (to each, pro-rata)	77,000 × 59.67%	45,948
Total Amount of Cash to Unsecured Creditors		$56,720

At the direction of the referee, the trustee makes the final distribution of cash as follows:

Transaction	Entry on Statement of Realization and Liquidation		
(z) Remaining cash paid to unsecured creditors	Notes Payable (Liabilities Liquidated)	$10,772	
	Accounts Payable (Liabilities Liquidated)	45,948	
	Cash (Cash Schedule)		$56,720

The final step in the bankruptcy proceedings of Summer Hardware, Inc., is its discharge by the referee. The firm is no longer liable for remaining debts and the discharge should be reflected in an entry similar to the one that follows:

Transaction		Entry on Statement of Realization and Liquidation		
(a–a)	Summer Hardware, Inc., discharged in bankruptcy from remaining indebtedness	Notes Payable—Debtor (Liabilities Liquidated)	$7,278	
		Accounts Payable—Debtor (Liabilities Liquidated)	31,052	
		Income from Discharge of Indebtedness (Revenue and Expense—Credits)		$38,330

From the entry above it may be seen that income arose from the discharge equal to the unpaid obligations. There appear to be no income taxes as a consequence, however, inasmuch as the income from the discharge did not render the firm solvent.

All transactions now completed, the revenue and expense portion of the statement (part III) is balanced by transferring the net gain or loss to retained earnings by the following entry:

Transaction		Entry on Statement of Realization and Liquidation		
(b–b)	To transfer net gains to retained earnings	Income Summary (Revenue and Expense—Debits)	$100	
		Retained Earnings		$100

Assuming that the firm yields its charter as a corporation and ceases its existence, one final entry is required:

(c–c)	Final dissoultion of corporation	Common Stock	$25,000	
		Additional Paid-in Capital	9,900	
		Retained Earnings		$34,900

Preparing Interim Statements During Liquidation

The example just completed of the preparation of the statement of realization and liquidation carried the entire process from the beginning of bankruptcy to the ultimate dissolution of the corporation without interruption. From time to time it may be necessary to prepare an interim statement showing how the process of liquidation is proceeding. At that point, a traditional balance sheet and income statement may be prepared as well as a statement of realization and liquidation. All that is required is to subtract assets realized on the Statement of Realization and Liquidation from assets to be realized and assets acquired. The remainder is, of course, assets not yet realized and this added to the cash balance constitutes the assets side of a balance sheet. Similarly, the balance sheet liabilities on the interim date may be determined by subtracting liabilities liquidated from those to be liquidated and those assumed. This procedure also completes parts I and II of the Statement of Realization and Liquidation showing the assets to be realized and liabilities to be liquidated. Of course, an income statement is prepared by reference to the revenue and expense portion (part III) of the Statement of Realization and Liquidation.

Because of the nature of a bankruptcy, accounting for it in all its aspects must be carefully aligned with the requirements of the law and reporting to the court, and the accountant has a responsibility to be familiar with both.

CHAPTER 9

A STREAMLINED APPROACH TO PRICE-LEVEL CONVERSION TECHNIQUES

THE PROBLEM OF INFLATION ACCOUNTING

BACKGROUND IN BRIEF

The whole matter of general price-level adjusted statements is currently one of the most controversial topics in the accounting profession. Arguments for and against conversion of conventional statements to remove (insofar as possible) the effects of an unstable money measuring unit are extensive. Many of the arguments on both sides are sound and involve accounting problems that will be difficult to overcome. Other arguments are often shaded by a lack of knowledge of the subject, personal or company financial axes to grind, and recognition of the additional costs involved. Another argument, perhaps a more important one, revolves around the matter of effectively communicating the restructured financial messages incorporated in the adjusted statements.

WHAT IS THE PRICE-LEVEL PROBLEM?

The general purchasing power of the dollar is measured by its ability to acquire goods and services. This power fluctuates as more or less dollars are required to obtain goods and services in general. In a period of rising prices, it takes more dollars to purchase goods and services and the purchasing power of the dollar falls. This is translated into inflation. Conversely, as the price-level goes down the increased purchasing power of the dollar is translated into deflation. In general, this latter case is rarely experienced. In specific instances, deflation may be experienced in the case of some goods and services while inflation is experienced in respect to the great majority of goods and services.

Conventional accounting assumes a stable monetary unit or assumes that changes in the value of money are immaterial. Since the accountant uses an assumed stable dollar as a unit of measurement, all the transactions recorded are done so with dollars of different purchasing power if the price-level is changing in the process. Crudely put, this is comparable to laying out the foundation for a house with a rubber measuring tape. It is easy to visualize the looks of the house built with a rubber measuring tape used to determine its dimension. This has been an ever-present problem from the very beginning of recorded business activity. Perhaps in most cases the "dimensions" were off so little that the accountant could not perceive the structural faults. To put the concept into sharper focus, consider the case of the company with a current year income statement showing a larger dollar amount for all accounts as compared with the previous year yet for the same period the physical volume of business transacted was *less* than that of the previous year. How can the proper financial interpretations be made in such a case, other factors being equal? These transactions are ultimately reflected in the balance sheet so the "measuring tape" differences are reflected there also.

Some Approaches to Solving the Problem

The general purchasing power or index number approach is accepted as the most theoretically sound, and therefore most comprehensive, method of converting conventional financial statements to eliminate the effects of price-level changes. This is the approach illustrated in this chapter.

Some other approaches are partial in nature only in that certain items on the financial statement are adjusted while others are not. One such approach is undertaken by use of the LIFO inventory method. Obviously, only inventories are adjusted. The use of accelerated depreciation in connection with relatively new assets is another approach and represents a partial adjustment for the inflation factor. Another approach makes use of the appropriation of retained earnings. This advises statement readers that management is aware of the inflation factor and is curtailing earnings available for dividends in order to provide for higher costs of replacing plant and equipment. None of these partial adjustments accomplishes the conversion in an effective manner. Each is relatively crude from a financial standpoint, destroys comparability in statement analysis, and there is no official consensus or agreement on them. Various methods of making partial adjustments are outlined below.

Current Replacement Value Approach

The S.E.C. has resolved the matter of accounting for inflation for very large companies by the issuance of Accounting Series Release No. 190, and subsequently, various Staff Accounting Bulletins. Under this approach, current replacement values for certain assets and operating items are to be developed and offered as supplementary information in connection with conventional statements by "qualifying" registrants. The rules apply to registrants whose total of inventories and gross property, plant and equipment as shown in the consolidated balance sheet at the beginning of the most recently completed fiscal year is $100,000,000 or more and where the total of inventories and gross property, plant and equipment is 10 per cent or more of the total assets as shown in the consolidated balance sheet at the beginning of the most recently completed fiscal year.

At this writing it can be safely stated that the rules have not been warmly received by the registrants who qualify. Over and above the cost of obtaining the data required, there remains the problem of too much subjectivity involved in the development of the data. In addition, the procedures as defined, and the data as developed, result in an incomplete picture of the inflation problem and its effect on the subject company. This approach is viewed as simply one more incomplete procedure for dealing with the problem of accounting for inflation.

Replacement Cost Information Requirements

The current replacement cost information required under A.S.R. No. 190 is quoted from Rule 3-17 as follows:

> (a) The current replacement cost of inventories at each fiscal year end for which a balance sheet is required shall be stated. If current replacement cost exceeds net realizable value at that date, that fact shall be stated and the amount of the excess disclosed.
> (b) For the two most recent fiscal years, state the approximate amount which cost of sales would have been if it had been calculated by estimating the current replacement cost of goods and services sold at the times when the sales were made.
> (c) State the estimated current cost of replacing (new) the productive capacity together with the current depreciated replacement cost of the productive capacity on hand at the end of each fiscal year for which a balance sheet is required. For purposes of this rule, assets held under financing leases as defined in Rule 3-16(q) shall be included in productive capacity. In the case of any major business segments which the company does not intend to maintain beyond the economic lives of existing assets, the disclosures set forth in Rules 3-17(c) and (d) are not required provided full disclosure of the facts, amounts and circumstances is made.
> (d) For the two most recent fiscal years, state the approximate amount of depreciation, depletion and amortization which would have been recorded if it were estimated on the basis of average current replacement cost of productive capacity. For purposes of this calculation, economic lives and salvage values currently used in calculating historical cost depreciation, depletion or amortization shall generally be used. For assets being depreciated, depleted or amortized on a time expired basis, the straight-line method shall be used in making this calculation. For assets depreciated, depleted or amortized on any other basis (such as use), that basis shall be used for this calculation.
> (e) Describe the methods used in determining the amounts disclosed in items (a) through (d) above. Describe what consideration, if any, was given in responding to items (a) and (b) to the related effects on direct labor costs, repairs and maintenance, utility and other indirect costs as a result of the assumed replacement of productive capacity. Where the economic lives or salvage values currently used in historical cost financial statements are not used in (d) above, an explanation of other bases used and the reasons therefor shall be disclosed. If depreciation, depletion or amortization expense is a component of inventory costs or cost of sales, indicate that fact and cross-reference the answer for this item in item (b) in order to avoid potential duplication in the use of these data.
> (f) Furnish any additional information—such as the historical customary relationships between cost changes and changes in selling prices, the difficulty and

related costs (such as those related to environmental regulations) which might be experienced in replacing productive capacity—of which management is aware and which it believes is necessary to prevent the above information from being misleading.

Rule 3-17 of Regulation S-X is effective for financial statements for fiscal years ending on or after December 25, 1976, except that the rule shall be initially applicable to the mineral resource assets of registrants engaged in the extractive industries and to registrants' assets located outside the North American continent and the countries of the European Economic Community in financial statements for fiscal years ending on or after December 25, 1977; provided that the historical cost and a description of any such assets excluded from the supplemental replacement cost data are disclosed.

Paragraph (f) above may be described as a "catch-all" requirement. It means that additional information may be necessary to adequately present the replacement cost data in an understandable fashion. At the present, it is up to the company accountants and the external auditors to determine the amount of such additional information necessary to accomplish the objective of preparing clear, understandable financial statements. Some additional degree of sophistication in the area of financial statement analysis is called for on the part of users of these statements. How far the companies can go in trying to simplify financial statements for the benefit of less sophisticated analysts remains to be determined and will present a real challenge.

Some Additional Information

When reporting replacement costs, it is good to make it clear to readers that the company does not necessarily plan to replace inventory and/or plant just because the replacement costs are stated. In addition, it is helpful to indicate that the replacement cost data does not necessarily represent the current market value of the respective assets. The impression should be discouraged that the data so presented represents the amounts for which the assets could be sold.

If there are certain assets for which replacement cost data is not prepared, such as obsolete inventories, discontinued product lines, exempt mineral resources and assets in foreign countries, a presentation should be made in some form. The normal historical relationships between changes in selling prices and changes in cost should also be described.

The reader of reports containing replacement cost data should be reminded that the data presented represents estimates based on subjective judgments and assumptions made by management. Usually, and this is very important, the readers should be advised that the replacement cost data does not account for all the effects of inflation on the respective company operations. It would not be appropriate to use the data in any attempt to calculate an "adjusted" net income.

Current Fair-Value Approach

The current fair-value accounting procedure is a fairly close theoretical relative of the index number procedure and is therefore complete in its application. It involves the same distinction between monetary and non-monetary items. In this procedure, current dollar values are substituted for the index number restatement of non-monetary amounts.

As yet no guidelines have been developed for fair-value accounting. There are a variety of views as to just what the guidelines should be. There are, of course, several ways of determining fair values, and no agreement has been reached or guidelines developed in this respect, either. These factors militate against its use for the present. There are many proponents of the procedure, and while not an accepted practice now, it could be researched and possibly developed into an acceptable procedure for accounting for (or perhaps "away") inflation in the future. After providing some historical background and technical information, a complete example of full price-level will be illustrated using the index number approach.

HISTORICAL DEVELOPMENT OF PRICE-LEVEL ADJUSTED STATEMENTS

Henry W. Sweeney's *Stabilized Accounting*[1] was the first book on the subject and was the product of a comprehensive study of the problem of restating conventional accounting statements. The American Accounting Association Committee on Concepts and Standards Underlying Corporate Financial Statements published a supplementary statement entitled "Price Level Changes and Financial Statements" in the October 1951 issue of *Accounting Review.* Earlier committees had reviewed the problem, also, but none prescribed any restatement procedures and techniques. The Association sponsored a research project which produced, in 1955, two monographs on the subject by Professor Ralph C. Jones and one monograph by Professor Perry Mason.[2] Specific conversion techniques were illustrated in Professor Mason's Monograph.

In the case of the AICPA, its Committee on Accounting Procedure, and subsequently its successor the Accounting Principles Board, have considered the whole matter of price-level changes in varying degrees since 1947. As the product of an authorized research study, AICPA published, in 1963, Accounting Research Study No. 6, "Reporting the Effects of Price-Level Changes." In 1969, the APB issued *Statement No., 3,* "Financial Statements Restated for General Price-Level Changes." *Statement No. 3* recommends the preparation of supplementary statements to accompany conventional statements and sets forth a series of specific guidelines to be followed. A detailed set of working papers and statements covering the conversion of conventional statements is also presented in *Statement No. 3*.

The Financial Accounting Standards Board issued an exposure draft, "Financial Reporting in Units of General Purchasing Power," December 31, 1974. The substance of the FASB proposal requires all entities to include supplemental financial information in units of general purchasing power as a part of their annual financial reports. This includes non-public companies, not-for-profit entities and regulated companies. The proposal calls for full conversion and the use of the Gross National Product Implicit Price Deflator as the general price-level index.

[1]Henry W. Sweeney, *Stabilized Accounting,* Harper & Brothers, (New York: 1936). Reprinted in 1964 by Holt, Rinehart and Winston, Inc., New York.

[2]Ralph C. Jones, *Price Level Changes and Financial Statements, Case Studies of Four Companies* and *Effects of Price Level Changes on Business Income, Capital, and Taxes;* Perry Mason, *Price-Level Changes and Financial Statements, Basic Concepts and Methods* (Columbus, Ohio: American Accounting Association, 1956).

In spite of the activities by the respective individuals and organizations just outlined, there has been no general acceptance of the concept and practically no actual policy adoption and use by companies in the United States. The only case involving actual application and publication in an annual report that has come to the attention of the authors is that of the Indiana Telephone Corporation.

The sharp inflation of the seventies in particular, along with the expectation that there will be continuing inflationary pressures, may provide motivation to examine the matter with renewed interest. Greater and greater distortions in financial statements will create pressures for developing some practical means of improving financial measurement in general.

This chapter does not debate the relative merits and demerits of the feasibility of preparing price-level adjusted statements as a general practice, nor does it attempt to encourage or discourage the adoption of the proposed practice. What it does do is illustrate a complete procedure with necessary working papers to accomplish the full conversion of a set of conventional financial statements. The guidelines of *Statement No. 3* of the APB are incorporated in the illustration making it easy to follow and then adapt to the accountant's own needs.

THE PRICE INDEX AS A BENCHMARK

A general-price-level index is an index which purports to measure the exchange ratio between money and a given set of goods and services at certain specific points in time. The larger the set of goods and services used in the calculations the more generally representative is the index, and the better it reflects the changes in the purchasing power of money. Specifically, if the year 19X1 is considered the base year with the price-level index at 100 (100%) and the index for year 19X5 stands at 125, it can be said that the purchasing power of the dollar has declined 20% (100/125) of what it was in the year 19X1, to approximately 80 cents. When the proper indices are applied to the dollar amounts in a given set of financial statements, the price-level changes are erased and a common-size dollar is then visible and measures on a comparable basis the indicated business activity.

The successful conversion of financial statements to eliminate the effects of price-level changes is dependent upon the validity of the index used. There are several price indices developed and used in various types of economic analysis. These include the Consumer Price Index, Composite Construction Index and the Gross National Product Implicit Price Deflator. The GNP Deflator is the index recommended for use in converting financial statements. This index is the only one that represents a weighted-average of all the goods and services exchanged in all segments of the United States economy. It is therefore the most representative of all the indices in terms of showing price-level changes in the economy.

It is appropriate to point out here that price-levels in some segments of the economy and, indeed, in certain industries may not change notably with the economy as a whole. In this event, proper conversion techniques will call for a specific index related to the particular segment or industry.

The GNP Implicit Price Deflator is developed on a quarterly and yearly basis. Normally, this is satisfactory for most conversions. If, in a given situation, the business activity pattern is such that a monthly index is needed to avoid distortions caused by using quarterly indices, the Consumer Price Index may be used for bridging the calendar quarter. The CPI is developed on a monthly basis and usually approximates the GNP Deflator. If the rates of change are reasonably close on a quarterly basis, the CPI monthly indices can be used to bridge the intra-quarterly period. The GNP Deflators are developed by the U.S. Department of Commerce, Office of Business Economics and are published in the *Survery of Current Business.* The Consumer Price Index is developed by the Bureau of Labor Statistics of the U.S. Department of Labor and is published in the *Monthly Labor Review* and the *Survey of Current Business.*

The GNP Deflator is reproduced in Figure 9A-26. The year 1958 is the base year (1958 Index = 100).[3] **The procedure that has received more general acceptance provides for** bringing prior period figures up to (or down to, if a deflationary situation) the current period level rather than taking current figures and shrinking them to a comparable basis for measurement against a prior period dollar considered to be "sound" and usable as a financial benchmark. As an example, a fixed asset purchased in the fourth quarter of 1956 for $12,000 would be restated as of December 31, 1974, at $22,392, by virtue of the following computation:

$$\frac{\text{(4th qtr 1974 Deflator) 177.97}}{\text{(4th qtr 1956 Deflator 95.4}} = 1.866 \text{ (multiplier)}$$

$12,000 (historical cost) × 1.866 (multiplier) = $22,392 (restated amount)

In the conversion process, after the proper ratios are determined, they should be turned into multipliers (as above) for convenience in developing restated amounts. Ratios and multipliers for the illustration developed in this chapter are listed in Figure 9A-25.

Monetary and Nonmonetary Classification of Assets and Liabilities

Another essential procedure in the conversion of financial statements for price-level changes is that of classifying the assets and liabilities of the company into monetary and nonmonetary assets and liabilities. Different techniques are used in the restatement of these two kinds of assets and liabilities.

In a period of inflation, holders of money and monetary claims representing fixed sums of money will suffer a general price-level loss since the purchasing power of the money and monetary claims has decreased. Conversely, the debtors will have a gain since they will be satisfying fixed dollar obligations with dollars of lower purchasing power. In the case of deflation, the effects are just the opposite.

The following represent some assets and liabilities which are or will be converted into a fixed number of dollars irrespective of changes in prices:

[3]**Since this illustration was developed, the deflators have been recalculated using as a base year 1972 = 100,** instead of 1958 = 100. This does not change any of the principles and procedures used in this illustration nor does it change the structure of any working papers.

Cash
Accounts and Notes Receivable
Marketable securities—Bonds
Prepaid Interest
Cash Surrender value—Life Insurance
Accounts and Notes Payable
Long-Term Debt
Accrued Expenses Payable.

A classification schedule of monetary and nonmonetary items is presented in Figure 9A-24.

AN ILLUSTRATION OF PURCHASING POWER LOSS

An example underscores the economic phenomenon of the disintegrating purchasing power of the dollar in a period of inflation. Assume a company has cash transactions as follows with a relatively even flow of receipts and disbursements:

Balance, beginning of period	$50,000
Receipts	90,000
	140,000
Disbursements	65,000
Balance, end of period	$ 75,000

Also, assume a deflator index of 150 at the beginning of the period, an average index of 175 for the period and an index of 200 at the end of the period. The cash position of the company, giving effect to price-level changes, is determined by the following computations:

	Historical Balances	Multiplier	Restated Balances
Cash balance, beginning of period	$50,000	1.3333*	66,667
Receipts	90,000	1.1429**	102,861
	140,000		169,528
Disbursements	65,000	1.1429	74,289
Cash balance end of period	$75,000		95,239
Cash balance end of period not restated			75,000
General price-level loss arising from the holding of cash			$20,239

*200/150 = 1.3333
**200/175 = 1.1429

The large loss in this example is due to the sharp price-level change as evidenced by the indices used. This was for emphasis only. The loss will not be a realized loss, however, until the cash is disbursed.

Continuing the illustration, a situation is presented in connection with notes payable using the same beginning and ending price-level indices as in the previous example. The quarterly indices for the year are as follows:

First Quarter	165
Second Quarter	175
Third Quarter	190

	Historical Balances	**Multiplier**	**Restated Balances**
Notes payable—Banks, beginning of period	$100,000	1.3333*	133,333
New Note, May 1	25,000	1.1429**	28,573
	125,000		161,906
Liquidation of Note, Aug. 1	40,000	1.0526***	42,104
Notes payable—Banks, end of period	$ 85,000		$ 119,802
Notes payable—Banks, end of period, not restated			85,000
General price-level gain arising from debtor status			$ 34,802

*200/150 = 1.3333
**200/175 = 1.1429
***200/190 = 1.0526

The restating of the accounts represents restated costs and involves price changes only. The restated accounts do not purport to represent current values such as appraisal values, replacement costs or any other type of measure.

In the case of monmonetary items such as inventories, plant and equipment, prepaid expense items and deferred charges, the holders thereof may or may not gain or lose general purchasing power. If the rates of general price-level change and the specific-item price change are the same, and in the same direction, there will be no resulting general purchasing power gain or loss. Should the price of a monmonetary item remain constant or change at a different rate, there will be a general purchasing power gain or loss. Since the gains and losses on nonmonetary items are composed of both general price level changes and specific-item price structure changes, they differ from those on monetary items which are price-level related only.

How to Handle the Foreign Currency Problem

There are two kinds of gains/losses likely to appear in the restatement of foreign currency. One kind represents price-level changes and the other represents foreign exchange rate changes. Both are not necessarily present in each case. The APB guidelines recommend that the foreign currency items be stated at the current foreign exchange rate in spite of the fact they are nonmonetary items. A few of the Board members were of the opinion that the effect of both the foreign exchange rate change and the general price-level change were measurable and should be reported separately. This assumes, of course, that the foreign exchange rate has actually changed.

Income Tax Restatement

General price-level restatements are not recognized for tax purposes by the income tax law. In restated financial statements the usual relationship between income tax expense and before-tax earnings is not maintained. The income tax expense as restated is based on the historical-dollar income tax expense reported in the conventional statements. Here again some board members were of the opinion that the restatement should be designed so as to develop a more direct relationship between the income tax expense and the related income elements.

Restatement of Investments and Bonds

There are some assets and liabilities that have both monetary and nonmonetary characteristics. For purposes of restatement it is necessary to resolve the problem by determining the purpose for which each item is held and use that as a basis for classification. Securities held in the marketable and investment classifications and in various funds are to be treated as monetary items if they are held primarily for income and return of fixed principal. Bonds held will usually fall into this category. If the market price is the primary consideration, the securities should be clarified as nonmonetary items. Also, if convertible bonds are held, and it is expected they will be converted into common stock, they should be considered as nonmonetary.

Investments in unconsolidated subsidiaries are considered to be nonmonetary if carried at cost and monetary if carried on the equity basis. If advances to unconsolidated subsidiaries are not of the current or working capital type but simply represent additional investments, they are treated as nonmonetary assets. When combined or consolidated financial statements involving foreign branches or subsidiaries are to be prepared, it is necessary to first convert the foreign units' statements into US dollars under the accepted procedures and then restate for the general price-level change in US dollars.

Estimated Liabilities

Provisions for warranties and for self-insurance would normally be treated as nonmonetary items. If, however, the adequacy of the provisions has been determined in terms of current costs at statement date, they may be treated as monetary items with no restatement necessary, the historical-dollar amounts being carried over to the restated statements without change.

INVENTORIES

All inventories except those manufactured under contract for a fixed price, and so valued, are nonmonetary. The restatement of inventories could involve a tremendous amount of detailed analysis work if carried out "by the book." The possibility of using abbreviated procedures should be investigated since the end result may not be very different from the more detailed approach. FIFO inventories may already be stated in current dollars; acquisition practices will be a determinant. Perhaps most of the purchases may be identified to specific quarter or quarters. The same approach may be taken in the case of weighted-average cost inventories. Where the rate of turnover is relatively low, use of the year's average deflator may give satisfactory results.

In the case of lower of cost or market inventories, the same rules apply in the restatement process as with conventional statements. On occasion, the restated inventory (from cost) will be higher than the market value thereof, necessitating a write-down to the market value.

If beginning LIFO inventories include several layers, use of the yearly average deflator for the respective "layer year" will usually give results close to those developed on a quarterly basis or by specific identification of purchases.

Of course, not all problems that might arise in the monetary-nonmonetary classification process are pointed up here nor can they be foreseen. Any study of a doubtful item must first consider the fixed-number-of-dollars claims receivable or payable aspect. This aspect will usually help resolve the matter since it is a key element in the generation of general price-level gains or losses. Once classification is established, the current accounts can be correctly restated and a general price-level gain or loss determined. In subsequent years, the accounts restated will be simply "rolled forward" to accomplish restatement in terms of the respective year's dollars. This applies, of course, to all accounts, monetary and nonmonetary.

A COMPLETE ILLUSTRATION OF PRICE-LEVEL CONVERSION

To assist in the practical application of a restatement of financial statements in order to eliminate the effects of general price-level changes, a series of steps are set forth below. References are made at each step to the illustrative statements and working papers. While any method of indexing may be used, the illustrative papers here will be indexed as follows: **Figures 9A-1 through 9A-4 are historical cost statements; working papers are shown in Figures 9A-5 through 9A-21 inclusive; and restated statements are illustrated in Figures** 9A-22 and 9A-23. Hopefully, this will facilitate quick reference. The reader is referred to Figure 9A-25 for a schedule of indices and multipliers used in the case.

The case presented here is an actual one. The years 1973 and 1974 were chosen for conversion since the general price-level increase was rather sharp during those years. The M.O.B. Company is a relatively small individual proprietorship with a little over half a million dollars in assets. To approximate the situation of a corporation, the proprietors' equity account was analyzed from 1961 (for practical reasons) to identify the initial investment, subsequent additional investments, net incomes (losses) and withdrawals. The net incomes (losses) and withdrawals were combined to develop a reinvested earnings account as the equivalent of the corporate retained earnings account.

Each year-end inventory is priced at the lower of cost or market and, because of its nature, is considered to have been acquired ratably throughout the respective years. In conversion, the respective years' average deflator is used because of the assumed uniform acquisition. Also, the assumption was made that costs and expenses were incurred, sales made, and payments received and made uniformly throughout the year (not unrealistic in this case).

Step 1—Classify as monetary and nonmonetary all asset, liability and equity accounts

The historical cost statements to be restated are Figures 9A-1 and 9A-4. With the exception of Figure 9A-3, these statements have been entered on working papers, Figures 9A-5 to 9A-7, in columnar form with column headings appropriate to the restatement process. The classification of each item is indicated in column 1 of Figures 9A-5 and 9A-6. The reader is referred to Figure 9A-24 for a listing of monetary and nonmonetary accounts. The restatement of the December 31, 1972 historical balances per working paper, Figure 9A-5, is necessary to obtain a starting balance for the Reinvested Earnings (retained earnings) account for 1973. In most cases, it is not practical to restate all the yearly statements from the inception of the company. The 1972 historical balances are restated in terms of December 31, 1973 dollars. The restated Reinvested Earnings amount for December 1, 1972 is literally a "plug" figure which is used to avoid restating all accounts from the inception of the company.

Step 2—Analyze all the nonmonetary asset and liability accounts and equity accounts for the years to be restated. Date of origination of each component money amount must be separately stated in the analysis. Restate the money amounts using the respective indices.

Of course, the analyst can use any type or style of working papers desired and/or appropriate to the particular analysis problem. The working papers used in this case (Figure 9A-8 to 9A-14) are designed to be used for analyzing almost any nonmonetary account so as to provide the restatement information needed, and they are recommended by the authors. The objective was to avoid both the development of a great variety of working papers, thereby slowing down the restatement task, and of more concern here, the greater difficulty for the reader in following the case. It is recommended that the reader not familiar with the general price level restatement process review Figures 9A-8 to 9A-14 for structural detail and tie in indicated historical balances with the conventional cost statements shown in Figures 9A-1 and 9A-2 at this point.

While acquisition dates for years prior to 1973 were broken down no more finely than annually in this case, it can and should be done where significant amounts are involved and the information is available. A *Statement No. 3* guideline recommends treating acquisitions prior to 1945 as though acquired in 1945.[4]

Because the inventory in this case did not require a detailed analysis for restatement purposes, the only analysis necessary involved the fixed asset, accumulated depreciation, and owner equity accounts. Figures 9A-8 to 9A-16 cover these accounts.

Step 3—Record the historical and restated balances for the years to be restated on the working balance sheets and working statements of income and retained earnings.

In this illustration, Step 3 was actually carried out in Figures 9A-5 and 9A-7 as a part of Step 1. Working paper totals for the nonmonetary accounts analyzed should be checked carefully against the working balance sheets to insure accuracy. Since a variety of indices will have been used to obtain multipliers, the column for recording indices on the working balance sheets should show the working paper index for each account instead of attempting to show each and every index used. As an example, reference to Figure 9A-5, column 4, Trucks and Autos account, will direct the reader to Figure 9A-8 as the source of indices actually used. Refer to Figure 9A-25 for a schedule of indices and multipliers used in this case.

Step 4—Analyze all operating accounts and all changes in retained earnings to determine dates of origin of the content of each account.

Practical judgment must be exercised in this step to avoid entrapment into the analysis of an enormous amount of detail. In the case at hand, it was found that sales and collections and disbursements were relatively uniform throughout the year. It did not appear that a restatement by quarters, using quarterly indices combined to obtain annual totals, would yield results significantly different from those obtained by using average annual indices. If the timing of transactions is such that peaks and valleys occur during the fiscal year, it may be necessary to restate by quarters or even monthly (using the CPI rate of change intra-quarterly). See the reference earlier in this chapter to the use of the monthly CPI indices for the purpose of obtaining a higher degree of preciseness in the restated money amounts.

In this case, the only analyses necessary involved the proprietor's capital account (Figures 9A-14 to 9A-16), the determination of the loss on the sale of an automobile (Figure 9A-17), and the separation of depreciation from total operating expenses (Figure 9A-18).

Step 5—Restate the prior years' money amounts in terms of the current year's dollars.

This procedure is known as a "roll-forward" process. It is accomplished by dividing the fourth quarter IPD of the prior year to get a multiplier to up-date all the prior year accounts.

[4]See A.P.B., "Financial Statements Restated for General Price-Level Changes," *Statement No. 3* (New York: AICPA, 1969), p. 35.

Reference to Figures 9A-5 and 9A-6 as well as analysis working papers will provide examples of the "roll-forward" procedure. The multiplier is used uniformly against all prior year amounts on these working papers. The prior years' statements are now stated in the current years' dollars which will facilitate comparative analysis. Differences due to price-level changes have been largely eliminated.

Step 6—Determine the general price-level gain or loss for the years being restated.

The income statements (restated) cannot be completed until the general price-level gain or loss has been determined (refer to Figures 9A-19 and 9A-20). This is the gain or loss resulting from holding monetary items. The total "inventory" of monetary items (historical balances) held at the beginning and end of each year can be taken from the working balance sheets (Figures 9A-5 and 9A-6). These items are restated from the fourth quarter of one year to the fourth quarter of the next year using the respective multipliers. Note, too, that operations and other monetary transactions are restated using identical multipliers as those used in Figure 9A-5 through 9A-16. The development of the general price-level losses represents the last items needed to complete the working income statements (Figure 9A-7).

The reinvested earnings portion of Figure 9A-7 can be completed now with the inclusion of historical and restated amounts developed in the analysis of proprietor's withdrawals (Figure 9A-16). The ending balances are carried forward to Figure 9A-6 for completion of the balance sheets.

Comparative conventional statements and general price-level basis statements taken from Figures 9A-6 and 9A-7 are presented and are indexed as Figures 9A-22 and 9A-23.

In many cases, the analytical working papers can be prepared on an extended basis so that subsequent years' analyses may be placed thereon. This dispenses with the copying over of much of the necessary material. The reader is referred to Figure 9A-21 as an example of continuing the worksheet into subsequent years. This paper is an extended version of Figure 9A-8 (Trucks and Autos only), assuming sales of vehicles in 1974 and 1975 as well as an acquisition in 1975. The amount of detail in the accounts being analyzed will determine whether or not such working papers are feasible.

SUMMARY

In view of the controversial nature of this topic, it is, of course, recommended that the reader review the latest relevant pronouncements of the FASB prior to an actual restatement for price-level changes of a company's financial statements. The complete restatement process should be carried out even if the restated accounts will be studied by management only. It is true that the restatement of certain assets and liabilities will account for most of the change in the over-all financial presentation in the majority of cases. However, different combinations and types of assets and liabilities and different dates of acquisition will materially affect the results of the restatement. If a partial restatement should be attempted to save time or for any other reason, the accountant is in the position of having limited the fields in which financial evaluations and decisions could be made by management.

A STREAMLINED APPROACH TO PRICE-LEVEL CONVERSION TECHNIQUES

When a restatement for price-level changes is to be carried out for the first time, the task is a fearsome one in terms of the analyses of accounts to be made, the classification process and choice of deflators to be used. Once the initial restatement is accomplished, it then becomes simply a matter of analyzing the current year nonmonetary accounts and "rolling forward" the prior year accounts where they are to be used on a comparative basis. The techniques and procedures developed and presented here, and especially the working balance sheet and statement of income and retained earnings, will simplify the accountant's task significantly. The work sheets, in skeletal form, may be used exactly as shown, the accountant simply filling in the particular firm's financial data and the indices he chooses. From there on it is merely a matter of following the steps as explained.

APPENDIX

Figure 9A-1

M.O.B. COMPANY
STATEMENT OF FINANCIAL CONDITION
DECEMBER 31, 1972

Assets

Current assets	
Cash	$ 5,734
Installment contracts receivable	171,255
Inventory	169,942
Other accounts receivable	1,008
Total current assets	347,939
Investments	
Cash surrender value of life insurance	22,355
Property and equipment	
Trucks and autos	17,690
Furniture and fixtures	4,875
Warehouse and leasehold improvements	57,831
Boat	2,183
	82,579
Less accumulated depreciation	55,090
Net property and equipment	27,489
Total assets	$397,783

Liabilities and Owner's Equity

Current liabilities	
Accounts payable	$ 58,667
Notes payable	34,569
Long-term debt due within one year	1,506
Accrued commissions	7,774
Payroll taxes payable	2,108
Sales tax payable	11,911
Total current liabilities	116,535
Long-term debt	38,291
Total liabilities	154,826
Owner's equity	242,957
Total liabilities and owner's equity	$397,783

Note: Conventional statement referred to as "Historical" in the working papers.

Figure 9A-2

M.O.B. COMPANY
BALANCE SHEETS
DECEMBER 31, 1974 AND 1973

Assets

	1974	1973
Current assets		
Cash	$ 7,053	$ 6,839
Installment contracts receivable	182,517	178,071
Inventory	268,000	238,814
Other accounts receivable	1,808	2,890
Total current assets	459,378	426,614
Investments		
Cash surrender value of life insurance	45,906	42,048
Property and equipment		
Trucks and autos	23,582	19,577
Furniture and fixtures	8,915	7,933
Warehouse and leasehold improvements	60,977	60,977
Boat	3,560	3,560
	97,034	92,047
Less accumulated depreciation	62,716	56,193
Net property and equipment	34,318	35,854
Total assets	$539,602	504,516

Liabilities and Owner's Equity

	1974	1973
Current liabilities		
Accounts payable	$ 64,236	$103,566
Notes payable	93,250	66,503
Accrued commissions	11,468	629
Payroll taxes payable	624	1,236
Sales tax payable	10,796	11,144
Total current liabilities	180,374	183,078
Long-term debt	37,538	37,538
Total liabilities	217,912	220,616
Owner's equity	321,690	283,900
Total liabilities and owner's equity	$539,602	$504,516

Note: Conventional statement referred to as "Historical" in the working papers.

Figure 9A-3

M.O.B. COMPANY
STATEMENTS OF OWNER'S EQUITY
YEARS ENDED DECEMBER 31, 1974 AND 1973

	1974	1973
Balance at beginning of year	$283,900	$242,957
Net income for the year	61,220	31,701
Additional investments	13,259	34,757
	358,379	309,415
Less owner's withdrawals	36,689	25,515
Balance at end of year	$321,690	$283,900

Note: Conventional statement referred to as "Historical" in the working papers.

Figure 9A-4

M.O.B. COMPANY
STATEMENTS OF INCOME
YEARS ENDED DECEMBER 31, 1974 AND 1973

	1974		1973	
	Amount	% of Sales	Amount	% of Sales
Net sales	$639,818	100.00%	$514,970	100.00%
Cost of sales				
Beginning inventory	238,814		169,942	
Purchases	353,411		350,410	
	592,225		520,352	
Less ending inventory	268,000		238,814	
Total cost of sales	324,225	50.67	281,538	54.68
Gross profit	315,593	49.33	233,432	45.32
Operating expenses	263,615	41.20	214,155	41.58
Operating profit	51,978	8.13	19,277	3.74
Other income and expense				
Recovery of bad accounts	1,188		3,968	
Finance charges	17,383		13,470	
	18,571	2.90	17,438	3.38
Interest paid	9,329	1.46	5,014	.97
Excess of other income over other expense	9,242	1.44	12,424	2.41
Net income before taxes	$61,220	9.57	$31,701	6.15

Note: Conventional statement referred to as "Historical" in the working papers.

Figure 9A-5

M.O.B. COMPANY
GENERAL PRICE-LEVEL RESTATEMENT—1973–74
WORKING BALANCE SHEET
DECEMBER 31, 1972

Classification: Monetary (M) or Nonmonetary (NM)	Accounts	Historical Balances 12-31-72	Indices Used to Obtain Multipliers or Working Paper Reference	Multipliers	Restated Balances 12-31-72
	Assets				
M	Cash	$ 5,734	158.93/147.63	1.077	$ 6,176
M	Install Accounts Rec.	171,255	158.93/147.63	1.077	184,442
N M	Inventory (LCM)	169,942	158.93/146.63	1.088	184,897
M	Other Accts. Rec.	1,008	158.93/147.63	1.077	1,086
	Total Current Assets	347,939			376,601
M	Cash Surrender Value—LI	22,355	158.93/147.63	1.077	24,076
N M	Trucks and Autos	17,690	Figure 9A-8		22,404
N M	Furniture & Fixtures	4,875	Figure 9A-8		6,358
N M	Whse. & Leasehold Impr.	57,831	Figure 9A-9		86,413
N M	Boat	2,183	Figure 9A-9		2,834
N M	Less Accum. Depr.	(55,090)	Figures 9A-10-13		(79,847)
	Total Assets	$397,783			$438,839
	Liabilities				
M	Accounts Payable	$ 58,667	158.93/147.63	1.077	$ 63,184
M	Notes Payable	36,075	158.93/147.63	1.077	38,853
M	Accrued Taxes & Expenses	21,793	158.93/147.63	1.077	23,471
M	Long-term Debt	38,291	158.93/147.63	1.077	41,239
	Owner Equity				
N M	Investments	220,875	Figure 9A-14		317,100
N M	Reinvested Earnings	22,082	Figure 9A-15	(To Balance)	(45,008)
	Total Liabilities and Owner Equity	$397,783			$438,839

NOTES

The purpose of this worksheet is to obtain a beginning Re-invested Earnings balance for the first year of the two year periods to be restated. The monetary accounts are restated from fourth quarter, 1972 dollars to fourth quarter, 1973 dollars. The non-monetary accounts are restated from years of origin dollars to fourth quarter, 1973 dollars. See individual working papers. The restated Reinvested Earnings is the amount necessary to balance the balance sheet as restated.

Figure 9A-6

M.O.B. COMPANY
GENERAL PRICE-LEVEL RESTATEMENT-1973-74
WORKING BALANCE SHEETS FOR THE DATES INDICATED

Classification: Monetary (M) Nonmonetary (NM)	Accounts	12-31-73 Historical Balances	12-31-73 Multipliers (Fig.)	12-31-73 Restated Balances 1973 $s	12-31-73 Restated Balances 1974 $s[1]	12-31-74 Historical Balances	12-31-74 Multipliers (Fig.)	12-31-74 Restated Balances 1974 $s
	Assets							
M	Cash	$ 6,839	—	$ 6,839	$ 7,660	$ 7,053	—	$ 7,053
M	Install Controls Receivable	178,071	—	178,071	199,440	182,517	—	182,517
NM	Inventory (LCM)	238,814	Fig. 9A-7	245,978	275,495	268,000	Fig. 9A-7	280,328
M	Other Accounts Receivable	2,890	—	2,890	3,236	1,808	—	1,808
	Total Current Assets	426,614		433,778	485,831	459,378		471,706
M	Cash Surrender Value-Life Insurance	42,048	—	42,048	47,094	45,906	—	45,906
NM	Trucks and Autos	19,577	Fig. 9A-8	21,986	24,624	23,582	Fig. 9A-8	28,885
NM	Furniture and Fixtures	7,933	Fig. 9A-8	9,587	10,737	8,915	Fig. 9A-8	11,719
NM	Whs. & Leasehold Impr.	60,977	Fig. 9A-9	89,600	100,352	60,977	Fig. 9A-9	100,352
NM	Boat	3,560	Fig. 9A-9	4,267	4,779	3,560	Fig. 9A-9	4,779
NM	Less: Accumulated Depreciation	(56,193)	Fig. 9A-10 -13	(79,952)	(89,546)	(62,716)	Fig. 10	(98,056)
	Total Assets	$504,516		$521,314	$583,871	$539,602		$565,291
	Liabilities							
M	Accounts Payable	$103,566	—	$103,566	$115,994	$ 64,236	—	$ 64,236
M	Notes Payable	66,503	—	66,503	74,483	93,250	—	93,250
M	Accrued Taxes & Expenses	13,009	—	13,009	14,570	22,888	—	22,888
M	Long-term Debts	37,538	—	37,538	42,043	37,538	—	37,538
	Owner Equity							
NM	Investments	255,632	Fig. 9A-14	352,900	395,248	268,891	Fig. 9A-14	409,117
NM	Reinvested Earnings	28,268	Fig. 9A-7	(52,202)	(58,467)	52,799	Fig. 9A-7	(61,738)
	Total Liabilities and Owner Equity	$504,516		$521,314	$583,871	$539,602		$565,291

NOTES

These working balance sheets are the vehicles for obtaining the restated account balances for the respective years. For 12-31-73, the monetary accounts are extended as is, no restatement being necessary. The non-monetary accounts are restated from year of origin dollar (except 1973 which is from quarter of origin dollars) to fourth quarter, 1973 dollars. See individual working papers.

If the balance sheet for 1973 is to be compared with that of 1974, all the accounts therein must be "rolled forward" to fourth quarter, 1974 dollars. See column 6 and footnote (1).

For 12-31-74, the monetary accounts are extended as is, no restatement being necessary. The non-monetary accounts are restated from year of origin dollars (except 1973 and 1974 which is from quarter of origin dollars) to fourth quarter, 1974 dollars. See individual working papers.

Of course, the balance sheets cannot be completed until the respective Reinvested Earnings balances have been determined per Figure 9A-7.

[1] "Rolled forward" by using 4th quarter, 1974/73 multiplier of 1.120 (177.97/158.93)

Figure 9A-7

M.O.B. COMPANY
GENERAL PRICE-LEVEL RESTATEMENT—1973-74
WORKING STATEMENTS OF INCOME AND RE-INVESTED EARNINGS
FOR THE PERIODS INDICATED

	1973				1974		
Accounts	**Historical Balances**	**Multipliers (Fig.)**	**Restated Balances 1973 $s**	**Restated Balances 1974 $s**	**Historical Balances**	**Multipliers (Fig.)**	**Restated Balances 1974 $s**
Net Sales	$514,970	1.030[1]	$530,419	$594,069	$639,818	1.046[3]	$669,250
Cost of Sales							
Beginning Inventory	169,942	1.088[2]	184,897	207,085	238,814	fwd.	275,495
Purchases	350,410	1.030	360,922	404,232	353,411	1.046	369,668
	520,352		545,819	611,317	592,225		645,163
Less Ending Inventory	238,814	1.030	245,978	275,495	268,000	1.046	280,328
Cost of Sales	281,538		299,841	335,822	324,225		364,835
Gross Profit	233,432		230,578	258,247	315,593		304,415
Operating Expenses							
Depreciation	7,067	Fig. 9A-13	8,475	9,492	5,479	Fig. 9A-13	8,510
Other (Fig. 9A-18)	207,088	1.030	213,301	238,897	258,136	1.046	270,010
Total Oper. Expenses	214,155		221,776	248,389	263,615		278,520
Operating Profit	19,277		8,802	9,858	51,978		25,895
Other Income and Expense							
Recovery of Bad Accounts	3,968	1.030	4,087	4,577	1,188	1.046	1,243
Finance Charges	13,470	1.030	13,874	15,539	17,382	1.046	18,183
	17,438		17,961	20,116	18,571		19,426
Loss on Sale of Auto	-0-	Fig. 9A-17	318	356	-0-		-0-
General Price Level Loss	-0-	Fig. 9A-19	2,264	2,536	-0-	Fig. 9A-20	1,549
Interest Paid	5,014	1.030	5,164	5,784	9,329	1.046	9,758
	5,014		7,746	8,676	9,329		11,307
Excess of Other Income over Other Expense	12,424		10,215	11,440	9,242		8,119
Net Income Before Taxes	31,701		19,017	21,298	61,220		34,014
Reinvested Earnings-beginning of Year	22,082	fwd.	(45,008)	(50,409)	28,268	fwd.	(58,467)
	53,783		(25,991)	(29,111)	89,488		(24,453)
Withdrawals	25,515	Fig. 9A-16	26,211	29,356	36,689	Fig. 9A-16	37,285
Reinvested Earnings-end of Year	$ 28,268		$ (52,202)	$ (58,467)	$ 52,799		$ (61,738)

NOTES

These working statements of income and reinvestment earnings are the vehicles for obtaining the restated account balances for the respective years. The historical amounts for 1973 are restated as indicated in column 3. If quarterly (or monthly) Deflators must be used instead of the annual average as in this case, the respective accounts will have to be assembled on preliminary working papers which combine the quarterly (monthly) restated amounts to obtain the annual amounts to be used on this working paper. See individual working papers where appropriate as indicated in column 3.

If the 1973 statement is to be compared with that of 1974, all the accounts therein must be "rolled forward" to fourth quarter, 1974 dollars. See column 5 and Footnote (4).

The historical amounts for 1974 are restated using the same technique as indicated above for the 1973 historical amounts.

[1]GNP -1 PD's—158.93/154.31
[2]GNP -1 PD's—158.93/146.12
[3]GNP -1 PD's—177.97/170.18
[4]"Rolled forward" by using 4th quarter, 1974/73 multipliers of 1.120 (177.97/158.93).

Figure 9A-8

M.O.B. COMPANY
GENERAL PRICE-LEVEL RESTATEMENT—1973-74
ANALYSES OF TRUCKS AND AUTOS, FURNITURE AND FIXTURES
FOR THE PERIODS INDICATED

Trucks and Autos

Date of Acq.	Notes	Yearly Historical Balances	GNP I P.D.'s Used	Multi-pliers	Restated Balances 1973 $s	"Roll Forward" Multi-pliers	Restated Balances 1974 $s
1966	(These years listed net	$ 6,730	158.93/114.15	1.395	$ 9,388		
1969	of reductions for	6,010	158.93/128.20	1.240	7,452		
1971	retirements)	4,950	158.93/141.35	1.124	5,564		
	Totals 12-31-72	17,690 (col. 3, Fig. 9A-5)			22,404 (col. 6, Fig. 9A-5)		
1973	**Additions**						
Qtr. 2		8,617	158.93/152/61	1.041	8,970		
1973	**Reductions**						
1966	(Retirements in the case of fixed assets)	(6,730)	(take out as put in)		(9,388)		
	Totals 12-31-73	19,577 (col. 3, Fig. 9A-6)			$21,986 (col. 5, Fig. 9A-6)	1.120	$24,624 (col. 6, Fig. 9A-6)
1974	**Additions**						
Qtr. 2		4,005	177.97/167.31	1.064			4,261
1974	**Reductions**						
	None						
	Totals 12-31-74	$23,582 (col. 7, Fig. 9A-6)					$28,885 (col. 9, Fig. 9A-6)

Furniture and Fixtures

Date of Acq.	Notes	Yearly Historical Balances	GNP I P.D.'s Used	Multi-pliers	Restated Balances 1973 $s
1953		$ 616	158.93/ 88.30	1.800	$ 1,109
1958		245	158.93/100.00	1.589	389
1964		128	158.93/108.90	1.459	187
1965		391	158.93/110.90	1.433	560
1967		517	158.93/117.30	1.355	701
1969		593	158.93/128.20	1.240	735
1971		2,279	158.93/141.35	1.124	2,562
1972		106	158.93/146.12	1.088	115
	Totals 12-31-72	4,875 (col. 3, Fig. 9A-5)			6,358 (col. 6, Fig. 9A-5)
1973	**Additions**				
Qtr. 1		2,822	158.93/149.95	1.060	2,991
Qtr. 3		106	158.93/155.67	1.021	108
Qtr. 4		130	158.93/158.93	1.000	130

Figure 9A-8 continued

1973	**Reductions**						
	None						
	Totals 12-31-73	7,933 (col. 3, Fig. 9A-6)			$ 9,587 (col. 5, Fig. 9A-6)	1.120	$10,737 (col. 6, Fig. 9A-6)
1974	**Additions**						
Qtr. 4		982	177.97/177.97	1.000			982
1974	**Reductions**						
	None						
	Totals 12-31-74	$ 8,915 (col. 7, Fig. 9A-6)					$11,719 (col. 9, Fig. 9A-6)

NOTES

Normally, the annual average Deflator will be used in restating amounts from years prior to 1973 (in this case), the first year of restatement. Quarterly or monthly Deflators could be used if the difference would be significant. All items up to and including the fourth quarter of 1973 must be restated in terms of fourth quarter, 1973 dollars. See columns 4 and 5.

All of the amounts restated as above will have to be "rolled forward" for use in the 1974 restated accounts. See columns 7 and 8. If the roll forward process is carried out on this working paper it is not repeated on the working balance sheet; the totals here are simply brought over to Figures 9A-5 and 9A-6.

Figure 9A-9

M.O.B. COMPANY
GENERAL PRICE-LEVEL RESTATEMENT
WAREHOUSE AND LEASEHOLD IMPROVEMENTS, BOAT
FOR THE PERIODS INDICATED

		Warehouse and Leasehold Improvements					
Date of Acq.	**Notes**	**Yearly Historical Balances**	**GNP I.P.D.'s Used**	**Multi-pliers**	**Restated Balances 1973 $s**	**"Roll Forward" Multi-pliers**	**Restated Balances 1974 $s**
1958		$19,438	158.93/100.00	1.589	$30,887		
1960		14,997	158.93/103.30	1.539	23,080		
1963		15,470	158.93/107.10	1.484	22,957		
1964		1,386	158.93/108.90	1.459	2,022		
1965		1,018	158.93/110.90	1.433	1,459		
1972		5,522	158.93/146.12	1.088	6,008		
	Totals 12-31-72	57,831 (col. 3, Fig. 9A-5)			86,413 (col. 6, Fig. 9A-5)		

Figure 9A-9 continued

1973	**Additions**						
Qtr. 2		1,960	158.93/155.67	1.021	2,001		
Qtr. 4		1,186	158.93/158.93	1.000	1,186		
1973	**Reductions**						
	None						
	Totals 12-31-73	$60,977 (col. 3, Fig. 9A-6)			$89,600 (col. 5, Fig. 9A-6)	1.120	$100,352 (col. 6, Fig. 9A-6)
1974	**Additions**						
	None						
1974	**Reductions**						
	None						
	Totals 12-31-74	60,977 (col. 7, Fig. 9A-6)					$100,352 (col. 9, Fig. 9A-6)

Boat

Date of Acq.	Notes	Yearly Historical Balances	GNP I P.D.'s Used	Multi-pliers	Restated Balances 1973 $s	"Roll Forward" Multi-pliers	Restated Balances 1974 $s
1968		$ 1,943	158.93/121.80	1.305	$ 2,536		
1969		240	158.93/128.20	1.240	298		
		2,183 (col. 3, Fig. 9A-5)			2,834 (col. 6, Fig. 9A-5)		
1973	**Additions**						
Qtr. 2		1,377	158.93/152.61	1.041	1,433		
1973	**Reductions**						
	None						
	Totals 12-31-72	3,560 (col. 3, Fig. 9A-6)			$ 4,267 (col. 5, Fig. 9A-6)	1.120	$ 4,779 (col. 6, Fig. 9A-6)
1974	**Additions**						
	None						
1974	**Reductions**						
	None						
	Totals 12-31-74	$ 3,560 (col. 7, Fig. 9A-6)					$ 4,779 (col. 9, Fig. 9A-6)

NOTES

See notes on Fig. 9A-8

Figure 9A-10

M.O.B. COMPANY
GENERAL PRICE-LEVEL RESTATEMENT—1973-74
ANALYSIS OF ACCUMULATED DEPRECIATION—TRUCKS AND AUTOS
FOR THE PERIODS INDICATED

Date of Acq.	Notes	Yearly Historical Balances	Multipliers (same as for related acq.)	Related Balances 1973 $s	"Roll Forward" Multipliers	Restated Balances 1974 $s
1966	(These years listed net	$ 6,000	1.395	$ 8,370		
1969	of reductions for	5,213	1.240	6,464		
1971	retirements)	2,719	1.124	3,056		
	Totals 12-31-72	$13,932		17,890		
1973	**Additions**					
1969		587	1.240	728		
1971		891	1.124	1,001		
1973 Qtr. 2		867	1.041	903		
	Sub-total-year	2,345		2,632		
1973	**Reductions**					
1966		(6,000)	1.395	(8,370)		
	Totals 12-31-73	10,277		$12,152	1.120	$13,610
1974	**Additions**					
1971		445	1.259			560
1973		1,300	1.166			1,516
1974 Qtr. 2		667	1.064			710
	Sub-total-year	2,412				2,786
1974	**Reductions**					
	None					
	Totals 12-31-74	$12,689				$16,396

NOTES

Deflators used here must be identical to those used with the respective assets. Refer to notes on Fig. 9A-8.

Figure 9A-11

M.O.B. COMPANY
GENERAL PRICE-LEVEL RESTATEMENT-1973-74
ANALYSIS OF ACCUMULATED DEPRECIATION-FURNITURE AND FIXTURES
FOR THE PERIODS INDICATED

Date of Acq.	Notes	Yearly Historical Balances	Multipliers (same as for related acq.)	Related Balances 1973 $s	"Roll Forward" Multipliers	Restated Balances 1974 $s
1953		$ 616	1.800	$1,109		
1958		245	1.589	389		
1964		103	1.459	150		
1965		274	1.433	393		
1967		284	1.355	385		
1969		576	1.240	714		
1971		1,502	1.124	1,688		
1972		5	1.088	5		
	Totals 12-31-72	3,605		4,833		
1973	**Additions**					
1964		13	1.459	19		
1965		39	1.433	56		
1967		52	1.355	70		
1969		18	1.240	22		
1971		439	1.124	493		
1972		10	1.088	11		
1973						
Qtr. 1		1,568	1.060	1,662		
3		8	1.021	8		
4		3	1.000	3		
	Sub-total-year	2,150		2,344		
1973	**Reductions**					
	None					
	Totals 12-31-73	5,755		$7,177	1.120	$8,038
1974	**Additions**					
1964		12	1.634			20
1965		39	1.605			63
1967		52	1.517			79
1971		163	1.259			205
1972		11	1.218			13
1973		828	1.187			
1973		15	1.143			
1973		13	1.120			1,015
1974						
Qtr. 4		20	1.000			20
	Sub-total-year	1,153				1,415
1974	**Reductions**					
	None					
	Totals 12-31-74	$6,908				$9,453

NOTES

See notes on Fig. 9A-10

Figure 9A-12

M.O.B. COMPANY
GENERAL PRICE-LEVEL RESTATEMENT-1973-74
ANALYSIS OF ACCUMULATED DEPRECIATION-WAREHOUSE AND LEASEHOLD IMPROVEMENTS
FOR THE PERIODS INDICATED

Date of Acq.	Notes	Yearly Historical Balances	Multipliers (same as for related acq.)	Related Balances 1973 $s	"Roll Forward" Multipliers	Restated Balances 1974 $s
1958		$14,408	1.589	$22,894		
1960		8,868	1.539	13,648		
1962		9,675	1.484	14,358		
1964		1,386	1.459	2,022		
1965		712	1.433	1,020		
1972		326	1.088	355		
	Totals 12-31-72	35,375		54,297		
1973	**Additions**					
1958		503	1.589	799		
1960		360	1.539	554		
1963		580	1.484	861		
1965		102	1.432	146		
1972		745	1.088	811		
1973						
Qtr. 2		163	1.021	166		
4		12	1.000	12		
	Sub-total-year	2,465		3,349		
1973	**Reductions**					
	None					
	Totals 12-31-73	37,840		$57,646	1.120	$64,563
1974	**Additions**					
1958		503	1.780			895
1960		360	1.723			620
1963		580	1.662			964
1965		102	1.605			164
1972		745	1.218			907
1973		245	1.143			
1973		148	1.120			446
	Sub-total-year	2,683				3,996
1974	**Reductions**					
	None					
	Totals 12-31-74	$40,523				$68,559

NOTES

See Notes on Fig. 9A-10

Figure 9A-13

M.O.B. COMPANY
GENERAL PRICE-LEVEL RESTATEMENT-1973-74
ANALYSIS OF ACCUMULATED DEPRECIATION-BOAT
FOR THE PERIODS INDICATED

Date of Acq.	Notes	Yearly Historical Balances	Multipliers (same as for related acq.)	Related Balances 1973 $s	"Roll Forward" Multipliers	Restated Balances 1974 $s
1968		$1,943	1.305	$2,536		
1969		235	1.240	291		
	Totals 12-31-72	2,178		2,827		
1973	**Additions**					
1969		5	1.240	6		
1973						
Qtr. 2		138	1.041	144		
	Sub-total-year	143		150		
1973	**Reductions**					
	None					
	Totals 12-31-73	2,321		$2,977	1.120	$3,335
1974	**Additions**					
1973		275	1.143			313
1974						
	None					
	Sub-total-year	275				313
1974	**Reductions**					
	None					
	Totals 12-31-74	$2,596				$3,648

Figure 9A-13 continued

M.O.B. COMPANY
GENERAL PRICE-LEVEL RESTATEMENT-1973-74
SUMMARY OF ACCUMULATED DEPRECIATION—ALL ACCOUNTS
FOR THE PERIODS INDICATED

Notes	Yearly Historical Balances	Multipliers (same as for related acq.)	Related Balances 1973 $s	"Roll Forward" Multipliers	Restated Balances 1974 $s
		1972 Restated			
Grand Totals 12-31-72	$55,090	$79,847			
	(col. 3, Fig. 9A-5)	(col. 6, Fig. 9A-5)			
12-31-73	$56,193		$79,952		$89,546
	(col. 3, Fig. 9A-6)		(col. 5, Fig. 9A-6)		(col. 6, Fig. 9A-6)
12-31-74	$62,716				$98,056
	(col. 7, Fig. 9A-6)				(col. 9, Fig. 9A-6)

Summary of Yearly Additions to Depreciation Expense—All Accounts

Depreciation—1973	$7,103				
Less personal charge	36				
Net (to Fig. 9A-18)	$7,067		$8,475		$9,492
Depreciation—1974	$6,523				
Less personal charge	1,044				
Net (to Fig. 9A-18)	$5,479				$8,510

NOTES

See Notes on Fig. 9A-10

Figure 9A-14

M.O.B. COMPANY
GENERAL PRICE-LEVEL RESTATEMENT—1973-74
ANALYSIS OF INVESTMENTS ACCOUNT
FOR THE PERIODS INDICATED

Date of Acq.	Notes	Yearly Historical Balances	G.N.P. I.P.D.'s Used	Multi-pliers	Restated Balances 1973 $s	"Roll Forward" Multi-pliers	Restated Balances 1974 $s
1961	Beg. Balances (for	$130,045	158.93/104.00	1.528	$198,709		
1963	convenience)	5,585	158.93/107.10	1.484	8,288		
1964	(These years listed	16,428	158.93/108.90	1.459	23,968		
1965	net of reductions)	6,942	158.93/110.90	1.433	9,948		
1966		7,500	158.93/114.15	1.395	10,462		
1967		10,889	158.93/117.30	1.355	14,755		
1968		4,571	158.93/121.80	1.305	5,965		
1969		10,508	158.93/128.20	1.240	13,030		
1970		7,150	158.93/135.24	1.175	8,401		
1971		12,387	158.93/141.35	1.124	13,923		
1972		8,870	158.93/146.12	1.088	9,651		
	Totals 12-31-72	220,875 (col. 3, Fig. 9A-5)			317,100 (col. 6, Fig. 9A-5)		
1973	**Additions** (Averaged)	34,757	158.93/154.31	1.030	35,800		
1973	**Reductions** None						
	Totals 12-31-73	255,632 (col. 3, Fig. 9A-6)			$352,900 (col. 5, Fig. 9A-6)	1.120	$395,248 (col. 6, Fig. 9A-6)
1974	**Additions** (Averaged)	13,259	177.97/170.18	1.046			13,869
1974	**Reductions** None						
	Totals 12-31-74	$268,891 (col. 7, Fig. 9A-6)					$409,117 (col. 9, Fig. 9A-6)

NOTES

In this case, it was assumed that the yearly additions to investment were made ratably throughout each year. Based on this assumption, the yearly average Deflator was used.

Figure 9A-15

M.O.B. COMPANY
GENERAL PRICE-LEVEL RESTATEMENT—1973-74
ANALYSIS OF REINVESTED EARNINGS
FOR THE PERIODS INDICATED

Date of Acq.	Notes	Yearly Historical Balances
1961		$ (843)
1962		33,270
1963		(6,929)
1964		3,836
1965		47,211
1966		(5,201)
1967		16,328
1968		(7,995)
1969		(44,397)
1970		520
1971		(17,643)
1972		3,925
	Total 12-31-72	$ 22,082
		(col. 3, Fig. 9A-5)

Figure 9A-16

M.O.B. COMPANY
GENERAL PRICE-LEVEL RESTATEMENT—1973-74
SCHEDULE OF WITHDRAWALS
FOR THE PERIODS INDICATED

		Historical Balance	Yearly Average Multiplier	Restated Balance
Withdrawals, 1973		25,515		
Deduct:		(col. 2,		
Depreciation adjustments		Fig. 9A-7)		
Boat	$ 36			
Auto	31	67		
		$25,448	1.030	$26,211
		(col. 2, Fig. 9A-19)		(col. 4, Fig. 9A-7) and Fig. 9A-19)
Withdrawals, 1974		36,689		
Deduct:		(col. 6,		
Depreciation adjustments		Fig. 9A-7)		
Boat	$ 69			
Auto	975	$ 1,044		
		$35,645	1.046	$37,285
		(col. 2, Fig. 9A-20)		(col. 8, Fig. 9A-7) and col. 4, Fig. 9A-20)

NOTES

It is necessary to adjust the withdrawal account for non-fund transactions for the purpose of determining the general price-level gain or loss.

Figure 9A-17

M.O.B. COMPANY
GENERAL PRICE-LEVEL RESTATEMENT—1973-74
ANALYSIS OF GAINS/LOSSES ON SALE OF ASSETS
1973

	Historical Cost	Restated	
Sale of 1967 Lincoln	$ 6,730	$ 9,388	(from Fig. 9A-8)
Depreciation	6,000	8,370	(from Fig. 9A-10)
Book value	730	1,018	
Sale to employee	700	700	
Less charged to Reinvested Earnings	$ 30		
Loss on sale (restated)		$318 (col. 4, Fig. 9A-7)	

Figure 9A-18

M.O.B. COMPANY
GENERAL PRICE-LEVEL RESTATEMENT—1973-74
ANALYSIS OF OPERATING EXPENSES
FOR THE PERIODS INDICATED

	1973 Historical Balances	1974 Historical Balances
Depreciation (Fig. 9A-13)	$ 7,067	$ 5,479
Other	207,088	258,136
Total	$214,155	$263,615
	(col. 2, Fig. 9A-7)	(col. 6, Fig. 9A-7)

Figure 9A-19

M.O.B. COMPANY
GENERAL PRICE-LEVEL RESTATEMENT—1973
GENERAL PRICE-LEVEL GAIN OR LOSS

	Historical	Multiplier (Schedule)	Restated
Net Monetary Items at beginning of year—1973			
Cash	5,734	1.077	6,176
Install. Contracts Receivable	171,255	1.077	184,442
Other Accounts Receivable	1,008	1.077	1,086
Cash Surrender Value-Life Insurance	22,355	1.077	24,076
Accounts payable	(58,667)	1.077	(63,184)
Notes payable	(36,075)	1.077	(38,853)
Accrued Taxes and Expenses	(21,793)	1.077	(23,471)
Long term debt	(38,291)	1.077	(41,239)
	45,526		49,033
Add:			
Additional investment	34,756	1.030	35,800
Sales	514,970	1.030	530,419
Sale of automobile	700	1.000	700
Bad debt recoveries	3,968	1.030	4,087
Finance charges	13,470	1.030	13,874
	567,864		584,880
Deduct:			
Purchases	350,410	1.030	360,922
Operating expenses-other	207,088	1.030	213,301
Purchases-property and equipment			
Trucks and autos	8,617	Fig. 9A-8	8,970
Furniture and fixtures	3,058	Fig. 9A-8	3,229
Warehouse-Leasehold improvements	3,146	Fig. 9A-9	3,187
Boat	1,377	Fig. 9A-9	1,433
Interest paid	5,014	1.030	5,164
Drawings (see Fig. 9A-16)	25,448	1.030	26,211
	604,158		622,417
Net Monetary items-Historical-at end of year-1973			
Cash	6,839		
Install. contracts receivable	178,071		
Other accounts receivable	2,890		
Cash surrender value-life insurance	42,048		
Accounts payable	(103,566)		
Notes payable	(66,503)		
Accrued taxes and expenses	(13,009)		
Long-term debt	(37,538)		
	$ 9,232		
Net monetary items-restated-at end of year-1973			11,496
Net monetary items-at end of year-1973			9,232
General Price-Level Loss			$ 2,264
			(col. 4, Fig. 9A-7)

Figure 9A-20

M.O.B. COMPANY
GENERAL PRICE-LEVEL RESTATEMENT-1974
GENERAL PRICE-LEVEL GAIN OR LOSS

	Historical	Multiplier (schedule)	Restated
Net monetary items at beginning of year, 1974			
Cash	6,839	1.120	7,660
Install. contracts receivable	178,071	1.120	199,440
Other accounts receivable	2,890	1.120	3,236
Cash surrender value-life insurance	42,048	1.120	47,094
Accounts payable	(103,566)	1.120	(115,994)
Notes payable	(66,503)	1.120	(74,483)
Accrued taxes and expenses	(13,009)	1.120	(14,570)
Long-term debt	(37,538)	1.120	(42,043)
	9,232		10,340
Add:			
Additional investment	13,259	1.046	13,869
Sales	639,818	1.046	669,250
Bad debt recoveries	1,188	1.046	1,243
Finance charges	17,383	1.046	18,183
	671,648		702,545
Deduct:			
Purchases	353,411	1.046	369,668
Operating expenses-other	258,136	1.046	270,010
Purchases-property and equipment			
Trucks and autos	4,005	Fig. 9A-8	4,261
Furniture and fixtures	982	Fig. 9A-8	982
Interest paid	9,329	1.046	9,758
Drawings (see Fig. 9A-16)	35,645	1.046	37,285
	661,508		691,964
Net Inventory Items-at end of year-1974			
Cash	$ 7,053		
Install. contracts receivable	182,517		
Other accounts receivable	1,808		
Cash surrender value-life insurance	45,906		
Accounts payable	(64,236)		
Notes payable	(93,250)		
Accrued taxes and expenses	(22,888)		
Long-term debt	(37,538)		
	$ 19,372		

Figure 9A-20 continued

Net monetary items-restated at end of year-1974	20,921
Net monetary items-historical at end of year-1974	19,372
General Price-Level Loss	$ 1,549
	(col. 8, Fig. 9A-7)

Figure 9A-21 **Sample Worksheet Carry—Forward To Subsequent Years**

M.O.B. COMPANY
GENERAL PRICE-LEVEL RESTATEMENT—1973-75
ANALYSIS OF TRUCKS AND AUTOS
FOR THE PERIODS INDICATED

Date of Acq.	Notes	Yearly Historical Balances	GNP I D.P's Used	"Roll Forward" Multi-pliers	Restated Balances 1973 $s	"Roll Forward" Multi-plier	Restated Balances 1974 $s	"Roll Forward" Multi-plier	Restated Balances 1975 $s
1966	(These years listed	$6,730	158.93/114.15	1.395	$9,388				
1969	net of retirements)	6,010	158.93/128.20	1.240	7,452				
1971		4,950	158.93/141.35	1.124	5,564				
	Totals 12-31-72	17,690			22,404				
1973	**Additions**								
Qtr. 1		8,617	158.93/152.61	1.041	8,970				
2									
3									
4									
1973	**Reductions**								
1966	(Retirements)	(6,730)	(take out as put in)		(9,388)				
	Totals 12-31-73	19,577			$21,986	1.120	$24,624		
1974	**Additions**								
Qtr. 1									
2		4,005	177.97/167.31	1.064			4,261		
3									
4									
1974	**Reductions**								
1971	(Retirements)	(4,950)	(take out as put in)		$(5,564)	1.120	(6,232)		
	Totals 12-31-73	18,632					$22,653	1.041	$23,582
1975	**Additions**								
Qtr. 1									
2									
3		7,500	185.32/182.15	1.017					7,628
4									
1975	**Reductions**								
1969	(Retirements)	(3,005)	(take out as put in)		(3,726)	1.120	$(4,173)	1.041	(4,344)
		$23,127							$26,866

Figure 9A-22

M.O.B. COMPANY
BALANCE SHEET
DECEMBER 31, 1974 and 1973

ASSETS			**General Price-Level Basis**	
	1974	**1973**	**1974**	**1973**
Current assets				
Cash	$ 7,053	$ 6,839	$ 7,053	$ 7,660
Installment contracts receivable	182,517	178,071	182,517	199,440
Inventory	268,000	238,814	280,328	275,495
Other accounts receivable	1,808	2,890	1,808	3,236
Total current assets	459,378	426,614	471,706	485,831
Investments				
Cash surrender value of life insurance	45,906	42,048	45,906	47,094
Property and equipment				
Trucks and autos	23,582	19,577	28,885	24,624
Furniture and fixtures	8,915	7,933	11,719	10,737
Warehouse and leashold improvements	60,977	60,977	100,352	100,352
Boat	3,560	3,560	4,779	4,779
	97,034	92,047	145,735	140,492
Less accumulated depreciation	62,716	56,193	98,056	89,546
Net property and equipment	34,318	35,854	47,679	50,946
Total assets	$539,602	$504,516	$565,291	$583,871

LIABILITIES AND OWNER'S EQUITY

Current liabilities				
Accounts payable	$ 64,236	$103,566	$ 64,236	$115,994
Notes payable	93,250	66,503	93,250	74,483
Accrued commissions	11,468	629	11,468	704
Payroll taxes payable	624	1,236	624	1,384
Sales tax payable	10,796	11,144	10,796	12,482
Total current liabilities	180,374	183,078	180,374	205,047
Long-term debt	37,538	37,538	37,538	42,043
Total liabilities	217,912	220,616	217,912	247,090
Owner's equity				
Initial investment plus additional investments	268,891	255,632	423,836	409,967
Reinvested earnings	52,799	28,268	(76,457)	73,186
	312,690	283,900	347,379	336,781
Total liabilities and owner's equity	$539,602	$504,516	$565,291	$583,871
	(from Fig. 9A-2)		(from Fig. 9A-6)	

Figure 9A-23

M.O.B. COMPANY
STATEMENT OF INCOME
YEARS ENDED DECEMBER 31, 1974 and 1973

					General Price-Level Basis			
	1974		1973		1974		1973	
	Amount	% of Sales	Amount	% of Sales	Amount	% of Sales	Amount	% of Sales
Net Sales	$639,818	100.00%	$514,970	100.00%	$669,250	100.00%	$594,069	100.00%
Cost of sales								
Beginning inventory	238,814		169,942		275,495		207,085	
Purchases	353,411		350,410		369,668		404,232	
	592,225		520,352		645,163		611,317	
Less ending inventory	268,000		238,814		280,328		275,495	
Total cost of sales	324,225	50.67	281,538	54.68	364,835	54.51	335,822	56.53
Gross profit	315,593	49.33	233,432	45.32	304,415	45.49	258,247	43.47
Depreciation	5,479	.85	7,067	1.37	8,510	1.27	9,492	1.60
Operating expenses	258,136	40.35	207,088	40.21	270,010	40.35	238,897	40.21
	263,615	41.20	214,155	41.58	278,520	41.62	248,389	41.81
Operating profit	51,978	8.13	19,277	3.74	25,895	3.87	9,858	1.66
Other income and expense								
Recovery of bad accounts	1,188		3,968		1,243		4,577	
Finance charges	17,383		13,470		18,183		15,539	
	18,571	2.90	17,438	3.38	19,426	2.90	20,116	3.39
Loss of sale of auto	-0-		-0-		-0-		356	.06
General Price-Level loss	-0-		-0-		1.549	.23	2,536	.43
Interest paid	9,329	1.46	5,014	.97	9,758	1.46	5,784	.97
	9,329	1.46	5,014	.97	11,307	1.69	8,676	1.46
Excess of other income over other expense	9,242	1.44	12,424	2.41	8,119	1.21	11,440	1.93
Net income before taxes	$ 61,220	9.57%	$ 31,701	6.15%	$ 34,014	5.08%	$ 21,298	3.59%

(From Fig. 9A-4) (From Fig. 9A-7)

***Figure 9A-24 Typical Classifications: Monetary and Nonmonetary Accounts**

Monetary

Assets

Accounts	**Special Considerations**
Cash on Hand	domestic currency
Bank Deposits-Demand	domestic currency
Bank Deposits-Time	domestic currency
Marketable Securities-Bonds	held primarily for income
Accounts Receivable	short- and long-term
Trade	
Officers and Employees	
Miscellaneous	
Notes Receivable	short- and long-term
Trade	
Officers and Employees	
Miscellaneous	
Allowance for uncollectible accounts and notes	
Contract inventories	produced and accounted for under a fixed price contract
Advances to Employees	
Prepaid Interest	
Refundable Deposits	
Cash Surrender Value-Life Insurance	
Investments in Convertible Bonds	held primarily for fixed principal and income
Unamortized Discount on Bonds Payable	
Various Funds	if comprised of bonds

Liabilities

Accounts payable	short- and long-term
Trade	
Officers	
Miscellaneous	
Notes payable	short- and long-term
Trade	
Officers	
Miscellaneous	
Accrued items payable	
Expenses	

*The appendices that follow list the monetary and nonmonetary accounts as well as the supporting indices and multipliers used in the actual example.

Figure 9A-24 continued

Losses on purchase commitments	
Pension costs	
Vacation pay	only if fixed contract
Miscellaneous	
Cash Dividends payable	
Refundable Deposits	
Bonds payable	
Reserve for self-insurance	if currently adequate
Provision for warranties	if currently adequate

Non-monetary

Assets

Foreign currency on hand and claims thereto	state at current foreign exchange rate
Marketable securities	
Stocks	
Bonds	if held for price speculation
Inventories	except contract inventories
Prepaid Expense items	
Unconsolidated subsidiaries	
Advances to	unless currently active
Investments in	
Advances on purchase contracts	
Land, plant and equipment	
Allowances for depreciation	
Deferred charges	
Goodwill	
Intangible assets	

Liabilities

Accounts and notes payable	in foreign currency; state at foreign exchange rate.
Advances on sales contracts	
Deferred items	
Taxes	deferred method
Investment credits	
Income	
Preferred stock	do not exceed call price in restatement
Common stock	
Other contributed capital accounts	
Minority interest	

Figure 9A-25

M.O.B. COMPANY
GENERAL PRICE LEVEL RESTATEMENT—1973-74
SCHEDULE OF RATIOS AND MULTIPLIERS

Year	Quarter	GNP Implicit Price Deflators	Multipliers
Quarterly		(Ratio: 4th quarter, 1973 to period indicated)	
1972	4th	158.93/147.63	1.077
1973	1st	158.93/149.95	1.060
	2nd	158.93/152.61	1.041
	3rd	158.93/155.67	1.021
	4th	158.93/158.93	1.000
		(Ratio: 4th quarter, 1974 to period indicated)	
1973	4th	177.97/158.93	1.120
1974	1st	177.97/163.61	1.088
	2nd	177.97/167.31	1.064
	3rd	177.97/172.07	1.034
	4th	177.97/177.97	1.000
		(Ratio: 4th quarter, 1973 to period indicated)	
Annual Average			
1953		158.93/ 88.30	1.800
1958		158.93/100.00	1.589
1960		158.93/103.30	1.539
1963		158.93/107.10	1.484
1964		158.93/108.90	1.459
1965		158.93/110.90	1.433
1966		158.93/114.15	1.395
1967		158.93/117.30	1.355
1968		158.93/121.80	1.305
1969		158.93/128.20	1.240
1970		158.93/135.24	1.175
1971		158.93/141.35	1.124
1972		158.93/146.12	1.088
1973		158.93/154.31	1.030
		(Ratio: 4th quarter, 1974 to period indicated)	
1974		177.97/170.18	1.046

Figure 9A-26

GROSS NATIONAL PRODUCT IMPLICIT PRICE DEFLATOR FOR THE PERIODS INDICATED

Year	Deflator Annual Average	Quarter	Deflator Quarterly Average
(1958 = 100.00)			
1929	50.6		
1930	49.3		
1931	44.8		
1932	40.3		
1933	39.3		
1934	42.2		
1935	42.6		
1936	42.7		
1937	44.5		
1938	43.9		
1939	43.2		
1940	43.9		
1941	47.2		
1942	53.0		
1943	56.8		
1944	58.2		
1945	59.7		
1946	66.7		
1947	74.6	1*	73.0
		2	73.7
		3	74.9
		4	77.0
1948	79.6	1	78.2
		2	79.2
		3	80.6
		4	80.3
1949	79.1	1	79.7
		2	79.1
		3	78.8
		4	78.9
1950	80.2	1	78.3
		2	79.0
		3	80.8
		4	82.3

*Not available prior to this date.

Figure 9A-26 continued

Year	Deflator Annual Average	Quarter	Deflator Quarterly Average
1951	85.6	1	84.8
		2	85.4
		3	85.6
		4	86.7
1952	87.6	1	86.7
		2	87.1
		3	87.7
		4	88.3
1953	88.3	1	88.4
		2	88.3
		3	88.4
		4	88.4
1954	89.6	1	89.5
		2	89.6
		3	89.5
		4	89.8
1955	90.9	1	90.2
		2	90.6
		3	91.0
		4	91.6
1956	94.0	1	92.6
		2	93.4
		3	94.6
		4	95.4
1957	97.5	1	96.4
		2	97.1
		3	98.0
		4	98.5
1958	100.00	1	99.3
		2	99.7
		3	100.1
		4	100.6
1959	101.6	1	101.1
		2	101.4
		3	101.9
		4	102.1

Figure 9A-26 continued

Year	Deflator Annual Average	Quarter	Deflator Quarterly Average
1960	103.3	1	102.6
		2	103.0
		3	103.4
		4	104.0
1961	104.6	1	104.3
		2	104.5
		3	104.5
		4	105.1
1962	105.7	1	105.4
		2	105.5
		3	105.8
		4	106.2
1963	107.1	1	106.6
		2	107.0
		3	107.1
		4	107.8
1964	108.9	1	108.3
		2	108.4
		3	109.0
		4	109.6
1965	110.9	1	110.0
		2	110.8
		3	111.2
		4	111.7
1966	114.2	1	112.6
		2	113.8
		3	114.7
		4	115.5
1967	117.3	1	116.0
		2	116.6
		3	117.7
		4	118.8
1968	121.8	1	120.0
		2	121.2
		3	122.3
		4	123.5

Figure 9A-26 continued

Year	Deflator Annual Average	Quarter	Deflator Quarterly Average
1969	128.20	1	125.68
		2	127.22
		3	128.97
		4	130.52
1970	135.24	1	132.82
		2	134.32
		3	135.97
		4	138.07
1971	141.35	1	139.84
		2	141.34
		3	142.35
		4	142.88
1972	146.12	1	144.85
		2	145.42
		3	146.42
		4	147.63
1973	154.31	1	149.95
		2	152.61
		3	155.67
		4	158.93
1974	170.18	1	163.61
		2	167.31
		3	172.07
		4	177.97
1975		1	181.65

SOURCE: United States Department of Commerce, *Survey of Current Business,* issued monthly.

Chapter 10

A Simplified Method for the Preparation of the Statement of Changes in Financial Position

The statement of changes in financial position represents a form of report evolution in the world of financial reporting. Now rather firmly established in the hierarchy of financial statements by virtue of APB Opinion No. 19, it takes the place of the statement of source and application of funds.[1] This earlier statement was recommended, but not specified as a requirement in financial reporting in APB Opinion No. 3.

The major thrust behind the advocacy of the revised statement is the recognition of the importance of non-fund financial activities to the presentation of the whole picture of financial resource generation and application. Examples of non-fund financial activities are the exchange of assets and the acquisition of assets by the issuance of stocks, bonds, notes and so forth. These items are included in the new statement whether it is prepared on the working capital or cash basis. The reader is referred to accounting theory texts offering more extensive presentation in respect to the history of the statement and theoretical aspects thereof if such information is needed and/or desired.

Purpose

The purpose of the statement of changes in financial position is to answer the rather plaintive cry of the businessman for information not easily available from the income statement and statement of financial position. These two statements do not give a clear picture of the total inflow of financial resources and the uses to which these resources were put. The statement of changes in financial position represents basically a recasting of

[1]A.I.C.P.A., Opinions of the Accounting Principles Board, No. 19, (New York, March 1971), pp. 371–379.

financial transactions to clearly present the total picture of financial resource inflows and outflows. Since the income statement provides information in respect to gross operating transactions, this detail is not incorporated in the changes in financial position statement. Net results of operations, adapted for non-working capital and/or noncash items, represent the take-off point.

Two Versions of the Statement

There are two well-recognized versions of the changes in financial position statement (hereinafter referred to as the "change statement"). One version concerns itself with reporting working capital changes in the total cash *and* credit aspect of the current assets and current liabilities. Noncash changes in these accounts are treated as cash in terms of regarding them all as "funds." The second version eliminates the short-term credit changes and other noncash changes in the current asset and current liabilities accounts in order to derive a net change in the cash position. Each version does incorporate the stream of nonworking capital resource inflow and outflow. The second version is generally considered more useful for management and outsiders who are more intimately concerned with the financial position of the company on a continuing basis.

The particular technique presented in this chapter is designed to facilitate the preparation of either version of the "change statement" from the worksheet. It is the simplest and easiest worksheet form in use today and is especially helpful to individuals not intimately familiar with the procedure of "change statement" preparation. Details of changes in current assets and current liabilities are incorporated in the worksheet with summaries provided to facilitate the preparation of the "change statement" on the working capital basis. Some accountants can prepare a "change statement" in certain cases without the use of a worksheet. It is not the intent of the writers to suggest dispensing with any workable shortcuts in statement preparation. The complexity of the financial structure and the professional skill of the accountant will dictate the use or nonuse of the worksheet technique.

A Comprehensive Illustration

The essential data for this illustration are presented in Figures 10A-1 and 10A-2 in the form of relatively condensed statements of financial position, an income statement and certain details of changes in account balances necessary to the completion of the worksheet. While these financial statements will most likely be readily available and usable in the regular form, some analysis will be necessary in order to obtain other important change information needed. In this connection, current asset and current liability accounts need to be examined to identify nontrade related accounts. Nontrade accounts will affect reporting on the cash basis. All other asset, liability and capital accounts need to be analyzed in order to determine the generation and application of resources whether or not working capital is involved. Disposition of assets must be analyzed in order to adjust for gains/losses and for removal from the records to net out the funds received needed for the "change statement." There may be entries not involving the movement of resources in and out such as the appropriation of retained earnings. Finally, the statement of operations must be analyzed to identify for later adjustment all nonfund cost and expense items such as depreciation, depletion, amortization of intangibles and other nonfund revisions.

ARRANGEMENT OF THE WORKSHEET

An analysis of transactions in the illustrative example has been presented at the bottom of Figure 10A-2, Statement of Income and Retained Earnings. This and a comparative balance sheet are the "place to begin" in setting up the worksheet. The worksheet, Figure 10A-3, is arranged so that balance sheet figures for the beginning and the end of the year are entered side by side leaving two (or more) columns for "Changes." Using the analysis of transaction data, completing the worksheet is simply a matter of explaining the changes from the balance sheet at the beginning of the year to the balance sheet at the end of the year. In so doing, the change automatically results in working capital generated or applied or in noncash, non-working capital items generated or applied. Account changes (Figure 10A-3) are keyed to the statement section of the worksheet by numbers, e.g., the change in cash from 6/30/X5 to 6/30/X6 is shown by entry No. 1. Cash increased, thereby requiring a debit in the "entries for changes" columns. The related credit appears in the statement portion of the worksheet as a "non-trade related item-increase in cash in the bank." Similarly, the debit aspect of entry No. 2 reflects an increase in accounts receivable. The credit is reflected as a "net change in working capital items-trade related items." Moreover, it appears as a *deduction* in the cash basis "change statement," from accrual net income. (Key letter Q in Figure 10A-4.) Further study of the worksheet will show that each balance sheet change in Figure 10A-3 except for key entry No. 22, is summarily reflected in the statement portion of the worksheet, the equivalent of the formal "change statement." Key entry 22 is merely an explanation of a portion of the change in retained earnings-unappropriated. The change resulted from an increase in some appropriation of retained earnings.

The worksheet should be set up allowing sufficient space for items in the respective catagories, and the asset, liability and capital accounts balances for the beginning and end of the year entered according to the classification used in the illustrative worksheet. While this classification is not absolutely essential to the completion of the worksheet and the preparation of the "change statement," it will aid in the process. It will be noted that the entries for the changes in the account section accomplish the changes as such and are made in the same order as the accounts are listed. This is a part of this particular worksheet technique and is very helpful in keeping the worksheet in balance. The entry key numbers will indicate this. It will be noted that the change entries are totaled and balanced at the end of the account section and the end of the statement section. This is simply a "built-in" worksheet aid. After the worksheet is completed and balanced, it will be helpful to develop the sub-totals and draw intra-column rulings in the statement of changes section as shown in the illustrative worksheet. This will also facilitate the preparation of the formal "change statement(s)."

Irrespective of the basis of presentation chosen, information pertinent to the other basis is readily available from the worksheet. To this extent, the worksheet presented here is unique in that it serves to aid in preparing a change statement on either a cash or a working capital basis. The key letters used to tie the worksheet statement of changes section to the formal "change statements" are, of course, for purposes of this illustration only and offer very little that is helpful in the usual preparation process (see Figures 10A-4 and 10A-5). The formal "change statements" are presented below and are taken directly from the statement section of the worksheet.

TRANSFERRING INFORMATION FROM WORKSHEET TO CHANGES STATEMENT

Key letters indicate the transference of the information contained in the statement section of the worksheet to the formalized change statements, either cash basis or working capital basis. By way of illustration, key letters A-C indicate the algebraic combination of the "bottom line" of the income statement, net income, with extra-ordinary gains to yield "income before extra-ordinary gains" which appears as the first "Resource Generated" on both the cash and working capital change statements. In like manner, key entries 8 and 12 are summed as key letters B & D and moved to the change statements as additions to "net income before extra-ordinary items." Each item on the second section of the worksheet is so lettered and may be traced to the change statement. Following this simplified illustration will result in a complete and accurate "change statement" with a minimum of time expenditure. It will be especially helpful to staff personnel with a minimum of experience in statement preparation.

REQUIREMENTS OF APB NO. 19

More or less detail can be presented on the formal statement than is shown in the illustrative examples. Opinion No. 19 of the Accounting Principles Board seems to indicate a preference for full reporting. If the working capital basis is preferred, the worksheet can be shortened by leaving out the details of the changes in the working capital items. The statement as shown here conforms to the requirements of APB No. 19 and is recommended over more abbreviated versions.

APPENDIX

Figure 10A-1

PRUDENCE CORPORATION
BALANCE SHEETS
FOR THE PERIODS INDICATED

Assets	**June 30, 19X1**	**June 30, 19X2**
Current Assets		
Petty Cash	$ 1,000	$ 1,000
Cash in Bank	19,000	36,000
Marketable Securities	3,000	5,000
Accounts Receivable (Net)	150,000	155,000
Merchandise Inventory	105,000	90,000
Prepaid Expenses	2,500	2,200
Fixed Assets		
Land	30,000	50,000
Building	100,000	140,000
Accumulated Depreciation-Building	(12,000)	(14,000)
Equipment	60,000	85,000
Accumulated Depreciation—Equipment	(10,000)	(16,000)
Intangible Assets		
Goodwill	20,000	16,000
Total Assets	$468,500	$550,200
Liabilities and Capital		
Current Liabilities		
Accounts payable	$ 83,400	$ 63,300
Notes Payable—Nontrade	20,000	15,000
Dividends payable	-0-	3,000
Accrued Expenses Payable	2,300	1,900
Accrued Taxes Payable	1,800	2,000
Long-term Liabilities		
Equipment Notes Payable	-0-	30,000
Mortgage Payable	60,000	50,000
Capital		
Common stock—par $100	200,000	250,000
Premium on Common Stock	-0-	10,000
Retained Earnings		
Appropriated	25,000	30,000
Unappropriated	76,000	95,000
Total Liabilities and Capital	$468,500	$550,200

Figure 10A-2

PRUDENCE CORPORATION
STATEMENT OF INCOME AND RETAINED EARNINGS
FOR THE FISCAL YEAR ENDED JUNE 30, 19X2

Sales		$400,000
Cost of Sales		242,000
Gross Profit		158,000
Expenses		122,000
Net Income before extra-ordinary items		36,000
Extra-ordinary items		
Gain on Sale of Equipment		3,000
Net Income		39,000
Unappropriated Retained Earnings, July 1, 19X1		76,000
		115,000
Less: Dividends	$15,000	
Appropriation	5,000	20,000
Unappropriated Retained Earnings, June 30, 19X2		$ 95,000
Appropriated Retained Earnings, July 1, 19X1		$ 25,000
Add:		
Current appropriation		5,000
Appropriated Retained Earnings, June 30, 19X2		$ 30,000

Analysis of financial transactions for the fiscal year ended June 30, 19X2

1. Depreciation Expense—Building, $2,000.
2. Depreciation Expense—Equipment, $10,000.
3. Amortization of Goodwill, $4,000.
4. Purchased equipment for $40,000; paid for by issuing 5-year equipment notes of $30,000 and a down payment of $10,000.
5. Purchased land for $20,000 by issuance of stock.
6. Built addition to plant for $40,000 by issuance of stock.
7. Equipment costing $15,000, with accumulated depreciation of $4,000, to date of sale, was sold for $14,000.
8. Purchased marketable securities for $2,000.

Figure 10A-3

PRUDENCE CORPORATION
WORKSHEET FOR STATEMENT OF CHANGES IN FINANCIAL POSITION
FOR THE FISCAL YEAR ENDED JUNE 30, 19X2

Asset Accounts	Balance Sheet June 30, 19X2	Entries for Changes Dr.	Entries for Changes Cr.	Balance Sheet June 30, 19X2
Working Capital Accounts—Trade Related				
Petty Cash	1,000			1,000
Cash in Bank	19,000	(1) 17,000		36,000
Accounts Receivable (Net)	150,000	(2) 5,000		155,000
Inventories	105,000		(3) 15,000	90,000
Prepaid Expenses	2,500		(4) 300	2,200
Working Capital Accounts—Nontrade Related				
Marketable Securities	3,000	(5) 2,000		5,000
Nonworking Capital Accounts				
Land	30,000	(6) 20,000		50,000
Building	100,000	(7) 40,000		140,000
Accum. Depr.—Bldg.	(12,000)		(8) 2,000	(14,000)
Equipment	60,000	(10) 30,000	(11) 15,000	85,000
		(9) 10,000		
Accumulated Depreciation —Equip.	(10,000)	(11) 4,000	(12) 10,000	(16,000)
Goodwill	20,000		(13) 4,000	16,000
Total	468,500			550,200
Liability and Equity Accounts				
Working Capital Accounts—Trade Related				
Accounts payable	83,400	(14) 20,100		63,300
Accrued Expenses Payable	2,300	(15) 400		1,900
Accrued Taxes Payable	1,800		(16) 200	2,000
Working Capital Accounts—Nontrade Related				
Notes Payable—Nontrade	20,000	(17) 5,000		15,000
Dividends Payable	-0-		(18) 3,000	3,000
Nonworking Capital Accounts				
Mortgage Payable	60,000	(19) 10,000		50,000
Equipment Notes Payable (Long-Term)	-0-		(20) 30,000	30,000
Common Stock	200,000		(21) 50,000	250,000
Premium on Common Stock	-0-		(21) 10,000	10,000
Approp. Retained Earn.	25,000		(22) 5,000	30,000
Unapprop. Re. Earn.	76,000	(22) 5,000	(25) 39,000	95,000
		(23) 12,000		
		(24) 3,000		
Total	468,500			550,200
Totals of Entries for Changes		183,500	183,500	

Figure 10A-3 continued

Statement of Changes	Entries for Changes Dr.			Cr.	
Resources Generated:					
Working Capital Resources generated:					
Net Income	(25)	39,000	(A)		
Adjustments to Net Income:					
Depreciation Expense—Building	(8)	2,000	(B)		
Gain on sale of equipment			(C)	(11)	3,000
Depreciation Expense—Equipment	(12)	10,000	(D)		
Amortization of Goodwill	(13)	4,000	(E)		
Net Income (DR) Loss (CR)) adjusted (sub-total)		52,000*	(F)		
Other items:					
Equipment sold	(11)	14,000*	(G)		
Liability for dividends declared but not paid (use on cash basis statement only)	(18)	3,000*	(H)		
Nonworking capital resources generated:					
Equipment notes issued to acquire equip.	(20)	30,000*	(I)		
Common stock issued to acquire land and addition to plant	(21)	60,000*	(J)		
Resources Applied:					
Working capital resources applied:					
Acquisition of equipment			(K)	(9)	10,000*
Reduction of mortgage principal			(L)	(19)	10,000*
Payment of dividends			(M)	(23)	12,000*
Nonworking capital resources applied					
Acquisition of land by issuance of common stock			(N)	(6)	20,000*
Acquisition of addition to plant by issuance of common stock			(0)	(7)	40,000*
Acquisition of equipment by issuance of notes			(P)	(10)	30,000*
Net Changes in Working Capital Items:					
Trade-related items:					
Increase in Accounts Receivable			(Q)	(2)	5,000
Decrease in Inventory	(3)	15,000	(R)		
Decrease Prepaid Expenses	(4)	300	(S)		
Decrease in Accounts Payable			(T)	(14)	20,100
Decrease in Accrued Expenses Payable			(U)	(15)	400
Increase in Accrued Taxes Payable	(16)	200	(V)		
Total of trade-related items—affecting income statement (sub-total)			(W)		10,000*
Nontrade-related items					
Increase in Cash in Bank			(X)	(1)	17,000
Acquisition of marketable securities			(Y)	(5)	2,000
Reduction in Notes-Payable-Nontrade			(Z)	(17)	5,000
Dividends declared but not paid			(AA)	(24)	3,000
Total of nontrade-related items (sub-total)			(BB)		27,000*
Net change in Working Capital (sub-total)			(CC)		31,000
Totals of entries for changes		159,000*			159,000*

Figure 10A-4

PRUDENCE CORPORATION
STATEMENT OF CHANGES IN FINANCIAL POSITION (CASH BASIS)
FOR THE FISCAL YEAR ENDED JUNE 30, 19X2

Resources Generated:			
Cash Resources generated from operations			
Income before extraordinary items	(A-C)	$36,000	
Add (deduct) items neither requiring nor generating cash in the fiscal year:			
Depreciation—Building and Equipment	(B+D)	12,000	
Amortization—Goodwill	(E)	4,000	
Increase in Accounts Receivable	(Q)	(5,000)	
Decrease in Inventories	(R)	15,000	
Decrease in Prepaid Expenses	(S)	300	
Decrease in Accounts Payable	(T)	(20,100)	
Decrease in Accrued Expenses Payable	(U)	(400)	
Increase in Accrued Taxes Payable	(V)	200	
Total cash generated by operations exclusive of extraordinary items:	(F-W)		$42,000
Cash Resources generated by extraordinary items:			
Sale of equipment	(G)		14,000
Total cash generated			56,000
Noncash resources generated			
Common stock issued to acquire land and plant addition	(J)	60,000	
Equipment notes issued to acquire equipment	(I)	30,000	
Liability for dividends declared but not paid	(H)	3,000	
Total noncash resources generated			93,000
Total Resources Generated			$149,000
Resources applied:			
Cash Resources applied for nonoperating items:			
Acquisition of equipment	(K)	$10,000	
Reduction in mortgage principal	(L)	10,000	
Payment of dividends	(M)	12,000	
Acquisition of marketable securities	(Y)	2,000	
Reduction of nontrade notes payable	(Z)	5,000	
Total cash applied for nonoperating items			39,000
Noncash resources applied:			
Acquisition of land and plant addition by issuance of common stock	(N+O)	60,000	
Acquisition of equipment by issuance of equipment notes	(P)	30,000	
Dividends declared but not paid	(AA)	3,000	
Total noncash resources applied			93,000
Increase in cash during the fiscal year	(X)		17,000
Total Resources applied			$149,000

Figure 10A-5

PRUDENCE CORPORATION
STATEMENT OF CHANGES IN FINANCIAL POSITION (WORKING CAPITAL BASIS)
FOR THE FISCAL YEAR ENDED JUNE 30, 19X2

Resources Generated:			
Working capital generated:			
Income before extraordinary items	(A-C)	$36,000	
Add (deduct) expenses not requiring working capital in the fiscal year:			
Depreciation—Building and Equipment	(B+D)	12,000	
Amortization—Goodwill	(E)	4,000	
Total working capital generated by operations exclusive of extraordinary items	(F)		52,000
Extraordinary items			
Sale of equipment	(G)		14,000
Total working capital generated			66,000
Nonworking capital resources generated			
Common stock issued to acquire land and plant addition	(J)	60,000	
Equipment notes issued to acquire equipment	(I)	30,000	
Total nonworking capital resources generated			90,000
Total Resources generated			$156,000
Resources Applied:			
Working capital applied for nonoperating items:			
Acquisition of equipment	(K)	$10,000	
Reduction of mortgage principal	(L)	10,000	
Declaration of dividends	(M + AA)	15,000	
Total working capital applied			35,000
Nonworking capital resources applied			
Acquisition of land and plant addition by issuance of common stock	(N+O)	60,000	
Acquisition of equipment by issuance of equipment notes	(P)	30,000	
Total nonworking capital resources applied			90,000
Increase in working capital during the fiscal year	(CC)		$31,000
Total Resources applied			$156,000

CHAPTER 11

USING JOB ORDER COST IN A SMALL MANUFACTURING PLANT

Every firm which manufactures, fabricates, assembles or installs a product must use some means of identifying and accumulating the associated costs. This is what cost accounting does. The reason for this identification and association is twofold: (1) management must know what product costs are to assist in establishing a selling price in order to have a satisfactory profit; and, (2) reporting to creditors, government agencies, and others necessitates an allocation of costs between work-in-progress, finished goods and the cost of goods sold. This is the nature of cost accounting. If all production were started, ended, and sold in one accounting period, cost accounting would be meaningless. It is because production is an on-going activity spanning more than one period, that cost accounting is essential.

JOB ORDER VS PROCESS COST SYSTEMS

Because not all production processes are identical, two conventional methods of cost accumulation have been widely used: process costing and job order costing. Process costing, as described fully in Chapter 12, lends itself to production processes which are more or less continuous. Job order costing, alternatively, is more readily applicable to those processes carried out according to batches, lots or contract order. An example of the former is petroleum refining, and of the latter a special order cabinet-maker. It is possible that a single firm may employ both process and job order costing. Applicability of the two methods is not a function of firm size. For example, a huge aircraft manufacturer may employ job order costing while a small bottling plant may use a process cost system. Standard costs may be superimposed on either job order or process cost systems.

What a Job Order Cost System Can Do for a Small Manufacturer

Quite frequently the accountant is called upon to recommend accounting systems, as well as to install and audit them. Justifying the recommendation to install a job order system is easy if the following advantages are offered:

1. All costs attributable to a given job accumulated in that job's subsidiary ledger account may be compared with its contract price, or a pre-determined standard cost. By its nature, a job order cost system affords management the ability to assess the profitability of each job, lot or batch.
2. Progress billings can be supported by cumulative cost-to-date figures. This is especially true when contract terms permit billings dependent upon the degree of completion.
3. The cost of each job can be monitored by management as the job progresses through its various stages. Excesses can be identified and immediate corrective action taken. Nothing is more frustrating than to complete a job only to discover that it has been unprofitable.
4. As each job progresses, costs accumulated to date can assist in determining priorities for labor and other effort. For example, if a job is progressing smoothly, as indicated by an analysis of its cost, effort may be redirected toward other more pressing commitments. Alternatively, a periodic analysis of job costs may indicate that a job is lagging behind schedule. Unnecessary delays are almost always accompanied by unnecessary costs.
5. Related to the fourth advantage is the ability to speed up completion of a job or to reallocate resources to begin another job and temporarily delay a job already in progress, assuming contract terms are fulfilled.
6. The choice of the percentage of completion method of recognizing revenue is contingent upon a ready determination of the degree of completion the job has reached. Cumulative cost to date compared with estimated total cost is an excellent method of estimating the percent of completion of a job. Short of a professional engineer's estimate, it may be the only method for such a determination.

The Manufacturing Cost Accumulation Cycle

Manufacturing costs include materials, labor and overhead. It is these costs which must be accounted for and assigned to either work-in-progress, finished goods, or cost of sales. Just as an overview of the entire cycle, consider the flow of data through the "T" accounts in Figure 11-1 according to the functional areas of the firm. From the illustration it may be seen that materials cost is determined by the Purchasing Department. The cost of materials is summarized in the raw materials inventory account. Both direct and indirect labor costs are determined by wage administration, personnel policy, and union contract. These costs are similarly summarized as between the two categories. Direct materials and direct labor, as incurred, are immediately associated with production, and are summarized as work-in-progress. Indirect materials, indirect labor and other manufacturing costs are temporarily accumulated as manufacturing overhead and are assigned to work-in-progress. Completed goods are transferred to the warehouse as "finished goods." Goods sold are turned over to customers; and their cost, consisting of labor, materials, and overhead is transferred to the "cost of goods sold" account.

Figure 11-1 describes any manufacturing cycle, irrespective of whether a process or a job order costing system is used. In job order costing, each cost, materials, labor and overhead, is accumulated by job. Thus, at the point a sales order is received, a job number is assigned and subsequent costs are identified and accumulated by that job number. The work-in-progress and finished goods accounts are in reality, controlling accounts, each supported by the sum of the accumulated cost by the individual job. The purpose of the job order cost accounting system, then, is to provide the cost of each job from the moment the order is received until it is delivered to the customer. Record-keeping must be adequate to accomplish this purpose.

Minimum Reporting Requirements According to GAAP and for the I.R.S.

All cost accounting systems, to meet the minimum reporting requirements of generally accepted accounting principles and the I.R.S. must utilize the "full costing" or "absorption costing" methods. This means that not only are direct materials and labor assigned to inventory (both work-in-progress and finished goods), but overhead must also be applied to inventory. Methods of applying overhead will be discussed later. Neither direct nor prime costing are acceptable for tax and reporting purposes.

Cost Accounting Terminology

From Figure 11-1 and the previous section it may be seen that direct materials, direct labor and manufacturing overhead are a part of job cost. The cost accumulated on unfinished jobs is *work-in-progress,* while the total cost of a job completed but unsold is classified as *finished goods.* Of course, the cost of jobs for which a sale is consummated is *cost of goods sold. Raw materials inventory* is the materials purchased either to become a part of the completed product, called *direct materials,* or as an adjunct to the production process, called *indirect materials.* Labor may be classified either as *direct labor,* the cost of labor which actually touches, handles or operates upon the product, or *indirect labor,* which is labor that supports the production process. Both indirect materials and indirect labor are classified as overhead. *Manufacturing overhead* consists of all costs which support the manufacturing process, but which cannot be directly traced to a job. Sometimes this classification is merely a convenience. As an example, consider the cost of nails or glue used to manufacture cabinets. Both become a part of the final product, but are either so small in relation to total cost, or so difficult to trace to a job, that they are treated as manufacturing overhead. Similarly, payroll taxes on direct labor are treated as overhead although they are obviously a cost of the direct labor. If all this seems somewhat imprecise, it is, and only serves to emphasize the importance of a proper accumulation and application of overhead.

A listing of costs properly includable as manufacturing overhead will contain the following:

Figure 11-1

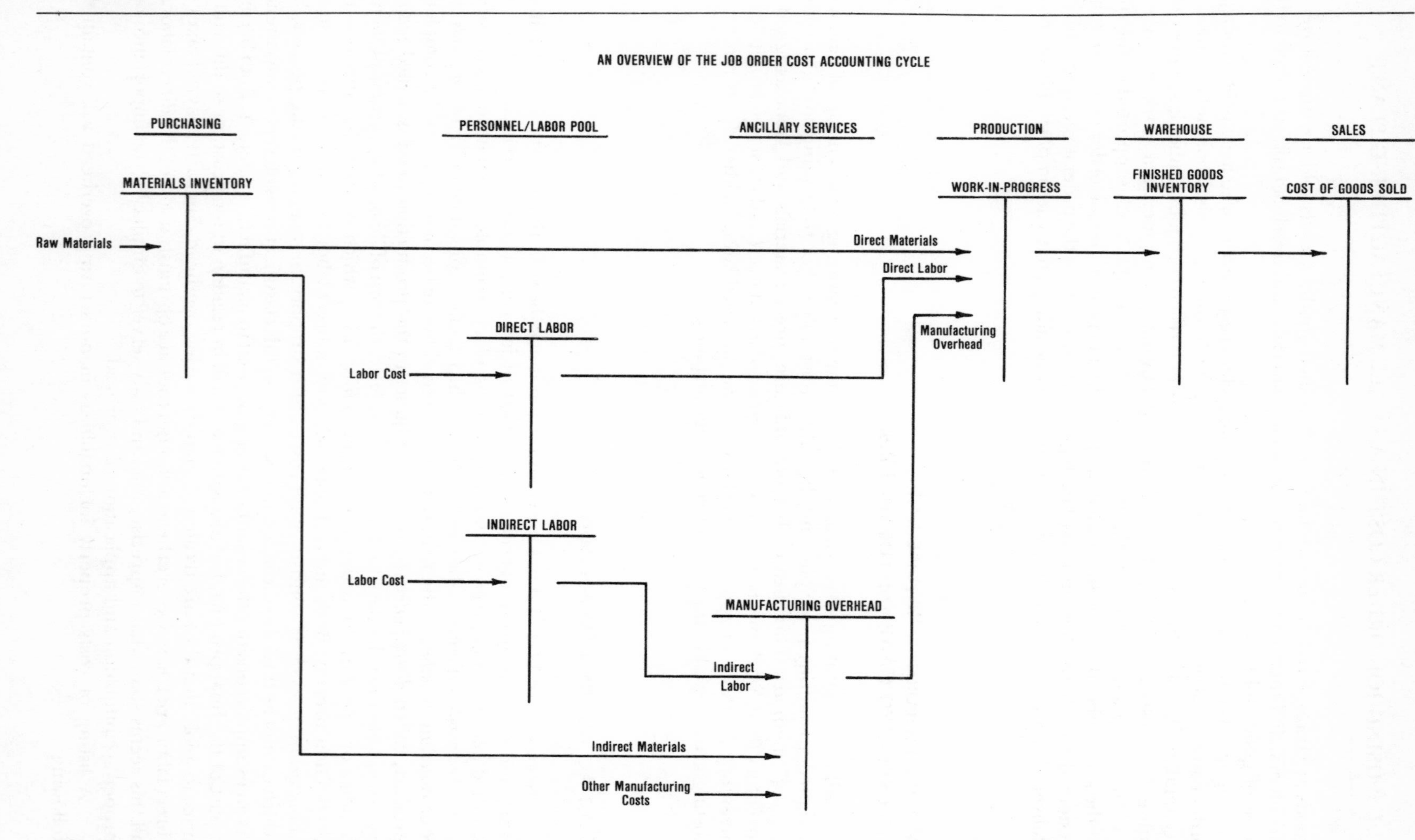

AN OVERVIEW OF THE JOB ORDER COST ACCOUNTING CYCLE
PURCHASING
PERSONNEL/LABOR POOL
ANCILLARY SERVICES
PRODUCTION
WAREHOUSE
SALES
MATERIALS INVENTORY
WORK-IN-PROGRESS
FINISHED GOODS INVENTORY
COST OF GOODS SOLD
Raw Materials
Direct Materials
Direct Labor
Manufacturing Overhead
DIRECT LABOR
Labor Cost
INDIRECT LABOR
Labor Cost
MANUFACTURING OVERHEAD
Indirect Labor
Indirect Materials
Other Manufacturing Costs

1. Salaries of foremen and manufacturing supervisors, maintenance and equipment servicing personnel.
2. Overtime premium.
3. Manufacturing supplies and small tools.
4. Payroll taxes, insurance, pension and vacation costs.
5. Factory utilities.
6. Taxes and insurance on factory property.
7. Equipment and manufacturing plant depreciation.
8. Maintenance and repair of plant and equipment.

How Much Record-Keeping in a Job Order Cost System?

One further advantage of a job order cost system is that necessary bookkeeping records and procedures can be relatively simple. In designing the system it should be remembered that the purpose is to accumulate materials, labor and overhead on a per job basis. To that end Figure 11-2 outlines the forms peculiar to a job order system, showing the source and movement of the information through the accounts as well as the supporting documents. An explanation of each document is in order.

Materials Requisition

This form supports the movement of raw materials from the stock of raw materials inventory into work-in-progress. It should be noted that a materials requisition form is used for each job, and that each requisition is numbered. Approval for the materials is required and receipt is also indicated by the initials of the recipient. This system of numbering and initialing is necessary for obvious control purposes. The materials requisition supports the following entry in the ledger:

Work-In-Progress (Job #808)	$112.00	
Raw Materials Inventory		$112.00

Time Ticket

Each employee in the manufacturing phase completes a daily time ticket showing his time spent on each job. Of course, one production worker may have time allocated to several jobs during the course of a day's time, as did employee No. 17, Joe Ames. Time tickets are supported by time cards, perhaps imprinted by some mechanical device such as a time clock. The cumulative time recorded on time cards for the payroll period determines the employee's gross pay. Each day's time ticket for each employee supports an entry similar to the one which follows for Joe Ames

Work-In-Progress (Job #808)	$17.55	
Work-In-Progress (Job #809)	$13.65	
Wages Payable		$31.20

The time on each job times his rate per hour is assigned to the cost of the job.

Figure 11-2

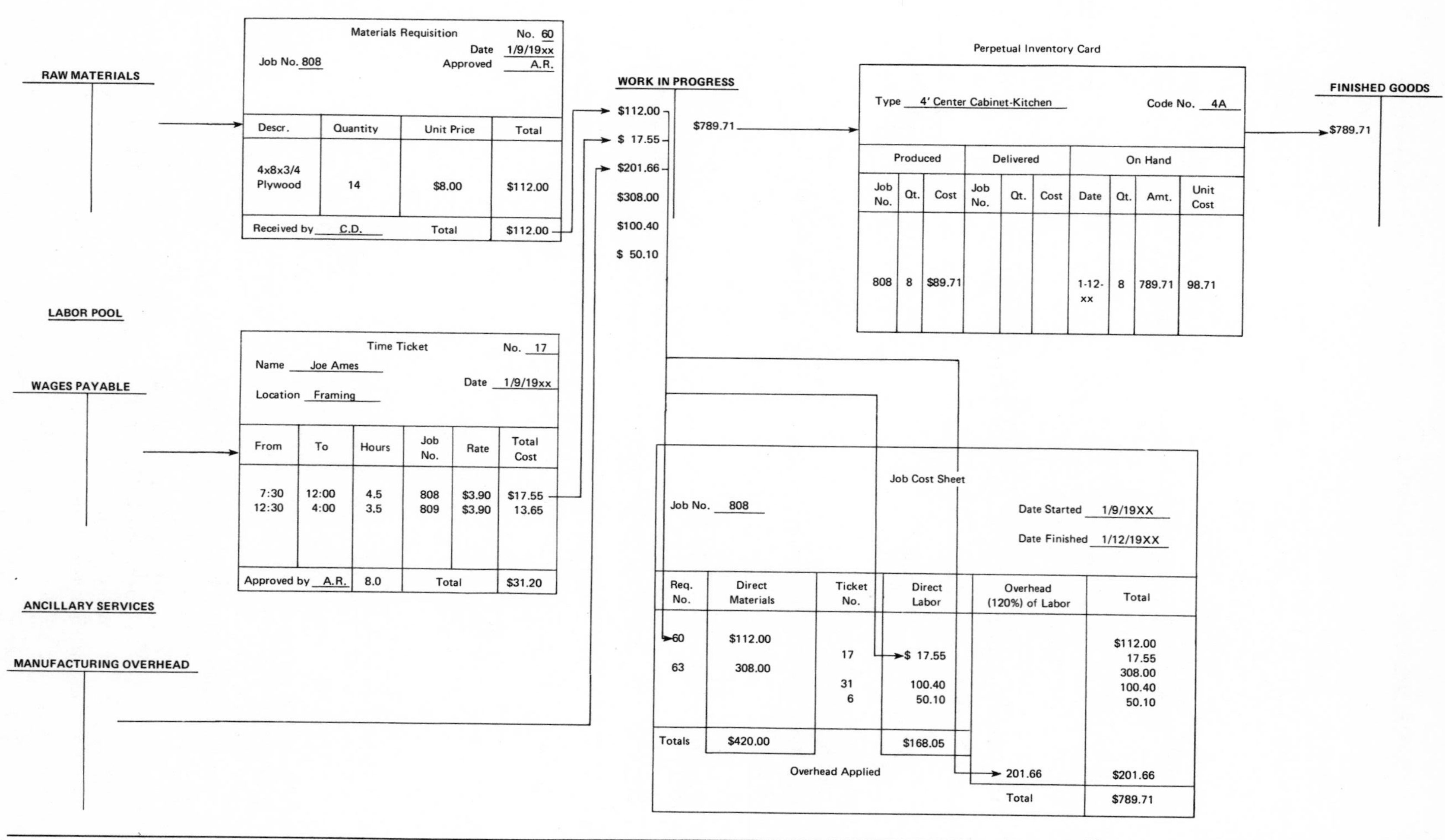
DATA FLOW THROUGH DOCUMENTS IN A JOB ORDER COST ACCOUNTING SYSTEM
RAW MATERIALS INVENTORY
RAW MATERIALS
Materials Requisition No. 60
Job No. 808 Date 1/9/19xx Approved A.R.
Descr. Quantity Unit Price Total
4x8x3/4 Plywood 14 $8.00 $112.00
Received by C.D. Total $112.00
LABOR POOL
WAGES PAYABLE
Time Ticket No. 17
Name Joe Ames
Location Framing Date 1/9/19xx
From To Hours Job No. Rate Total Cost
7:30 12:00 4.5 808 $3.90 $17.55
12:30 4:00 3.5 809 $3.90 13.65
Approved by A.R. 8.0 Total $31.20
ANCILLARY SERVICES
MANUFACTURING OVERHEAD
WORK IN PROGRESS
$112.00
$ 17.55
$201.66
$308.00
$100.40
$ 50.10
$789.71
Perpetual Inventory Card
Type 4' Center Cabinet-Kitchen Code No. 4A
Produced Delivered On Hand
Job No. Qt. Cost Job No. Qt. Cost Date Qt. Amt. Unit Cost
808 8 $89.71 1-12-xx 8 789.71 98.71
FINISHED GOODS
$789.71
Job Cost Sheet
Job No. 808
Date Started 1/9/19XX
Date Finished 1/12/19XX
Req. No. Direct Materials Ticket No. Direct Labor Overhead (120%) of Labor Total
60 $112.00 $112.00
17 $ 17.55 17.55
63 308.00 308.00
31 100.40 100.40
6 50.10 50.10
Totals $420.00 $168.05
Overhead Applied 201.66 $201.66
Total $789.71

JOB COST SHEET

Each job has a job cost sheet which performs two functions: (1) It is (along with all other job cost sheets) the subsidiary work-in-progress ledger, supporting the general ledger account "work-in-progress." Sometimes, another column is provided at the right of the "total" column showing accumulated cost-to-date, making a trial balance of the subsidiary ledger easier; and (2) The job cost sheet shows the cost-to-date on each job and its status toward completion. The total cost, upon completion, supports an entry to finished goods as:

Finished Goods - 8′ Center Kitchen-Cabinets	$789.71	
Work-In-Progress (Job#808)		$789.71

It is important to observe that overhead is applied on the job cost sheet, as well as labor and materials. In the illustration, overhead is applied at a rate of 120% of labor. Methods of applying overhead will be discussed more fully later in this chapter. The application of overhead shown in the job cost sheet is accomplished with the following entry:

Work-In-Progress (Job #808)	$201.66	
Manufacturing Overhead		$201.66

Information on the job cost sheet, as is indicated, includes the starting and finishing dates of the job, and the source of entries for materials and labor costs by identification of materials requisition number and time ticket number. It is obvious that other materials were used on Job #808 (from materials requisition #63), and that other labor was employed (from time tickets #31 and #6).

FINISHED GOODS PERPETUAL RECORD CARD

When completed, a job is identified (in this case, as 8-foot center kitchen-cabinets) and recorded on a perpetual record card. The cards themselves are the subsidiary finished goods ledger. Unit costs as computed in the example may be important if the cabinets were manufactured for individual sale. If, however, they were produced for one customer, a unit cost computation may be unnecessary. When the job or a portion of it is sold or delivered, an entry is made on the inventory card under the "delivered" column. In addition, a ledger entry recording the sale and the diminution of inventory is necessary.

ACCOUNTING FOR MATERIALS AND LABOR COST

Accounting for direct materials, direct labor, and overhead has been treated only in general terms at this point. A few procedures peculiar to materials and labor may be of help, and they will be described here. Manufacturing overhead is covered in the section which follows.

Inventory control techniques described in Chapter 7 are applicable in any firm, including those with job order cost accounting systems. Traditional accounting theory books adequately treat the methods of inventory costings, Lifo and Fifo and average, and will not be dealt with here. Peculiar to manufacturing is the matter of handling scrap, spoiled work and waste. Ideally, all three are to be avoided, but usually they cannot be.

The least avoidable of the three mentioned above are waste and scrap, although carefully designed quality control techniques can minimize both. In larger firms, scrap and waste often are rather sizable amounts, and consequently receive more than cursory attention.

Scrap or waste reports are required, describing the amount of and reason for the scrap or waste, the job on which either occurred, and the kind of materials involved. Frequently, scrap and waste are predetermined for the period and comparisons are made with actual figures. Materials falling in these categories are accumulated and periodically sold or disposed of.

Several methods of accounting for scrap and waste are acceptable, but for saleable materials, it is preferable to use the simple procedure of crediting manufacturing overhead at the time of sale when the amounts are considered immaterial. When scrap or waste has a relatively high value, scrap should be stored and costed at current scrap prices, and inventory record cards should be prepared and maintained. At this time an entry is made to charge a scrap inventory account and to credit manufacturing overhead. Upon its sale the entry is a charge to cash and a credit to scrap inventory.

The cost of goods spoiled during the process of a job should be charged to that job. As an example of accounting for spoiled units, assume that a cabinet manufacturer has received an order for 50, eight foot kitchen cabinets, and that in the cutting department ten of the fifty sheets of plywood split so as to be unusable except as scrap and are saleable at $2.00 a sheet. Further assume the total cost of the job (including the 10 spoiled sheets) was recorded as follows:

Work-In-Progress (Job #110)	$3,400	
Raw Materials Inventory		$1,640
Wages Payable		800
Manufacturing Overhead (120% of direct labor of $800)		960

The entry to record the spoilage is as follows:

Scrap Inventory (spoilage) (10 × $2)	$20.00	
Work-In-Progress-Materials (Job #110)		$9.60
Work-In-Progress-Labor (Job #110)		4.70
Work-In-Progress-Overhead (Job #110)		5.70[1]

When spoilage cannot be identified with a particular job, the spoiled goods cost should be allocated to the total production cost. This is accomplished by the following entry:

Scrap Inventory (Spoiled Goods)	$20.00	
Manufacturing Overhead	60.00	
Work-In-Progress (Materials)		38.40
Work-In-Progress (Labor)		18.80
Work-In-Progress (Overhead)		22.80[2]

[1]The percent of each of labor, materials and overhead cost to total cost of the job is:

$$\frac{\text{Materials Cost (\$1,640)}}{\text{Total Cost (\$3,400)}} = 48\% \times \text{Spoilage Recovery (\$20)} = \$9.60$$

$$\frac{\text{Labor Cost (\$800)}}{\text{Total Cost (\$3,400)}} = 23.5\% \times \$20 = \$4.70$$

$$\frac{\text{Manufacturing Overhead (\$960)}}{\text{Total Cost (\$3,400)}} = 28.5\% = \$20 = \$5.70$$

[2]Total spoilage is $80 (10 sheets x the cost per sheet of $8.00). The sales value of spoiled goods is $20 (10 × $2.00). The remainder of $60.00 is unrecoverable cost.

Charging manufacturing overhead with the unrecoverable cost will result in assigning the cost to all production through the overhead rate. Of course, the overhead rate should include a factor for spoilage, along with other indirect costs, to be allocated to work-in-progress inventory.

LABOR COST RECORD-KEEPING AND IDLE TIME

Direct labor cost must be charged either to a particular job or to idle time. Consequently, record-keeping and other accounting procedures should facilitate accomplishment of this objective. What this means is that each worker must keep a daily record of his time by job and of that time lost for whatever reason but paid. The worker's daily record should account for the entire time for which he is paid. The time ticket for Joe Ames in Figure 11-2 shows how Ames spent his time on a particular day. All eight hours are accounted for and charged to jobs. Support for the time ticket, as stated earlier, may be a time clock with a clock card for each employee. Aside from the cost control afforded by the clock card, federal labor laws make use of it or a similar record mandatory. The clock card and daily time ticket, as stated, are used to prepare each employee's payroll. As an example of the use of the time sheet for costing jobs and recording idle time, assume the following time sheet for Joe Ames on 1/10/19XX:

Figure 11-3

TIME TICKET

No. 29

Name: Joe Ames

Location: Framing | Date: 1/10/19XX

From	To	Hours	Job No.	Rate	Total Cost
7:30	8:10	.67	821	$3.90	$2.61
8:10	9:00	.83	Idle	3.90	3.24
9:00	12:00	3.0	821	3.90	11.70
12:30	4:00	3.5	822	3.90	13.65
Approved By: A. R.		8.0	Totals		$31.20

Ames' clock card will be compared with his time ticket for correctness. Analysis of the time sheet results in the following entry:

Work-In-Progress (Job #821)	$14.31	
Work-In-Progress (Job #822)	13.65	
Manufacturing Overhead	3.24	
Wages Payable		$31.20[3]

Idle time, as shown, is charged to manufacturing overhead. Some firms use idle time reports showing the amount of time and the reason for the stoppage. Such reports are an excellent device for controlling idle time.

Incentive wage systems, productivity and efficiency measurement, and other more complex topics affecting the accounting for labor costs are more frequently useful in larger manufacturing operations, and as such, are outside the scope of this book. The reader is respectfully referred to texts written exclusively and in depth on the subject of cost accounting. One such text is *Cost Accounting: A Managerial Emphasis,* 4th edition, by Charles T. Horngren, and published by Prentice-Hall, Inc.

One final point needs mentioning under the labor cost topic, and that is fringe benefits and other costs associated with wages and salaries. Examples of these costs are: payroll taxes, workmen's compensation insurance, vacation pay and other allowed time off with pay, overtime premium, pensions, medical and life insurance plans, and the cost of services provided employees, such as parking, legal and tax advice, etc. In the aggregate, wage associated costs are no small matter, often amounting to as much as 30% of regular pay. In general these costs are treated as manufacturing overhead, the subject of the next section. One exception to this generality is that, not infrequently, overtime premium that arises because of a particular job is charged to that job. For example, a job brought in late Friday and wanted Monday morning will likely involve overtime which should be part of its cost and included in the selling price.

ACCOUNTING FOR MANUFACTURING OVERHEAD

Accounting for manufacturing overhead involves consideration of the following factors: How to select the basis for applying overhead; choosing the level of activity to be used; and when to use a flexible overhead budget.

HOW TO SELECT THE BASIS FOR APPLYING OVERHEAD

Incurring expenses properly classified as manufacturing overhead is often a random event, and as a consequence, charging units of output as the expense occurs will likely result in unit costs of one period being substantially different from those of another period. This cost differential is true simply because of the volitional act of committing assets rather than that the units indeed cost more. For example, a large expenditure for machine repair in June will cause units produced in June to cost more than units produced in July, resulting in an

[3]This entry is illustrative only. The more likely approach is to accumulate time tickets by department, assuming there is more than one, and to record labor cost in one aggregative entry for the day's work.

unrealistic unit cost. For this reason, overhead should be estimated for the year and applied to the cost of units produced on a uniform basis.

Estimating overhead is much like traditional budgeting described in Chapter 4 in that expenses are planned taking into account prior years' experience and influencing factors expected to occur in the year being considered. The formula for the overhead rate is:

$$\frac{\text{Planned (or Estimated) Overhead}}{\text{Selected Basis}} = \text{Rate of Overhead}$$

Several bases are in use. The most common ones are:

1. Direct Labor Cost.
2. Direct Labor Hours.
3. Materials Cost.
4. Planned Units of Production.
5. Machine Hours.

Choosing the base is dependent on the factors contributing most to the incurrence of overhead. For example, manufacturing processes which are highly capital intensive suggest the use of machine hours. When materials contribute the greatest to ultimate cost, the cost of materials is the most apt. Alternatively, in labor intensive firms either labor cost or labor hours result in the most accurate application of overhead. The choice between them will hinge on whether labor cost is relatively uniform. If labor cost is relatively uniform, then that is the best choice. When labor cost is widely divergent then labor hours is appropriate. The simplest basis is planned units of production, but this is limited to cases where only one product is made. The accountant is in the best position to advise on the selection of the basis for overhead application, and he will consider each of these mentioned remembering that the objective is to obtain the most accurate unit cost of product. If, for example, labor cost is chosen as the basis for allocating overhead, expected overhead is \$120,000 and direct labor cost estimated to be \$100,000 for the coming year, then the overhead rate is:

$$\frac{\text{Planned overhead \$120,000}}{\text{Direct labor cost \$100,000}} = \text{Overhead rate 120\% of direct labor cost}$$

It is important to note that both the planned overhead and the basis, whichever chosen, are estimates of the costs for the coming year. The cost estimates are obviously dependent on the expected level of activity, or volume, for the year.

Choosing the Level of Activity to be Used

The significance of the choice of the level of activity, or volume, to be used is found in its effect on the amount of fixed overhead assigned to each unit of product. It will be recalled that fixed overhead is a period charge, not related to output, whereas variable overhead is definitionally tied to production. A good deal more will be said on the subject of fixed and variable overhead later in this chapter. An example of the impact of the level of activity on unit cost of fixed overhead will illustrate this point. Assume the firm expects planned production of 11,000 units and that the fixed overhead for the year is \$96,000. The per unit cost of fixed overhead is \$8.73. On the other hand, should production be expected to equal last year's production of 9,000 units, fixed overhead assigned to each unit would be \$10.67.

The Internal Revenue Code allows any one of three levels of activity for allocating fixed overhead: normal capacity, expected actual capacity, or practical capacity. Normal capacity is a long-run view while expected capacity is short-run in outlook. The difference between the two is essentially that normal capacity smoothes the effect of year-to-year variations due to cyclical or seasonal surges in demand. Expected actual capacity on the other hand, looks forward only one year considering all factors likely to affect production in that period. It is obvious that variances between actual overhead and applied overhead will be more likely using normal capacity than using expected actual.

Practical capacity is determined by first establishing the volume that is theoretically possible if production proceeded continually without interruptions. This is sometimes referred to as engineering or theoretical capacity. Realistically, no firm can operate at this level, because there are unavoidable interruptions. Engineering capacity less an allowance for these unavoidable delays equals practical capacity.

The various capacities may be seen more clearly from the following diagram:

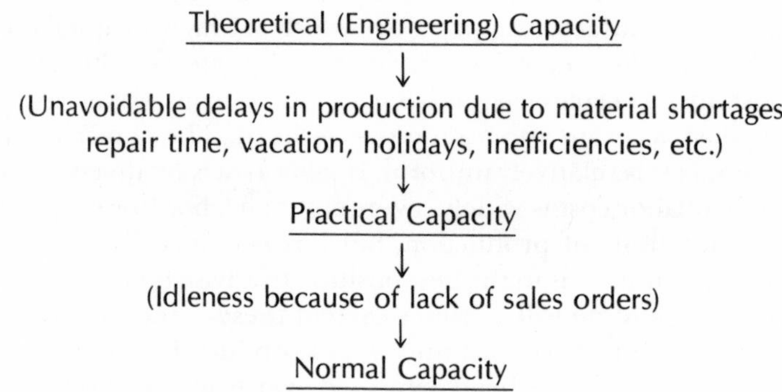

Normal capacity is in widest use as the level of activity for applying fixed overhead primarily because of its long-run approach and smoothing effect. If these are its advantages, they are also the chief contributors to making a determination of the firm's normal capacity difficult.

STEPS IN ESTIMATING NORMAL CAPACITY

Normal capacity is the expected volume which can be sold over a period long enough to smooth seasonal and cyclical variations. Consequently, normal capacity must be simultaneously viewed both from the standpoint of sales expectancy and from that of physical capability. The point at which they converge is normal capacity. The following steps have proven useful in estimating normal capacity:

Step 1. Determine the firm's theoretical capacity. Management may have a fairly refined idea of the plant's capacity, operating 24 hours a day without interruption. If not, then a production specialist or engineer may be called upon for an estimate.

Step 2. Compute down time because of repairs, materials shortages and inactivity due to vacations, holidays and normal nonworking days. Make allowances for unavoidable (in a practical sense) inefficiencies. This is the firm's practical capacity.

Step 3. Project a sales budget (as described in Chapter 4) for an extended period, say five years, and convert into production units.

Step 4. Add a factor for production for inventory if desirable. Reconcile the production figures obtained in Steps 2 and 3. It is likely that the practical capacity determined in Step 2 will differ from the annualized sales and inventory production figure projected in Step 3. The reconciliation should involve consideration of advertising campaigns, additional sales personnel, expanded sales territories, and other approaches to increase sales. Alternatively, consideration should be given to correcting inefficiencies in production, additional production work shifts, overtime, subcontracting work, or ultimately adding production capacity. The reconciled production figure obtained and annualized, is normal capacity.

The process described in steps one through four is an excellent device for firm self study, and is an integral part of management planning.

Cost Behavior—Fixed and Variable Costs

From an overview, the determination of normal overhead is the initial, and possibly the most important, step in establishing an overhead rate. Analyzing the behavior of the firm's cost is the next step, the purpose of which is to identify the fixed and variable cost elements of the firm. Fixed costs, it will be recalled, are those which do not change with changes in activity. On the other hand, variable costs, as the name implies, vary directly with volume changes. Analysis will show that all costs cannot be conveniently categorized as either fixed or variable. Some costs have elements of both and are called "stair-stepped" costs because of their appearance when observed on a chart, or semi-variable costs. More on this topic later.

Rent, property taxes and insurance, and depreciation are typical fixed costs. Indirect labor and supplies are typical variable costs. Some administrative salaries, such as maintenance personnel and supervisors are examples of semi-variable costs. The semi-variable characteristic exists because of the need for one maintenance worker, for example, for a given range of volume beyond which another maintenance worker is needed and so on.[4]

Why Does Each Firm's Cost Need Analysis?

It is not adequate to take a list of examples of fixed and variable (semi-variable, too) costs, no matter how exhaustive, and use it to establish the nature of a particular firm's cost. The reason is that management intent can make a seemingly fixed cost variable. Depreciation is a good illustration. A policy of straight line depreciation renders it a fixed cost; however, using the units of production method makes it variable. Moreover, each firm has a range of output within which it expects to operate, this range is called the "relevant range," and it is within this parameter that the firm's cost behavior must be analyzed and classified. A good rule of thumb for categorizing costs as either fixed or variable is to ask the question: Will management, through necessity or otherwise, allow or require this cost to change as activity changes? If the answer is "no," it is a fixed cost to this firm.

[4]It may be well to note that adding an employee permanently is not always required or desirable; rather, the firm may use existing personnel on an overtime basis or use temporary help.

THE HIGH-LOW METHOD OF SEGREGATING FIXED AND VARIABLE ELEMENTS OF SEMI-VARIABLE COSTS

Semi-variable costs are identified as having both an element of fixed cost and one of variable cost. Each must be isolated from the other. A simple, yet practical, approach to segregating the fixed and variable elements of a semi-variable cost is commonly called the high-low method. Using historical data, the cost being analyzed and the activity level for each segment of a period of time, usually a year, are arrayed side by side as in the illustration which follows:

	Salaries Expense-Supervisory and Maintenance	Units of Output
January	$24,408	1,863
February	31,916	2,109
March	31,060	2,216
April	23,320	1,480
May	28,091	2,007
June	37,119	3,115
July	34,300	2,193
August	26,040	1,644
September	28,146	1,916
October	23,633	1,495
November	23,900	1,506
December	24,323	1,522

The salaries expense of the high volume month (June) is compared with the salaries expense of the low volume month (April) in a ratio as follows:

$$\frac{\Delta \text{ Salaries Expense}}{\Delta \text{ In Volume}}$$

The change (Δ) in salaries from low to high is $13,799 ($37,119 – $23,320), while the change in volume is 1,635 (3,115 – 1,480).

$$\frac{\$13{,}799}{1{,}635} = \$8.44$$

From this ratio, the variable cost rate per unit of output is determined to be $8.44. The fixed overhead portion is:

High Cost	$37,119
Less Variable Cost ($8.44 × 3,115)	26,290
Fixed Cost	$10,829

Figure 11-4

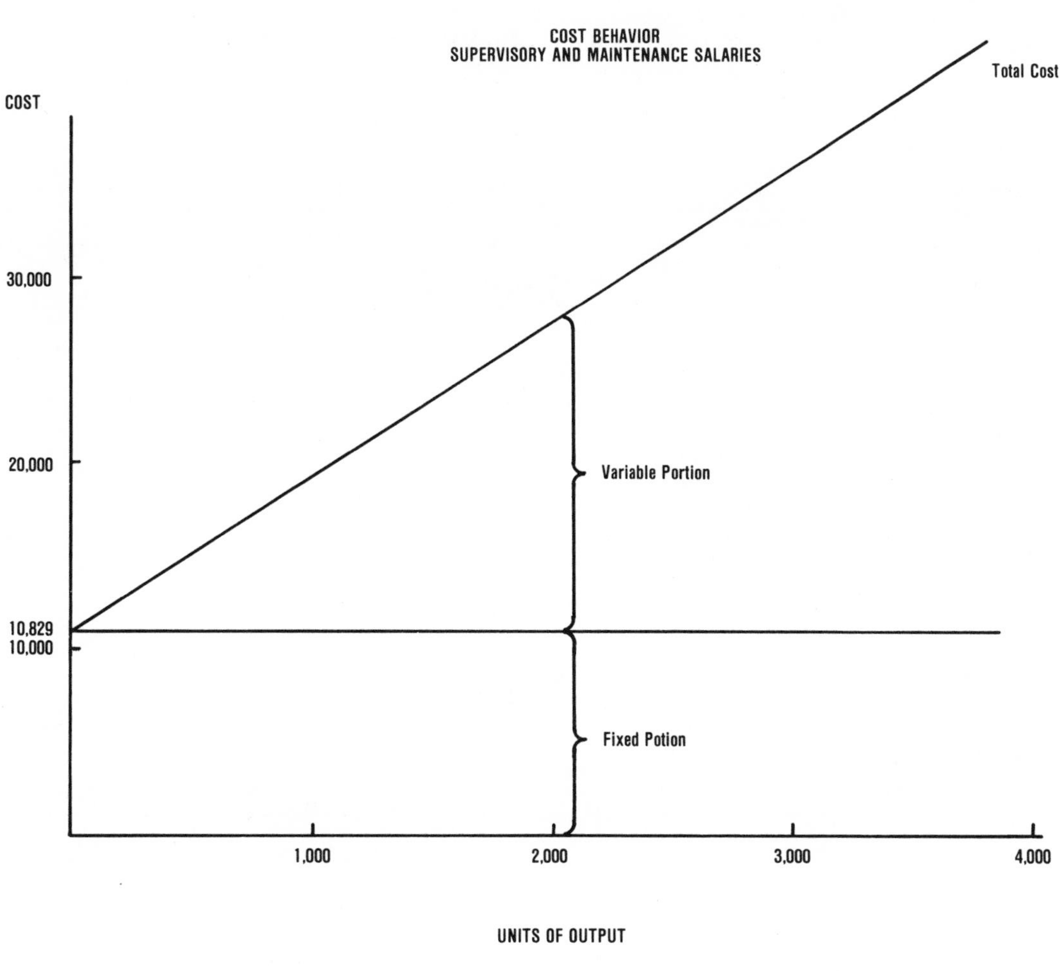

A chart showing the behavior of supervisory and maintenance salaries expense will take form as shown in Figure 11-4. The line in Figure 11-4 describing total cost has a slope equivalent to $8.44 cost for every unit of output. This is, of course, the variable cost rate.

The high-low method is reasonably accurate and simple to use. Other methods, such as least squares or scatter graphs, while yielding slightly more accuracy, sacrifice simplicity. Circumstances will dictate which technique is most appropriate, but the authors prefer the high-low method for the reasons mentioned. Traditional statistics texts may be consulted if another method is preferable.

Finally, on the subject of semi-variable costs, the accountant analyzing cost behavior is likely to discover that many of the firm's costs are semi-variable, containing both fixed and variable elements. This only seems to emphasize the need for analysis of each of the firm's costs.

Figure 11-5

MONTHLY FLEXIBLE BUDGET—PRODUCTION DEPARTMENT

	LEVEL OF ACTIVITY			
Number of Units	1,000	2,000	3,000*	4,000
Direct Labor Hours (3 hrs. per unit)	3,000	6,000	9,000	12,000
Variable Overhead: Indirect Labor (Supervisory and Maintenance)	$ 8,444	$16,888	$25,332	$33,776
Office & Administrative	300	600	900	1,200
Manufacturing Supplies	150	300	450	600
Payroll Taxes & Other Employment Costs	1,750	3,500	5,250	7,000
Power	200	400	600	800
Other Variable (Including Spoiled Goods)	1,600	3,200	4,800	6,400
Total Variable Overhead	$12,444	$24,888	$37,332	$49,776
Fixed Overhead: Depreciation	$ 1,000	$ 1,000	$ 1,000	$ 1,000
Insurance & Property Taxes	700	700	700	700
Fixed Portion of Semi-Variable	14,936	14,936	14,936	14,936
Other Fixed	2,000	2,000	2,000	2,000
Total Fixed Overhead	$18,636	$18,636	$18,636	$18,636
Total Manufacturing Overhead	$31,080	$43,524	$55,968	$68,412

*NORMAL CAPACITY

Figure 11-5 continued

Rate Per Direct Labor Hour:				
Total	$10.36	$7.25	6.21	$5.70
Fixed	6.22	3.11	2.07	1.56
Variable	4.14	4.14	4.14	4.14

When to Use a Flexible Budget

The earlier discussion in this chapter on capacity and analysis of cost behavior is directed toward developing and using flexible budgets. Simply said, a flexible budget allows for the realistic assignment of overhead on the basis of any level of activity. Logic indicates that the more output a firm has, the smaller the per unit cost, because of fixed costs and the fixed portion of semi-variable costs. Use of a flexible budget recognizes this fact.

Developing a Flexible Budget

Using the figures developed from the analysis of costs, a flexible budget can be prepared. Figure 11-5 is a condensed example of a flexible budget for a one production department manufacturer. In firms with more than one department, a flexible budget should be prepared for each.

Several observations need to be made concerning Figure 11-5. It will be noted that the flexible budget is prepared according to volume (number of units), the limits of which are what the firm believes to be its relevant range of production. However, overhead is applied on the basis of direct labor hours, and this requires an estimate of the number of direct labor hours needed per unit of production, in this instance—three. The manufacturing overhead accounts have been analyzed as already illustrated and the fixed and variable elements in each cost account separated. It will be observed that variable overhead, as a rate per direct labor hour, is constant throughout the entire relevant range, indicating perfect variability, while fixed overhead, as a rate of direct labor, decreases. This behavior of both variable and fixed costs is consistent with the assumptions made and discussed previously about their behavior. The assumption of the perfect variability of variable costs is unaltered by possible additional variable overhead at higher production levels, although the rate may be different. As an example, consider the possibility of overtime required of employees at production levels over 3,000 units. This would add to total variable cost and increase its rate for these volumes. It is assumed, in this example, that 3,000 units is normal capacity, and that the firm uses normal capacity as the basis for applying fixed overhead.

Ordinarily a flexible budget, such as Figure 11-5 should be allowed to stand for at least one year without revision. At that time, a review of all the factors considered in preparing it should be undertaken.

THE MECHANICS OF APPLYING OVERHEAD—AN EXAMPLE

Once the flexible budget has been prepared, and variable and fixed overhead rates have been computed, overhead can be applied to individual jobs as well as to the general ledger account "Work-in-Progress." Fixed overhead is assigned on the basis of normal capacity, irrespective of the actual level of operations, while variable overhead is assigned at $4.14 per direct labor hour.

As an example of the mechanics of applying overhead, and using the flexible budget illustrated, assume a firm with the following operating data for November, 19XX:

Actual Volume:	
Units Produced	2,890
Direct Labor Hours	8,731
Actual Factory Overhead:	
Variable	$37,907
Fixed	18,491
Total	$56,398
Predetermined Overhead:	
Variable (8,670 hrs. × $4.14)[5]	$35,894
Fixed (8,670 hrs. × $2.07)	17,947
Total	$53,841
Total Overhead Variance (Unfavorable)	
($56,398—$53,841)	$ 2,557

OVERHEAD VARIANCE—DIFFERENCES BETWEEN ACTUAL AND PREDETERMINED OVERHEAD

As is the case in the example above, differences, called variances, between actual and predetermined overhead will likely occur. Variance analysis can be quite useful to management as a control device. Both the efficiency of the firm's manufacturing process and its care in allocating resources can be evaluated by an analysis of variances.[6]

[5]Overhead is applied on the basis of direct labor hours allowed (3) for the actual number of units produced (2,890). 3 × 2,890 = 8,670 hours.

[6]Although this chapter's subject is job order costing, a standard cost system is not assumed. If it were, variances between standard labor and materials costs as well as variances between predetermined and actual overhead, would exist and need analysis. Standard cost is the subject of Chapter 13, and a complete discussion of analysis of labor and materials variances in included there.

UNDERSTANDING OVERHEAD VARIANCES

Any difference between actual and predetermined overhead may be isolated into a spending variance and a capacity variance. A spending variance occurs because of changes due to efficiency, indirect labor wage rates, or other factors which make actual costs for a particular volume differ from budgeted costs for that volume. Ordinarily, spending variances arise from variable costs rather than fixed costs because the latter tend to vary little from budgeted figures. (In the example used here, there is a spending variance attributable to fixed costs.)

A capacity variance arises because the firm operated at a level of output different from the level used to establish the fixed overhead rate (in this illustration, normal capacity). Obviously, the capacity variance is associated exclusively with fixed overhead.

The relationship and computation of the two variances may be demonstrated as follows, using the flexible budget and operating data presented earlier:

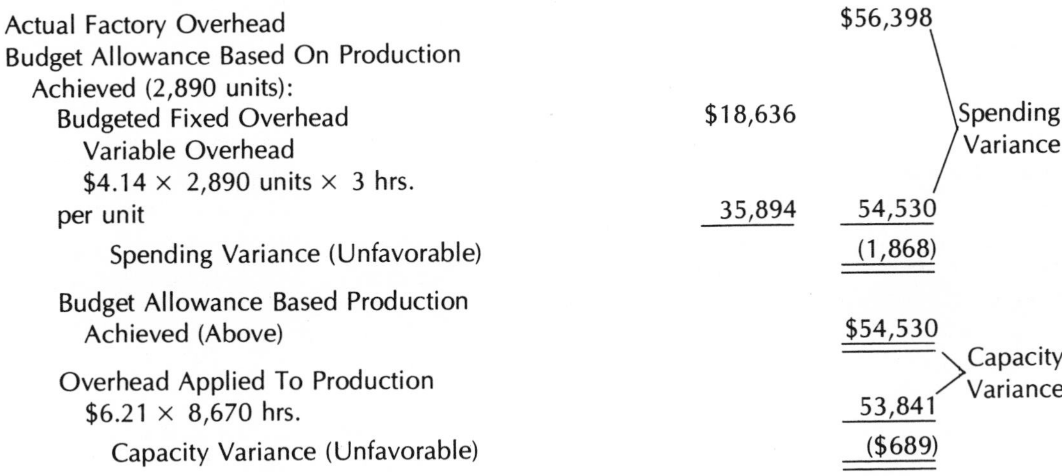

Actual Factory Overhead		$56,398	Spending Variance
Budget Allowance Based On Production Achieved (2,890 units):			
Budgeted Fixed Overhead	$18,636		
Variable Overhead $4.14 × 2,890 units × 3 hrs. per unit	35,894	54,530	
Spending Variance (Unfavorable)		(1,868)	
Budget Allowance Based Production Achieved (Above)		$54,530	Capacity Variance
Overhead Applied To Production $6.21 × 8,670 hrs.		53,841	
Capacity Variance (Unfavorable)		($689)	

A further analysis and proof of the two variances may be as follows:

Spending Variance		
Fixed portion:		
Budgeted Fixed Overhead	$18,636	
Actual Fixed Overhead	18,491	
Spending Variance Attributable to Fixed Overhead (Favorable)		$145
Variable portion:		
Budgeted Variable Overhead 8,670 hrs. × $4.14	$35,894	
Actual Variable Overhead	37,907	

Spending Variance Attributable to Variable Overhead (Unfavorable)	(2,013)
Total Spending Variance (Unfavorable)	($1,868)

Proof of Capacity Variance:

	Direct Labor Hours
Capacity Available (Normal Capacity)	9,000
Capacity Used (Allowed for Production Achieved)	8,670
Unused Capacity	330
Unused Capacity × Fixed Overhead Rate (330 hrs. × $2.07)	$ 683*

*Difference of $6 due to rounding.

What Do the Variances Mean?

A variance, favorable or unfavorable, means that the production department did not operate as planned. An unfavorable capacity variance is the cost of capacity available but unused. It could have arisen because supervisors did not maintain a steady flow of work or because of faulty materials, causing lost effort. Alternatively, a capacity variance occurs when orders created in the sales department simply were insufficient to operate fully. Appropriate corrective action should be taken by management.

An account-by-account analysis of spending variances should be made, comparing actual figures with predetermined amounts. Unfavorable variances are indicative of excess spending, and while excesses may be acceptable, they should be investigated and reasons for the excesses understood.

A common fallacy held by laymen is that favorable variances are good and hence desirable, while the opposite is true of unfavorable variances. As an example, a favorable variance can, in reality, be undesirable. Consider a firm which uses service department labor (indirect labor) of a lower grade, and consequently pays a lower rate. If a higher level of personnel is planned and needed than is used, poor or even faulty work can result. Now indirect labor cost will show a favorable variance, but substandard maintenance can have long-term harmful effects on profitability. The point of this is that each variance from predetermined levels should be viewed both independently and from the standpoint of the productivity and profitability of the firm as a whole. Precipitous action on the part of management using a month's, or even a year's, results is seldom justified. Moreover, predetermined overhead rates should not be altered within a given year. Trends should be noted, of course, and variances understood. Some firms change overhead rates only after two, three, or even five years' experience.

How to Account for Variances

Accounting for overhead variances is quite simple, and the following rule of thumb is recommended: If the variance is deemed immaterial, write it off as a period cost in the cost of goods sold section of the income statement. If the variance is material, allocate it to cost of goods sold, work-in-progress, and finished goods on the basis of the relative values of each account for the period. An example may help.

An Example of Allocating Variances

Referring to the flexible budget, Figure 11-5, and the operating data of the illustrative firm, the entries indicated are as follows, assuming the variance to be material:

	Debit	Credit
Manufacturing Overhead Control	$56,398	
Cash (Accounts Payable, etc.)		$56,398
To record actual overhead for November 19XX.		
Work-In-Progress	53,841	
Manufacturing Overhead Control		53,841
To apply overhead to production on the basis of 8,670 allowed direct labor hours at $6.21 per hour.		

The manufacturing overhead account at this point appears as:

Manufacturing	Overhead-Control
56,398	53,841
Bal. 2,557	

The debit balance of $2,557 is the unfavorable variance already identified. Further, assume that the following additional data in the accounts is available for November (These are account balances considering the entries above):

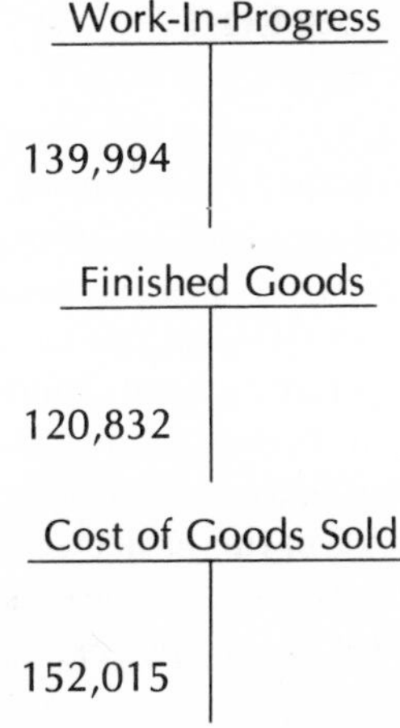

Work-In-Progress	
139,994	

Finished Goods	
120,832	

Cost of Goods Sold	
152,015	

Allocation of the overhead variance would be made as:

	Account Balance	Percent of Total
Work-In-Progress	$139,994	33.9%
Finished Goods	120,832	29.3%
Cost of Goods Sold	152,015	36.8%
Totals	$412,841	100.0%

Allocated to:

	Percent	Variance Allocated
Work-In-Progress	33.9%	$ 867
Finished Goods	29.3%	749
Cost of Goods Sold	36.8%	941
Totals	100.0%	$2,557

The entry is:

	Debit	Credit
Work-In-Progress	867	
Finished Goods	749	
Cost of Goods Sold	941	
Manufacturing Overhead-Control		2,557

A Comprehensive Example of Job Order Cost Accounting

The example which follows is necessarily condensed, but an attempt has been made to include the normal accounting procedures and techniques common to most small manufacturing firms which have been found useful. A particular effort has been made to inject realism, but the reader should remember that companies are unique, each with its own set of problems and environment. Consequently, what follows should be viewed from the standpoint that it illustrates *principles* and that modifications will almost surely have to be made by accountants in the field. If the reader needs a further refresher for his or her cost accounting knowledge, an excellent text on the subject, carefully written in much detail with illustrations of complexities outside the scope of this book, is *Cost Accounting—A Managerial Emphasis,* 4th edition by Charles T. Horngren, published by Prentice-Hall, Inc.

A Description of the Illustrative Firm and Its Operation

King Kabinets manufactures custom kitchen cabinets primarily for residential construction contractors. Cabinets are made only on order and a job order cost accounting system is used. The firm hires about 250 employees, most of whom are production workers. Between 30,000 and 40,000 wooden cabinets are manufactured in a year's time and sales approximate three million dollars annually.

A typical floor cabinet base is 4 feet long, although special size cabinets are constructed for corners and ends. Wall cabinets are made in three standard sizes and few orders are received for odd sizes. Counter tops are wooden, covered with a plastic laminate. All cabinet fronts are veneered in traditionally popular wood grains and colors. Hardware, consisting of hinges and pulls, is added according to the color and style requested by the contractor. These materials are purchased in quantity and merely installed by the company's employees.

The Accounting Process

Following is a description of the transactions of King Kabinets for the month of November, 19XX, and entries indicated thereby. The entries are, of course, in summary form, highly condensed for this illustration.

A trial balance for King Kabinets at November 1, 19XX, the beginning of its fiscal year, shows the following accounts and their balances:

KING KABINETS, INC.
Trial Balance
November 1, 19XX

Cash	$60,000	
Accounts Receivable	100,000	
Raw Materials	37,000	
Work-In-Progress	190,300	
Finished Goods	97,700	
Prepayments	4,800	
Plant And Equipment	366,000	
Accumulated Depreciation		$ 176,000
Accounts Payable		128,000
Salaries Payable		9,500
Common Stock		400,000
Retained Earnings		142,300
	$ 855,800	$ 855,800

A trial balance of the Job Cost Ledger shows:

Job #1906	$ 50,692
#1907	33,775
#1908	42,481
#1909	63,352
	$ 190,300

Figure 11-6

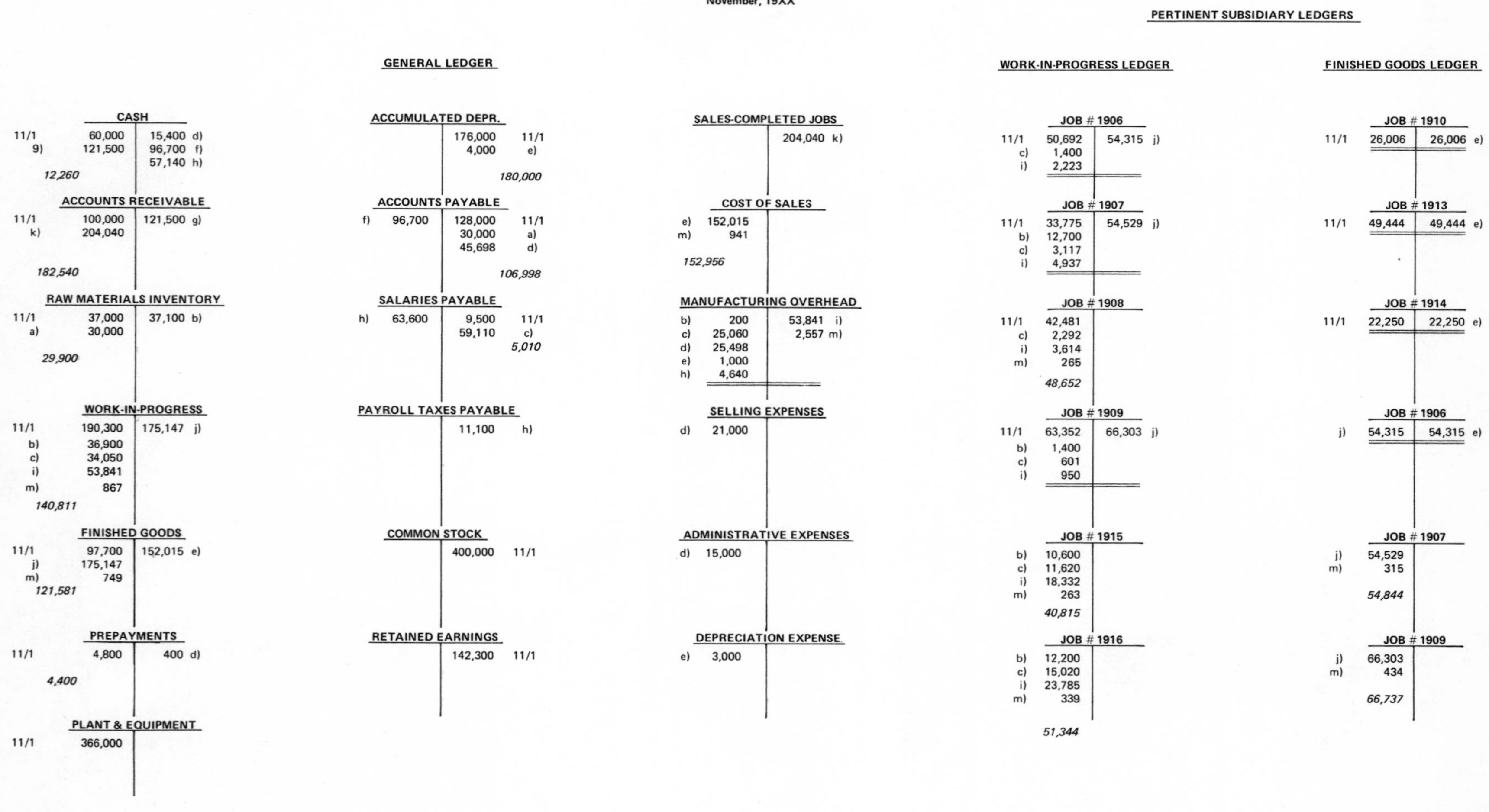

GENERAL AND SUBSIDIARY LEDGERS
KING KABINETS, INC.
November, 19XX

GENERAL LEDGER

CASH

	Dr.	Cr.	
11/1	60,000	15,400	d)
9)	121,500	96,700	f)
		57,140	h)
	12,260		

ACCOUNTS RECEIVABLE

	Dr.	Cr.	
11/1	100,000	121,500	g)
k)	204,040		
	182,540		

RAW MATERIALS INVENTORY

	Dr.	Cr.	
11/1	37,000	37,100	b)
a)	30,000		
	29,900		

WORK-IN-PROGRESS

	Dr.	Cr.	
11/1	190,300	175,147	j)
b)	36,900		
c)	34,050		
i)	53,841		
m)	867		
	140,811		

FINISHED GOODS

	Dr.	Cr.	
11/1	97,700	152,015	e)
j)	175,147		
m)	749		
	121,581		

PREPAYMENTS

	Dr.	Cr.	
11/1	4,800	400	d)
	4,400		

PLANT & EQUIPMENT

	Dr.	Cr.	
11/1	366,000		

ACCUMULATED DEPR.

	Dr.	Cr.	
		176,000	11/1
		4,000	e)
		180,000	

ACCOUNTS PAYABLE

	Dr.	Cr.	
f)	96,700	128,000	11/1
		30,000	a)
		45,698	d)
		106,998	

SALARIES PAYABLE

	Dr.	Cr.	
h)	63,600	9,500	11/1
		59,110	c)
		5,010	

PAYROLL TAXES PAYABLE

	Dr.	Cr.	
		11,100	h)

COMMON STOCK

	Dr.	Cr.	
		400,000	11/1

RETAINED EARNINGS

	Dr.	Cr.	
		142,300	11/1

SALES-COMPLETED JOBS

	Dr.	Cr.	
		204,040	k)

COST OF SALES

	Dr.	Cr.	
e)	152,015		
m)	941		
	152,956		

MANUFACTURING OVERHEAD

	Dr.	Cr.	
b)	200	53,841	i)
c)	25,060	2,557	m)
d)	25,498		
e)	1,000		
h)	4,640		

SELLING EXPENSES

	Dr.	Cr.	
d)	21,000		

ADMINISTRATIVE EXPENSES

	Dr.	Cr.	
d)	15,000		

DEPRECIATION EXPENSE

	Dr.	Cr.	
e)	3,000		

PERTINENT SUBSIDIARY LEDGERS

WORK-IN-PROGRESS LEDGER

JOB # 1906

	Dr.	Cr.	
11/1	50,692	54,315	j)
c)	1,400		
i)	2,223		

JOB # 1907

	Dr.	Cr.	
11/1	33,775	54,529	j)
b)	12,700		
c)	3,117		
i)	4,937		

JOB # 1908

	Dr.	Cr.	
11/1	42,481		
c)	2,292		
i)	3,614		
m)	265		
	48,652		

JOB # 1909

	Dr.	Cr.	
11/1	63,352	66,303	j)
b)	1,400		
c)	601		
i)	950		

JOB # 1915

	Dr.	Cr.	
b)	10,600		
c)	11,620		
i)	18,332		
m)	263		
	40,815		

JOB # 1916

	Dr.	Cr.	
b)	12,200		
c)	15,020		
i)	23,785		
m)	339		
	51,344		

FINISHED GOODS LEDGER

JOB # 1910

	Dr.	Cr.	
11/1	26,006	26,006	e)

JOB # 1913

	Dr.	Cr.	
11/1	49,444	49,444	e)

JOB # 1914

	Dr.	Cr.	
11/1	22,250	22,250	e)

JOB # 1906

	Dr.	Cr.	
j)	54,315	54,315	e)

JOB # 1907

	Dr.	Cr.	
j)	54,529		
m)	315		
	54,844		

JOB # 1909

	Dr.	Cr.	
j)	66,303		
m)	434		
	66,737		

Finished Goods Consist of:	
Job #1910	$ 26,006
#1913	49,444
#1914	22,250
	$ 97,700

Overhead is accumulated in a manufacturing overhead account on the basis of direct labor hours. The overhead rate is as shown in Figure 11-5 presented earlier.

Jobs are assigned a number when the contract is agreed upon with the builder, and an account is opened in the job ledger at that time. The form of the ledger account is similar to that shown in Figure 11-2. Overhead is ordinarily applied monthly to uncompleted jobs. Hence, the jobs in process at October 31, 19XX, already have included overhead based on direct labor hours to date.

Finished goods, jobs completed but not delivered, are supported by perpetual inventory cards similar to that in Figure 11-2.

Transactions for November, 19XX, follow and are posted to the general ledger "T" accounts, Figure 11-6.

(a) Raw Materials Purchased			
General Ledger Entry:			
Raw Materials		30,000	
Accounts Payable			30,000
Perpetual Raw Materials Inventory Cards:			
4′ × 8′ × ¾″ plywood (2,600 @ $8)	$20,800		
1″ × 4″ × 16′ fir (19,000 BF $.30)	5,700		
Plastic Laminate (500 @ $6)	3,000		
Glue (50 gals. @ $10)	500[7]		
	$30,000		

(b) Raw Materials Requisitioned for Production			
Manufacturing Overhead		200[8]	
Work-In-Progress		36,900	
Raw Materials			37,100
Work-In-Progress Ledger			

Job		
Job	#1907	$ 12,700
	#1909	1,400
	#1915	10,600
	#1916	12,200
	Total	$ 36,900

[7]For purposes of this illustration, no further entries will be shown to raw materials inventory perpetual records because of the need for brevity. The reader will understand that these entries must be made in practice. Because the work-in-progress and finished goods accounts are more important to understanding the example, subsidiary ledgers will be maintained.

[8]Because of the difficulty in tracing glue to an individual cabinet, it is treated as manufacturing overhead. Nails, when used, are handled similarly.

	Debit	Credit
(c) Labor Use (From Time Tickets)		
Work-In-Progress (8,731 hrs. @ $3.90)	34,050	
Manufacturing Overhead (6,961 hrs. @ 3.60)	25,060	
Accrued Payroll		59,110

Work-In-Progress Ledger:

	Hours	Amount
Job #1906	360	$ 1,400
#1907	799	3,117
#1908	588	2,292
#1909	154	601
#1915	2,979	11,620
#1916	3,851	15,020
	8,731	$34,050

	Debit	Credit
(d) Various Expenses Paid or Accrued for November		
Manufacturing Overhead	25,498	
Selling Expense	21,000	
Administrative Expense	15,000	
Cash		15,400
Accounts Payable		45,698
Prepaid Expense		400
e) November Depreciation		
Manufacturing Overhead	1,000	
Depreciation Expense	3,000	
Accumulated Depreciation		4,000
(f) Payments on Account		
Accounts Payable	96,700	
Cash		96,700
(g) Collections on Account		
Cash	121,500	
Accounts Receivable		121,500
(h) Payment of the Wages Accrued		
Accrued Payroll	63,600	
Manufacturing Overhead	4,640	
Payroll Taxes Payable		11,100
Cash		57,140
(i) To Apply Overhead for the Month		
Work-In-Progress	53,841	
Manufacturing Overhead (8,670 allowed direct labor hours @ $6.21 per hour)		53,841

Job Number	Allowed Hours	Amount
1906	358	$ 2,223
1907	795	4,937
1908	582	3,614
1909	153	950
1915	2,952	18,332
1916	3,830	23,785
	8,670	$53,841

		Debit	Credit
(j) To Record Completed Jobs			
Finished Goods		175,147	
Work-In-Progress			175,147

Job Number	Cost
1906	$54,315
1907	54,529
1909	66,303
	$175,147

		Debit	Credit
(k) To Record Delivery of Completed Jobs			
Accounts Receivable		204,040	
Sales-Completed Jobs			204,040
(l) Cost of Completed Jobs			
Cost of Sales		152,015	
Finished Goods			152,015

Job Number	Cost
1910	$ 26,006
1913	49,444
1914	22,250
1906	54,315
	$152,015

	Debit	Credit
(m) To Allocate Under-applied Overhead[9]		
Work-In-Progress	867	
Finished Goods	749	
Cost of Sales	941	
Manufacturing Overhead		2,557

Under-applied overhead is allocated to jobs, both those complete and those incomplete, on the basis of the number of direct labor hours charged to the job. Open jobs and direct labor hours charged to each are:

Job No.	Direct Labor Hours	% Of Total
1908	3,007	30.6%
1915	2,979	30.3%
1916	3,851	39.1%
	9,837	100.0%

Under-applied overhead allocated is:

Job No.	% of Total	Under-applied Overhead Allocated
1908	30.6%	$ 265
1915	30.3%	263
1916	39.1%	339
TOTALS	100.0%	$ 867

[9]Some firms carry under-applied or over-applied overhead balances until the end of the fiscal period and make one entry to allocate at that time. Little objection to that practice can be found assuming the allocation is based on total cost of sales, year-to-date, added to finished goods and work-in-progress account balances at the year's end. Obviously, most of the under-applied or over-applied balance will come to rest in cost of sales whether done monthly or annually.

A similar approach may be taken to allocate that portion of the under-applied overhead assigned to finished goods.

Job No.	Direct Labor Hours	% Of Total	Under-applied Overhead Allocated
1907	2,741	42.1%	$ 315
1909	3,772	57.9%	434
	6,513	100.0%	$ 749

A general trial ledger balance at November 30, 19XX, after giving effect to these transactions follows, along with schedules of work-in-progress and finished goods.

KING KABINETS, INC.
Trial Balance
November 30, 19XX

Cash	$ 12,260	
Accounts Receivable	182,540	
Raw Materials	29,900	
Work-In-Progress	140,811	
Finished Goods	121,581	
Prepayments	4,400	
Plant And Equipment	366,000	
Accumulated Depreciation		$ 180,000
Accounts Payable		106,998
Salaries Payable		5,010
Payroll Taxes Payable		11,100
Common Stock		400,000
Retained Earnings		142,300
Sales-Completed Contracts		204,040
Cost of Sales	152,956	
Selling Expense	21,000	
Administrative Expense	15,000	
Depreciation Expense	3,000	
	$1,049,448	$1,049,448

Schedule Of Work-In-Progress

Job No.	Amount
1908	$ 48,652
1915	40,815
1916	51,344
	$140,811

Schedule Of Finished Goods

Job No.	Amount
1907	$ 54,844
1909	66,737
	$121,581

A Note to Practitioners

The example shown, while comprehensive, is fairly simple. The only complication introduced was an allocation of under-applied overhead. This is not unrealistic, however, because the complications in a job order cost accounting system, once installed, are few. The necessary preliminaries of analyzing cost behavior and producing a flexible budget are much more complex than the accounting process. One further complication, not addressed directly earlier, is that of establishing the allowed direct labor hours for a given number of units of production. All three of these, cost behavior, flexible budgets, and allowed hours, are invaluable management control tools, and have much usefulness quite apart from the accounting process flowing therefrom for reasons already mentioned.

The matter of determining allowed direct labor hours is covered in Chapter 13 on Standard Costing.

Chapter 12

A Quick Review of Process Cost Analysis

Characteristics of Process Costing

Process cost reports are complex by nature and users tend to shy away from those that are so weighed down with intricate calculations as to hamper their effective use in the control process. While some industrial processes present enormous costing problems, it is possible to identify the cost elements without producing a report that is impressive but not functional. This chapter presents such a streamlined process cost analysis system. It will assist in effectively controlling the manufacturing process using the least possible amount of complex computation.

Industries that can effectively use process costing are usually those which produce their product(s) in a more or less steady flow through one or more manufacturing departments. Examples include assembly type industries manufacturing such items as small electrical parts and appliances of the household variety, washing machines, dryers, television sets, refrigerators, typewriters and automobiles. Of course, producers of sugar, flour, chemicals, pharmaceuticals, cement, steel, rubber and textiles find process costing methods very effective. These are only a few examples of industries using process costing, but they should serve to illustrate the manufacturing processes for which this type of cost analysis is most suitable.

In process cost accounting, costs are accumulated by manufacturing departments rather than by specific product jobs as in the case of job order cost accounting. In most cases where process costs are used, it would not be feasible or even possible to assign costs by specific lots. Average unit costs for each department are obtained by dividing the departmental costs by the units produced. These unit costs can be identified as to material, labor, and overhead costs for control purposes. The sum of the departmental unit costs constitutes the total unit cost of the product. They may be accomplished by accumulating the costs as the product moves through the manufacturing process or by totaling the individual department costs upon completion.

Departmental costs must also be identified by time periods to be really meaningful. If unit costs are to be compared to standards and/or previous time periods, there ought to be some degree of comparability between the periods, and the units produced must be identified with costs of the same period.

In those manufacturing processes where there is work in process at the beginning and/or the end of an accounting period, it will be necessary to calculate the number of equivalent whole units processed. This involves determining the percentage of completion in each case. The accuracy of the unit costs will, of course, be a function of the accuracy in determining percentage of completion. The determination of equivalent units will be discussed later in this chapter.

Process Cost Plans—General

The variety of routes taken by different kinds of products through their respective manufacturing processes presents the accountant with a comparable variety of process cost assembly problems. Three different cost flows are illustrated here as examples. With the exception of the lineal cost flow, they are subject to almost infinite variation themselves. The departmental breakdown used should be closely related to the manufacturing steps or phases encountered that will represent logical cost accumulation centers. The idea is to develop a departmentalization permitting accurate determination of material, labor and overhead costs by time periods.

The simplest and probably most common process cost flow is the lineal flow. Refer to Figure 12-1 for an example. Here the product moves through successive departments for processing straight to finished goods storage. Material may or may not be added along the way; the number of units started in process may increase or decrease along the way depending upon the nature of the manufacturing process. In Figure 12-1, two methods of cost accumulation are indicated.

The first method carries the cost forward from one department to the next, the unit cost increasing as the units progress through the several manufacturing stages. The second method accumulates costs by department with no carry-forward, the intent being to add the several departments' costs to arrive at a total unit cost for the period covered. This second method is not recommended where there are work-in-process inventories to be dealt with as well as frequent changes in the number of units in process. Units in process can change because of material added, increasing the volume, and because of shrinkage or lost units.

Another fairly common process cost flow is the concurrent process cost flow as illustrated in Figure 12-1. In this situation, two or more batches of material are started separately and processed separately through one or more departments. The materials ultimately come together in a final assembly process. In the case illustrated in Figure 12-1, costs for three independent processes ((A), (B) and (C)) are accumulated separately and are combined in process (D), Dept. 8, for finishing. Costs may be gathered cumulatively or by separate departments as in the case of the lineal process cost flow.

In more complex manufacturing processes, processed material may follow different routes for special processing and possibly combining as well as splitting apart to form different products. Meat packing, chemicals, petroleum, and assembly processes using common components are examples of industries having multi-product process cost flows. Refer to Figure 12-2 for an example. Gathering costs accumulatively would probably work

Figure 12-1

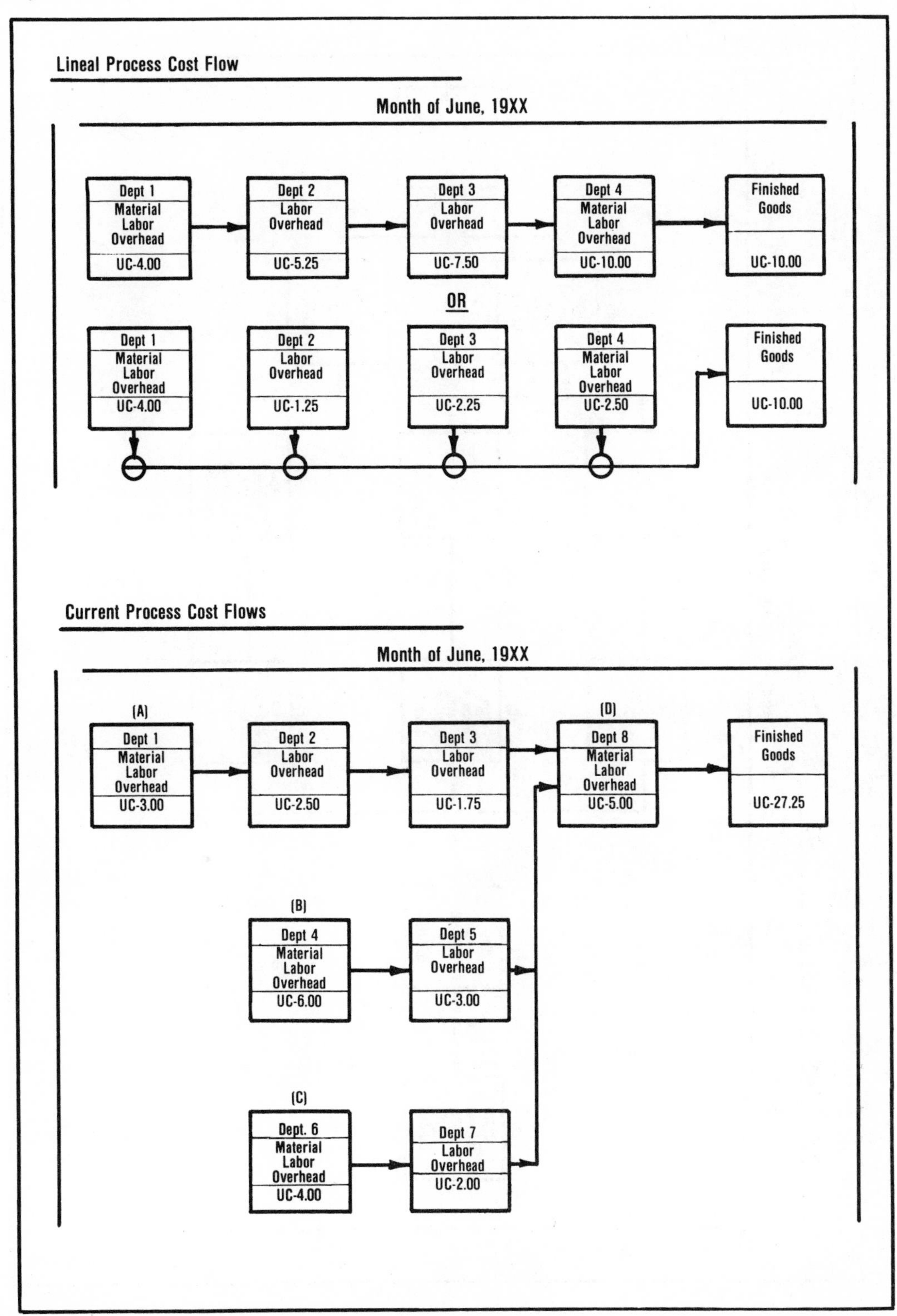
Lineal Process Cost Flow
Month of June, 19XX
Dept 1
Material
Labor
Overhead
UC-4.00
Dept 2
Labor
Overhead
UC-5.25
Dept 3
Labor
Overhead
UC-7.50
Dept 4
Material
Labor
Overhead
UC-10.00
Finished
Goods
UC-10.00
OR
Dept 1
Material
Labor
Overhead
UC-4.00
Dept 2
Labor
Overhead
UC-1.25
Dept 3
Labor
Overhead
UC-2.25
Dept 4
Material
Labor
Overhead
UC-2.50
Finished
Goods
UC-10.00
Current Process Cost Flows
Month of June, 19XX
(A)
Dept 1
Material
Labor
Overhead
UC-3.00
Dept 2
Labor
Overhead
UC-2.50
Dept 3
Labor
Overhead
UC-1.75
(D)
Dept 8
Material
Labor
Overhead
UC-5.00
Finished
Goods
UC-27.25
(B)
Dept 4
Material
Labor
Overhead
UC-6.00
Dept 5
Labor
Overhead
UC-3.00
(C)
Dept. 6
Material
Labor
Overhead
UC-4.00
Dept 7
Labor
Overhead
UC-2.00

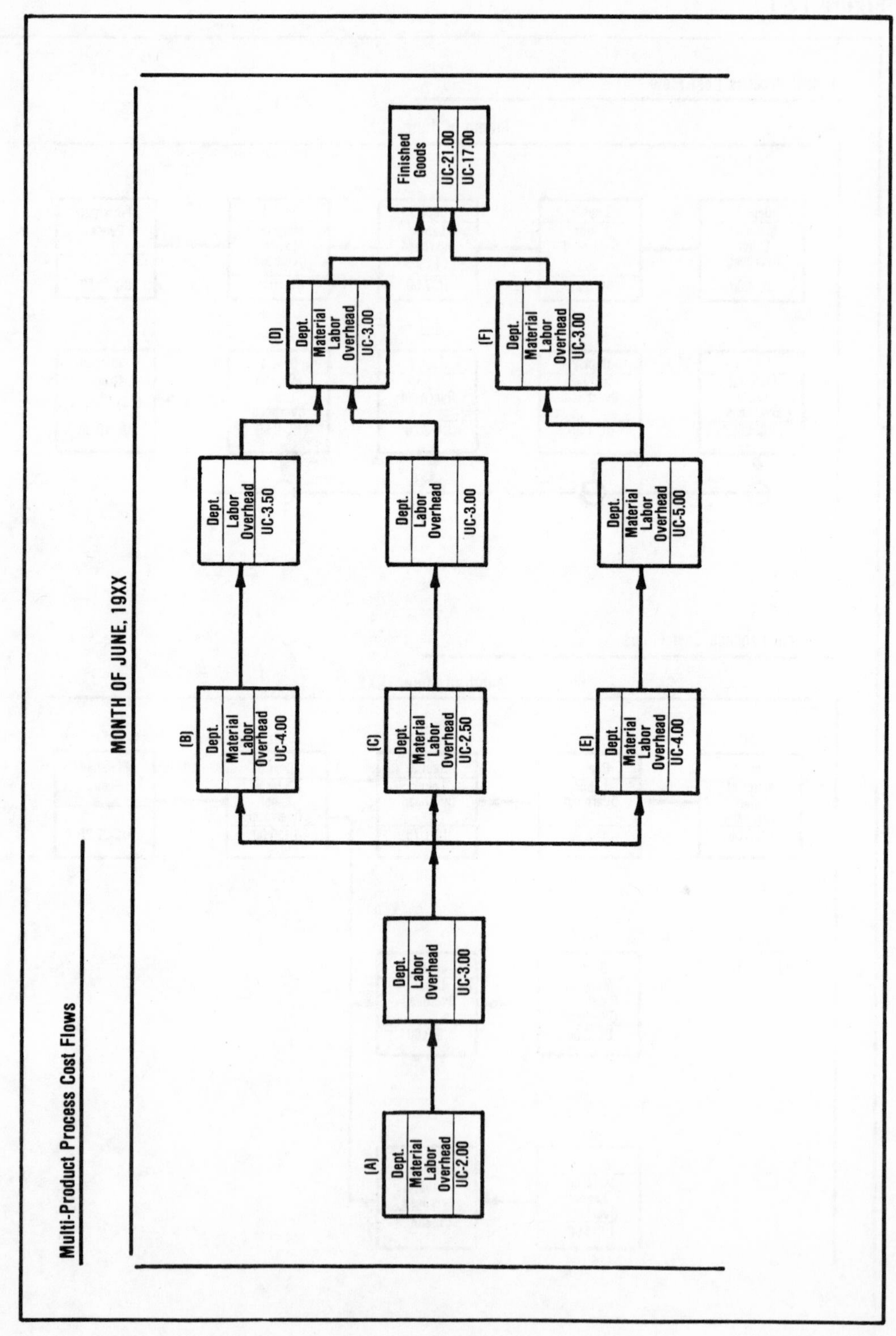

Figure 12-2

Multi-Product Process Cost Flows

better in this case because of the product split after processing initially and the later recombining of the separately costed elements.

Calculation of Equivalent Units

In those manufacturing processes where there are work in process inventories to be considered at the beginning and end of each cost accounting period, it will probably be necessary to translate the partially completed work in process into the equivalents of completed work, all in terms of units. As a simple illustration, take the case of the manufacture of 100 pairs of roller skates and assume 100% completion thereof. Costs accumulated can be divided by the 100 pairs of roller skates (100 units) to obtain the total unit cost of one pair of skates.

Using the same example, assume that the 100 pairs of skates are only 50% complete as to material, labor and overhead at the end of the period. The 100 pairs of skates multiplied by the 50% completion factor results in 50 pairs of skates completed on an *equivalent* basis. The work done on the 100 planned units represents the same amount of work as though 50 pairs of skates had been started and finished (100% completion). The 50 equivalent units divided into the respective accumulated costs will provide a comparable unit cost and a basis for allocation of a portion of the total processing costs to the work in process inventory.

Occasionally it will be necessary to calculate two equivalencies, a material equivalency and a labor and overhead equivalency. In the example at hand, assume that the 100 planned units are 75% complete as to materials and 60% complete as to labor and overhead. The respective equivalencies are determined by multiplying the 100 units by the 75% completion factor to obtain a 75-unit material equivalency and by multiplying the 100 units by the 60% completion factor to obtain a 60-unit labor and overhead equivalency. These equivalencies will provide comparable unit costs and a basis for allocating a portion of the total material and labor and overhead costs to material and labor and overhead costs in the work in process inventory. For additional examples, the reader is referred to Figures 12-3 through 12-8, representing illustrative cost of production reports.

While it is apparently a rather rare situation, there could be a need for three separate equivalencies because of the fact that labor and overhead percentages of completion were actually different. There is more likelihood of this occurring where overhead is allocated on some basis other than labor hours or labor costs.

It is very important to the process cost accounting computations to determine percentages of completion as accurately as possible. The difficulty involved in obtaining equivalent units from the percentages of completion varies greatly from industry to industry. The accuracy of the unit costs, period-to-period, and the accuracy of costs allocated to work in process inventories, will be a function of the accuracy of the production equivalencies developed and used. The larger the work in process inventories the greater will be the effect on unit costs, and cost allocations, of any inaccuracies in the percentages of completion used to develop equivalencies.

Procedures for Accumulating Costs

The primary difference in accumulating costs in a process system as compared with a job order system is that costs are accumulated by processing departments (centers, divisions, units, steps) rather than by individual jobs. This greatly reduces the amount of detailed data processing required in the case of the job order system.

Materials are charged out to the departments requiring them during a specifically designated accounting period (weekly, bi-weekly, semi-monthly, monthly). This may be done in terms of quantities only at the time of issue, with unit costing to come later. If standard costs have been developed for the various processes, materials will probably be issued on so-called standard requisitions for quantities only as determined by formula. Materials issued in excess of the standard quantity formula, or materials returned because of less than standard usage will be readily identified as material usage variances. There are cases in which material usage can be more easily determined by inventorying materials on hand at the end of each accounting period. In any case, identification and computation are usually easier because the detailed breakdown by jobs is non-existent in process costing.

Labor costs are easier to account for since, again, individuals are identified to departments for a specific time period rather than to jobs. Job time tickets are not required. It is usually just a matter of calculating elapsed time from time clock cards or a timekeeper's record. The problem is complicated a bit if men move between departments because of the nature of the process and/or because of the plant layout. Obviously, some basis of allocation to departments will have to be worked out and used. Here again, standard labor costs may be used as a measure against actual labor costs to determine rate and/or efficiency variances in a given accounting period.

The determination and application of factory overhead was dealt with at length in Chapter 11 in connection with job order costing. The same principles apply in the case of process costing. Again, overhead is somewhat easier to apply since the overhead is identified to specific departments. In some situations it is feasible to charge actual overhead to the departments for a given accounting period. This makes it unnecessary to estimate the overhead and then apply it to departments (or jobs) on some more or less arbitrary basis.

If production is not relatively uniform or stable from period to period, if the actual hours of operation available vary from period to period, or if the fixed portion of overhead is quite significant, the use of actual overhead in calculating departmental costs may not be practical. Many accountants feel that cost control is much more effective if predetermined rates are used to apply overhead rather than using actual costs. Spending variances and volume variances can be identified more easily when measured against applied overhead developed from good overhead budgets.

The Cost of Production Report

The cost of production report, prepared for each operating department for each accounting period, provides information for handling costs in the accounts and is also a very useful control statement for management. The report is, of course, historical in its timing, and while useful in cost analysis, it takes second place as a control instrument when compared to standard costs. Variances from standards will normally have already been detected and the abnormalities corrected before sufficient information is available to complete a cost of production report.

A considerable amount of supporting detail is needed with a cost of production report which is rather condensed by nature. While the amount of detail needed will depend upon the nature of the manufacturing process, a rather complete breakdown of the material and labor elements in each operating department will be required for effective cost control. This

Figure 12-3

VIBRA-CLEAN CHEMICALS, INC.
REFINING DEPARTMENT
COST OF PRODUCTION REPORT
FOR THE MONTH OF JUNE, 19XX

Quantity Schedule:		
Units in process, BOM (40% Labor & Overhead)	4,000	
Units transferred in	25,000	29,000
Units transferred out	26,000	
Units in process, EOM (30% Labor & Overhead)	3,000	29,000
	Total Cost	Unit Cost
Chargeable Costs:		
Cost transferred in:		
Work in process, BOM	$ 13,020	$3.255
Transferred in this month	83,125	3.355
Total costs transferred in	$ 96,145	$3.315[1]
Cost added by department:		
Work in process, BOM:		
Labor	$ 2,000	
Overhead	1,640	
During the month:		
Labor	31,032	$1.228[2]
Overhead	27,830	1.096[3]
Total costs added by department	$ 62,502	$2.324
Total chargeable costs	$158,647	$5.639
Chargeable Costs Accounted For:		
Transferred out (26,000 × $5.639)		$146,611*
Work in process, EOM		
Costs transferred in (3,000 × $3.315)	$ 9,945	
Labor (3,000 × 30% × $1.228)	1,105	
Overhead (3,000 × 30% × $1.096)	986	12,036
Total chargeable costs accounted for		$158,647

Supporting Computations:
[1]Unit cost from preceding department—$96,145 ÷ 29,000 = $3.315
Unit Costs:
[2]Labor —($2,000 + $31,032) ÷ 26,900 = $1.228
[3]Overhead —($1,640 + $27,830) ÷ 26,900 = $1.096
Equivalent Production:
Labor and Overhead —26,000 + (3,000 × 30%) = 26,900 units

* $3 difference due to rounding

information is essential, anyway, in determining reasonably precise work in process inventories. The cost of production report itself provides only total figures by major cost elements for the period stated.

There are generally four major sections in a cost of production report:

1. Schedule of quantities
2. Charges to the department
3. Costs to be accounted for
4. Supporting computations

These four sections are to be found in the illustrative report, Figure 12-3. This illustration includes opening and closing work in process inventories but does not include any adjustments for lost units or an increase in units. Special problems of this type will be taken up in later illustrations.

The quantity schedule sets the stage, more or less, for the detailed costs which follow. In Figure 12-3, there were 4,000 units in process at the beginning of the month (BOM) with 25,000 transferred in from the preceding department during the month. The units could represent gallons, pounds, hundredweight, barrels, drums, or a pair of roller skates. There were 26,000 units transferred to the next department, leaving 3,000 units still in process at the end of the month (EOM). The percentages of completion, as far as the Refining Department is concerned, for the beginning and ending work in process inventories is indicated in the quantity schedule by the respective titles.

The next section, which covers costs chargeable to the department, is comprised of two parts, one indicating costs transferred in from the preceding department and the other indicating costs added during the accounting period, the month of June in this case. The costs transferred in are identified to the work in process, BOM, and to the current month's units transferred in. In this illustration the two unit costs are averaged (weighted) to determine the carry-forward unit cost, i.e., $3.315 per unit. The calculation is set forth in the supporting computation section.

It will be noted that costs in the work in process inventory, BOM, are split between the costs from the previous department ($13,020) and the costs added by the Refining Department in the previous period, labor amounting to $2,000, and overhead amounting to $1,640. As will be seen in the supporting computations section, these latter two costs are added to the costs of $31,032 for labor and $27,830 for overhead, and divided by the equivalent units for labor and overhead (26,900) to obtain the unit costs of $1.228 (rounded) for labor and $1.096 (rounded) for overhead. Total chargeable costs included both the costs transferred in from the previous department and costs added by the Refining Department. Since there were work in process inventories at the beginning of the month, the unit costs in all elements, as well as the total unit cost, are all the result of weighted averages. It should be obvious, too, that this illustrative report is prepared on the accumulative cost basis by virtue of bringing forward prior department costs and including those costs in the totals.

The total chargeable costs in the Refining Department for the month of June, 19XX, are accounted for in the third section of the report under the heading, *Chargeable Costs Accounted For*.

There were 26,000 units at a unit cost of $5.639 (rounded) transferred to the succeeding department. A difference of $3.00, due to the rounding of the unit cost figures to three decimal places, is deducted from the amount transferred out in order to balance. Prior department costs and Refining Department costs in the work in process inventory, EOM, are indicated separately and will be brought forward separately to the July, 19XX cost of production report to be set forth as costs transferred in and costs added by the department as that period's beginning work in process inventory.

The supporting computations in the fourth section of the report have already been identified to the respective cost elements. Any computations that would help clarify the report for the reader can and should be set forth here. If too many computations are included in the body of the report it may make it more difficult to read and evaluate.

Illustrative Case—Description

The illustrative case used here involves a five-process chemical manufacturing plant with a variety of processing situations. The material addition problem varies with departments; there are work in process inventories to be considered; some completed work may be held in the department and not passed on. Factory overhead is applied on the basis of labor cost and varies with departments. Cost of production reports are presented for each of the five departments as well as the entries, in general journal form, for material, labor, and applied overhead and the work in process inventory and the ledger accounts.

A listing of the departments, including pertinent characteristics follows:

1. Grinding Department—material is added at the beginning of the process; there are no work in process inventories to be considered in this department.
2. Mixing Department—material is added at the beginning of the process; the material added causes an increase in the number of units being processed; there are work in process inventories, beginning and ending.
3. Cooking Department—no material is added to this process; the physical volume of the unit changes in this process from a unit of 100 pounds to a unit of one gallon; some units complete as to this process are held over; there are work in process inventories, beginning and ending.
4. Refining Department—no material is added in this process; some units are lost in the process, and this is a normal situation; there are work in process inventories, beginning and ending.
5. Packaging Department—material is added during the process; some units complete as to this process are held over; there are work in process inventories, beginning and ending.

During the month of July, 19XX, the schedule of units, and costs of material, labor, and factory overhead, put into process were as follows:

Costs Added During the Month

Departments	Units Started	Material	Labor	Overhead	Work in Process
Grinding	30,000	$45,000	$ 4,800	$ 9,600	$ -0-
Mixing	2,500	8,000	4,260	10,650	4,836
Cooking	-0-	-0-	24,566	72,225	6,812
Refining	-0-	-0-	44,280	127,965	10,674
Packaging	-0-	$41,846	$61,625	$ 29,750	$35,960

Costs will be accumulated and carried forward from one department to the next. In this illustration, costs are averaged throughout the process. The opening inventory costs are added to the current period costs to obtain the unit costs used in determining closing work in process inventories and in costing the completed work transferred to subsequent departments. The subject of first-in, first-out costing will be discussed briefly later in this chapter.

GRINDING DEPARTMENT

Since this department does not normally have work in process inventories, there is no balance in Work in Process-Grinding Department accounts on July 1, 19XX. Costs were added by the department as shown by the following entry:

Work in Process-Grinding Department	59,400	
Raw Materials Inventory		45,000
Payroll Clearing		4,800
Factory Overhead Applied (see Figure 12-4)		9,600

The 30,000 units (1 unit equals 100 pounds of raw material) were started in process during the month. The Grinding Department Cost of Production Report is set forth in Figure 12-4. Reference to the quantity schedule on the report will provide the reader with a complete accountability for all units brought in and transferred out. Since there are no work in process inventories and no units held over or lost, all units started are transferred out.

As this is the first operating department, there is no cost transferred in to be accounted for. Also, with no work in process inventories, there are no inventory costs. Total chargeable costs, $59,400, consist only of the costs of material, labor and overhead added during the month. Again, with no inventories, chargeable costs are accounted for as being transferred to the next department, $59,400 (30,000 units multiplied by a unit cost of $1.9800).

In the last section of the report, captioned *Supporting Computations,* the unit costs for the month are calculated based on the equivalent production for the month. With no work in process inventories, all units started are 100% complete as to material and as to labor and overhead. The calculations of the unit costs, presented in abbreviated form on Figure 12-4, are as follows:

$$\text{Material Unit Cost} = \frac{\$45{,}000 \text{ material cost}}{30{,}000 \text{ equivalent units}} = \$1.5000$$

$$\text{Labor Unit Cost} = \frac{\$\ 4{,}800 \text{ labor cost}}{30{,}000 \text{ equivalent units}} = 0.1600$$

$$\text{Overhead Unit Cost} = \frac{\$\ 9{,}600 \text{ overhead applied}}{30{,}000 \text{ equivalent units}} = 0.3200$$

Total Unit Cost in Grinding Department $1.9800

Figure 12-4

MAGIC CHEMICAL COMPANY, INC.
GRINDING DEPARTMENT
COST OF PRODUCTION REPORT
FOR THE MONTH OF JULY, 19XX

Quantity Schedule: (1 unit = 100 lbs)			
Units in process, BOM		-0-	
Units transferred in		30,000	
Units added to process		-0-	30,000
Units transferred out		30,000	
Units completed—on hand		-0-	
Units in process, EOM		-0-	
Units lost in process		-0-	30,000
		Total Cost	**Unit Cost**
Chargeable Costs:			
Cost from preceding department:			
Work in process, BOM		$ -0-	$ -0-
Cost transferred in this month		-0-	-0-
Total		$ -0-	$ -0-
Cost added by department:			
Work in process, BOM			
Material		-0-	-0-
Labor		-0-	-0-
Overhead		-0-	-0-
Added during this month:			
Material		$45,000	$1.5000[1]
Labor		4,800	0.1600[2]
Overhead		9,600	0.3200[3]
Total cost added		$59,400	$1.9800
Lost units adjustment			-0-
Total chargeable costs		$59,400	$1.9800
Chargeable Costs Accounted For:			
Transferred to next department (30,000 × $1.9800)			$59,400
Work in process, EOM			
Cost from preceding department		$ -0-	
Completed—on hand		-0-	
Material	$ -0-		
Labor	-0-		
Overhead	$ -0-	-0-	-0-
Total chargeable costs accounted for			$59,400

Figure 12-4 continued

Supporting Computations:
Equivalent Production:

Material	- 30,000 × 100% = 30,000 units
Labor and Overhead	- 30,000 × 100% = 30,000 units

Unit Costs:

[1]Material	- $45,000 ÷ 30,000 = $1.5000
[2]Labor	- $ 4,800 ÷ 30,000 = $0.1600
[3]Overhead	- $ 9,600 ÷ 30,000 = $0.3200

An entry to transfer the Grinding Departmental costs of completed work to the Mixing Department would be made as indicated below:

Work in Process-Mixing Department	59,400	
Work in Process-Grinding Department		59,400

At the close of the month, the Work in Process-Grinding Department account appears as follows:

Work in Process-Grinding Department			
(Cost for material, labor and overhead)	59,400	59,400	(Cost of material transferred to Mixing Department

MIXING DEPARTMENT

The Cost of Production Report for the Mixing Department is illustrated in Figure 12-5. Reference to the quantity schedule in Figure 12-5 will reveal that there are work in process inventories and an addition of material which causes an increase in the total number of units of 2,500 units. In this process, material is added at the very beginning. It will be seen by reference to Note 1 that the beginning inventory (BOM) is 100% complete as to materials and 40% complete as to labor and overhead. The ending inventory (EOM) is 100% complete as to materials and 60% complete as to labor and overhead (See Note 2).

Costs from the preceding department (Grinding) total $63,400. This amount is made up of beginning work in process of $4,000 and costs transferred in during the month from the Grinding Department of $59,400. It will be noted that the unit cost determined from the total cost is lower than either of the unit costs brought forward. While the unit cost for the total is usually determined on a weighted average basis here, it is necessary to consider the overall increase in the units in process caused by the addition of material in the department. The total cost of $63,400 is divided by the expanded number of units, 34,500, to obtain the revised unit cost of $1.8377. Note 3 in Figure 12-5 makes reference to this situation.

During the month, costs were added by the department as shown by the following entry:

Work in Process-Mixing Department	22,910	
Raw Materials Inventory		8,000
Payroll Clearing		4,260
Factory Overhead Applied (see Figure 12-5)		10,650

The material cost of $8,000 covers the 2,500 additional units of material added at the beginning of the mixing process. The quantity schedule accounts for all material on hand in that 31,500 units are transferred to the next operating department with 3,000 remaining in process. The units are lost in this department. There are beginning work in process inventory costs of $836 added by this department in the previous month. These are averaged with the costs added during this month to obtain the unit costs per month.

In the last section of the report, captioned *Supporting Computations,* the unit costs for the month are calculated based on the equivalent production for the month. Since material is added at the beginning of the process, the units are all 100% complete as to material, so equivalent production is equal to actual production, 34,500 units. Equivalent production for labor and overhead amounts to 33,300 units, comprising 31,500 units completed and transferred to the next department and 3,000 units in process only 60% complete (1,800 equivalent units). The calculations of the unit costs, presented in abbreviated form in Figure 12-5 are as follows:

$$\text{Material Unit Cost} = \frac{\$500 + \$8{,}000 \text{ material costs}}{34{,}500 \text{ equivalent units}} = \$0.2464$$

$$\text{Labor Unit Cost} = \frac{\$96 + \$4{,}260 \text{ labor costs}}{33{,}300 \text{ equivalent units}} = 0.1308$$

$$\text{Overhead Unit Cost} = \frac{\$240 + \$10{,}650 \text{ overhead applied}}{33{,}300 \text{ equivalent units}} = 0.3270$$

Total unit cost in mixing department	$0.7042
Add: Unit cost from preceding department	1.8377
Total Unit Cost to End of Mixing Department Process	$2.5419

Figure 12-5

MAGIC CHEMICAL COMPANY, INC.
MIXING DEPARTMENT
COST OF PRODUCTION REPORT
FOR THE MONTH OF JULY, 19XX

Quantity Schedule: (1 unit = 100 lbs)		
Units in process, BOM (Note 1)	2,000	
Units transferred in	30,000	
Units added to process (beginning of process)	2,500	34,500
Units transferred out	31,500	
Units completed—on hand	-0-	
Units in process, EOM (Note 2)	3,000	
Units lost in process	-0-	34,500

Chargeable Costs:	Total Cost	Unit Cost
Cost from preceding department:		
Work in process, BOM	$ 4,000	$2.0000
Cost transferred in this month	59,400	1.9800
Total ($63,400 ÷ 34,500 units) (Note 3)	$63,400	$1.8377
Cost added by department:		
Work in process, BOM		
Material	$ 500	$
Labor	96	
Overhead	240	
Added during this month:		
Material	8,000	0.2464[1]
Labor	4,260	0.1308[2]
Overhead	10,650	0.3270[3]
Total cost added	$23,746	$0.7042
Lost units adjustment		-0-
Total chargeable costs	$87,146	$2.5419

Chargeable Costs Accounted For:		
Transferred to next department (31,500 × $2.5419)		$80,071
Work in process, EOM		
Cost from preceding department (3,000 × $1.8377)	$ 5,513	
Completed—on hand	-0-	
Material (3,000 × 100% × $0.2464)	739	
Labor (3,000 × 60% × $0.1308)	235	
Overhead (3,000 × 60% × $0.3270)	588	7,075
Total chargeable costs accounted for		$87,146

Figure 12-5 continued

Supporting Computations:
Equivalent Production:

Material	— (2,000 + 30,000 + 2,500) × 100% = 34,500 units
Labor and Overhead	— 31,500 + (3,000 × 60%) = 33,300 units

Unit Costs:

[1]Material	— ($500 + $8,000) ÷ 34,500 = $0.2464
[2]Labor	— ($96 + $4,260) ÷ 33,300 = $0.1308
[3]Overhead	— ($240 + $10,650) ÷ 33,300 = $0.3270

Note 1—100% complete as to material, 40% complete as to labor and overhead.
Note 2—100% complete as to material, 60% complete as to labor and overhead.
Note 3—To distribute preceding department cost over increase in units.

Total costs of $87,146 are accounted for by the transfer of 31,500 completed units at a unit cost of $2.5419 to the Cooking Department for a total cost of $80,071 and by a work in process inventory consisting of the following items:

Cost from preceding department (3,000 units × $1.8377)	$5,513
Material (3,000 × 100% × $0.2464)	739
Labor (3,000 × 60% × $0.1308)	235
Overhead (3,000 × 60% × $0.3270)	588
Total Work in Process Inventory	$7,075

Any difference due to rounding of unit costs is added to (or subtracted from) the cost transferred to the next department. An entry to transfer the Mixing Department costs (cumulative) of completed work to the Cooking Department would be made as indicated below:

Work in Process—Cooking Department	80,071	
Work in process—Mixing Department		80,071

At the close of the month the Work in Process-Mixing Department account will appear as follows:

Work in Process—Mixing Department

Inventory, BOM-			
Prior Dept. Cost	4,000	80,071	Cost Transferred to Cooking Department
Mixing Dept. Cost	836		
Sub Total	4,836		
Transferred from Grinding Dept.	59,400		
Charges for Material, Labor, and Overhead	22,910		
Inventory, EOM	7,075		

Cooking Department

Financial details of the month's operations of this department are set forth in Figure 12-6. As indicated in the quantity schedule, the beginning and ending work in process inventories (Notes 1 and 3) are 30% and 50% complete, respectively, as to labor and overhead. It is also to be observed that there has been a change in the constitution of the units as processed by the Cooking Department. In this process the original unit of 100 pounds is converted to 15 units of 1 gallon each. In effect, 6⅔ pounds of material from the Mixing Department becomes 1 gallon of material in the Cooking Department. This is explained by the indicated computation for units transferred in and by Note 2. A new consideration here is the fact that 20,500 units are completed by the Cooking Department and retained in the department. No new material is added in this department nor are any units lost.

Costs from the preceding department (Mixing) total $85,083. This amount is made up of beginning work in process of $5,012 and costs transferred in during the month from the Mixing Department of $80,071. It will be noted that the unit cost determined from the total cost is lower than either of the unit costs brought forward. Instead of determining a new unit cost on a weighted average basis as usual at this point, the total cost from the preceding department must be divided by the total of the new units. In this case, the total cost of $85,083 is divided by 502,500 units (gallons) to obtain the new unit costs of $0.1693 per gallon.

During the month, costs were added by the department as shown by the following entry:

Work in Process—Cooking Department	96,791	
Payroll Clearing		24,566
Factory Overhead Applied		72,225

There are beginning work in process inventory costs of $1,800 added by this department in the previous month. These are averaged with the costs added during this month to obtain the unit costs for the month.

In the last section of the report, captioned *Supporting Computations,* the unit costs for the month are calculated based on the equivalent production for the month. Equivalent production for labor and overhead amounts to 490,500 units, comprising 458,000 units completed

Figure 12-6

MAGIC CHEMICAL COMPANY, INC.
COOKING DEPARTMENT
COST OF PRODUCTION REPORT
FOR THE MONTH OF JULY, 19XX

Quantity Schedule: (1 unit—1 gallon)		
Units in process, BOM (Note 1)	30,000	
Units transferred in (31,000 × 100 ÷ 6²/₃) Note 2)	472,500	
Units added to process	-0-	502,500
Units transferred out	458,000	
Units completed—on hand	20,500	
Units in process, EOM (Note 3)	24,000	
Units lost in process	-0-	502,500

Chargeable Costs:	Total Cost	Unit Cost
Cost from preceding department:		
Work in process, BOM	$ 5,012	$2.5600
Cost transferred in this month	80,071	2.5419
Total ($85,083 ÷ 502,500 units) (Note 2)	$ 85,083	$0.1693
Cost added by department:		
Work in process, BOM		
Material	$ -0-	$
Labor	450	
Overhead	1,350	
Added during this month:		
Material	-0-	
Labor	24,566	0.0510[1]
Overhead	72,225	0.1500[2]
Total cost added	$ 98,591	$0.2010
Lost units adjustment		-0-
Total chargeable costs	$183,674	$0.3703

Chargeable Costs Accounted For:		
Transferred to next department (458,000 × $0.3703)		$169,608
Work in process, EOM		
Cost from preceding department (24,000 × $0.1693)	$ 4,063	
Completed—on hand (20,500 × $0.3703)	7,591	
Material	-0-	
Labor (24,000 × 50% × $0.0510)	612	
Overhead (24,000 × 50% × $0.1500)	1,800	14,066
Total chargeable costs accounted for		$183,674

Figure 12-6 continued

Supporting Computations:
Equivalent Production:
Labor and Overhead — 458,000 + 20,500 + (24,000 × 50%) = 490,500 units
Unit Costs:
[1]Labor — ($450 + $24,566) ÷ 490,500 = $0.0510
[2]Overhead — ($1,350 + $72,225) ÷ 490,500 = $0.1500
Note 1—30% complete as to labor and overhead.
Note 2—Units converted in Cooking Department from 100 lbs. to 15 gallons.
Note 3—50% complete as to labor and overhead.

and transferred to the next department, 20,500 units completed and retained in the department and 24,000 units in process only 50% complete (12,000 equivalent units). The calculations of the unit costs, presented in abbreviated form in Figure 12-6 are as follows:

Labor Unit Cost =	$\dfrac{\$450 + \$24{,}566 \text{ labor costs}}{490{,}500 \text{ equivalent units}}$ =	$0.0510
Overhead Unit Cost =	$\dfrac{\$1{,}350 + \$72{,}225 \text{ overhead applied}}{490{,}500 \text{ equivalent units}}$ =	0.1500
Total unit cost in Cooking Department		$0.2010
Add: Unit cost from preceding department		0.1693
(As revised because of changes in composition of units)		
Total Unit Cost to End of Cooking Department Process		$0.3703

Total costs of $183,674 are accounted for by the transfer of 458,000 completed units at a unit cost of $0.3703 to the Refining Department for a total cost of $169,608 and by a work in process inventory consisting of the following items:

Completed and on hand in department—	
(20,500 × $0.3703)	$ 7,591
Still in process:	
Cost from preceding department (24,000 × $0.1693)	4,063
Labor (24,000 × 50% × $0.0510)	612
Overhead (24,000 × 50% × $0.1500)	1,800
Total Work in Process Inventory	$14,066

Any difference due to rounding of unit costs is added to (or subtracted from) the cost transferred to the next department. An entry to transfer the Cooking Department costs (cumulative) of completed work to the Refining Department would be made as indicated below:

Work in Process—Refining Department	169,608	
Work in Process—Cooking Department		169,608

At the close of the month the Work in Process—Cooking Department will appear as follows:

Work In Process—Cooking Department

Inventory, BOM			
Prior Dept. Cost	5,012	169,608	Cost transferred to Refining Department
Cooking Dept. Cost	1,800		
Sub Total	6,812		
Transferred from Mixing Dept.	80,071		
Charges for Labor and Overhead	96,791		
Inventory, EOM	14,066		

REFINING DEPARTMENT

Figure 12-7 illustrates the Cost of Production Report for the Refining Department. Reference to the quantity schedule in Figure 12-7 will reveal that there are beginning and ending work in process inventories (Notes 1 and 2) 40% and 70% complete, respectively, as to labor and overhead. In this department, 12,000 units are lost in the processing as waste material which is considered normal in this operation. No new material is added. Since average costing is being used in this illustration, the unit costs are increased to absorb the accumulated cost of the lost units.

Costs from the preceding department (Cooking) total $177,208. This amount is made up of beginning work in process of $7,600 and costs transferred in during the month of $169,608. The reader's attention is directed to the new higher unit cost ($0.3707) based on total costs from the preceding department as compared with the unit cost of material transferred in ($0.3703). The increase is due to the higher unit cost of the work in process inventory costs from the preceding department. The calculation of the unit cost of the last units adjustment is set forth in Note 3 in Figure 12-7.

During the month, costs were added by the department as shown by the following entry:

Work in Process—Refining Department	172,245	
Payroll Clearing		44,280
Factory Overhead Applied		127,965

Figure 12-7

MAGIC CHEMICAL COMPANY, INC.
REFINING DEPARTMENT
COST OF PRODUCTION REPORT
FOR THE MONTH OF JULY, 19XX

Quantity Schedule: (1 unit—1 gallon)		
Units in process, BOM (Note 1)	20,000	
Units transferred in	458,000	
Units added to process	-0-	478,000
Units transferred out	436,000	
Units completed—on hand	-0-	
Units in process, EOM (Note 2)	30,000	
Units lost in process	12,000	478,000

Chargeable Costs:	Total Cost	Unit Cost
Cost from preceding department:		
Work in process, BOM	$ 7,600	$0.3800
Cost transferred in this month	169,608	0.3703
Total ($177,208 ÷ 478,000)	$177,208	$0.3707
Cost added by department:		
Work in process, BOM		
Material	$ -0-	$
Labor	794	
Overhead	2,280	
Added during this month:		
Material	-0-	
Labor	44,280	0.0986[1]
Overhead	127,965	0.2850[2]
Total Cost added	$175,319	$0.3836
Lost units adjustment		.0096
Total chargeable costs (Note 3)	$352,527	$0.7639

Chargeable Costs Accounted For:		
Transferred to next department (436,000 × $0.7639)		$333,062
Work in process, EOM		
Cost from preceding department		
(30,000 × ($0.3707 + $0.0096))	$ 11,409	
Completed—on hand	-0-	
Material	-0-	
Labor (30,000 × 70% × $0.0986)	2,071	
Overhead (30,000 × 70% × $0.2850)	5,985	19,465
Total chargeable costs accounted for		$352,527

Figure 12-7 continued

Supporting Computation:
Equivalent Production:
Labor and Overhead — 436,000 + (30,000 × 70%) = 457,000 units
Unit Costs:
[1]Labor — ($794 + $44,280) ÷ 457,000 = $0.0986
[2]Overhead — ($2,280 + 127,965) ÷ 457,000 = $0.2850
Note 1—40% complete as to labor and overhead.
Note 2—70% complete as to labor and overhead.
Note 3—$177,208 ÷ 466,000 units = $0.3803 (revised for lost units); $0.3803 − $0.3707 − $0.0096.

There are beginning work in process inventory costs of $3,074 added by this department in the previous month. These costs are averaged with the costs added during this month to obtain the unit costs for the month.

In the Supporting Computations section of Figure 12-7, the unit costs for the month are calculated based on the equivalent production for the month. Equivalent production for labor and overhead amounts to 457,000 units, comprised of 436,000 units completed and transferred to the next department and 30,000 units in process only 70% complete (21,000 equivalent units). The calculations of the unit costs, presented in abbreviated form in Figure 12-7 are as follows:

$$\text{Labor Unit Cost} = \frac{\$794 + \$44{,}280 \text{ labor costs}}{457{,}000 \text{ equivalent units}} = \$0.0986$$

$$\text{Overhead Unit Cost} = \frac{\$2{,}280 + \$127{,}965 \text{ overhead applied}}{457{,}000 \text{ equivalent units}} = 0.2850$$

Total unit cost in Refining Department	$0.3836
Add: Unit cost from preceding department	0.3707
Lost units adjusted (Note 3, Figure 12-7)	0.0096
Total Unit Cost to End of Refining Department Process	$0.7639

Total costs of $352,527 are accounted for by the transfer of 436,000 completed units at a unit cost of $0.7639 to the Packaging Department for a total cost of $333,062 and by a work in process inventory consisting of the following items:

Cost from preceding department (30,000 × ($0.3707 + $0.0096))	$11,409
Labor (30,000 × 70% × $0.0986)	2,071
Overhead (30,000 × 70% × $0.2850)	5,985
Total Work in Process Inventory	$19,465

Any difference due to rounding of unit costs is added to (or subtracted from) the cost transferred to the next department. An entry to transfer the refining department costs (cumulative) of completed work to the Packaging Department would be made as indicated below:

Work in Process—Packaging Department	333,062	
Work in Process—Refining Department		333,062

At the close of the month the Work in Process—Refining Department account will appear as follows:

Work in Process—Refining Department			
Inventory, BOM			
Prior Dept. Cost	7,600	333,062	Cost transferred to Packaging Dept.
Refining Dept. Cost	3,074		
Sub Total	10,674		
Transferred from Cooking Cept.	169,608		
Charges for Labor and Overhead	172,245		
Inventory, EOM	19,465		

PACKAGING DEPARTMENT

The Cost of Production Report for the Packaging Department is set forth in Figure 12-8. The quantity schedule in Figure 12-8 lists beginning and ending work in process inventories (Notes 1 and 2) 60% and 50% complete, respectively, as to material and 50% and 30% complete respectively, as to labor and overhead. Material is added throughout the process but does not increase the number of units as indicated. There were 6,000 units completed during the month retained in the department.

Costs from the preceding department (Refining) total $363,262. This amount is made up of beginning work in process of $30,200 and costs transferred in during the month of $333,062. The revised average unit cost, based on the total cost is $0.7632. During the month, costs were added by the department as shown by the following entry:

Work in Process—Packaging Department	133,221	
Raw Material Inventory		41,846
Payroll Clearing		61,625
Factory Overhead Applied		29,750

Figure 12-8

MAGIC CHEMICAL COMPANY, INC.
PACKAGING DEPARTMENT
COST OF PRODUCTION REPORT
FOR THE MONTH OF JULY, 19XX

Quantity Schedule: (1 unit = 1 gallon)		
Units in process, BOM (Note 1)	40,000	
Units transferred in	436,000	
Units added to process	-0-	476,000
Units transferred out	420,000	
Units completed—on hand	6,000	
Units in process, EOM	50,000	
Units lost in process	-0-	476,000

Chargeable Costs:	Total Cost	Unit Cost
Cost from preceding department:		
Work in process, BOM	$ 30,200	$0.7550
Cost transferred in this month	333,062	0.7639
Total ($363,262 ÷ 476,000)	$363,262	$0.7632
Cost added by department:		
Work in process, BOM		
Material	$ 2,400	
Labor	2,240	
Overhead	1,120	
Added during this month:		
Material	41,846	0.0981[1]
Labor	61,625	0.1448[2]
Overhead	29,750	0.0700[3]
Total cost added	$138,981	$0.3129
Lost units adjustment		-0-
Total chargeable costs	$502,243	$1.0761

Chargeable Costs Accounted For:		
Transferred to next department (420,000 × $1.0761)		$451,951
Work in process, EOM		
Cost from preceding department (50,000 × $0.7632	$ 38,160	
Completed—on hand (6,000 × $1.0761)	6,457	
Material (50,000 × 50% × $0.0981)	2,453	
Labor (50,000 × 30% × $0.1448)	2,172	
Overhead (50,000 × 30% × $0.0700)	1,050	50,292
Total chargeable costs accounted for		$502,243

Figure 12-8 continued

Supporting Computations:
Equivalent Production:
Material — 420,000 + 6,000 + (50,000 × 50%) = 451,000 units
Labor and Overhead — 420,000 + 6,000 + (50,000 × 30%) = 441,000 units
Unit Costs:
[1]Material — ($2,400 + $41,846) ÷ 451,000 = $0.0981
[2]Labor — ($2,240 + $61,625) ÷ 441,000 = $0.1448
[3]Overhead — ($1,120 + $29,750) ÷ 441,000 = $0.0700
Note 1—60% complete as to material, 40% complete as to labor and overhead
Note 2—50% complete as to material, 30% complete as to labor and overhead

There are beginning work in process inventory costs of $5,760 added by this department in the previous month. These costs are averaged with the costs added during this month to obtain the unit costs for the month.

In the Supporting Computations section of Figure 12-8, the unit costs for the month are calculated based on the equivalent production for the month. Equivalent production for material amounts to 451,000 units, comprised of 420,000 units completed and transferred to the next department, 6,000 completed and remaining in the department and 50,000 units in process only 50% complete (25,000 equivalent units). Equivalent production for labor and overhead amounts to 441,000 units, comprised of 420,000 units completed and transferred to the next department, 6,000 units completed and remaining in the department and 50,000 units in process only 30% complete (15,000 equivalent units).

The calculations of the unit costs, presented in abbreviated form on Figure 12-8 are as follows:

$$\text{Material Unit Cost} = \frac{\$2{,}400 + \$41{,}846 \text{ material costs}}{451{,}000 \text{ equivalent units}} = \$0.0981$$

$$\text{Labor Unit Cost} = \frac{\$2{,}240 + \$61{,}625 \text{ labor costs}}{441{,}000 \text{ equivalent units}} = 0.1448$$

$$\text{Overhead Unit Cost} = \frac{\$1{,}120 + \$29{,}750 \text{ overhead applied}}{441{,}000 \text{ equivalent units}} = 0.0700$$

Total unit cost in Packaging Department	$0.3129
Add: Unit cost from preceding department	0.7632
Total Unit Cost to End of Packaging Department Process	$1.0761

Total costs of $502,243 are accounted for by the transfer of 420,000 completed units at a unit cost of $1.0761 to the Finished Goods warehouse for a total cost of $451,951 and by a work in process inventory consisting of the following items:

Completed and on hand in department	
(6,000 × $1.0761)	$ 6,457
Still in Process:	
Cost from preceding department (50,000 × $0.7632)	38,160
Material (50,000 × 50% × $0.0981)	2,453
Labor (50,000 × 30% × $0.1448)	2,172
Overhead (50,000 × 30% × $0.0700)	1,050
Total Work in Process Inventory	$50,292

Any difference due to rounding of unit costs is added to (or subtracted from) the cost transferred to Finished Goods Inventory. An entry to transfer the Packaging Department costs (cumulative) of completed work to the Finished Goods Inventory would be made as indicated below:

Finished Goods Inventory	451,951	
Work in Process—Packaging Department		451,951

At the close of the month the Work in Process—Packaging Department account will appear as follows:

Work in Process—Packaging Department

Inventory, BOM			
Prior Dept. Cost	30,200	451,951	Cost transferred to Finished Goods Inventory
Packaging Dept. Cost	5,760		
Sub Total	35,960		
Transferred from Refining Dept.	333,062		
Chgs. for Labor and Overhead	133,221		
Inventory, EOM	50,292		

COSTING OF INVENTORIES

As previously indicated, this illustrative case has used average costing throughout for all inventories and all completed work. Some accountants prefer to use the first-in, first-out method of costing completed work. This requires the determination of the cost of completing the work in process at the beginning of the period first, then determining the cost of the units started and finished within the period. If this procedure is followed, two sets of unit costs have to be calculated. Under the average cost method, only one set of unit costs needs to be developed.

In most process cost type industries, the manufacturing operations are fairly uniform from period to period. The difference in unit costs as between the FIFO and average cost methods in a given period is usually not significant, especially at the accumulative stage in the cost of production reports. While it is a management choice as to the costing method used, the approach here was to use the simplest possible methods in arriving at unit costs under the various situations of increased volume, lost units and change of unit size.

A Final Word

The reader is reminded again that the more detailed cost summaries of material, labor and actual overhead which provide the information for the departmental cost of production reports and provide the basis for developing overhead application rates are probably more helpful to management in the day-to-day control of operations. The use of standard process costs would be very helpful in that the material and labor variances could be more easily and quickly determined. This more timely information will be more useful in control than will the average cost of production report which by its nature and content is "after the fact."

This treatment of process costs is not exhaustive nor is it intended to be. It is intended to illustrate the basic theory of process costing in the so-called average cost situation. For a more extensive treatment and presentation of unique problems, the reader is referred to the publications listed in the bibliography provided by the authors.

CHAPTER 13

A PRACTICAL APPROACH TO STANDARD COSTING

WHAT ARE THE ADVANTAGES OF USING STANDARD COSTING?

The primary purposes of the use of standard costs are to improve cost control, promote cost reduction, provide a basis for setting selling prices, and improve the general budgetary control system. A really good budget cannot be developed unless standard costs can be incorporated therein. Anything less becomes a matter of estimates which may be fair at best.

A secondary purpose of the use of standard costs is to reduce the clerical work involved in recording cost information. The volume of clerical work required to assemble cost data and develop unit costs is cut down. The unit costs have already been determined and the variances of actual costs from standard costs are cast out in the cost assembly process. There is less summarizing and allocating required, and the variances are pointed up on a more timely basis. Detailed job cost sheets do not have to be kept. Material requisitions can be prepared in advance. Labor requirements can be planned more effectively and in advance.

Standard costs may be used in both job order costing and process costing. The determination of the standards to be used will probably be easier in process cost systems. This is because the manufacturing process will tend to be more uniform with fewer variations in types of products being manufactured. Job lot manufacturing for inventory needs will represent a less difficult standard setting situation than will manufacturing by customer specifications on an irregular basis. Detailed standards may still be developed for such jobs especially if the jobs are quite sizable in terms of cost. The development of these standards will provide a basis for bidding or price setting and will provide a means of manufacturing cost control when manufacturing has actually started.

The Two Elements Composing Standard Costs

Standard costs are composed of two elements, standards and costs. The standards represent uniquely identified measurements which will be used as gauges or scales for control purposes. Standards are primarily thought of as physical or quantity standards. A material standard will indicate the quantity, and possibly the quality of the material that is to be consumed in making a given product. A labor standard will indicate the time requirement (broken down by specific operations) to manufacture a given product. Variations from these standards will usually be identified as usage, quantity or efficiency variances.

Cost or price standards represent specific costs assigned to material and labor on a per unit basis, e.g., a material costs will be assigned on a per pound, per gallon, or possibly per square foot basis. A labor cost will usually be assigned on an hourly basis.

The quantity standard and the price standard make up the standard cost of the product as related to material, labor and factory overhead. In order to properly evaluate actual performance against the standards, it will be necessary to analyze and identify the variances from standard in terms of the quantity standard and the price standard for materials and labor. With respect to overhead, the variances of actual from standard can be analyzed in terms of the two-, three- or four-variance methods. Overhead variance analysis will be illustrated in detail later in this chapter.

Who Sets the Standards?

Industrial engineers usually set the physical or quantity standards after thorough study of the drawings (blue-prints), production layout sheets, types of materials to be used and, after an analysis of the operations related to the manufacture of the products in question. The cost accounting, personnel, and purchasing departments will collaborate with the engineers in developing price standards for material, labor and overhead. Since overhead will be applied to the jobs and/or processes on a rate per hour or per dollar of cost, a factory overhead budget will have to be prepared. This budget will probably be prepared on the basis of several possible operating volumes, described in Chapter 11 as a flexible budget.

The Philosophy of Standards—How High?

Standards may be developed and used which range from rather "loose" standards to what might be called "ideal" standards, generally almost impossible to attain. If the standards are to be used in any way as a basis for remuneration of labor, they obviously must be fair if any attention is expected to be paid to the standards. An efficient worker, doing a good job without exhausting himself in the process, should be able to "beat" the standard and, accordingly, derive some benefit therefrom. When materials and/or manufacturing processes change, the standards will have to be revised to accommodate the new working environment. The direction of the philosophy of modern management in setting standards is toward a realistic standard reflecting "good" performance rather than "ideal" performance.

Use of Standard Cost Card

Developed standard costs are maintained in a variety of ways on various types of records

Figure 13-1

STANDARD COST CARD

		1. Date 9/7/XX by J.C.D.
Item Hand Pump	No. 270	2. Rev. ____ by ____
		3. Rev. ____ by ____
Standard Quantity per Run	1,000	

Material		Standard	Unit Cost			Total Cost		
Stock No.	Desc.	Quantity	1	2	3	1	2	3
A—271		1 pc.	.55			.55		
A—295		2 pc.	1.40			2.80		
C—420		4 pc.	.30			1.20		
D—361		1 pc.	5.60			5.60		
F—241		2 pc.	.75			1.50		
Material—Total Cost						$11.65		
Direct Labor		**Standard**						
Oper. #	Desc.	Hours						
1—89		.10	5.00			.50		
1—101		.15	5.00			.75		
2—63		.25	5.75			1.44		
2—69		.30	5.75			1.73		
3—122		1.55	7.50			11.63		
4—190		.40	6.25			2.50		
4—195		.60	6.25			3.75		
4—201		1.10	6.75			7.43		
Direct Labor—Total Cost						$29.73		
Factory Overhead		**Standard**						
Dept. #	Type	Hours						
1	F	.25	4.00			1.00		
	V	.25	3.60			.90		
2	F	.55	3.00			1.65		
	V	.55	2.80			1.54		
3	F	1.55	3.00			4.65		
	V	1.55	3.20			4.96		
4	F	2.10	2.50			5.25		
	V	2.10	2.90			6.09		
Factory Overhead—Total Cost						$26.04		
Total Cost						$67.42		

ranging from cards to storage in a computer. The method used is normally a function of the complexity of the cost structure, the size of the company, frequency of revision and accounting office use. Figure 13-1 is an illustration of a standard cost card. The card sets forth details as to materials and labor in terms of quantity and price and as to overhead in terms of rates and rate bases. This design makes provision for two revisions.

The card in this illustration provides detail as to type and quantity of all material elements used in manufacturing the item. The assigned costs are determined from the best price information available at the date of preparation or date of revision as the case may be.

Standard hours allowed for each operation in the manufacturing process and the hourly rate for each operation are entered on the card. The standard hours allowed are determined by a scientific analysis of the manufacturing operations, which will include time and motion studies by the industrial engineers. The time allowances are normally based on the results of studies of the average worker of average skill putting forth an average effort while working with machines operating normally. The allowances will ordinarily include time for personal needs, a fatigue factor and possibly time for mechanical adjustment delays.

The hourly rates, as a rule, represent the average hourly rate for the job skill required for the particular operation. The assignment of hourly rates is made easier if a program of job rating (evaluation) has been carried out in the plant. Such a program is of great help in fairly assigning rates to the various operations. The end result will be more accurate standard costs for direct labor.

The factory overhead rates are taken from the flexible factory overhead budget on the basis of a normal operating level of production (normal capacity). In this example, the overhead is related to and applied on the basis of direct labor hours.

Standard Costs and Financial Accounting

It seems to be the practice of most companies to close out all variances from standard costs developed during the fiscal year to the cost of goods sold account. This results from permitting standard costs of production to flow through the work in process accounts to the finished goods inventory. In this case, the various inventories will not be stated in the books or on the financial statements at actual cost; rather they will be stated at standard cost to manufacture, which will be above or below actual cost depending upon the net variance from standard, the direction of price-level changes, replacement costs, and the age of at least part of the inventories. There could be a sizable difference between the actual and stated (standard cost) value of the inventories.

In many cases, it would be feasible to assign a ratable portion of the net annual variance to the inventories by book adjustments. This might represent the best of two worlds from a cost control and financial reporting standpoint if not too difficult to accomplish.

A Simplified Illustration of Standard Cost Flows

Figure 13-2 provides an illustration of the flow of costs through the accounts on the basis of standard cost only, sometimes referred to as the *single plan.*

Figure 13-2

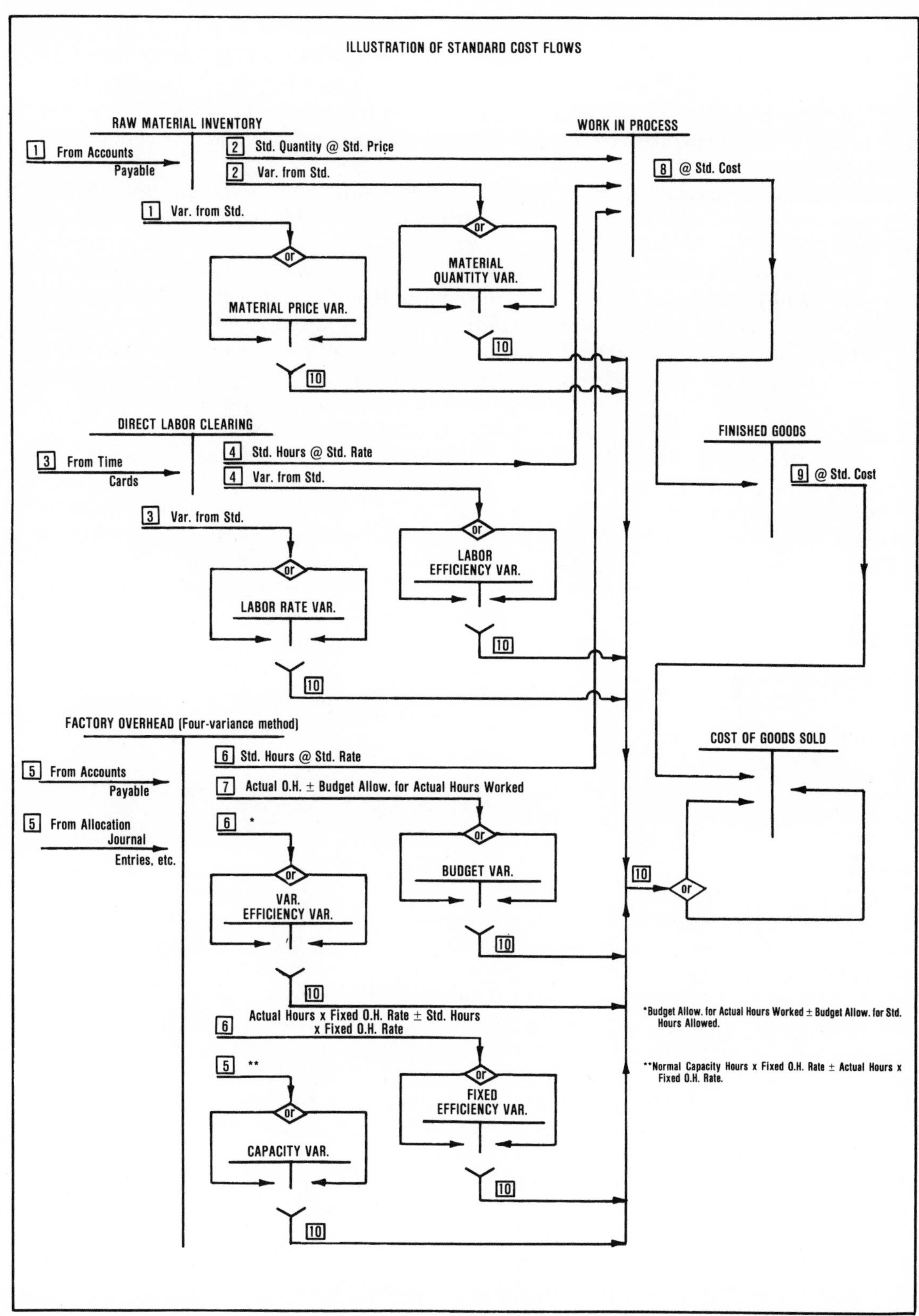
ILLUSTRATION OF STANDARD COST FLOWS
RAW MATERIAL INVENTORY
1 From Accounts Payable
2 Std. Quantity @ Std. Price
2 Var. from Std.
1 Var. from Std.
MATERIAL PRICE VAR.
MATERIAL QUANTITY VAR.
WORK IN PROCESS
8 @ Std. Cost
DIRECT LABOR CLEARING
3 From Time Cards
4 Std. Hours @ Std. Rate
4 Var. from Std.
3 Var. from Std.
LABOR RATE VAR.
LABOR EFFICIENCY VAR.
FINISHED GOODS
9 @ Std. Cost
FACTORY OVERHEAD (Four-variance method)
5 From Accounts Payable
5 From Allocation Journal Entries, etc.
6 Std. Hours @ Std. Rate
7 Actual O.H. ± Budget Allow. for Actual Hours Worked
6 *
VAR. EFFICIENCY VAR.
BUDGET VAR.
6 Actual Hours x Fixed O.H. Rate ± Std. Hours x Fixed O.H. Rate
5 **
CAPACITY VAR.
FIXED EFFICIENCY VAR.
COST OF GOODS SOLD
10
or
*Budget Allow. for Actual Hours Worked ± Budget Allow. for Std. Hours Allowed.
**Normal Capacity Hours x Fixed O.H. Rate ± Actual Hours x Fixed O.H. Rate.

The numbers in the squares at various points in the illustration are keyed to the respective journal entries presented later in the chapter for reference purposes. It will be noted that the Raw Material Inventory account is charged and credited at standard prices. Variations from standard are charged or credited to the appropriate variance accounts at the point of entry.

Direct labor time and rate variances are likewise charged or credited to variance accounts at the point of entry. The Direct Labor Clearing account is charged and credited at standard as is the Raw Material Inventory account. Work in Process is accordingly charged at standard for material and labor. As a result of the standard charges, finished goods will move out of the Work in Process account and into the Finished Goods account at standard and then into the Cost of Goods Sold account at standard.

The Factory Overhead account is charged for the actual cost of overhead items. Overhead is applied to work in process on the basis of standard direct labor hours at standard overhead rates determined from the flexible factory overhead budget. The difference in actual and applied overhead represents several variances (using the four variance method), and this difference is removed from the Factory Overhead account and is charged or credited to the respective variance accounts.

In this illustration, all variance account balances are closed to the Cost of Goods Sold account. For statement preparation purposes, this can be done periodically by worksheet or other temporary adjustment technique.

The single plan is probably the easiest and least costly method of handling the cost accounting when standard costs are to be developed and used. From a clerical standpoint, the inventories can probably be kept on a physical unit basis only. Since variances are cast out at the inception of each operating phase (with the exception of factory overhead), cost summaries for material and labor can be easily prepared by physical counts from material requisitions and labor rate and time records.

STANDARD COSTS IN THE ACCOUNTS— THE "PARTIAL" PLAN

There are other methods for handling standard costs in the accounts. Some accountants prefer to use a procedure wherein the raw materials inventory is carried at actual cost and the work in process account is charged for actual costs (material and direct labor) but is credited for standard costs. Finished goods inventory will be charged and credited at standard cost and cost of goods sold is charged at standard cost. This particular procedure is usually referred to as the *partial plan* for accumulating costs. Variances are determined in connection with the inventorying and/or analysis of the work in process at the end of an accounting period. This procedure requires some information that necessarily comes from supporting documents such as material requisitions, labor time records and summaries thereof.

Factory overhead is applied by using the budgeted overhead rates with actual hours of direct labor (or other basis). This is a sort of hybrid method for applying overhead in that actual overhead is not charged to work in process because of the use of the predetermined rates, and the standard cost of overhead is not charged to work in process because the rates are applied to actual rather than standard hours.

THE "DUAL" PLAN

Another method of procedure for accumulating cost information where standards are to be used is known as the dual plan. Under this plan, inventory accounts are carried at both actual and standard cost. The cost of goods sold account will be charged only for actual costs. Inventories will be carried on the financial statements at actual costs. Under the dual plan, variances are not segregated in the accounts but are determined as percentages rather than as absolute accounts. It is possible to convert the percentages to dollar amounts if desired.

Basically, the dual plan is more complex than the partial and single plans. It is more difficult to explain to management the procedures used in developing the variance percentages and relating them to the respective manufacturing processes. Depending upon the cost accounting system design, there may be some loss of detail with respect to the several variances concerned with usage or efficiency. Because much more clerical work is involved, this plan would be more feasible where a computer is available and a carefully tested computer program is developed to handle this type of complex data processing. One big advantage of using this plan is that the problem of dealing with standard costs in the financial statements no longer exists.

The examples, illustrations and discussion in this chapter are directed primarily to the *single plan.* The reason is that from clerical and accounting standpoints, this plan is the simplest procedure for handling standard costs in the accounts. Also, it is assumed that for most companies any adjustments necessary to bring inventories from standard cost to actual cost will not be so involved and complex as to negate the advantages derived from the use of the simpler system.

ACCOUNTING FOR STANDARD COSTS OF MATERIALS

In measuring actual material costs against standard material costs, two types of variances may appear. The first variance to appear would be the material price variance, the difference between the actual price paid for the material and the standard price to be used in charging the inventory. The second variance to appear would be the material quantity (usage, efficiency) variance, the difference between the standard cost of the actual quantity used in the manufacturing process and the standard cost of the quantity previously determined to be the standard or normal amounts of material to be used in the manufacturing process.

COMPUTING AND RECORDING PRICE AND QUANTITY VARIANCES

An example of computing a material price variance follows:

Material Price Variance

Cost of material purchased—	
1,000 pieces @ \$2.74 (actual price)	\$2,740.00
Standard cost of this material—	
1,000 pieces @ \$2.65 (standard)	\$2,650.00
Price variance (unfavorable)	\$ 90.00

The journal entry to record the purchase of materials and the variance from standard in the above example follows:[1]

1. To record the purchase of materials:

Raw Material Inventory	2,650.00	
Material Price Variance (credited if favorable variance)	90.00	
Accounts Payable		2,740.00

Material Quantity Variance

Material actually used—230 pieces @ $2.65 (standard)	$ 609.50
Material allowed by standard—220 pieces @ $2.65 (standard)	$ 583.00
Quantity variance (unfavorable)	$ 26.50

The journal entry to record the issuance of materials to processing departments and the variance from the standard quantity in the above example follows:

2. To record the issuance of materials from inventory:

Work in process (appropriate department)	583.00	
Material Quantity Variance (credited if favorable variance)	26.50	
Raw Material Inventory		609.50

Material price variances are cast out before the raw material inventory account is charged with any material cost. Consequently, the raw material inventory control account is charged with standard costs. The subsidiary inventory records will also be charged with standard costs. It may be feasible to carry these individual material item records on the basis of physical units only. Standard costs can be picked up from the standard cost cards for the purpose of pricing inventories and costing material requisitions covering issuances to the factory. The data processing system can be easily designed so that the purchasing agents will have ready reference to the standard price lists. In effect, management can be alerted to price variances before they become a financial fact.

The procedure for handling material requisitions will be a function of the manufacturing processes and the methods of controlling them. Here again it may be feasible to prepare the material requisitions in terms of physical units only. Later the issuances (perhaps summarized) could be costed using the standard unit costs for the materials.

[1]Keyed to Figure 13-2 here and in the following entries by number.

Material efficiency variances arise as a result of material consumption over or under standard allowances. Material issuances over standard (or returns to inventory for credit) could likewise be handled on a physical unit basis using easily identified special requisition forms. This could give the appropriate management personnel the opportunity to review the variance reports almost at the actual occurrence of the situation creating the variance. The nature of the manufacturing process will more or less dictate the timing involved here.

ACCOUNTING FOR STANDARD COSTS OF DIRECT LABOR

As in the case of material costs, the measurement of actual direct labor costs against standard labor costs may produce two types of variances from standards. The first variance to appear would be the labor rate variance, the difference between the actual hourly rates paid labor and the standard hourly rates to be used in charging the work in process inventory (or direct labor clearing account). The second variance (usage, quantity) is the difference between the standard cost of the actual labor hours used in the manufacturing process and the standard cost of the actual labor hours allowed for the particular manufacturing process.

COMPUTING AND RECORDING RATE AND EFFICIENCY VARIANCES

An example of computing and recording labor rate and efficiency variances follows, keyed by number to Figure 13-2.

Labor Rate Variance

Cost of labor used—	
500 hrs. @ $5.25 per hr. (actual rate)	$2,625.00
Standard cost of this labor—	
500 hrs. @ $5.00 per hour (standard)	$2,500.00
Rate Variance (unfavorable)	$ 125.00

The journal entry to record the payment of labor and variance from standard in the above example follows:

3. To record payment of salaries and wages:

Direct Labor Clearing (work in process)	2,500.00	
Labor Rate Variance (credited if favorable variance)	125.00	
Payroll Clearing		2,625.00

The labor efficiency variance is computed below:

Labor Efficiency Variance

Labor actually used—	
200 hrs. @ $5.00 (standard)	$1,000.00
Labor allowed by standard—	
195 hrs. @ $5.00 (standard)	$ 975.00
Efficiency variance (unfavorable)	$ 25.00

The journal entry to record the application of labor to processing departments and the variance from the standard allowance in the above example follows:

4. To record labor applied to process:

Work in process	975.00	
Labor Efficiency Variance (credited if favorable variance)	25.00	
Direct Labor Clearing		1,000.00

Some Causes of Labor Variances and How to Identify Them

Labor rate variances are not as readily identifiable as material price variances. The labor rate variances can come from two sources. One source involves a difference in rates resulting from new agreements with labor or their union representatives. If agreements are made for a definite contract period, the standards can be set or adjusted accordingly. Rate variances from these sources should not be too common. The other source involves the assignment of labor paid at different rates than the standard rates set for the respective job skills. Where the shifting of personnel from one department to another or within the same department becomes necessary, it is likely rate variances will occur. Time keeping methods and the general routine of the manufacturing process will determine how timely the reports of labor rate variances will be to concerned management personnel.

The labor efficiency variances may ordinarily be determined and reported on a very timely basis. The procedure to be used and the related difficulty will be a function of the availability of daily time records for measurement against standard labor allowances. If sound time standards are to be established, there must be a thorough study of the manufacturing operations. Humans cannot be expected to perform in the same manner as machines. Tolerances for a variety of human needs must be provided for in the establishment of the labor time standards.

Efficiency variances in the case of direct labor may result from the following causes:

1. Physical condition of worker.
2. Mental attitude of worker.

3. Degree of training and experience of worker.
4. Mechanical condition of equipment.
5. Condition of materials (or substitutes).
6. Environmental changes.
7. Volume of work.

While not all inclusive, the above list identifies most of the causes of labor efficiency variances. Material quantity variances may likewise be attributed to the above causes in many situations, in addition to the usual material substitute, mix and yield causes. There will often be both a material quantity variance and a labor efficiency variance in the same direction. For example, a worker in poor physical condition will usually work somewhat more slowly and will occasionally spoil material during the manufacturing process. In some cases, it may be difficult to pinpoint the causative factors since several will be involved simultaneously. Variance report forms should be designed so as to facilitate the identification of the causes of the variances, favorable and unfavorable, to the extent possible.

Accounting for Standard Costs and Factory Overhead

The development of factory overhead budgets for standard costing follows the general procedure as in the case of job order and process costing. The identification of fixed and variable expenses is essential to the building of a good budget for factory overhead. This topic was covered in Chapter 11 and consequently will not be repeated here. The use of a flexible budget is very helpful for dealing with variances in the application of factory overhead to work in process. Since the flexible budget makes provision for fixed overhead application rates that are related to production volume, fixed expenses can be more readily absorbed. Variances due to volume will be largely eliminated. The more important spending and efficiency variances will then be highlighted in the variance analyses.

The journal entry(ies) to record the actual factory overhead expenses incurred as illustrated in Figure 13-2 follows:

5. To record actual factory overhead incurred during the month:

Factory overhead	XXXX	
Accounts Payable		xx
Various prepayments		xx
Various accruals		xx
Accumulated Depreciation		xx

Three Methods of Analyzing and Recording Overhead Variances

While Figure 13-2 illustrates the use of four-variance overhead analysis, the two-variance and three-variance overhead analyses will be reviewed and illustrated here as well.

The data to be used in the illustrations will be the same in each case in order to help point out the basic differences in each method. The factory overhead rates will be applied on the basis of direct labor hours in these examples. The data for the examples follows:

Department A

From Department A Flexible Budget:

Variable overhead for month	$10,500.00
Fixed overhead for month	12,000.00
Total overhead for month	22,500.00
Standard direct labor hours	6,000.00

$$\text{Variable overhead rate} = \frac{\$10{,}500}{6{,}000} = \$1.75 \text{ per DLH}$$

$$\text{Fixed overhead rate} = \frac{\$12{,}000}{6{,}000} = \$2.00 \text{ per DLH}$$

$$\text{Total standard overhead rate} = \$3.75 \text{ per DLH}$$

Actual overhead for month	$23,300.00
Standard DLH for actual production	5,600
Actual DLH for month	5,744
Overhead applied to production—5,600 DLH × $3.75 per DLH	$21,000.00
Net overhead variance (unfavorable) $23,300.00 (actual)—$21,000.00 (applied)	$ 2,300.00

The above budget amounts are based on so-called "normal production" which is approximately 15% less than the physical capacity limit of the manufacturing facilities.

1. The Two-Variance Overhead Analysis

The two variances to be identified in this method of analysis are a controllable variance and a plant capacity (volume) variance. The controllable variance measures the actual factory overhead against the sum of the budget allowance for variable expenses on actual work performed and the total fixed expenses budgeted for the month.

An example of controllable variance analysis follows:

Budget allowances:

Variable expenses allowance—5600 allowed for actual production × $1.75 (variable overhead rate per DLH)	$ 9,800.00	
Fixed expenses for the month	12,000.00	
Total Budget Allowances		$21,800.00
Actual overhead for the month		23,300.00
Controllable variance (unfavorable)		$ 1,500.00

The plant capacity (volume) variance measures the total budget allowances for the month against the overhead applied to production for the month.

Example of plant capacity variance analysis:

Total budget allowances (as computed above)	$21,800.00
Overhead applied to production	21,000.00
Plant capacity variance (unfavorable)	$ 800.00

The two variances as computed above account for the net overhead variance for the month as follows:

Actual overhead for the month	$23,300.00
Overhead applied to production	21,000.00
Net overhead variance (unfavorable)	2,300.00

Consisting of the following:

Controllable variance (unfavorable)	$ 1,500.00
Plant capacity variance (unfavorable)	800.00
Total	$ 2,300.00

The entry to separate the variances when the two-variance method is used is as follows:

Controllable variance	1,500.00	
Plant capacity variance	800.00	
Factory overhead		2,300.00

2. The Three-Variance Overhead Analysis

The three variances to be identified in this method of analysis are a budget (spending) variance, an idle plant capacity variance and an efficiency variance. The budget variance measures the actual factory overhead against the sum of the fixed expenses budgeted for the month and the variable expense allowance for actual hours worked during the month.

An example of budget (spending) variance analysis follows:

Budget allowance:	
Variable expense allowance for actual hours worked—5,744 DLH × $1.75 (variable overhead rate per DLH)	$10,052.00
Fixed expenses for the month	12,000.00
Total budget allowances	$22,052.00
Actual overhead for month	23,300.00
Budget variance (unfavorable)	$ 1,248.00

The idle plant capacity variance measures the budget allowance for actual hours worked against an overhead amount developed by multiplying actual hours worked against the standard overhead rate.

An example of idle plant capacity variance analysis follows:

Total budget allowances (as computed above)	$22,052.00
Actual hours worked (5,744) × standard overhead rate ($3.75 per DLH)	21,540.00
Idle Plant Capacity Variance (unfavorable)	$ 512.00

This variance sets forth the portion of the total unfavorable overhead variance caused by underabsorbed fixed overhead. The standard direct labor hours for the month (6,000) exceed the actual direct labor hours (5,744) by 256 hours. The 256 hours multiplied by the standard overhead rate of $2.00 per DLH will also develop the idle plant capacity variance of $512.00.

The efficiency variance measures the total of the actual hours of the standard rate against the overhead applied to production (standard hours allowed for work done multiplied by the standard overhead rate of $3.75 per DLH).

An example of efficiency variance analysis follows:

Actual hours worked (5,744) × standard	$21,540.00
Overhead rate ($3.75 per DLH)	
Overhead applied to production	21,000.00
Efficiency variance (unfavorable)	$540.00

This variance sets forth the portion of the total unfavorable overhead variance caused by the necessity of working 144 hours over the standard hours allowed for the production accomplished. The 144 hours multiplied by the standard overhead rate of $3.75 per DLH will also develop the efficiency variance of $540.00.

The three variances as computed above account for the $2,300 net overhead variance for the month.

Budget variance (unfavorable)	$ 1,248.00
Idle plant capacity variance (unfavorable)	512.00
Efficiency variance (unfavorable)	540.00
Total	$ 2,300.00

The journal entries needed to separate the variances when the three variance method is used are as follows:

Work in process	$21,000.00	
Efficiency Variance	$ 540.00	
Factory Overhead		$21,540.00
Budget Variance	$ 1,248.00	
Idle Plant Capacity Variance	$ 512.00	
Factory Overhead		$ 1,760.00

3. The Four-Variance Overhead Analysis

The four variances to be identified in this method of analysis are a budget (spending) variance, an idle plant capacity variance and an efficiency variance broken down into fixed and variable efficiency variances. The budget variance measures the actual factory overhead against the sum of the fixed expenses budgeted for the month and the variable expense allowance for actual hours worked during the month. It is computed in the same manner as it is in the three-variance method. The idle plant capacity variance measures the budget allowance for actual hours worked against an overhead amount developed by multiplying actual hours worked against the standard overhead rate. It is computed in the same manner as it is in the three-variance method.

The fixed efficiency variance measures the actual hours at the fixed overhead rate per DLH against the standard hours allowed at the fixed overhead rate per DLH.

An example of fixed efficiency variance analysis follows:

Actual hours worked (5,744) × standard fixed overhead rate ($2.00 per DLH)	$11,488.00
Standard hours allowed (5,600) × standard fixed overhead rate ($2.00 per DLH)	11,200.00
Fixed efficiency variance (unfavorable)	$ 288.00

This variance sets forth the fixed portion of the total unfavorable overhead variance caused by the necessity of working 144 hours over the standard hours allowed for the production accomplished. The 144 hours multiplied by the standard fixed overhead rate of $2.00 per DLH will also develop the fixed efficiency variance of $288.00.

The variable efficiency variance measures the budget allowance for actual hours worked against the budget allowance for standard hours allowed.

An example of variable efficiency variance analysis follows:

Budget allowances (actual):		
Variable expense allowance for actual hours worked—5,744 DLH × $1.75 (variable overhead rate per DLH)	$10,052.00	
Fixed expenses for the month	12,000.00	
Total budget allowances (actual)		$22,052.00
Budget allowances (standard):		
Variable expense allowance for standard hours allowed—5,600 DLH × $1.75 (variable overhead rate per DLH)	$ 9,800.00	
Fixed expenses for the month	12,000.00	
Total budget allowances (standard)		$21,800.00
Variable efficiency variance (unfavorable)		$ 252.00

This variance sets forth the variable position of the total unfavorable overhead variance caused by the necessity of working 144 hours over the standard hours allowed for the production accomplished. The 144 hours multiplied by the standard variable overhead rate of $1.75 per DLH will also develop the variable efficiency variance of $252.00.

The four variances as computed above account for the $2,300 net overhead variance for the month.

Budget variance (unfavorable)	$1,248.00
Idle plant capacity variance (unfavorable)	512.00
Fixed efficiency variance (unfavorable)	288.00
Variable efficiency variance (unfavorable)	252.00
Total	$2,300.00

The journal entries needed to separate the variances when the four-variance method is used are as follows:

6. To record the application of overhead to work in process and clear the Factory Overhead account of the efficiency variances:

Work in Process	21,000.00	
Fixed Efficiency Variance	288.00	
Variable Efficiency Variance	252.00	
Factory Overhead		21,540.00

7. To clear the Factory Overhead account of the budget and idle plant capacity variances:

Budget Variance	1,248.00	
Idle Plant Capacity Variance	512.00	
Factory Overhead		1,760.00

Completing the Standard Cost Accounting Process

Under the single plan, the balance of the standard cost accounting process is relatively simple. Costs flow from Work in Process to Finished Goods Inventory to Cost of Goods Sold at standard. The variance accounts will normally be closed, at the end of the company fiscal year, to the Cost of Goods Sold account. If an allocation of the net variance from standard appears to be in order, then the various inventory accounts will share in the variances with the Cost of Goods Sold account.

The journal entries needed to complete the standard cost flow are as follows:

8. To transfer work in process to Finished Goods:

Finished Goods	xxx	
Work in Process		xxx

9. To record Cost of Goods Sold:

Cost of Goods Sold	xxx	
Finished Goods		xxx

10. To close the variance accounts to Cost of Goods Sold:

Cost of Goods Sold	xxx	
Material Price Variance		xx
Material Quantity Variance		xx
Labor Rate Variance		xx
Labor Efficiency Variance		xx
Variable Efficiency Variance		xx
Fixed Efficiency Variance		xx
Budget Variance		xx
Capacity Variance		xx

(Any of the above variance accounts could have credit balances to be closed to Cost of Goods Sold).

Some accountants feel that the variances representing waste and inefficiency should not be charged to Cost of Goods Sold but should be treated as a separate item to develop an "adjusted" gross profit figure. If the accounting is to be consistent, favorable variances would have to be treated in the same manner, even if an addition to gross profit results.

Some Reporting Considerations

In most cases where standard costing is used, the single plan as illustrated here is followed. As a result, the raw materials, work in process and finished goods inventories will be stated at standard cost unless allocated a portion of the net variance from standard. This problem was discussed earlier in this chapter. For practical reasons, the inventories should be left at standard unless the inventories are large and the net variance is materially distorting in which case it should be allocated as described in Chapter 11.

Standards are to be taken seriously, and they represent a sound production plan in the overall manufacturing operation. It is not unrealistic to equate the net variance write-off to cost of goods sold with the concept of absorbing the current year's mistakes in the current year's operating results. To prorate the net variance to the inventories is to, in effect, pass on a portion of these "mistakes" to the next year's operations. In the authors' opinion this does not appear to be in line with the concept of conservatism or the matching principle as generally defined.

In the matter of disposition of variances to inventories and cost of goods sold, the AICPA Committee on accounting procedures has taken the following position:

> Standard costs are acceptable if adjusted at reasonable intervals to reflect current conditions so that at the balance-sheet date standard costs reasonably approximate costs computed under one of the recognized bases. In such cases descriptive language should be used which will express this relationship, as, for instance, "approximate costs determined on the first-in first-out basis," or, if it is desired to mention standard costs, "at standard costs, approximating average costs."[2]

Accounting Principles Board Opinion #28 provides some interim financial reporting guidelines as quoted below from Paragraph 14, Section d.

> Companies that use standard cost accounting systems for determining inventory and product costs should generally follow the same procedures in reporting purchase price, wage rate, usage or efficiency variances from standard cost at the end of an interim period at the end of a fiscal year. Purchase price variances or volume or capacity cost variances that are planned and expected to be absorbed by the end of the annual period, should ordinarily be deferred at interim reporting dates. The effect of unplanned or unanticipated purchase price or volume variances, however, should be reported at the end of an interim period following the same procedures used at the end of a fiscal year.[3]

These guidelines relate to the consistency and reporting principles without taking a position as to the ultimate disposition of the net variance(s).

The present Internal Revenue Service regulations permit the writing off of variances annually without any allocation to the inventories if the amounts are not significant in relation to the total of the factory overhead; financial reporting must handle the variances in the same manner as they are handled on the tax returns. Favorable and unfavorable variances must be treated consistently.

---

[2] AICPA Committee on Accounting Procedures, "Inventory Pricing," *Accounting Research Bulletin* No. 43, p. 30.

[3] AICPA Accounting Principles Board, "Interim Financial Reporting," Opinions of the Accounting Principles Board #28, p. 525.

The Cost Accounting Standards Board has promulgated Standard 407, among others, which relates to the use of standard costs for direct material and direct labor.[4] It became effective on October 1, 1974. The Standard requires the following: (a) That standard costs be entered into the books of account; (b) That standard cost and related variances be accounted for at the production unit level; (c) That all practices that relate to the setting and revision of standards, use of standard costs and disposition of variances be stated in writing and consistently followed. The regulations set forth some techniques for application and give several illustrations as well. There are no exemptions for this cost accounting standard which applies, of course, only to companies subject to CASB regulations.

SUMMARY

The whole value of standard costing lies in the timely identification of variances from standards in all areas and the effective analysis of the causes of those variances. The single plan system is simple enough in application and reduces greatly the clerical work normally involved in standard cost accounting. The identification and analysis of the variances on a timely basis represents the real benefit of the standard cost information system.

[4]Code of Federal Regulations, Title 4, Chapter III, Paragraph 407.40; U.S. Government Printing Office, Washington D.C., 1976.

BIBLIOGRAPHY

American Institute of Certified Public Accountants. *An Auditors' Approach to Statistical Sampling.* Volumes 1–6, New York: American Institute of Certified Public Accountants, 1974.

American Institute of Certified Public Accountants. *Management Advisory Services Technical Studies, Study No. 6 Practical Techniques and Policies for Inventory Control—1968.* New York: American Institute of Certified Public Accountants, c1968.

American Institute of Certified Public Accountants. *Statements of the Accounting Principles Board, Statement No. 3 Financial Statements Restated for General Pricing Level Changes—1969.* New York: American Institute of Certified Public Accountants, c1969.

American Institute of Certified Public Accountants. *Management Advisory Services Technical Studies, Study No. 4 Analysis for Purchasing and Financing Productive Equipment—1967.* New York: American Institute of Certified Public Accountants, c1967.

Anthony, Robert M. and Welsch, Glenn A. *Fundamentals of Management Accounting.* Rev. ed. Homewood: Richard D. Irwin, Inc., c1977.

Beyer, Robert and Trawicki, Donald J. *Profitability Accounting—For Planning and Control.* 2nd ed. New York: The Ronald Press Company, c1972.

Bruns, William J., Jr. and Vancil, Richard N. *A Primer on Replacement Cost Accounting.* Glen Ridge: Thomas Horton and Daughters, c1977.

Buchan, Joseph and Ernest Koenigsberg. *Scientific Inventory Management.* Englewood Cliffs: Prentice-Hall, Inc.

Burns, David C. and James K. Loebbecke, "Internal Control Evaluation: How The Computer Can Help." *Journal of Accountancy,* (August, 1975), 60.

Canadian Institute of Chartered Accountants. *Computer Control Guidelines.* 1970. (May be obtained through the American Institute of Certified Public Accountants, 1211 Avenue of the Americas, New York, New York 10036.)

Canadian Institute of Chartered Accountants. *Computer Audit Guidelines.* 1975. (Order through AICPA)

Childs, John R. *Encyclopedia of Long-Term Financing and Capital Management.* Englewood Cliffs: Prentice-Hall, Inc., c1976.

Crowningshield, Gerald and Gorman, Kenneth. *Cost Accounting Principles and Managerial Applications,* 3rd ed. Boston: Houghton Mifflin, c1974.

Dopuch, Nicholas; Birnberg, Jacob G. and Demski, Joel. *Cost Accounting Data for Management's Decisions.* 2nd ed. New York: Harcourt Brace Jovanovich, Inc., c1974.

BIBLIOGRAPHY

Griffin, Charles H.; Williams, Thomas H. and Larson, Kermit D. *Advanced Accounting.* 3rd ed. Homewood: Richard D. Irwin, Inc., c1977.

Henrici, Stanley B. *Standard Costs for Manufacturing.* 3rd ed. New York: McGraw-Hill Book Company. c1960.

Horngren, Charles T. *Accounting for Management Control: An Introduction.* 3rd ed. Englewood Cliffs: Prentice-Hall, Inc., c1974.

Horngren, Charles T. *Cost Accounting: A Managerial Emphasis.* 4th ed. Englewood Cliffs: Prentice-Hall, Inc., c1977.

Johnson, Glenn L. and Gentry, James A. *Finney and Miller's Principles of Accounting Intermediate.* 7th ed. Englewood Cliffs: Prentice-Hall, Inc., c1974.

Larson, Stanley E. *Inventory Control Systems Handbook,* Englewood Cliffs: Prentice-Hall, Inc., 1976.

Livingstone, John L. and Kerrigan, Harry D. *Modern Accounting Systems,* 4th ed. New York: The Ronald Press Company, 1975.

Matz, Adolph and Usry, Milton F. *Cost Accounting-Planning and Control.* 6th ed. Cincinnati: South-Western Publishing Company, c1976.

Moore, Carl L. and Jaedicke, Robert R. *Managerial Accounting.* 4th ed. Cincinnati: South-Western Publishing Company, c1976.

National Association of Accountants. *Techniques In Inventory Management Research Report No. 4,* New York: National Association of Accountants, 1964.

Neuner, John J. W. *Cost Accounting: Principles and Practice.* 9th ed. Homewood: Richard D. Irwin, Inc., c1977.

Newton, Grant W. *Bankruptcy and Insolvency Accounting-Practice and Procedure.* New York: The Ronald Press Company, c1975.

Porter, Thomas W. "Generalized Computer-Audit Programs," *Journal of Accounting,* (January, 1969), 54.

Fremgen, James M. *Accounting For Managerial Analysis.* 3rd ed. Homewood: Richard D. Irwin, Inc., c1976.

Shillinglaw, Gordon. *Managerial Cost Accounting,* 4th ed. Homewood: Richard D. Irwin, Inc., c1977.

Smith, Jay and Skousen, Fred. *Intermediate Accounting Comprehensive Volume.* 6th ed. Cincinnati: South-Western Publishing Company, c1977.

Stringer, Kenneth W. "Conceptual Aspects of Internal Control Evaluation." Haskins & Sells, *Collected Papers* 1970, 177.

Summers, Edward L. *An Introduction to Accounting for Decision Making and Control.* Homewood: Richard D. Irwin, Inc., c1974.

Thomas, William E. *Readings in Cost Accounting, Budgeting, and Control.* 4th ed. Cincinnati: South-Western Publishing Company, c1973.

Welsch, Glenn A. *Budgeting: Profit Planning and Control.* 4th ed. Englewood Cliffs: Prentice-Hall, Inc., c1976.

Welsch, Glenn A.; Zlatkovich, Charles T. and White, John Arch. *Intermediate Accounting.* 4th ed. Homewood: Richard D. Irwin, Inc., c1976.

Wiener, Robert A. and Christian, Roger. *Insolvency Accounting.* New York: McGraw-Hill Book Company, c1976.

INDEX

A

ABC Method, 198–199
Accumulation of Costs (see Cost accumulation)
Acts of bankruptcy, 216–217
Arrangement, 218
Attributes, sampling for, 102–119

B

Bank Relations, 192–193
Bankruptcy:
  accountant's role in, 218–219
  acts of bankruptcy, 216–217
  arrangement, 218
  attorney, need for, 217
  Chapter XI of Federal Bankruptcy Act, 216–217
    steps for relief under, 217–218
    claims with priority, 219
  composition, 215
  creditors' committee, 216
  deficiency statement, 221–223
    example of, 223
    purpose of, 221
  discharge under, 218
    debts not discharged, 218
  extension, 215
  Federal Bankruptcy Act, 215–218
  general assignment for benefit of creditors, 216
  general equity receiver, 216
  insolvency, definition, 215
  involuntary bankruptcy, 216
  liquidating the firm, 232–243
  partly secured creditors, 221, 242
  receiver, 217
    duties of, 217
  referee in bankruptcy, 217
  secured claims, 219
  statement of affairs, 219–222
    example of, 222
  statement of realization and liquidation, 232–243
    computation of payments to unsecured creditors, 242
    form of, 232–233
    steps in preparing, 233, 236
    transactions put into statement format, 236, 238–243
  trustee (see Trustee)
  unsecured claims, 219
  voluntary bankruptcy, 217
    petition, 217–218
Bankruptcy, acts of (see Acts of bankruptcy)
Benchmark, 250
Block diagram, 67
Budget variance, 359, 369–371 (see also Spending variance)
Budgeting, 129–130
  administrative expense, 138–139, 148
  assembly, 152
  cash (see Cash budget)
  capital additions, 156–157
  distribution expense, 139, 148
  labor, direct, 138
  manufacturing expense, 138, 146
  manufacturing overhead (see Manufacturing expense)
  master budget, 140
  materials, 137–138
  other income and expense, 139
  overhead (see Manufacturing expense)
  planning information, 130–135
  production, 137–138, 142
  sales, 137, 141–142

C

Capital additions:
  alternative investments, 163–168
  basis of evaluation:
    arithmetic basis, 161
    discounted basis, 161–163
    payback, 159–161
  budgeting, 156–157
  control of, 156–157
  financing, 168
    bank loans, 168–169, 171–173
    leasing, 168, 170–173
    manufacturer financing, 168, 170
  keep or replace, 173–177
  post-completion audit, 157
  projects, 156
  tax shield, 169–176
Capital expenditure management, 156
Cash budget, 139–140, 148, 184–185
Cash management (see Cash planning and control)
Cash planning and control:
  cash control schedule, 186–191
  collection patterns, 180–183
  daily cash balance, 186–191
  "float," 188, 193
  general, 179–180
  investments, 184
  long-range projections, 194–195
  other receipts and disbursements, 183–184
  payables, 184–185, 187
  receipts and disbursements, schedule of, 181, 185, 195
  savings, 184
  short-term loans, 184, 187–191

INDEX

Causes of labor variances (see Labor variances, causes of)
Chargeable costs, 335
Chargeable costs accounted for, 335
Chart of accounts, 18–19, 42
 evaluating, 59
 functions of, 42
 understanding of, 52
Capacity variance, 317–318, 359, 366–371
Composite construction index, 250
Composition, 215
Computerized internal control systems, 64–67
Confidence level, 100
Confirmation sample, accounts receivable, 116–118
Consumer price index, 250–251
Controllable variance, 367–368
Conventional accounting, 246
Conventional statements, 260
Cost accounting terminology:
 direct labor, 301, 360
 direct materials, 301, 361
 finished goods, 301, 353, 372
 indirect labor, 301
 indirect materials, 301
 manufacturing overhead, 301, 303
  examples of, 302–303
 raw materials, 301
 work-in-progress, 301
Cost accumulation, 333–334
Cost accumulation cycle, 300–302
Cost added by department, 335
Cost behavior, 313
Cost flows, 330–333
Cost from preceding department, 339
Cost of capital, 203–204
Cost of goods completed on hand, 345
Cost of holding inventory, 196
Cost of production report, 334–337
Costs, standard (see Standard costs)
Costs to be accounted for, 336
Costs transferred in, 335
Costs transferred to next department, 339
Current fair value, 248–249
Current replacement value, 246–248
 Accounting Series Release, 190, 246–248
 qualifying registrants, 246–247
 rule, 3–17, 247–248

D

Debit memorandum, 201
Deficiency statement (see Bankruptcy)
Deflation, 245
Deflator (see Gross National Product Implicit Price Deflator)
Department charges, 336
Direct labor, 138, 301, 305, 360
Direct materials, 301, 305, 361
Direct materials, budgeting of, 137–138
Discharge in bankruptcy, 218
Discounted cash flow, 161–163
Discovery sampling, 107–108, 113–114
Distribution expense (see Budgeting, distribution expense)
Documents in an internal control system, 55–57

E

EOP, 209
EOQ, 202
Equivalent production (see Equivalent units)
Equivalent units, 333
Error rate, 100
Estimation sampling for variables, 108–111
Extension, 215

F

Facilities planning, 155–156
Federal Bankruptcy Act, 215–218
Fixed costs, 311–314
Flexible budget, 314–315
Float (see Cash planning and control: "float")
Flow charting:
 cash receipts function, 39–42
  flow chart of collections on account, 41
  flow chart of other cash receipts, 43
 disbursements function, 30–34
  flow chart of payment of freight, travel expense and truck maintenance, 31–32
  flow chart of payment of vendor's invoices, 29
  flow chart of petty cash, 33
 evaluating, 55, 57–58
 example of, 24
 payroll function, 57–59
 purchasing function, 25–29
  flow chart of, 26–27
 sales function, 34–39
  flow chart of cash sales, 40
  flow chart of charge sales, 35–38
 standard symbols used, 45
Forecasting, 131–134
 controller role, 134–135
 economic, 131–132
  information, sources of, 132
 sociological, 132–133
 technological, 133–134
Four-variance analysis, 369–371

G

Generalized audit programs, 66
Gross National Product Implicit Price Deflator, 249–251, Fig. 9A–26

INDEX

H

High-low method, 312–313
Historical cost, 247, 255
Historical statements (see Conventional statements)

I

Idle time, accounting for, 307–308
Implicit price deflator (see Gross National Product Implicit Price Deflator)
Index numbers, 246, 249–251, 256, Fig. 9A–26
Inflation (see Inflation accounting)
Inflation accounting, 245–249
Input controls, 64–65
Insolvency, 215
Internal control questionnaire, 64, 69–98
Internal control system:
  applying statistical sampling in audit of, 119
  chart of accounts (see Chart of accounts)
  computerized systems, 64–67
    block diagram, 67
    generalized audit programs, 66
    input controls, 64–65
    output controls, 65
    parallel simulation, 66
    processing controls, 65–66
    reasonableness, test of, 65
    redundancy, 66
    steps in evaluating, 66–67
    test deck, 66
  design of, 17
    "links" in, 18–19
  difficulties of evaluating, 47–48
  documents in, 55–57
  evaluation of, 52–62
  flow charting (see Flow charting)
  information flow, detecting weaknesses, 55–57
  organization plan, 49 (see also Organization chart)
    evaluating, 54
    job responsibility worksheet, 51
    line function, 49–50
    "originators" of accounting information, identification of, 23–24
    staff function, 49–50
    understanding of, 49–50
  overcoming resistance to installation, 42, 44
  periodic review of, 44
  personnel, evaluation of, 60–62
  principles of design of, 17–18
  "selling" an ICS to management, 44
  small businesses—checklist of techniques for, 68
  standard for measurement, 48–49
  working paper documentation, 62–63
Inventory:
  applying statistical sampling in audit of, 119
Inventory (cont'd.)
  control techniques:
    ABC method, 198–199
    account analysis as a control device, 199–200
    carrying costs, measuring, 203–204
    controlling the number of orders, 202
    EOQ formula, 205
    economic order quantity, 202–207
    evaluating the inventory control system, 213
    guidelines for recommending, 213–214
    insurance, 200–201
    manufacturing inventories, 202
    ordering costs, measuring, 204–206
    record-keeping, 201
      debit memorandum, 201
      materials requisition, 201, 303–304
      purchase order, 201
      purchase request, 201
      receiving report, 201
    storage as a control device, 200
    when to order, 208–211
      average usage, 209–211
      economic order point method, 209–211
      lead time, 209–210
      minimum-maximum method, 208–209
      reserve stock system, 208
      safety stock, 209–211
      sales frequency distribution, 210–211
      visual inspection method, 208
  cost of holding inventory, 196
  cost of stock outs, 196
  obtaining at favorable prices, 196
  perpetual inventories, 197–198
    advantages, 198
    disadvantages of, 198
    inventory record card, 197
  price-level conversion, 255
Inventory control (see Inventory: control techniques)
Inventories, costing of, 353–354
Involuntary bankruptcy, 216

J

Job order cost systems:
  advantages of, 300
  example of, 320–327
  finished goods perpetual record card, 304–305
  flow of accounting information through, 302, 304
  fringe benefits, 308
  idle time, 307–308
  job cost sheet, 304–305
  labor, 305
    accounting for, 305, 321–327
  manufacturing overhead, 308–320
    accounting for, 308–320
  materials, 305
    accounting for, 305, 321–327

INDEX

Job order cost systems (cont'd.)
  materials requisition, 201, 303–304
  record-keeping necessary, 303–305
  scrap, 305–306
  spoilage, allocation of, 306
  time ticket, 303–304, 307
Job responsibility worksheet, 51
Judgment sampling, 99

L

Labor efficiency variance (see Standard costs: labor variances)
Labor rate variance (see Standard costs: labor variances)
Labor unit cost, 335–338
Labor usage variance (see Standard costs: labor variances)
Labor variances, causes of, 364–365
Lead time, 209–210
Leasing (see Capital additions: financing, leasing)
Line function, 49–50
Lineal process cost flow, 330–331
Long-range planning:
  capital additions, 155
  cash (see Cash planning and control: long-range projections)
Lost units, 330, 337, 348

M

Manufacturing overhead (see Overhead)
Material price variance (see Standard costs: material variances)
Material quantity variance (see Standard costs: material variances)
Material usage variance (see Standard costs: material variances)
Material unit cost, 335–338
Materials requisition, 201, 303–304, 362
Mini-Max system, 208–209
Monetary items, 248, 251–256, Fig. 9A–24
Multiplier, 251
Multi-Product cost flow, 330, 332

N

Non-Monetary items, 248, 251–256, Fig. 9A–24
Normal capacity, 309–311

O

Occurrence rate, 100
Ordering costs, 204–206
Organization chart, 18 (see also Internal control system: organization plan)
  construction of, 19
  description of duties and responsibilities, 20–22
Organization chart (cont'd.)
  example of, 20, 53
  importance of, 22–23
  originators of accounting data, identification of, 23–24
  recognizing weaknesses, 53–55
  understanding of, 49–52
  working paper documentation, 50–51
Output controls, 65
Overhead:
  accounting for variances, 318–320
  analyzing costs, 311–313
  basis for applying overhead, 308–311
  budgeting, 314–315
    manufacturing expense, 138, 146
  capacity variance, 317–318
  cost behavior, chart showing, 313
  example of allocating variances, 319–320
  fixed costs, 311–314
  flexible budget, 314–315
    example of, 314
    how to construct, 315
    when to use, 315
  high-low method, 312–313
  in a job order cost system, 308
  Internal Revenue Code, requirements of, 301, 309
  level of activity, 309–311
  normal capacity, 309–311
    steps in estimating, 310–311
  planned overhead, 309
  practical capacity, 309–310
  semi-variable cost, 311–312
  spending variance, 317–318
  theoretical capacity, 309
  understanding overhead variances, 317–318
  variable cost, 311–314
  variance analysis, 316–320
Overhead efficiency variance, 369–370
  fixed efficiency variance, 359, 370–371
  variable efficiency variance, 359, 369–371
Overhead unit cost, 335–338

P

Parallel simulation, 66
Payback, 159–161
Perpetual inventories, 197–198
Personnel, evaluation of, in an ICS, 60–62
Petition in bankruptcy, 217–218
Plant expansion (see Capital additions)
Practical capacity, 309–310
Precision interval, 100
Price-Level adjustments (see Price-Level conversion)
Price-Level change (see Price-Level conversion)
Price-Level conversion, 245–246, 249–259
  estimated liabilities, 254–255
  foreign currency, 254

Price-Level conversion (cont'd.)
general price level gain/loss, 258
historical development, 249–250
illustration, 255–281
income tax, 254
inventories, 255
investments and bonds, 254
"roll-forward," 257–258
Priority claims, 219
Process costs analysis, definition of, 329–330
Process costing (see Process cost analysis)
Processing controls, 65–66
Production report (see Cost of production report)
Purchase order, 201
Purchase request, 201
Purchasing power, 245, 250

Q

Quantity schedule, 336

R

Random number table, 104
Random sampling, 103
Receivables, analyzing collection of, 180–183
Receiver, 217
Receiving report, 201
Referee in bankruptcy, 217
Replacement cost (see Current replacement value)
Reserve stock system, 208
Resources:
applied, 291, 296–298
nonworking capital, 291, 296, 298
working capital, 291–292, 296, 298
generated, 292, 296–298
nonworking capital, 291, 298
working capital, 291, 298
Restated balances, 251–255
Return on investment:
discounted basis, 161–163
arithmetic basis, 161

S

Safety stock, 209–211
Sales frequency distribution, 210–211
Sample size, determining, 114–119, 120–121
Sampling (see Statistical sampling)
Scrap and spoilage, 305–306
Semi-variable costs, 311–312
Skip interval, 103
Small businesses, internal control systems for, 68
Source and application of funds (see Statement of changes in financial position)
Spending variance, 317–318 (see also Budget variance)
Staff function, 49–50
Standard cost card, 357–358
Standard cost flows, 359–360
Standard costing (see Standard costs)
Standard costs, 355–356
accounting for finished goods, 371–372
accounting for labor, 363–365
accounting for materials, 361–363
accounting for overhead, 365–371
Cost Accounting Standards Board, 374
definition of, 355–356
dual plan, 361
labor variances, 363–365, 372
material variances, 361–363, 372
overhead variances, 365–372
four-variance analysis, 369–371
three-variance analysis, 368–369
two-variance analysis, 366–368
partial plan, 360
reporting considerations, 373–374
Standard costs—financial accounting, 358, 373–374
Standards, 356
Statement of affairs (see Bankruptcy)
Statement of changes in financial position:
cash basis, 290–291, 297
general, 289, 290
working capital basis, 290–291, 298
Statement of realization and liquidation (see Bankruptcy)
Statistical sampling:
applying statistical sampling—accounts payable audit, 119
applying statistical sampling—accounts receivable audit, 114–119, 121–123
steps in selecting confirmation sample, 116–118
applying statistical sampling—cash audit, 111–114, 123–128
applying statistical sampling—expense audit, 119
applying statistical sampling—internal control audit, 119
applying statistical sampling—inventory audit, 119
applying statistical sampling—sales audit, 119
attributes, sampling for, 102, 119
cash disbursements, testing of, 112–113
cash receipts, testing of, 113–114
confidence level defined, 100
discovery sampling, 107–108, 113–114
example of, 126–128
steps in using, 113–114
tables for, 107, 115
error rate, 100
example of, 102, 124
estimating totals, 108–111
example of, 120–121
tables for, 110
estimation sampling for variables, 108–111
evaluation of sample results, 105–106, 122–123
tables for, 106, 118

Statistical sampling (cont'd.)
judgment sampling, 99
precision, definition of, 100
purpose of, 99–100
random number table, 104
random sampling, 103
example of using, 120–122
sample size, example of determining, 114–119, 120–121
sample size, steps in determining, 100–102
tables for, 101
stratified random sampling, 105, 121
systematic sampling, 103–105
skip interval, 103
working paper documentation, 102–128
accounts receivable aging schedule, testing of, 120–121
accounts receivable confirmation, 121–123
cash disbursements, testing of, 123–126
cash receipts, testing of, 126–128
Stratified random sampling, 105, 121
Stock outs, cost of, 196
Symbols used in flow charting, 45
Systematic sampling, 103–105

T

Test deck, 66
Theoretical capacity, 309
Three-variance analysis, 368–369
Trustee, 217
accounting for, 223–244
financial statements prepared for, 229–232
interim statements during liquidation, 244
interpreting statements of, 231–232
recording transactions of, 224–226, 229
worksheet, example, of, 227–228
duties of, 217
Two-variance analysis, 366, 368

U

Units added to process, 342
Units completed on-hand, 345
Unit costs, 336
Units in process, 335
Units lost in process (see Lost units)
Units transferred in, 335
Units transferred out, 335

V

Variable costs, 311–314
Variance analysis (see Standard costs: material variances, labor variances, overhead variances)
Variance analysis—job order costing, 316–320
Voluntary bankruptcy, 217

W

"Where Got—Where Gone" statement (see Statement of changes in financial position)
Working capital:
accounts, 291
trade related, 291, 295
nontrade related, 291, 295
basis, 290, 298
changes, 291, 296, 298
items, (see Working capital: accounts)
Working papers:
budget, financial:
administrative expense, 149
applied manufacturing expense, 147
budget worksheet (assembly), 153
direct labor, 144–145
distribution expense, 148
journal entries (for finalizing budget), 154
manufacturing expense, 146
manufacturing expense distribution, 147
material purchases, 143
materials, requirements, 143
production, 142
sales, 141
schedule of cash receipts and disbursements, 151–152
schedule of collections on accounts receivable, 150
capital additions:
financing by bank loan vs manufacturer's installment plan, 171
schedule for determining rate of return, 172
schedule of comparative cash flows, 172
schedule of comparative costs, 171
schedule of depreciation tax-shield, 169
schedule of installment payments—manufacturer financing, 170
schedule of leasing costs, 170
schedule of principal and interest—bank loan for equipment payments, 169
cash planning and control:
cash control schedule, 186–190
long-range projections, cash and marketable securities derived from operations, 192
long-range projections—cash receipts and disbursements, 193
schedule of cash receipts and disbursements, 181, 185
schedule of collections of receivables, 182–183
general price-level restatement:
analysis of accumulated depreciation—boat, 272
analysis of accumulated depreciation—furniture and fixtures, 270
analysis of accumulated depreciation—trucks and autos, 269
analysis of accumulated depreciation—warehouse and leasehold improvements, 271

Working papers (cont'd.)
general price-level restatement (cont'd.)
analysis of gains/losses on sale of assets, 276
analysis of investment account, 274
analysis of operating expenses, 276
analysis of reinvested earnings, 275
analysis of trucks and autos, furniture and fixtures, 266–267
general price-level gain or loss, 277–278
sample worksheet—carry forward to subsequent years, 279
schedule of withdrawals, 275
summary of accumulated depreciation—all accounts, 273
warehouse and leasehold improvements, boat, 267–268
working balance sheets, 263–264

Working papers (cont'd.)
general price-level restatement (cont'd.)
working statements of income and reinvested earnings, 265
internal control system documentation, 51, 62–63
organization plan, documentation of, 50–51
process cost analysis:
cost of production report, 335, 339, 342, 345, 348, 351
standard costs card, 357
statement of changes in financial position (cash basis), 297
statement of changes in financial position (working capital basis), 298
statistical sampling, documentation of, 102–128
worksheet for statement of changes in financial position, 295–296